Programming Robots with ROS

*Morgan Quigley, Brian Gerkey,
and William D. Smart*

Beijing · Boston · Farnham · Sebastopol · Tokyo

Programming Robots with ROS

by Morgan Quigley, Brian Gerkey, and William D. Smart

Printed in the United States of America.

Published by O'Reilly Media, Inc., 1005 Gravenstein Highway North, Sebastopol, CA 95472.

O'Reilly books may be purchased for educational, business, or sales promotional use. Online editions are also available for most titles (*http://safaribooksonline.com*). For more information, contact our corporate/institutional sales department: 800-998-9938 or *corporate@oreilly.com*.

Acquisitions Editor: Mike Loukides	**Indexer:** WordCo Indexing Services, Inc.
Editors: Meghan Blanchette and Dawn Schanafelt	**Interior Designer:** David Futato
Production Editor: Matthew Hacker	**Cover Designer:** Ellie Volckhausen
Copyeditor: Rachel Head	**Illustrator:** Rebecca Demarest
Proofreader: Amanda Kersey	

December 2015:   First Edition

Revision History for the First Edition

2015-11-18   First Release

See *http://oreilly.com/catalog/errata.csp?isbn=9781449323899* for release details.

978-1-4493-2389-9

[LSI]

Table of Contents

Part II.   Moving Around Using ROS

Part IV.   Bringing Your Own Stuff into ROS

Part V.   Tips and Tricks

Preface

ROS, the Robot Operating System, is an open source framework for getting robots to do things. ROS is meant to serve as a common software platform for people who are building and using robots. This common platform lets people share code and ideas more readily and, perhaps more importantly, means that you do not have to spend years writing software infrastructure before your robots start moving!

ROS has been remarkably successful. At the time of writing, in the official distribution of ROS, there are over 2,000 software packages, written and maintained by almost 600 people. Approximately 80 commercially available robots are supported, and we can find at least 1,850 academic papers that mention ROS. We no longer have to write everything from scratch, especially if we're working with one of the many robots that support ROS, and can spend more time thinking about *robotics*, rather than bit-fiddling and device drivers.

ROS consists of a number of parts:

1. A set of drivers that let you read data from sensors and send commands to motors and other actuators, in an abstracted, well-defined format. A wide variety of popular hardware is supported, including a growing number of commercially available robot systems.

2. A large and growing collection of fundamental robotics algorithms that allow you to build maps of the world, navigate around it, represent and interpret sensor data, plan motions, manipulate objects, and do a lot of other stuff. ROS has become very popular in the robotics research community, and a lot of cutting-edge algorithms are now available in ROS.

3. All of the computational infrastructure that allows you to move data around, to connect the various components of a complex robot system, and to incorporate your own algorithms. ROS is inherently distributed and allows you to split the workload across multiple computers seamlessly.

4. A large set of tools that make it easy to visualize the state of the robot and the algorithms, debug faulty behaviors, and record sensor data. Debugging robot software is notoriously difficult, and this rich set of tools is one of the things that make ROS as powerful as it is.

5. Finally, the larger ROS ecosystem includes an extensive set of resources, such as a wiki that documents many of the aspects of the framework, a question-and-answer site where you can ask for help and share what you've learned, and a thriving community of users and developers.

So, why should you learn ROS? The short answer is because it will save you time. ROS provides all the parts of a robot software system that you would otherwise have to write. It allows you to focus on the parts of the system that you care about, without worrying about the parts that you don't care about.

Why should you read this book? There's a lot of material on the ROS wiki, including detailed tutorials for many aspects of the framework. A thriving user community is ready to answer your questions on *http://answers.ros.org*. Why not just learn ROS from these resources? What we've tried to do in this book is to lay things out in a more ordered way and to give comprehensive examples of how you can use ROS to do interesting things with real and simulated robots. We've also tried to include tips and hints about how to structure your code, how to debug your code when it causes the robot to do something unexpected, and how to become part of the ROS community.

There's a fair amount of complexity in ROS, especially if you're not a seasoned programmer; distributed computation, multithreading, event-driven programming, and a host of other concepts lie at the heart of the system. If you're not already familiar with at least some of these, ROS can have a daunting learning curve. This book is an attempt to flatten out that curve a bit by introducing you to the basics of ROS and giving you some practical examples of how to use it for real applications on real (and simulated) robots.

Who Should Read This Book?

If you want to make your robots do things in the real world, but don't want to spend time reinventing the wheel, then this book is for you. ROS includes all of the computational infrastructure you'll need to get your robots up and running and enough robotics algorithms to get them doing interesting things quickly.

If you're interested in some particular aspect, like path planning, and want to investigate it in the context of a larger robot system, then this book is for you. We'll show you how to get your robot doing interesting things using the infrastructure and algorithms in ROS and how to swap out some of the existing algorithms for your own.

If you want to get an introduction to the basic mechanisms of ROS and an overview of some of the things that are possible, but you're a bit daunted by the scale of the information on the wiki, then this book is for you. We'll give you a tour of the basic mechanisms and tools in ROS and concrete examples of complete systems that you can build on and adapt.

Who Should Not Read This Book?

Although we don't want to exclude anyone from reading this book, it's probably not the right resource for everyone. We make certain implicit assumptions about the robots that you will be using. They are probably running Linux, and have decent computational resources (at least equivalent to a laptop computer). They have sophisticated sensors, such as a Microsoft Kinect. They are ground-based, and probably can move about the world. If your robots don't fall into at least some of these categories, the examples in this book might not be immediately relevant to you, although the material on the underlying mechanisms and tools should be.

This book is primarily about ROS, and not about robotics. While you will learn a bit about robotics here, we don't go into great depth about many of the algorithms in ROS. If you're looking for a broad introduction to robotics, then this book isn't the one you're looking for.

What You'll Learn

This book is meant to be a broad introduction to programming robots with ROS. We'll cover the important aspects of the basic mechanisms and tools that make up the core of ROS and show you how to use them to create software to control your robots. We'll show you concrete examples of how you can use ROS to do some interesting things with your robots and give you advice on how to build on these examples to create your own systems.

In addition to the technical material, we'll also show you how to navigate the larger ROS ecosystem, such as the wiki and the Q&A forum, and how to become a part of the global ROS community, sharing your code and newly found knowledge with other roboticists across the world.

Prerequisites

There are a few things that you need to know before you can really use the material in this book. Since ROS is a software framework, you really need to know how to program to properly understand it. Although it's possible to program in ROS in a variety of languages, in this book we're going to be using Python. If you don't know Python, then a lot of the code here isn't going to make much sense. Fortunately, Python is an easy language to learn! There are many excellent reference books and free websites available for learning Python, starting with the official Python website: *http://python.org*.

ROS works best in an Ubuntu Linux environment, and having some previous exposure to Linux will make your life a lot easier. We'll try to introduce the important parts of Linux as we go, but having a basic understanding of the filesystem, the bash command shell, and at least one text editor will help you concentrate on the ROS-specific material.

A basic understanding of robotics, while not strictly necessary to learn ROS, will also be helpful. Knowing something about the underlying mathematics used by robotics, such as coordinate transforms and kinematic chains, will be useful for understanding some of the ROS mechanisms that we talk about. Again, we'll try to give a brief introduction to some of this material, but if you're not familiar with it, you might want to take a side track and dig into the robotics literature to fill in some background.

Conventions Used in This Book

The following typographical conventions are used in this book:

Italic
> Indicates new terms, URLs, email addresses, directory and pathnames, filenames, and file extensions.

`Constant width`
> Used for program listings, as well as within paragraphs to refer to program elements such as variable or function names, namespaces, data types, environment variables, statements, and keywords. Also used for commands, command-line utilities, and ROS packages, nodes, topics, etc.

`Constant width bold`
> Shows commands or other text that should be typed literally by the user.

`Constant width italic`
> Shows text that should be replaced with user-supplied values or by values determined by context.

This icon indicates a general note.

 This icon signifies a tip or suggestion.

 This icon indicates a warning or caution.

Using Code Examples

Supplemental material (code examples, exercises, etc.) is available for download: *https://github.com/osrf/rosbook*.

This book is here to help you get your job done. To that end, the examples in the above-linked repository are available under the Apache 2.0 License, which permits very broad reuse of the code.

We appreciate, but do not require, attribution. An attribution usually includes the title, author, publisher, and ISBN. For example: "*Programming Robots with ROS* by Morgan Quigley, Brian Gerkey, and William D. Smart (O'Reilly). Copyright 2015 Morgan Quigley, Brian Gerkey, and William D. Smart, 978-1-4493-2389-9."

If you feel your use of code examples falls outside fair use or the permission given above, feel free to contact us at *permissions@oreilly.com*.

Safari® Books Online

 *Safari Books Online* is an on-demand digital library that delivers expert content in both book and video form from the world's leading authors in technology and business.

Technology professionals, software developers, web designers, and business and creative professionals use Safari Books Online as their primary resource for research, problem solving, learning, and certification training.

Safari Books Online offers a range of plans and pricing for enterprise, government, education, and individuals.

Members have access to thousands of books, training videos, and prepublication manuscripts in one fully searchable database from publishers like O'Reilly Media, Prentice Hall Professional, Addison-Wesley Professional, Microsoft Press, Sams, Que, Peachpit Press, Focal Press, Cisco Press, John Wiley & Sons, Syngress, Morgan Kaufmann, IBM Redbooks, Packt, Adobe Press, FT Press, Apress, Manning, New Riders, McGraw-Hill, Jones & Bartlett, Course Technology, and hundreds more. For more information about Safari Books Online, please visit us online.

How to Contact Us

Please address comments and questions concerning this book to the publisher:

> O'Reilly Media, Inc.
> 1005 Gravenstein Highway North
> Sebastopol, CA 95472
> 800-998-9938 (in the United States or Canada)
> 707-829-0515 (international or local)
> 707-829-0104 (fax)

We have a web page for this book, where we list errata, examples, and any additional information. You can access this page at *http://bit.ly/prog_robots_w_ros*.

To comment or ask technical questions about this book, send email to *bookquestions@oreilly.com*.

For more information about our books, courses, conferences, and news, see our website at *http://www.oreilly.com*.

Find us on Facebook: *http://facebook.com/oreilly*

Follow us on Twitter: *http://twitter.com/oreillymedia*

Watch us on YouTube: *http://www.youtube.com/oreillymedia*

Acknowledgments

First and foremost, we would like to thank our editors at O'Reilly, Mike Loukides, Meg Blanchette, and Dawn Schanafelt, all of whom showed great patience and uncommon restraint with us as we put this book together. We'd also like to thank everyone who gave us feedback on early drafts of the book, especially Andreas Bihlmaier, Jon Bohren, Zach Dodds, and Kat Scott. Their comments and suggestions made this a much better book.

Thanks, also, to everyone who's helped us figure out how to make ROS do the right thing on our robots. Mike Ferguson helped with the Fetch examples. Steve Peters, Nate Koenig, and John Hsu from the Open Source Robotics Foundation (OSRF) answered some gnarly Gazebo simulation questions. William Woodall and Tully Foote (both from the OSRF) fielded a number of general ROS hacking questions.

Thanks as well to Dylan Jones, who caught a code bug at the last minute before the book went to press.

Finally, we'd like to thank all of the authors, maintainers, and users in the worldwide ROS community. If it wasn't for them, ROS would not be what it is today, and we would not be writing this preface.

PART I

Fundamentals

## CHAPTER 1

Introduction

The Robot Operating System (ROS) is a framework for writing robot software. It is a collection of tools, libraries, and conventions that aim to simplify the task of creating complex and robust robot behavior across a wide variety of robotic platforms.

Why? Because creating truly robust, general-purpose robot software is *hard*. From the robot's perspective, many problems that seem trivial to humans can actually encompass wild variations between instances of tasks and environments.

Consider a simple "fetch an item" task, where an office-assistant robot is instructed to retrieve a stapler. First, the robot must understand the request, either verbally or through some other modality, such as a web interface, email, or even SMS. Then, the robot must start some sort of planner to coordinate the search for the item, which will likely require navigating through various rooms in a building, perhaps including elevators and doors. Once arriving in a room, the robot must search desks cluttered with similarly sized objects (since all handheld objects are roughly the same size) and find a stapler. The robot must then retrace its steps and deliver the stapler to the desired location. Each of those subproblems can have arbitrary numbers of complicating factors. And this was a relatively simple task!

Dealing with real-world variations in complex tasks and environments is so difficult that no single individual, laboratory, or institution can hope to build a complete system from scratch. As a result, ROS was built from the ground up to encourage *collaborative* robotics software development. For example, in the "fetch a stapler" problem, one organization might have experts in mapping indoor environments and could contribute a complex yet easy-to-use system for producing indoor maps. Another group might have expertise in using maps to robustly navigate indoor environments. Yet another group might have discovered a particular computer vision approach that works well for recognizing small objects in clutter. ROS includes many features specifically designed to simplify this type of large-scale collaboration.

Brief History

ROS is a large project that has many ancestors and contributors. The need for an open collaboration framework was felt by many people in the robotics research community. Various projects at Stanford University in the mid-2000s involving integrative, embodied AI, such as the STanford AI Robot (STAIR) and the Personal Robots (PR) program, created in-house prototypes of the types of flexible, dynamic software systems described in this book. In 2007, Willow Garage, Inc., a nearby robotics incubator, provided significant resources to extend these concepts much further and create well-tested implementations. The effort was boosted by countless researchers who contributed their time and expertise to the core of ROS and its fundamental software packages. Throughout, the software was developed in the open using the permissive BSD open source license, and it gradually became widely used in the robotics research community.

From the start, ROS was being developed at multiple institutions and for multiple robots. At first, this seemed like a headache, since it would have been far simpler for all contributors to place their code on the same servers. Ironically, over the years, this has emerged as one of the great strengths of the ROS ecosystem: any group can start their own ROS code repository on their own servers, and they will maintain full ownership and control of it. They don't need anyone's permission. If they choose to make their repository publicly visible, they can receive the recognition and credit they deserve for their achievements and benefit from specific technical feedback and improvements like all open source software projects.

The ROS ecosystem now consists of tens of thousands of users worldwide, working in domains ranging from tabletop hobby projects to large industrial automation systems.

Philosophy

All software frameworks impose their development philosophies on their contributors directly or indirectly, through their idioms and common practices. Broadly speaking, ROS follows the Unix philosophy of software development in several key aspects. This tends to make ROS feel "natural" for developers coming from a Unix background but somewhat "cryptic" at first for those who have primarily used graphical development environments on Windows or Mac OS X. The following paragraphs describe several philosophical aspects of ROS:

Peer to peer
> ROS systems consist of numerous small computer programs that connect to one another and continuously exchange *messages*. These messages travel directly from one program to another; there is no central routing service. Although this

makes the underlying "plumbing" more complex, the result is a system that scales better as the amount of data increases.

Tools-based

As demonstrated by the enduring architecture of Unix, complex software systems can be created from many small, generic programs. Unlike many other robotics software frameworks, ROS does not have a canonical integrated development and runtime environment. Tasks such as navigating the source code tree, visualizing the system interconnections, graphically plotting data streams, generating documentation, logging data, etc. are all performed by separate programs. This encourages the creation of new, improved implementations, since (ideally) they can be exchanged for implementations better suited for a particular task domain. Recent versions of ROS allow many of these tools to be composed into single processes for efficiency or to create coherent interfaces for operators or debugging, but the principle remains the same: the individual tools themselves are relatively small and generic.

Multilingual

Many software tasks are easier to accomplish in "high-productivity" scripting languages such as Python or Ruby. However, there are times when performance requirements dictate the use of faster languages, such as C++. There are also various reasons that some programmers prefer languages such as Lisp or MATLAB. Endless email flame wars have been waged, are currently being waged, and will doubtless continue to be waged over which language is best suited for a particular task. Acknowledging that all of these opinions have merit, that languages have different utilities in different contexts, and that each programmer's unique background is hugely important when choosing a language, ROS chose a *multilingual* approach. ROS software modules can be written in any language for which a *client library* has been written. At the time of writing, client libraries exist for C++, Python, LISP, Java, JavaScript, MATLAB, Ruby, Haskell, R, Julia, and others. ROS client libraries communicate with one another by following a convention that describes how messages are "flattened" or "serialized" before being transmitted over the network. This book will use the Python client library almost exclusively, to save space in the code examples and for its general ease of use. However, the tasks described in this book can be accomplished with any of the client libraries.

Thin

The ROS conventions encourage contributors to create standalone libraries and then *wrap* those libraries so they can send and receive messages to and from other ROS modules. This extra layer is intended to allow the reuse of software outside of ROS for other applications, and it greatly simplifies the creation of automated tests using standard continuous integration tools.

Free and open source

The core of ROS is released under the permissive BSD license, which allows commercial and noncommercial use. ROS passes data between modules using interprocess communication (IPC), which means that systems built using ROS can have fine-grained licensing of their various components. Commercial systems, for example, often have several closed source modules communicating with a large number of open source modules. Academic and hobby projects are often fully open source. Commercial product development is often done completely behind a firewall. All of these use cases, and more, are common and perfectly valid under the ROS license.

Installation

Although ROS has been made to work on a wide variety of systems, in this book we will be using Ubuntu Linux, a popular and relatively user-friendly Linux distribution. Ubuntu provides an easy-to-use installer that allows computers to dual-boot between the operating system they were shipped with (typically Windows or Mac OS X) and Ubuntu itself. That being said, it is important to back up your computer before installing Ubuntu, in case something unexpected happens and the drive is completely erased in the process.

Although there are virtualization environments such as VirtualBox and VMware that allow Linux to run concurrently with a host operating system such as Windows or Mac OS X, the simulator used in this book is rather compute- and graphics-intensive, and might be overly sluggish in a virtualized environment. As such, we recommend running Ubuntu Linux natively by following the instructions on the Ubuntu website.

Ubuntu Linux can be downloaded freely from *http://ubuntu.com*. The remainder of this book assumes that ROS is being run on Ubuntu 14.04 LTS, also known as Ubuntu Trusty Tahr, and will use the ROS Indigo distribution.

The ROS installation steps require a few shell commands that involve some careful typing. These can be either hand-copied from the following block (note that the first command has been broken across lines to fit the page margins; you can enter this on a single line, without the backslashes), or copied and pasted from the ROS wiki (*http://wiki.ros.org/indigo/Installation/Ubuntu*). The following commands will add *ros.org* to the system's list of software sources, download and install the ROS packages, and set up the environment and ROS build tools:

```
user@hostname$ sudo sh -c \
  'echo "deb http://packages.ros.org/ros/ubuntu trusty main" > \
  /etc/apt/sources.list.d/ros-latest.list'
user@hostname$ wget http://packages.ros.org/ros.key -O - | sudo apt-key add -
user@hostname$ sudo apt-get update
user@hostname$ sudo apt-get install ros-indigo-desktop-full python-rosinstall
user@hostname$ sudo rosdep init
```

```
user@hostname$ rosdep update
user@hostname$ echo "source /opt/ros/indigo/setup.bash" >> ~/.bashrc
user@hostname$ source ~/.bashrc
```

That seems like a gnarly block of shell commands! Some of them are indeed a bit unusual, but others will be commonly used when using ROS and other large software packages on Ubuntu systems. In particular, the apt-get command is a commonly used command on Ubuntu Linux distributions (among others), and it will be used frequently throughout the book to install additional software packages. This command will install the desired software package(s) requested on the command line, as well as their dependencies, and their dependencies' dependencies, and so on. If you'd rather use a graphical application to install and manage your Ubuntu package files, you can install synaptic. Of course, you might have to do this on the command line:

```
user@hostname$ sudo apt-get install synaptic
```

The last two lines of the installation sequence add the ROS environment setup script, *setup.bash*, to the current and future shells on this system. This means that commands and shell scripts provided by ROS, such as the many command-line tools described in future chapters, are now accessible to the shell interpreters on this system. Without those two lines, users would have to manually source the */opt/ros/ indigo/setup.bash* file for each command shell they opened. Adding the ROS *setup.bash* file to the user's *~/.bashrc* ensures that this step happens automatically for all future command shells.

Throughout the book, we will refer to various operating system features as "POSIX," such as "POSIX processes," "POSIX environment variables," and so on. This is meant to indicate that much of ROS is written with *portability* in mind between POSIX-compliant systems, such as Linux or Mac OS X. That being said, in this book we will be focusing specifically on Ubuntu Linux, since it is a popular Linux distribution for the desktop and since the ROS build farm produces easy-to-install binaries for Ubuntu.

Summary

This chapter has provided a high-level overview of ROS and its guiding philosophical ideas. ROS is a *framework* for developing robotics software. The software is structured as a large number of small programs that rapidly pass messages to one another. This paradigm was chosen to encourage the reuse of robotics software outside the particular robot and environment that drove its creation. Indeed, this loosely coupled structure allows for the creation of *generic* modules that are applicable to broad classes of robot hardware and software pipelines, facilitating code sharing and reuse among the global robotics community.

## CHAPTER 2

Preliminaries

Before we start writing code in ROS, we're going to take a moment to introduce some of the key concepts that underlie the framework. ROS systems are comprised of a large number of independent programs that are constantly communicating with each other. In this chapter, we'll discuss this architecture and look at the command-line tools that interact with it. We'll also discuss the details of the naming schemes and namespaces used by ROS, and how these can be employed to promote reuse of your code.

The ROS Graph

One of the original "challenge problems" that motivated the design of ROS was fondly referred to as the "fetch an item" problem. Imagine a relatively large and complex robot with several cameras and laser scanners, a manipulator arm, and a wheeled base. In the "fetch an item" problem, the robot's task is to navigate a typical home or office environment, find the requested item, and deliver it to the requested location. This task, like many robotics tasks, led to several observations about many robotics software applications, which became some of the design goals of ROS:

- The application task can be decomposed into many independent subsystems, such as navigation, computer vision, grasping, and so on.
- These subsystems can be used for other tasks, such as doing security patrols, cleaning, delivering mail, and so on.
- With proper hardware and geometry abstraction layers, the vast majority of the application software can run on *any* robot.

These goals can be illustrated by the fundamental rendering of a ROS system: its *graph*. A ROS system is made up of many different programs running simultaneously and communicating with one another by passing *messages*. It is convenient to use a mathematical *graph* to represent this collection of programs and messages: the programs are the graph *nodes*, and programs that communicate with one another are connected by *edges*. A sample ROS graph appears in Figure 2-1, which represents one of the earliest implementations of the "fetch an item" application using ROS. The details of this graph are not particularly important; it is just provided to illustrate the general concept of a ROS system as a collection of nodes passing messages to one another. We can represent any ROS system, large or small, in this way. In fact, this representation is so useful for software development that we actually refer to ROS programs as *nodes*, to help us remember that each program is just one piece of a much larger system.

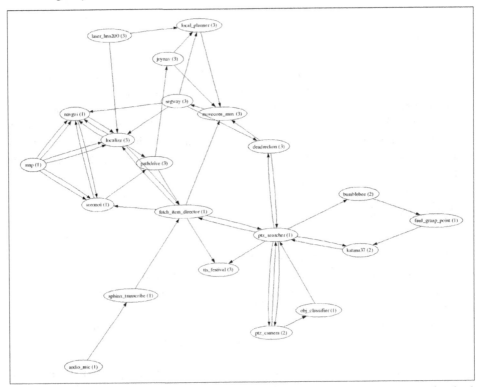

Figure 2-1. ROS graph of a fetch-an-item robot—nodes in the graph represent individual programs; edges represent message streams communicating sensor data, actuator commands, planner states, intermediate representations, and so on

To reiterate: a ROS graph *node* represents a software module that is sending or receiving messages, and a ROS graph *edge* represents a stream of messages between two nodes. Although things can get more complex, typically nodes are POSIX processes, and edges are TCP connections. This offers additional fault tolerance: a software crash will typically only take down its own process. The rest of the graph will stay up, passing messages and functioning as normal. The circumstances leading up to the crash can often be recreated by logging the messages entering a node and simply playing them back at a later time inside a debugger.

However, perhaps the greatest benefit of a loosely coupled, graph-based architecture is the ability to rapid-prototype complex systems with little or no software "glue" required for experimentation. Single nodes, such as the object recognition node in a "fetch an item" system, can be trivially swapped by simply launching an entirely different process that accepts images and outputs labeled objects. Not only can a single node be swapped, but entire chunks of the graph (*subgraphs*) can be torn down and replaced, at runtime, with other subgraphs. Real-robot hardware drivers can be replaced with simulators, navigation subsystems can be swapped, algorithms can be tweaked and recompiled, and so on. Since ROS is creating all of the required network backend on the fly, the entire system is interactive and designed to encourage experimentation.

Up to this point, we have assumed that nodes somehow find each other but have not described how that process works. Among all the traffic flying around a busy network, how do nodes find one another, so they can start passing messages? The answer lies in a program called roscore.

roscore

roscore is a service that provides connection information to nodes so that they can transmit messages to one another. Every node connects to roscore at startup to register details of the message streams it publishes and the streams to which it wishes to subscribe. When a new node appears, roscore provides it with the information that it needs to form a direct peer-to-peer connection with other nodes publishing and subscribing to the same message topics. Every ROS system needs a running roscore, since without it, nodes cannot find other nodes.

However, a key aspect of ROS is that the messages between nodes are transmitted peer-to-peer. The roscore is only used by nodes to know where to find their peers. This is a bit subtle, and can lead to some misunderstandings, as programmers coming from web-based backgrounds are often familiar with client/server systems, such as web-browsers talking to web servers, where the roles of clients and servers are clearly defined. The ROS architecture is a hybrid between a classical client/server system and a fully distributed one, due to the presence of a central roscore that provides a name service for the peer-to-peer message streams.

When a ROS node starts up, it expects its process to have an environment variable named ROS_MASTER_URI. This variable is expected to contain a string of the form http://*hostname*:11311/, which in this case would imply that there is a running instance of roscore accessible on port 11311 somewhere on a host called *hostname* that can be accessed over the network.

 Port 11311 was chosen as the default port for roscore because it was a palindromic prime that was not being used by other popular applications in the early days of ROS, circa 2007. It has no particular significance. Any user space port number (1025–65535) can be used instead. Different ports can be specified in the roscore startup command and in the ROS_MASTER_URI environment variable to allow multiple ROS systems to coexist on a single network.

With knowledge of the location of roscore on the network, nodes register themselves at startup with roscore and then query roscore to find other nodes and data streams by name. Each ROS node tells roscore which messages it provides and which it would like to subscribe to. roscore then provides the addresses of the relevant message producers and consumers. Viewed in a graph form, every node in the graph can periodically call on services provided by roscore to find its peers. This is represented by the dashed lines shown in Figure 2-2, which show that in this minimalist two-node system, the talker and listener nodes can periodically make calls to roscore while exchanging peer-to-peer messages directly themselves.

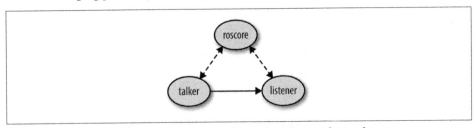

Figure 2-2. roscore connects only ephemerally to the other nodes in the system

roscore also provides a *parameter server*, which is used extensively by ROS nodes for configuration. The parameter server allows nodes to store and retrieve arbitrary data structures, such as descriptions of robots, parameters for algorithms, and so on. As with everything in ROS, there is a simple command-line tool to interact with the parameter server: rosparam, which will be used throughout the book.

We'll see examples of how to use roscore soon. For now, all you really need to remember is that roscore is a program that allows nodes to find other nodes. The last thing you need to know about before we start running some nodes is how ROS organizes packages and a little bit about how the ROS build system, known as catkin, works.

catkin, Workspaces, and ROS Packages

catkin is the ROS build system: the set of tools that ROS uses to generate executable programs, libraries, scripts, and interfaces that other code can use. If you use C++ to write your ROS code, you need to know a fair bit about catkin. Since we're going to be using Python for the examples in this book, we can get away without delving into all the details. We will, however, have to interact with it a bit, so we'll spend some time now talking about how it works. If you're interested in learning more, the catkin wiki page (*http://wiki.ros.org/catkin?distro=indigo*) is a good place to start. If you want to know why ROS has its own build system in the first place, there's a good discussion on the catkin conceptual overview wiki page (*http://wiki.ros.org/catkin/concep tual_overview?distro=indigo*).

catkin

catkin comprises a set of CMake macros and custom Python scripts to provide extra functionality on top of the normal CMake workflow. CMake is a commonly used open source build system. If you're going to master the subtleties of catkin, it really helps if you know a bit about CMake. However, for the more casual catkin user, all you really need to know is that there are two files, *CMakeLists.txt* and *package.xml*, that you need to add some specific information to in order to have things work properly. You then call the various catkin tools to generate the directories and files you're going to need as you write code for your robots. These tools will be introduced as we need them throughout the book. Before we get to any of this, though, we need to introduce you to workspaces.

Workspaces

Before you start writing any ROS code, you need to set up a *workspace* for this code to live in. A workspace is simply a set of directories in which a related set of ROS code lives. You can have multiple ROS workspaces, but you can only work in one of them at any one time. The simple way to think about this is that you can only see code that lives in your current workspace.

Start by making sure that you've added the system-wide ROS setup script to your *.bashrc* file, as described in "Installation" on page 6. If you haven't done that already, do it now, or source the file by hand:

```
user@hostname$ source /opt/ros/indigo/setup.bash
```

Now, we're going to make a catkin workspace and initialize it:

```
user@hostname$ mkdir -p ~/catkin_ws/src
user@hostname$ cd ~/catkin_ws/src
user@hostname$ catkin_init_workspace
```

This creates a workspace directory called *catkin_ws* (although you can call it anything you like), with a *src* directory inside it for your code. The `catkin_init_workspace` command creates a *CMakeLists.txt* file for you in the *src* directory, where you invoked it.[1] Next, we're going to create some other workspace files:

```
user@hostname$ cd ~/catkin_ws
user@hostname$ catkin_make
```

Running `catkin_make` will generate a lot of output as it does its work. When it's done, you'll end up with two new directories: *build* and *devel*. *build* is where `catkin` is going to store the results of some of its work, like libraries and executable programs if you use C++. We'll largely ignore *build* since we don't need it much when using Python. *devel* contains a number of files and directories, the most interesting of which are the *setup* files. Running these configures your system to use this workspace, and the code that's (going to be) contained inside it. Assuming you're using the default command-line shell (`bash`) and are still in the top-level directory of your workspace, you can do this with:

```
user@hostname$ source devel/setup.bash
```

Congratulations! You've just created your first ROS workspace. You should put all the code for this book, and any additional code you write that's based on it, into this workspace, in the *src* directory, organized as ROS packages.

 If you open a new shell (or Linux terminal), you have to `source` the *setup.bash* file for the workspace you want to work with. If you don't do this, then the shell won't know where to find your code. This can be annoying, since it's an easy thing to forget. One way to get around this if you only have one workspace is to add the `source ~/catkin_ws/devel/setup.bash` command to your *.bashrc* file (with the appropriate filename, of course). This will automatically set up your workspace for you when you open a new shell.

ROS Packages

ROS software is organized into *packages*, each of which contains some combination of code, data, and documentation.[2] The ROS ecosystem includes thousands of pub-

---

1 Actually, it creates a symbolic link to a system-wide *CMakeLists.txt* file.

2 Unfortunately, Ubuntu software is also organized into packages. The ROS Ubuntu packages (the things you install with `apt-get`) are conceptually different from ROS packages. In this book, we'll use "ROS package" or simply "package" when referring to a ROS package. We'll use "Ubuntu package" to refer to an Ubuntu package.

licly available packages in open repositories, and many thousands more packages are certainly lurking behind organizational firewalls.

Packages sit inside workspaces, in the *src* directory. Each package directory *must* include a *CMakeLists.txt* file and a *package.xml* file that describes the contents of the package and how `catkin` should interact with it. Creating a new package is easy:

```
user@hostname$ cd ~/catkin_ws/src
user@hostname$ catkin_create_pkg my_awesome_code rospy
```

This changes the directory to *src* (where packages live) and invokes `catkin_cre ate_pkg` to make the new package called `my_awesome_code`, which depends on the (already existing) `rospy` package. If your new package depends on other existing packages, you can also list them on the command line. We'll talk about package dependencies later in the book, so don't worry if that bit doesn't make a lot of sense to you just yet.

The `catkin_create_pkg` command makes a directory with the same name as the new package (*my_awesome_code*) with a *CMakeLists.txt* file, a *package.xml* file, and a *src* directory in it. The *package.xml* file contains a bunch of metadata about your new package, as shown in Example 2-1.

Example 2-1. An example empty package file

```
<?xml version="1.0"?>
<package>
  <name>my_awesome_code</name> ❶
  <version>0.0.0</version> ❷
  <description>The my_awesome_code package</description>        ❸

  <!-- One maintainer tag required, multiple allowed, one person per tag -->
  <!-- Example:  -->
  <!-- <maintainer email="jane.doe@example.com">Jane Doe</maintainer> -->
  <maintainer email="user@todo.todo">user</maintainer>        ❹


  <!-- One license tag required, multiple allowed, one license per tag -->
  <!-- Commonly used license strings: -->
  <!--    BSD, MIT, Boost Software License, GPLv2, GPLv3, LGPLv2.1, LGPLv3 -->
  <license>TODO</license>        ❺


  <!-- Url tags are optional, but multiple are allowed, one per tag -->
  <!-- Optional attribute type can be: website, bugtracker, or repository -->
  <!-- Example: -->
  <!-- <url type="website">http://wiki.ros.org/my_awesome_code</url> -->        ❻


  <!-- Author tags are optional, multiple are allowed, one per tag -->
  <!-- Authors do not have to be maintainers, but could be -->
```

```
<!-- Example: -->
<!-- <author email="jane.doe@example.com">Jane Doe</author> -->          ❼


<!-- The *_depend tags are used to specify dependencies -->
<!-- Dependencies can be catkin packages or system dependencies -->
<!-- Examples: -->
<!-- Use build_depend for packages you need at compile time: -->
<!--    <build_depend>message_generation</build_depend> -->
<!-- Use buildtool_depend for build tool packages: -->
<!--    <buildtool_depend>catkin</buildtool_depend> -->
<!-- Use run_depend for packages you need at runtime: -->
<!--    <run_depend>message_runtime</run_depend> -->
<!-- Use test_depend for packages you need only for testing: -->
<!--    <test_depend>gtest</test_depend> -->
<buildtool_depend>catkin</buildtool_depend>          ❽
<build_depend>rospy</build_depend>
<run_depend>rospy</run_depend>


<!-- The export tag contains other, unspecified, tags -->
<export>          ❾
  <!-- Other tools can request additional information be placed here -->

</export>
</package>
```

❶   The name of your package. You shouldn't change this.

❷   The version number.

❸   A short description of what's in the package and what it's for.

❹   Who's responsible for maintaining the package and fixing bugs?

❺   What license are you releasing the code under?

❻   A URL, often pointing at the ROS wiki page for the package.

❼   Who wrote the package? One set of tags per author.

❽   What dependencies does the package have? We'll cover this later.

❾   This is for information used by other tools external to catkin.

We're going to ignore the *CMakeLists.txt* file for now, since we'll return to it later. You can take a look at it if you like, but unless you are already familiar with CMake it might not make a lot of sense to you.

Once you have a created package, you can put your Python nodes in the *src* directory. Other files go in directories under the package directory, too. For instance, launch files, which we'll talk about soon, conventionally go in a directory called *launch*.

Now that you know what a package directory looks like, we're going to talk about the tools that you're going to use to run nodes from your packages.

rosrun

Since ROS has a large, distributed community, its software is organized into packages that are independently developed by community members. The concept of a ROS package will be described in greater detail in subsequent chapters, but a package can be thought of as a collection of resources that are built and distributed together. Packages are just locations in the filesystem, and because ROS nodes are typically executable programs, one could manually cd around the filesystem to start all the ROS nodes of interest.

For example, the talker program lives in a package named rospy_tutorials, and its executable programs are found in */opt/ros/indigo/share/rospy_tutorials*. However, chasing down these long paths would become tiresome in large filesystems, since nodes can be deeply buried in large directory hierarchies. To automate this task, ROS provides a command-line utility called rosrun that will search a package for the requested program and pass it any parameters supplied on the command line. The syntax is as follows:

    user@hostname$ *rosrun PACKAGE EXECUTABLE [ARGS]*

To run the talker program in the rospy_tutorials package, no matter where one happened to be in the filesystem, one would first start a roscore instance in a terminal emulator window:

    user@hostname$ **roscore**

Then, in another terminal window, run:

    user@hostname$ **rosrun rospy_tutorials talker**

This will create the ROS graph in Figure 2-3.

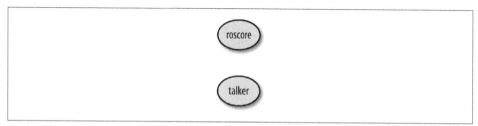

Figure 2-3. A ROS graph with only one node

In the terminal with `talker`, there will be a sequence of timestamp messages printing to the console:

```
user@hostname$ rosrun rospy_tutorials talker

[INFO] [WallTime: 1439847784.336147] hello world 1439847784.34
[INFO] [WallTime: 1439847784.436334] hello world 1439847784.44
[INFO] [WallTime: 1439847784.536316] hello world 1439847784.54
[INFO] [WallTime: 1439847784.636319] hello world 1439847784.64
```

The `talker` program is the ROS equivalent of the canonical first program whose task is to print "Hello, world!" to the console. In the ROS case, since we are dealing with message streams rather than single statements, `talker` sends a stream of "hello world" messages 10 times per second, appending the Unix timestamp so that it's easy to tell that the messages are changing over time. `talker` prints these messages to the console as well as sending them via ROS to any nodes who are listening.

It is instructive to think about how this is implemented. In Unix, every program has a stream called "standard output," or `stdout`. When an interactive terminal runs a "Hello, world!" program, its `stdout` stream is received by its parent terminal program, which renders the text in a *terminal emulator* window. In ROS, this concept is extended so that programs have an arbitrary number of streams, connected to an arbitrary number of other programs running on machines anywhere in the network, any of which can start up or shut down at any time.

Therefore, creating a minimal "Hello, world!" system in ROS requires two nodes, with one node sending a stream of string messages to the other nodes. As we have seen, `talker` will periodically send "hello world" as a text message. Simultaneously, we will start a `listener` node, which will await new string messages and print them to the console as they arrive. Whenever both of these programs advertise themselves to the same `roscore`, ROS will connect them as shown in Figure 2-4. Note that in Figure 2-4 and all future ROS graph renderings, we will omit `roscore` from the graph, since it is implied by the existence of the graph itself (i.e., without `roscore`, there could be no ROS graph).

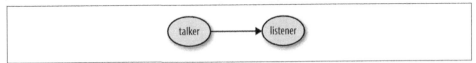

Figure 2-4. "Hello, world!" in ROS: talker sends messages to listener

To create this graph on your own computer, you'll need three terminal windows. The first two, as before, will run `roscore` and `talker`, and the third one will run `listener`:

```
user@hostname$ rosrun rospy_tutorials listener

[INFO] [WallTime: 1439848277.141546] /listener_14364_1439848276913 \
  I heard hello world 1439848277.14
[INFO] [WallTime: 1439848277.241519] /listener_14364_1439848276913 \
  I heard hello world 1439848277.24
[INFO] [WallTime: 1439848277.341668] /listener_14364_1439848276913 \
  I heard hello world 1439848277.34
[INFO] [WallTime: 1439848277.441579] /listener_14364_1439848276913 \
  I heard hello world 1439848277.44
```

Hooray! The `talker` node is now sending messages to the `listener` node. We can now use some ROS command-line tools to query the system and understand more about what's happening. First, we can use the command-line tool `rostopic`, which is an extremely useful tool for introspecting running ROS systems. `rostopic` has many subcommands that will be introduced in later chapters, but its simplest and most-commonly used subcommand is to print the list of current message topics to the console. While leaving the other three terminals open and running (that is, the terminals with, `roscore`, `talker`, and `listener`), open a fourth terminal window and launch the ROS Qt-based graph visualizer, `rqt_graph`:

```
user@hostname$ rqt_graph
```

This will bring up a display that produces renderings similar to those shown in Figure 2-4. The renderings will not autorefresh, but you can click the refresh icon in the upper-left corner of the `rqt_graph` window when you add a node to or remove one from the ROS graph by terminating (e.g., pressing Ctrl-C) or running (via `ros run`) its program, and the graph will be redrawn to represent the current state of the system.

Now that we have a ROS graph up and running, we can demonstrate some of the benefits of this message-passing architecture. Imagine that you wanted to create a log file of these "hello world" messages. Typical ROS development follows the pattern of an *anonymous* publish/subscribe system: nodes generally do not receive or use any details about the identity or function of the peer nodes, where their inbound messages are coming from, or where they are going. There are special cases (for example, debugging tools) that acquire and use this information, but generally speaking, typical ROS development does not, with the goal that software modules will work with a wide variety of peer nodes.

We can thus create a generic `logger` program that writes all incoming messages to disk, and tie that to `talker`, as shown in Figure 2-5.

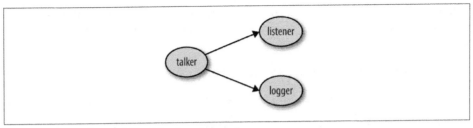

Figure 2-5. "Hello, world" with a logging node

Perhaps we want to run our "Hello, world!" program on two different computers and have a single node receive both of their messages. Without having to modify any source code, we can just start `talker` twice, calling the nodes `talker1` and `talker2`, respectively, and ROS will connect them as shown in Figure 2-6.

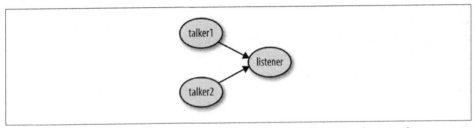

Figure 2-6. Instantiating two "Hello, world!" programs and routing them to the same receiver

Perhaps we want to simultaneously log and print both of those streams? Again, this can be accomplished without modifying any source code; ROS will happily route the streams as shown in Figure 2-7.

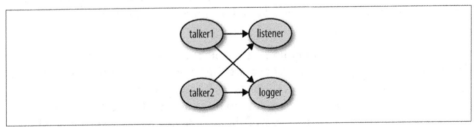

Figure 2-7. Two "Hello, world!" programs with two listeners

Of course, a typical robot is more complicated than this "Hello, world!" example. For example, the "fetch an item" problem described at the beginning of this chapter was implemented on Stanford's STAIR robot in the early days of ROS development, using the exact graph previously shown as Figure 2-1 and reprinted as Figure 2-8 for convenience. This system included 22 programs running on 4 computers and would now be considered a relatively simple software system.

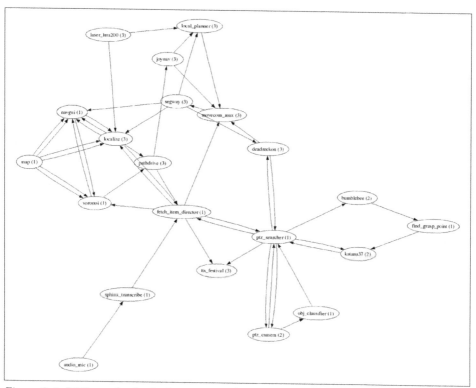

Figure 2-8. ROS graph of a fetch-an-item robot

In Figure 2-8, the STAIR navigation system is approximately the upper half of the graph, and its vision and grasping systems are in the lower-right corner. It is interesting to note that this graph is *sparse*, with most nodes connecting to a very small number of other nodes. This property is commonly seen in ROS graphs and can serve as a check on a software architecture: if a ROS graph starts looking like a star, where most nodes are streaming data to or from a central node, it is often worthwhile to re-assess the flow of data and separate functions into smaller pieces. The goal is to create small, manageable functional units, which ideally can be reused in other applications on other robots.

Although rosrun is great for starting single ROS nodes during debugging sessions, most robot systems end up consisting of tens or hundreds of nodes, all running at the same time. Since it wouldn't be practical to call rosrun on each of these nodes, ROS includes a tool for starting collections of nodes, called roslaunch. We'll look at roslaunch shortly, but first we need to talk about how things are named in ROS.

Names, Namespaces, and Remapping

Names are a fundamental concept in ROS. Nodes, message streams (often called "topics"), and parameters must all have unique names. For example, the camera node on a robot could be named camera, and it could output a message topic named image and read a parameter named frame_rate to know how fast to send images.

So far, so good. But, what happens when a robot has two cameras? We wouldn't want to have to write a separate program for each camera, nor would we want the output of both cameras to be interleaved on the image topic, since that would require all subscribers to image to have logic that separates the image streams.

More generally, namespace collisions are extremely common in robotic systems, which often contain identical hardware or software subsystems to simplify their engineering, such as identical left and right arms, cameras, or wheels. ROS provides two mechanisms to handle these situations: *namespaces* and *remapping*.

Namespaces are a fundamental concept throughout computer science. Following the convention of Unix paths and Internet URIs, ROS uses the forward slash (/) to delimit namespaces. Just like how two files named *readme.txt* can exist in separate paths, such as */home/user1/readme.txt* and */home/user2/readme.txt*, ROS can launch identical nodes into separate namespaces to avoid name collisions.

In the previous example, a robot with two cameras could launch two camera drivers in separate namespaces, such as left and right, which would result in image streams named left/image and right/image.

This avoids a topic name collision, but how could we send these data streams to another program that was still expecting to receive messages on the topic image? One answer would be to launch this other program in the same namespace as the first, but perhaps this program needs to "reach into" more than one namespace. Enter *remapping*.

In ROS, any string in a program that defines a name can be *remapped* at runtime. As one example, there is a commonly used program in ROS called image_view that renders a live video window of images being sent on the image topic. At least, that is what is written in the source code of the image_view program. Using remapping, we can instead cause the image_view program to render the right/image topic, or the left/image topic, without having to modify the source code of image_view!

Because ROS design patterns try to encourage reuse of software, remapping names is very common when developing and deploying ROS software. To simplify this operation, ROS provides a standard syntax to remap names when starting nodes on the command line. For example, if the working directory contains the image_view program, one could type the following to map image to right/image:

```
user@hostname$ ./image_view image:=right/image
```

This command-line remapping would produce the graph shown in Figure 2-9.

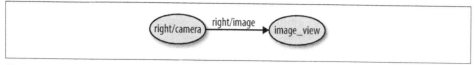

Figure 2-9. Image topic has right/image using command-line remapping

Pushing a node into a namespace can be accomplished with a special __ns namespace-remapping syntax (note the double underscore). For example, if the working directory contains the camera program, the following shell command would launch camera into the namespace right:

```
user@hostname$ ./camera __ns:=right
```

Just as for filesystems, web URLs, and countless other domains, ROS names must be unique. If the same node is launched twice, roscore directs the older node to exit to make way for the newer instance of the node.

Earlier in this chapter, a graph was shown that had two nodes, talker1 and talker2, sending data to a node named listener. To change the *name* of a node on the command line, the special __name remapping syntax can be used. This changes the name of a program when it is launched (again, note the double underscore). The following two shell commands would launch two instances of talker, one named talker1 and one named talker2, as was shown in Figure 2-6:

```
user@hostname$ ./talker __name:=talker1
```

```
user@hostname$ ./talker __name:=talker2
```

The previous examples demonstrated that ROS topics can be remapped quickly and easily on the command line. This is useful for debugging and for initially hacking systems together when experimenting with various ideas. However, after typing long command-line strings a few times, it's time to automate them! The roslaunch tool was created for this purpose.

roslaunch

roslaunch is a command-line tool designed to automate the launching of collections of ROS nodes. On the surface, it looks a lot like rosrun, needing a package name and a filename:

```
user@hostname$ roslaunch PACKAGE LAUNCH_FILE
```

However, roslaunch operates on *launch files*, rather than nodes. Launch files are XML files that describe a collection of nodes along with their topic remappings and parameters. By convention, these files have a suffix of *.launch*. For example, here is *talker_listener.launch* in the `rospy_tutorials` package:

```
<launch>
  <node name="talker" pkg="rospy_tutorials"
        type="talker.py" output="screen" />
  <node name="listener" pkg="rospy_tutorials"
        type="listener.py" output="screen" />
</launch>
```

Each <node> tag includes attributes declaring the ROS graph name of the node, the package in which it can be found, and the *type* of node, which is simply the filename of the executable program. In this example, the `output="screen"` attributes indicate that the `talker` and `listener` nodes should dump their console outputs to the current console, instead of only to log files. This is a commonly used setting for debugging; once things start working, it is often convenient to remove this attribute so that the console has less noise.

`roslaunch` has many other important features, such as the ability to launch programs on other computers across the network via `ssh`, to automatically respawn nodes that crash, and so on. These features will be described throughout the book as they are necessary to accomplish various tasks. One of the most useful features of `roslaunch` is that it closes all of its nodes when Ctrl-C is pressed in the console containing `roslaunch`. Ctrl-C is a common way to force programs to exit on the Linux/Unix command line, and `roslaunch` follows this convention by closing its collection of launched nodes and then finally exiting `roslaunch` itself when Ctrl-C is typed into its console. For example, the following command would cause `roslaunch` to spawn two nodes to form a talker-listener pair, as described in the *talker_listener.launch* file listed previously:

```
user@hostname$ roslaunch rospy_tutorials talker_listener.launch
```

And, equally importantly, pressing Ctrl-C would cause the nodes to exit. Virtually every time you use ROS, you'll be invoking `roslaunch` and eventually typing Ctrl-C in the `roslaunch` terminal(s) to create and destroy various collections of nodes.

`roslaunch` will automatically instantiate a `roscore` if one does not exist when `roslaunch` is invoked. However, this `roscore` will exit when Ctrl-C is pressed in the `roslaunch` window. If you have more than one terminal open when launching ROS programs, it's often easier to remember to launch a `roscore` in a separate terminal, which is left open during the entire ROS session. Then, you can `roslaunch` and Ctrl-C with abandon in all other consoles, without risk of losing the `roscore` tying the whole system together.

Before we start to look at writing some code with ROS, there's one more thing to cover that will save you time and heartache as you try to remember the names of packages, nodes, and launch files: tab completion.

The Tab Key

The ROS command-line tools have tab-completion support. When using `rosrun`, for example, hitting the Tab key in the middle of typing a package name will auto-complete it for you; or, if there are multiple potential completions, pressing Tab again will present you with a list of possible completions. As with many other Linux commands, using tab completion with ROS will save you a massive amount of typing, and help avoid spelling errors when trying to type long package or message names. For example, typing:

```
user@hostname$ rosrun rospy_tutorials ta[TAB]
```

will autocomplete to:

```
user@hostname$ rosrun rospy_tutorials talker
```

since no other programs in the `rospy_tutorials` package begin with `ta`. Additionally, `rosrun` (like virtually all ROS core tools) will autocomplete package names. For example, typing:

```
user@hostname$ rosrun rospy_tu[TAB]
```

will autocomplete to:

```
user@hostname$ rosrun rospy_tutorials
```

since no other packages currently loaded begin with `rospy_tu`.

 It's hard to emphasize this enough: pound the Tab key *furiously* when using the core ROS tools, or other standard Unix command-line tools. The Tab key is a huge time-saver!

tf: Coordinate Transforms

The "fetch an item" task described in "The ROS Graph" on page 9 includes many, many problems to tackle, encompassing nearly every aspect of robotics and artificial intelligence (that's one reason that it made such a great challenge problem to drive the design of ROS). One problem that might not be immediately obvious, but is extremely important, is the management of *coordinate frames*. Seriously, coordinate frames are a big deal in robotics.

Poses, Positions, and Orientations

Your average item-fetching robot will have a bunch of subsystems, such as a mobile base, a laser scanner attached to the base to allow it to navigate through the world, a camera (visual and/or depth) attached elsewhere to the base to find items to be fetched, and a manipulator arm with a hand that will do the actual grabbing of those items. A really good item-fetching robot might have many more features, but these are already plenty to make coordinate frames an important concern.

Let's start with the laser on the base. To correctly interpret a range scan produced by the laser, we need to know exactly *where* on the base the laser is attached. Is it mounted at the front of the base? The back? Is it facing backward? Is it mounted upside-down (which is not uncommon)? More generally, we could ask: what are the position and orientation of the laser with respect to the base?

We actually need to be a bit more careful than that, asking: what are the position and orientation of the *origin* of the laser with respect to the *origin* of the base? Before we can talk about physical relationships between components on our robot, we need to pick for each component a coordinate frame of reference, or *origin*. In general, you can choose the origin arbitrarily, though there's usually a widely used convention that should be followed. For example, a mobile base should have its origin at the geometric centroid of the base, with the positive x-axis pointing forward, the positive y-axis pointing left, and the positive z-axis pointing up (you could have inferred the z-axis direction because we always use righthanded coordinate systems). Other than following such conventions, the important thing is that everyone understand and agree on (usually via documentation) where each component's origin is.

Let's establish some terminology. In our 3D world, a *position* is a vector of three numbers (x, y, z) that describe how far we have translated along each axis, with respect to some origin. Similarly, an *orientation* is a vector of three numbers (roll, pitch, yaw) that describe how far we have rotated about each axis, again with respect to some origin.[3] Taken together, a (position, orientation) pair is called a *pose*. For clarity, this kind of pose, which varies in six dimensions (three for translation plus three for rotation) is sometimes called a *6D pose*. Given the pose of one thing relative to another, we can *transform* data between their frames of reference, a process that usually involves some matrix multiplications.

Restating our earlier question, we need to know: what is the *pose* (of the origin) of the laser with respect to the *pose* (of the origin) of the base? That's not all, of course. And if we're going to use the base-mounted camera to find items in the environment, then we likely need to know the camera's pose with respect to the base. If we're going to use

---

3 For a variety of reasons, we actually represent orientation using a *quaternion*, which comprises four numbers, but we can ignore that for the purpose of this discussion.

the locations of items found by the camera to send goals to the hand, then we further need to know the pose of the camera with respect to the hand. This case is especially interesting because the camera-to-hand relationship might be changing all the time as the arm moves the hand with respect to the camera. Then you have the mobile base moving around in the world (e.g., defined by a map), so there's a base-to-world relationship that is also constantly changing.

We could go on, but by now the point should be clear: you will, eventually, want to be able to compute the pose of every component of your robot with respect to every other pose. Some relationships are static (e.g., a laser bolted to a base), while others are dynamic (e.g., a hand reaching to grasp an item). We need to capture and combine all of these relationships, ideally in such a way that we can easily convert sensor data and actuator commands among them, while doing as little math as possible (because if we do the math ourselves, we'll just get it wrong). Enter tf.

tf

There are many ways to manage coordinate frames and transforms between them. In ROS, continuing with the philosophy of keeping things small and modular, we take a distributed approach, using ROS topics to share transform data. Any node can be the authority that publishes the current information for some transform(s), and any node can subscribe to transform data, gathering from all the various authorities a complete picture of the robot. This system is implemented in the tf (short for transform) package, which is extremely widely used throughout ROS software.

This approach makes a lot of sense when you consider that there's usually one place where the information for a given transform is most easily acquired or computed. For example, the driver that talks to a robot arm and has direct access to its joint encoder data might be the best node to publish the information about the transform from the start of the arm to the hand at the other end.[4] Similarly, the node that is performing localization of the base with respect to a map is the best authority for the base-to-world transform.

We need names for coordinate frames. In tf, we use strings. The frame of the laser attached to the base might be called "laser" or, if there's the potential for confusion, "front_laser". You can pick any names you like, so long as they're unique (and you should follow established naming conventions wherever they exist).

---

4 In practice, an arm driver will publish just the joint encoder data and let the robot_state_publisher compute the full 6D transforms, as described in "Verifying Transforms" on page 335.

We also need a message format to use when publishing information about transforms. In tf, we use tf/tfMessage, sent over the /tf topic. You don't need to know the details of this message, because you're unlikely to ever manipulate one manually. It's enough to know that each tf/tfMessage message contains a list of transforms, specifying for each one the names of the frames involved (referred to as *parent* and *child*), their relative position and orientation, and the time at which that transform was measured or computed.

Time turns out to be extremely important when we talk about sensor data and coordinate frames. If you want to combine a laser scan from one second ago with a scan from five seconds ago, then you had better keep track of where that laser was over time and be able to convert the scan data between its one-second-ago pose and its five-seconds-ago pose.

We don't want every node that works with transform data to reinvent the publishing, subscribing, remembering, or computing of transforms. So, tf also provides a set of libraries that can be used in any node to perform those common tasks. For example, if you create a tf *listener* in your node, then, behind the scenes, your node will subscribe to the /tf topic and maintain a buffer of all the tf/tfMessage data published by other nodes in the system. Then you can ask questions of tf, like: Where is the laser with respect to the base? Or, where was the hand with respect to the map two seconds ago? Or, how does this point cloud taken from the depth camera look in the frame of the laser? In each case, the tf libraries handle all the matrix manipulations for you, chaining together transforms and going back in time through its buffer as needed.

As is often the case for a powerful system, tf is relatively complex, and there are a variety of ways in which things can go wrong. Consequently, there a number of tf-specific introspection and debugging tools to help you understand what's happening, from printing a single transform on the console to rendering a graphical view of the entire transform hierarchy.

There is much, much more to know about the tf system, but for the work that we'll do in the rest of this book, this introduction should be enough for you to understand what's happening. When you get to the point that you want to start publishing and manipulating transforms yourself, start with the tf documentation (*http://wiki.ros.org/tf?distro=indigo*).

Summary

In this chapter, we looked at the ROS graph architecture and introduced you to the tools such as `catkin`, `rosrun`, and `roslaunch` that you'll be using to interact with the ROS graph. We also introduced the ROS namespace conventions and showed how namespaces can be remapped to avoid collisions. We further discussed the importance of coordinate transforms and how they're handled in ROS by the `tf` system.

Now that you understand the underlying architecture of a ROS system, it's time to look at what sorts of messages the nodes might send to one another and how these messages are composed, sent, and received, and to think about some of the computations that the nodes might be doing. That brings us to *topics*, the fundamental communication method in ROS.

## CHAPTER 3

Topics

As we saw in the previous chapter, ROS systems consist of a number of independent *nodes* that comprise a *graph*. These nodes by themselves are typically not very useful. Things only get interesting when nodes communicate with each other, exchanging information and data. The most common way to do that is through *topics*. A topic is a name for a stream of messages with a defined type. For example, the data from a laser range-finder might be sent on a topic called scan, with a message type of LaserScan, while the data from a camera might be sent over a topic called image, with a message type of Image.

Topics implement a *publish/subscribe* communication mechanism, one of the more common ways to exchange data in a distributed system. Before nodes start to transmit data over topics, they must first announce, or *advertise*, both the topic name and the types of messages that are going to be sent. Then they can start to send, or *publish*, the actual data on the topic. Nodes that want to receive messages on a topic can *subscribe* to that topic by making a request to roscore. After subscribing, all messages on the topic are delivered to the node that made the request. One of the main advantages to using ROS is that all the messy details of setting up the necessary connections when nodes advertise or subscribe to topics is handled for you by the underlying communication mechanism so that you don't have to worry about it yourself.

In ROS, all messages on the same topic *must* be of the same data type. Although ROS does not enforce it, topic names often describe the messages that are sent over them. For example, on the PR2 robot, the topic /wide_stereo/right/image_color is used for color images from the rightmost camera of the wide-angle stereo pair.

We'll start off by looking at how a node advertises a topic and publishes data on it.

In this section, and in much of the rest of the book, we're going to assume that you know how to create workspaces and packages, and how to structure the files in them. If you can't remember how to do this, you should refresh your memory by looking at "catkin, Workspaces, and ROS Packages" on page 13 again. If you're unsure about things, you can take a look at the code that goes along with this book, since things should be laid out correctly there.

Publishing to a Topic

Example 3-1 shows the basic code for advertising a topic and publishing messages on it. This node publishes consecutive integers on the topic counter at a rate of 2 Hz.

Example 3-1. topic_publisher.py

```python
#!/usr/bin/env python

import rospy

from std_msgs.msg import Int32


rospy.init_node('topic_publisher')

pub = rospy.Publisher('counter', Int32)

rate = rospy.Rate(2)

count = 0
while not rospy.is_shutdown():
    pub.publish(count)
    count += 1
    rate.sleep()
```

The first line:

```
#!/usr/bin/env python
```

is known as the *shebang*. It lets the operating system know that this is a Python file, and that it should be passed to the Python interpreter. Since we're going to be running the nodes we write as programs, we also have to set *execute permissions* on them using the Linux chmod command:

```
user@hostname$ chmod u+x topic_publisher.py
```

This particular invocation of chmod will allow the owner of the file to execute it. You should take a moment to look up the documentation for chmod to understand permissions and how to set them, either using the Linux man pages or by searching for chmod on the Web.

The second line:

```
import rospy
```

appears in every ROS Python node and imports all of the basic functionality that we'll need. The next line imports the definition of the message that we're going to send over the topic:

```
from std_msgs.msg import Int32
```

In this case, we're going to use a 32-bit integer, defined in the ROS standard message package, std_msgs. For the import to work as expected, we need to import from *<package name>.msg*, since this is where the package definitions are stored (more on this later). Since we're using a message from another package, we have to tell the ROS build system about this by adding a *dependency* to our *package.xml* file:

```
<depend package="std_msgs" />
```

Without this dependency, ROS will not know where to find the message definition, and the node will not be able to run.

After initializing the node, we advertise it with a Publisher:

```
pub = rospy.Publisher('counter', Int32)
```

This gives the topic a name (counter) and specifies the type of message that will be sent over it (Int32). Behind the scenes, the publisher also sets up a connection to roscore and sends some information to it. When another node tries to subscribe to the counter topic, roscore will share its list of publishers and subscribers, which the nodes will then use to create direct connections between all publishers and of all subscribers to each topic.

At this point, the topic is advertised and is available for other nodes to subscribe to. Now we can go about actually publishing messages over the topic:

```
rate = rospy.Rate(2)

count = 0
while not rospy.is_shutdown():
    pub.publish(count)
    count += 1
    rate.sleep()
```

First, we set the rate, in hertz, at which we want to publish. For this example, we're going to publish twice a second. The is_shutdown() function will return True if the node is ready to be shut down and False otherwise, so we can use this to determine if it is time to exit the while loop.

Inside the while loop, we publish the current value of the counter, increment its value by 1, and then sleep for a while. The call to rate.sleep() will sleep for long enough to make sure that we run the body of the while loop at approximately 2 Hz.

And that's it. We now have a minimalist ROS node that advertises the `counter` topic and publishes integers on it.

Checking That Everything Works as Expected

Now that we have a node set up, let's verify that it works. We can use the `rostopic` command to dig into the currently available topics. Open a new terminal, and start up `roscore`. Once it's running, you can see what topics are available by running `rostopic list` in another terminal:

```
user@hostname$ rostopic list
/rosout
/rosout_agg
```

These topics are used by ROS for logging and debugging; don't worry about them. If you ever forget what the arguments to `rostopic` are, then you can use the `-h` flag to list them. This generally works for the other ROS command-line tools, too:

```
user@hostname$ rostopic -h
rostopic is a command-line tool for printing information about ROS Topics.

Commands:
        rostopic bw      display bandwidth used by topic
        rostopic echo    print messages to screen
        rostopic find    find topics by type
        rostopic hz      display publishing rate of topic
        rostopic info    print information about active topic
        rostopic list    list active topics
        rostopic pub     publish data to topic
        rostopic type    print topic type

Type rostopic <command> -h for more detailed usage, e.g. 'rostopic echo -h'
```

Now, run the node we've just looked at in yet another terminal. Make sure that the `basics` package is in a workspace, and you've sourced the setup file for that workspace:

```
user@hostname$ rosrun basics topic_publisher.py
```

Remember that the *basics* directory has to be in your `catkin` workspace, and that, if you typed in the code for the node yourself, the file will need to have its execute permissions set using `chmod`. Once the node is running, you can verify that the `counter` topic is advertised by running `rostopic list` again:

```
user@hostname$ rostopic list
/counter
/rosout
/rosout_agg
```

Even better, you can see the messages being published to the topic by running `rostopic echo`:

```
user@hostname$ rostopic echo counter -n 5
data: 681
---
data: 682
---
data: 683
---
data: 684
---
data: 685
---
```

The -n 5 flag tells rostopic to only print out five messages. Without it, it will happily go on printing messages forever, until you stop it with a Ctrl-C. We can also use rostopic to verify that we're publishing at the rate we think we are:

```
user@hostname$ rostopic hz counter
subscribed to [/counter]
average rate: 2.000
        min: 0.500s max: 0.500s std dev: 0.00000s window: 2
average rate: 2.000
        min: 0.500s max: 0.500s std dev: 0.00004s window: 4
average rate: 2.000
        min: 0.500s max: 0.500s std dev: 0.00006s window: 6
average rate: 2.000
        min: 0.500s max: 0.500s std dev: 0.00005s window: 7
```

rostopic hz has to be stopped with a Ctrl-C. Similarly, rostopic bw will give information about the bandwidth being used by the topic.

You can also find out about an advertised topic with rostopic info:

```
user@hostname$ rostopic info counter
Type: std_msgs/Int32

Publishers:
 * /topic_publisher (http://hostname:39964/)

Subscribers: None
```

This reveals that counter carries messages of type std_msgs/Int32, that it is currently being advertised by topic_publisher, and that no one is currently subscribing to it. Since it's possible for more than one node to publish to the same topic and for more than one node to be subscribed to a topic, this command can help you make sure things are connected in the way that you think they are. Here, the publisher topic_publisher is running on the computer hostname and is communicating over

TCP port 39964.[1] `rostopic type` works similarly but only returns the message type for a given topic.

Finally, you can find all of the topics that publish a certain message type using `rostopic find`:

```
user@hostname$ rostopic find std_msgs/Int32
/counter
```

Note that you have to give both the package name (`std_msgs`) and the message type (`Int32`) for this to work.

So, now we have a node that's happily publishing consecutive integers, and we can verify that everything is as it should be. Now let's turn our attention to a node that subscribes to this topic and uses the messages it is receiving.

 As you work through this book, you'll probably notice that we use a number of Linux command-line tools and talk about some of the underlying mechanisms in Linux, such as the use of TCP ports. You can use ROS with only a vague idea of what these things are. However, if you're going to be using ROS a lot, then it's probably a good idea to learn some more about Linux and what's going on under the hood. Knowing a bit about the operating system and how to work on the command line will make you more efficient, and will often help you debug problems with your ROS system *much* faster.

Subscribing to a Topic

Example 3-2 shows a minimalist node that subscribes to the counter topic and prints out the values in the messages as they arrive.

Example 3-2. topic_subscriber.py

```python
#!/usr/bin/env python


import rospy
from std_msgs.msg import Int32


def callback(msg):
    print msg.data
```

---

1 Don't worry if you don't know what a TCP port is. ROS will generally take care of this for you without you having to think about it.

```
rospy.init_node('topic_subscriber')

sub = rospy.Subscriber('counter', Int32, callback)

rospy.spin()
```

The first interesting part of this code is the *callback* that handles the messages as they come in:

```
def callback(msg):
    print msg.data
```

ROS is an event-driven system, and it uses callback functions heavily. Once a node has subscribed to a topic, every time a message arrives on it the associated callback function is called, with the message as its parameter. In this case, the function simply prints out the data contained in the message (see "Defining Your Own Message Types" on page 39 for more details about messages and what they contain).

After initializing the node, as before, we subscribe to the counter topic:

```
sub = rospy.Subscriber('counter', Int32, callback)
```

We give the name of the topic, the message type of the topic, and the name of the callback function. Behind the scenes, the subscriber passes this information on to roscore and tries to make a direct connection with the publishers of this topic. If the topic does not exist, or if the type is wrong, there are no error messages: the node will simply wait until messages start being published on the topic.

Once the subscription is made, we give control over to ROS by calling rospy.spin(). This function will only return when the node is ready to shut down. This is just a useful shortcut to avoid having to define a top-level while loop like we did in Example 3-1; ROS does not necessarily need to "take over" the main thread of execution.

Checking That Everything Works as Expected

First, make sure that the publisher node is still running and that it is still publishing messages on the counter topic. Then, in another terminal, start up the subscriber node:

```
user@hostname$ rosrun basics topic_subscriber.py
355
356
357
358
359
360
```

It should start to print out integers published to the counter topic by the publisher node. Congratulations! You're now running your first ROS system: Example 3-1 is sending messages to Example 3-2. You can visualize this system by typing rqt_graph, which will attempt to draw the publishers and subscribers in a logical manner.

We can also publish messages to a topic from the command line using rostopic pub. Run the following command, and watch the output of the subscriber node:

```
user@hostname$ rostopic pub counter std_msgs/Int32 1000000
```

We can use rostopic info again to make sure things are the way we expect them to be:

```
user@hostname$ rostopic info counter
Type: std_msgs/Int32

Publishers:
 * /topic_publisher (http://hostname:46674/)

Subscribers:
 * /topic_subscriber (http://hostname:53744/)
```

Now that you understand how basic topics work, we can talk about a special type of topics designed for nodes that publish data only infrequently, called *latched topics*.

Latched Topics

Messages in ROS are fleeting. If you're not subscribed to a topic when a message goes out on it, you'll miss it and will have to wait for the next one. This is fine if the publisher sends out messages frequently, since it won't be long until the next message comes along. However, there are cases where sending out frequent messages is a bad idea.

For example, the map_server node advertises a map (of type nav_msgs/Occupancy Grid) on the map topic. This represents a map of the world that the robot can use to determine where it is, such as the one shown in Figure 3-1. Often, this map never changes and is published only once, when the map_server loads it from disk. However, this means if another node needs the map, but starts up after map_server publishes it, it will never get the message.

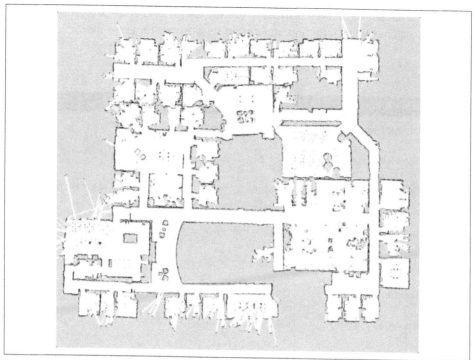

Figure 3-1. An example map

We could periodically publish the map, but we don't want to publish the message more often than we have to, since it's typically huge. If we did decide to republish it, we would have to pick a suitable frequency, which might be tricky to get right.

Latched topics offer a simple solution to this problem. If a topic is marked as latched when it is advertised, subscribers automatically get *the last message sent* when they subscribe to the topic. In our `map_server` example, this means that we only need to mark it as latched and publish it once. Topics can be marked as latched with the optional `latched` argument:

```
pub = rospy.Publisher('map', nav_msgs/OccupancyGrid, latched=True)
```

Now that we know how to send messages over topics, it's time to think about what to do if we want to send a message that isn't already defined by ROS.

Defining Your Own Message Types

ROS offers a rich set of built-in message types. The `std_msgs` package defines the primitive types, shown in Table 3-1 and documented more fully on the ROS wiki `msg` page (*http://wiki.ros.org/msg#Field_Types?distro=indigo*). Arrays of these types, both fixed and variable length, are returned (from the lower-level communications deserialization code) as tuples in Python and can be set as either tuples or lists.

Table 3-1. ROS primitive message types, how they are serialized, and their corresponding C and Python types

ROS type	Serialization	C++ type	Python type	Notes
bool	Unsigned 8-bit integer	uint8_t	bool	
int8	Signed 8-bit integer	int8_t	int	
uint8	Unsigned 8-bit integer	uint8_t	int	uint8[] is treated as a string in Python
int16	Signed 16-bit integer	int16_t	int	
uint16	Unsigned 16-bit integer	uint16_t	int	
int32	Signed 32-bit integer	int32_t	int	
uint32	Unsigned 32-bit integer	uint32_t	int	
int64	Signed 64-bit integer	int64_t	long	
uint64	Unsigned 64-bit integer	uint64_t	long	
float32	32-bit IEEE float	float	float	
float64	64-bit IEEE float	double	float	
string	ASCII string	std::string	string	ROS does not support Unicode strings; use a UTF-8 encoding
time	secs/nsecs unsigned 32-bit ints	ros::Time	rospy.Time	duration

C++ has more native data types than Python, which can lead to subtle problems when nodes written in C++ and Python exchange data. For example, the ROS UInt8 is represented as an 8-bit unsigned integer in C++ and will behave normally. However, in Python it is represented as an integer, which means you can set it negative, or to a value greater than 255. When this out-of-range value is subsequently published as a ROS message, it will be interpreted as an 8-bit unsigned value. This will often lead to an unpredictable value being received and a hard-to-find error. Be careful when using range-limited ROS types in Python.

These primitive types are used to build all of the messages used in ROS. These messages are contained in the `std_msgs` package (*http://wiki.ros.org/std_msgs?distro=indigo*) and the `common_msgs` package (*http://wiki.ros.org/common_msgs?distro=indigo*). These message types are part of what gives ROS its power. Since (most) laser range-finder sensors publish `sensor_msgs/LaserScan` messages, we can write control code for our robots without having to know the specific details of the laser range-finder hardware. Furthermore, most robots can publish their estimated locations in a standard way. Using standardized message types for laser scans and location estimates enables nodes can be written that provide navigation and mapping (among many other things) for a wide variety of robots.

However, there are times when the built-in message types are not enough, and we have to define our own messages. These messages are "first-class citizens" in ROS, and there is no distinction between the message types that are defined in the core of ROS and those you define yourself.

Defining a New Message

ROS messages are defined by special message-definition files in the *msg* directory of a package. These files are then compiled into language-specific implementations that can be used in your code. This means that, even if you're using an interpreted language such as Python, you need to run `catkin_make` if you're going to define your own message types. Otherwise, the language-specific implementation will not be generated, and Python will not be able to find your new message type. Furthermore, if you don't rerun `catkin_make` after you change the message definition, Python will still be using the older version of the message type. Although this sounds like an extra layer of complexity, there is a good reason to do things this way: it allows us to define a message once and have it automatically available in all languages that ROS supports, without having to manually write the (extremely tedious) code that "deflates" and "inflates" messages as they come across the network.

Message-definition files are typically quite simple and short. Each line specifies a type and a field name. Types can be built-in ROS primitive types, message types from other packages, arrays of types (either primitive or from other packages, and either fixed or variable length), or the special `Header` type.

 A message-definition file comprises a list of types that make up the message. These types can either be ones that are built into ROS, such as those defined in the `std_msgs` package, or types that you have defined yourself.

As a concrete example, suppose we wanted to modify Example 3-1 to publish random complex numbers, instead of integers. A complex number has two parts, real and imaginary, both of which are floating-point numbers. The message-definition file for our new type, called Complex, is shown in Example 3-3.

Example 3-3. Complex.msg

```
float32 real
float32 imaginary
```

The file *Complex.msg* is in the *msg* directory of the basics package. It defines two values, real and imaginary, both with the same type (float32).[2]

Once the message is defined, we need to run catkin_make to generate the language-specific code that will let us use it. This code includes a definition of the type, and code to marshal and unmarshal it for transmission down a topic. This allows us to use the message in all of the languages that ROS supports; nodes written in one language can subscribe to topics from nodes written in another. Moreover, it allows us to use messages to communicate seamlessly between computers with different architectures.

To get ROS to generate the language-specific message code, we need to make sure that we tell the build system about the new message definitions. We can do this by adding these lines to our *package.xml* file:

```
<build_depend>message_generation</build_depend>
<run_depend>message_runtime</run_depend>
```

Next, we need to make a few changes to the *CMakeLists.txt* file. First, we need to add message_generation to the end of the find_package() call, so that catkin knows to look for the message_generation package:

```
find_package(catkin REQUIRED COMPONENTS
   roscpp
   rospy
   std_msgs
   message_generation    # Add message_generation here, after the other packages
)
```

Then we need to tell catkin that we're going to use messages at runtime, by adding message_runtime to the catkin_package() call:

```
catkin_package(
   CATKIN_DEPENDS message_runtime    # This will not be the only thing here
)
```

We tell catkin which message files we want to compile by adding them to the add_message_files() call:

---

2 The two primitive floating-point types, float32 and float64, both map to the Python float type.

```
add_message_files(
  FILES
  Complex.msg
)
```

Finally, still in the *CMakeLists.txt* file, we need to make sure the `generate_mes sages()` call is uncommented and contains all the dependencies that are needed by our messages:

```
generate_messages(
  DEPENDENCIES
  std_msgs
)
```

Now that we've told `catkin` everything that it needs to know about our messages, we're ready to compile them. Go to the root of your `catkin` workspace, and run `cat kin_make`. This will generate a message type with the same name as the message-definition file, with the *.msg* extension removed. By convention, ROS types are capitalized and contain no underscores.

You'll probably never need to see the details of the Python class that `catkin_make` generates in order to use it in your ROS code. However, for the sake of completeness, Example 3-4 shows (parts of) the class generated from our complex number example.

Example 3-4. Part of the Python message definition generated by catkin_make for our complex number example

```
"""autogenerated by genpy from basics/Complex.msg. Do not edit."""
import sys
python3 = True if sys.hexversion > 0x03000000 else False
import genpy
import struct


class Complex(genpy.Message):
  _md5sum = "54da470dccf15d60bd273ab751e1c0a1"
  _type = "basics/Complex"
  _has_header = False #flag to mark the presence of a Header object
  _full_text = """float32 real
float32 imaginary

"""
  __slots__ = ['real','imaginary']
  _slot_types = ['float32','float32']

  def __init__(self, *args, **kwds):
    """
    Constructor. Any message fields that are implicitly/explicitly
    set to None will be assigned a default value. The recommend
    use is keyword arguments as this is more robust to future message
    changes.  You cannot mix in-order arguments and keyword arguments.
```

```
    The available fields are:
        real,imaginary

    :param args: complete set of field values, in .msg order
    :param kwds: use keyword arguments corresponding to message field names
    to set specific fields.
    """
    if args or kwds:
        super(Complex, self).__init__(*args, **kwds)
        #message fields cannot be None, assign default values for those that are
        if self.real is None:
            self.real = 0.
        if self.imaginary is None:
            self.imaginary = 0.
    else:
        self.real = 0.
        self.imaginary = 0.

def _get_types(self):
    """
    internal API method
    """
    return self._slot_types

def serialize(self, buff):
    ...

def deserialize(self, str):
    ...

def serialize_numpy(self, buff, numpy):
    ...

def deserialize_numpy(self, str, numpy):
    ...
```

The important thing to notice here is that you can provide parameters to the constructor to initialize the values in the class. You can do this in two ways. You can give values for each of the elements of the class (real and imaginary in this example), in the order that they're listed in the message-definition file. In this case, you need to give values for *all* of the fields. Alternatively, you can use keyword arguments to give values to some of the fields, like this:

```
c = Complex(real=2.3)
```

and have default values be assigned to the remaining fields.

Generated message definitions contain an MD5 checksum. This is used by ROS to make sure that it's using the correct version of a message. If you modify your message-definition files and run catkin_make over them, you might also have to run catkin_make over any code that uses these messages, to make sure that the checksums match up. This is generally more of a problem with C++ than with Python, since the checksums are compiled into the executables. However, it can be an issue with Python with compiled byte code (*.pyc* files).

Using Your New Message

Once your message is defined and compiled, you can use it just like any other message in ROS, as you can see in Example 3-5.

Example 3-5. message_publisher.py

```python
#!/usr/bin/env python

import rospy

from basics.msg import Complex

from random import random


rospy.init_node('message_publisher')

pub = rospy.Publisher('complex', Complex)

rate = rospy.Rate(2)

while not rospy.is_shutdown():
    msg = Complex()
    msg.real = random()
    msg.imaginary = random()

    pub.publish(msg)
    rate.sleep()
```

Importing your new message type works just like including a standard ROS message type and allows you to create a message instance just like any other Python class. Once you've created the instance, you can fill in the values for the individual fields. Any fields that are not explicitly assigned a value should be considered to have an undefined value.

Subscribing to and using your new message is similarly easy, as Example 3-6 demonstrates.

Example 3-6. message_subscriber.py

```
#!/usr/bin/env python


import rospy
from basics.msg import Complex


def callback(msg):
    print 'Real:', msg.real
    print 'Imaginary:', msg.imaginary
    print


rospy.init_node('message_subscriber')

sub = rospy.Subscriber('complex', Complex, callback)

rospy.spin()
```

The `rosmsg` command lets you look at the contents of a message type:

```
user@hostname$ rosmsg show Complex
[basics/Complex]:
float32 real
float32 imaginary
```

If a message contains other messages, they are displayed recursively by `rosmsg`. For example, `PointStamped` has a `Header` and a `Point`, each of which is a ROS type:

```
user@hostname$ rosmsg show PointStamped
[geometry_msgs/PointStamped]:
std_msgs/Header header
  uint32 seq
  time stamp
  string frame_id
geometry_msgs/Point point
  float64 x
  float64 y
  float64 z
```

`rosmsg list` will show all of the messages available in ROS. `rosmsg packages` will list all of the packages that define messages. Finally, `rosmsg package` will list the messages defined in a particular package:

```
user@hostname$ rosmsg package basics
basics/Complex

user@hostname$ rosmsg package sensor_msgs
sensor_msgs/CameraInfo
sensor_msgs/ChannelFloat32
sensor_msgs/CompressedImage
```

```
sensor_msgs/FluidPressure
sensor_msgs/Illuminance
sensor_msgs/Image
sensor_msgs/Imu
sensor_msgs/JointState
sensor_msgs/Joy
sensor_msgs/JoyFeedback
sensor_msgs/JoyFeedbackArray
sensor_msgs/LaserEcho
sensor_msgs/LaserScan
sensor_msgs/MagneticField
sensor_msgs/MultiEchoLaserScan
sensor_msgs/NavSatFix
sensor_msgs/NavSatStatus
sensor_msgs/PointCloud
sensor_msgs/PointCloud2
sensor_msgs/PointField
sensor_msgs/Range
sensor_msgs/RegionOfInterest
sensor_msgs/RelativeHumidity
sensor_msgs/Temperature
sensor_msgs/TimeReference
```

When Should You Make a New Message Type?

The short answer is, "Only when you absolutely have to." ROS already has a rich set of message types, and you should use one of these if you can. Part of the power of ROS is the ability to combine nodes together to form complex systems, and this can only happen if nodes publish and receive messages of the same type. So, before you go and create a new message type, you should use rosmsg to see if there is already something there that you can use instead. ROS messages define the public interface between nodes. Nodes that use the same messages can easily be combined into a running system. However, if every node uses a different message for similar data, then you'll have to do a lot of (pointless) work translating between these messages in order to get something working. You should prefer existing message types whenever you can, since this will make your code fit in more seamlessly with the existing ROS code base. Similarly, you should use SI units (meters, kilograms, seconds, etc.) whenever possible, since this is what the rest of ROS uses.

Mixing Publishers and Subscribers

The previous examples showed nodes that have a single publisher and a single subscriber, but there's no reason why a node can't be both a publisher and a subscriber or have multiple publications and subscriptions. In fact, one of the most common things nodes in ROS do is to transform data by performing computations on it. For example, a node might subscribe to a topic containing camera images, identify faces in those images, and publish the positions of those faces in another topic. Example 3-7 shows an example of a node like this.

Example 3-7. doubler.py

```python
#!/usr/bin/env python

import rospy

from std_msgs.msg import Int32


rospy.init_node('doubler')


def callback(msg):
    doubled = Int32()
    doubled.data = msg.data * 2

    pub.publish(doubled)

sub = rospy.Subscriber('number', Int32, callback)
pub = rospy.Publisher('doubled', Int32)

rospy.spin()
```

The subscriber and publisher are set up as before, but now we're going to publish data in the callback, rather than periodically. The idea behind this is that we only want to publish when we have new data coming in, since the purpose of this node is to transform data (in this case, by doubling the number that comes in on the subscribed topic).

Summary

In this chapter, we covered *topics*, the fundamental ROS communication mechanism. You should now know how to advertise a topic and publish messages over it, how to subscribe to a topic and receive messages from it, how to define your own messages, and how to write simple nodes that interact with topics. You should also know how to write nodes that transform data that comes in on one topic and republish it on another. This sort of node is the backbone in many ROS systems, performing computations to transform one sort of data into another, and we'll be seeing examples of this throughout the book.

Topics are probably the communication mechanism that you will use most often in ROS. Whenever you have a node that generates data that other nodes can use, you should consider using a topic to publish that data. Whenever you need to transform data from one form to another, a node like the one shown in Example 3-7 is often a good choice.

While we covered most of what you can do with topics in this chapter, we didn't cover everything. For further details, you should look at the topic's API documentation (*http://wiki.ros.org/Topics?distro=indigo*).

Now that you've got the hang of topics, it's time to talk about the second main communication mechanism in ROS: *services*.

## CHAPTER 4

Services

Services are another way to pass data between nodes in ROS. Services are just synchronous remote procedure calls; they allow one node to call a function that executes in another node. We define the inputs and outputs of this function similarly to the way we define new message types. The server (which provides the service) specifies a callback to deal with the service request, and advertises the service. The client (which calls the service) then accesses this service through a local proxy.

Service calls are well suited to things that you only need to do occasionally and that take a bounded amount of time to complete. Common computations, which you might want to distribute to other computers, are a good example. Discrete actions that the robot might do, such as turning on a sensor or taking a high-resolution picture with a camera, are also good candidates for a service-call implementation.

Although there are several services already defined by packages in ROS, we'll start by looking at how to define and implement our own service, since this gives some insight into the underlying mechanisms of service calls. As a concrete example in this chapter, we're going to show how to create a service that counts the number of words in a string.

Defining a Service

The first step in creating a new service is to define the service call inputs and outputs. This is done in a *service-definition file*, which has a similar structure to the message-definition files we've already seen. However, since a service call has both inputs and outputs, it's a bit more complicated than a message.

Our example service counts the number of words in a string. This means that the input to the service call should be a `string` and the output should be an integer. Although we're using messages from `std_msgs` here, you can use *any* ROS message, even ones that you've defined yourself. Example 4-1 shows a service definition for this.

Example 4-1. WordCount.srv

```
string words
---
uint32 count
```

 Like message-definition files, service-definition files are just lists of message types. These can be built in, such as those defined in the std_msgs package, or they can be ones you have defined yourself.

The inputs to the service call come first. In this case, we're just going to use the ROS built-in string type. Three dashes (---) mark the end of the inputs and the start of the output definition. We're going to use a 32-bit unsigned integer (uint32) for our output. The file holding this definition is called *WordCount.srv* and is traditionally in a directory called *srv* in the main package directory (although this is not strictly required).

Once we've got the definition file in the right place, we need to run catkin_make to create the code and class definitions that we will actually use when interacting with the service, just like we did for new messages. To get catkin_make to generate this code, we need to make sure that the find_package() call in *CMakeLists.txt* contains message_generation, just like we did for new messages:

```
find_package(catkin REQUIRED COMPONENTS
  roscpp
  rospy
  message_generation   # Add message_generation here, after the other packages
)
```

We also have to make an addition to the *package.xml* file to reflect the dependencies on both rospy and the message system. This means we need a build dependency on message_generation and a runtime dependency on message_runtime:

```
<build_depend>rospy</build_depend>
<run_depend>rospy</run_depend>

<build_depend>message_generation</build_depend>
<run_depend>message_runtime</run_depend>
```

Then, we need to tell catkin which service-definition files we want compiled, using the add_service_files() call in *CMakeLists.txt*:

```
add_service_files(
  FILES
  WordCount.srv
)
```

Finally, we must make sure that the dependencies for the service-definition file are declared (again in *CMakeLists.txt*), using the `generate_messages()` call:

```
generate_messages(
  DEPENDENCIES
  std_msgs
)
```

With all of this in place, running `catkin_make` will generate three classes: `WordCount`, `WordCountRequest`, and `WordCountResponse`. These classes will be used to interact with the service, as we will see. Just like with messages, you will probably never have to look at the details of the generated classes. However, just in case you're interested, (part of) the classes generated by the `WordCount` example are shown in Example 4-2.

Example 4-2. The Python classes generated by catkin_make for the WordCount example (code in functions removed for clarity)

```
"""autogenerated by genpy from basics/WordCountRequest.msg. Do not edit."""
import sys
python3 = True if sys.hexversion > 0x03000000 else False
import genpy
import struct


class WordCountRequest(genpy.Message):
  _md5sum = "6f897d3845272d18053a750c1cfb862a"
  _type = "basics/WordCountRequest"
  _has_header = False #flag to mark the presence of a Header object
  _full_text = """string words

"""
  __slots__ = ['words']
  _slot_types = ['string']

  def __init__(self, *args, **kwds):
    """
    Constructor. Any message fields that are implicitly/explicitly
    set to None will be assigned a default value. The recommend
    use is keyword arguments as this is more robust to future message
    changes.  You cannot mix in-order arguments and keyword arguments.

    The available fields are:
       words

    :param args: complete set of field values, in .msg order
    :param kwds: use keyword arguments corresponding to message field names
```

```
    to set specific fields.
    """
    if args or kwds:
      super(WordCountRequest, self).__init__(*args, **kwds)
      #message fields cannot be None, assign default values for those that are
      if self.words is None:
        self.words = ''
    else:
      self.words = ''

  def _get_types(self):
    ...        """

  def serialize(self, buff):
    ...

  def deserialize(self, str):
    ...

  def serialize_numpy(self, buff, numpy):
    ...

  def deserialize_numpy(self, str, numpy):
    ...

class WordCountResponse(genpy.Message):
  ...

class WordCount(genpy.Message):
  ...
```

The details of the definitions for WordCountResponse and WordCount are similar to those for WordCountRequest. All of these are just ROS messages.

We can verify that the service call definition is what we expect by using the rossrv command:

```
user@hostname$ rossrv show WordCount
[basics/WordCount]:
string words
---
uint32 count
```

You can see all available services using rossrv list, all packages offering services with rossrv packages, and all the services offered by a particular package with rossrv package.

Implementing a Service

Now that we have a definition of the inputs and outputs for the service call, we're ready to write the code that implements the service. Like topics, services are a callback-based mechanism. The service provider specifies a callback that will be run when the service call is made, and then waits for requests to come in. Example 4-3 shows a simple server that implements our word-counting service call.

Example 4-3. service_server.py

```python
#!/usr/bin/env python

import rospy

from basics.srv import WordCount,WordCountResponse


def count_words(request):
    return WordCountResponse(len(request.words.split()))


rospy.init_node('service_server')

service = rospy.Service('word_count', WordCount, count_words)

rospy.spin()
```

We first need to import the code generated by `catkin`:

```python
from basics.srv import WordCount,WordCountResponse
```

Notice that we need to import both `WordCount` and `WordCountResponse`. Both of these are generated in a Python module with the same name as the package, with a *.srv* extension (*basics.srv*, in our case).

The callback function takes a single argument of type `WordCountRequest` and returns a single argument of type `WordCountResponse`:

```python
def count_words(request):
    return WordCountResponse(len(request.words.split()))
```

The constructor for `WordCountResponse` takes parameters that match those in the service-definition file. For us, this means an unsigned integer. By convention, services that fail, for whatever reason, should return `None`.

After initializing the node, we advertise the service, giving it a name (`word_count`) and a type (`WordCount`), and specifying the callback that will implement it:

```python
service = rospy.Service('word_count', WordCount, count_words)
```

Finally, we make a call to `rospy.spin()`, which gives control of the node over to ROS and exits when the node is ready to shut down. You don't actually have to hand control over by calling `rospy.spin()` (unlike in the C++ API), since callbacks run in their own threads. You could set up your own loop, remembering to check for node termination, if you have something else you need to do. However, using `rospy.spin()` is a convenient way to keep the node alive until it's ready to shut down.

Checking That Everything Works as Expected

Now that we have the service defined and implemented, we can verify that everything is working as expected with the `rosservice` command. Start up a `roscore` and run the service node:

```
user@hostname$ rosrun basics service_server.py
```

First, let's check that the service is there:

```
user@hostname$ rosservice list
/rosout/get_loggers
/rosout/set_logger_level
/service_server/get_loggers
/service_server/set_logger_level
/word_count
```

In addition to the logging services provided by ROS, our service seems to be there. We can get some more information about it with `rosservice info`:

```
user@hostname$ rosservice info word_count
Node: /service_server
URI: rosrpc://hostname:60085
Type: basics/WordCount
Args: words
```

This tells us the node that provides the service, where it's running, the type that it uses, and the names of the arguments to the service call. We can also get some of this information using `rosservice type word_count` and `roservice args word_count`.

Other Ways of Returning Values from a Service

In the previous example, we explicitly created a `WordCountResponse` object and returned it from the service callback. There are a number of other ways to return values from a service callback that you can use. In the case where there is a single return argument for the service, you can simply return that value:

```
def count_words(request):
    return len(request.words.split())
```

If there are multiple return arguments, you can return a tuple or a list. The values in the list will be assigned to the values in the service definition, in order. This works even if there's only one return value:

```
def count_words(request):
    return [len(request.words.split())]
```

You can also return a dictionary, where the keys are the argument names (given as strings):

```
def count_words(request):
    return {'count': len(request.words.split())}
```

In both of these cases, the underlying service call code in ROS will translate these return types into a `WordCountResponse` object and return it to the calling node, just as in the initial example code.

Using a Service

The simplest way to use a service is to call it using the `rosservice` command. For our word-counting service, the call looks like this:

```
user@hostname$ rosservice call word_count 'one two three'
count: 3
```

The command takes the `call` subcommand, the service name, and the arguments. While this lets us call the service and make sure that it's working as expected, it's not as useful as calling it from another running node. Example 4-4 shows how to call our service programmatically.

Example 4-4. service_client.py

```
#!/usr/bin/env python

import rospy

from basics.srv import WordCount

import sys


rospy.init_node('service_client')

rospy.wait_for_service('word_count')

word_counter = rospy.ServiceProxy('word_count', WordCount)

words = ' '.join(sys.argv[1:])

word_count = word_counter(words)

print words, '->', word_count.count
```

First, we wait for the service to be advertised by the server:

```
rospy.wait_for_service('word_count')
```

If we try to use the service before it's advertised, the call will fail with an exception. This is a major difference between topics and services. We can subscribe to topics that are not yet advertised, but we can only use advertised services. Once the service is advertised, we can set up a local proxy for it:

```
word_counter = rospy.ServiceProxy('word_count', WordCount)
```

We need to specify the name of the service (`word_count`) and the type (`WordCount`). This will allow us to use `word_counter` like a local function that, when called, will actually make the service call for us:

```
word_count = word_counter(words)
```

Checking That Everything Works as Expected

Now that we've defined the service, built the support code with `catkin`, and implemented both a server and a client, it's time to see if everything works. Check that your server is still running, and run the client node (make sure that you've sourced your workspace setup file in the shell in which you run the client node, or it will not work):

```
user@hostname$ rosrun basics service_client.py these are some words
these are some words -> 4
```

Now, stop the server and rerun the client node. It should stop, waiting for the service to be advertised. Starting the server node should result in the client completing normally, once the service is available. This highlights one of the limitations of ROS services: the service client can potentially wait forever if the service is not available for some reason. Perhaps the service server has died unexpectedly, or perhaps the service name is misspelled in the client call. In either case, the service client will get stuck.

Other Ways to Call Services

In our client node, we are calling the service through the proxy as if it were a local function. The arguments to this function are used to fill in the elements of the service request, in order. In our example, we only have one argument (`words`), so we are only allowed to give the proxy function one argument. Similarly, since there is only one output from the service call, the proxy function returns a single value. If, on the other hand, our service definition were to look like this:

```
string words
int min_word_length
---
uint32 count
uint32 ignored
```

then the proxy function would take two arguments, and return two values:

```
c,i = word_count(words, 3)
```

The arguments are passed in the order they are defined in the service definition. It is also possible to explicitly construct a service request object and use that to call the service:

```
request = WordCountRequest('one two three', 3)
count,ignored = word_counter(request)
```

Note that, if you choose this mechanism, you will have to also import the definition for WordCountRequest in the client code, as follows:

```
from basics.srv import WordCountRequest
```

Finally, if you only want to set some of the arguments, you can use keyword arguments to make the service call:

```
count,ignored = word_counter(words='one two three')
```

While this mechanism can be useful, you should use it with care, since any arguments that you do not explicitly set will remain undefined. If you omit arguments that the service needs to run, you might get strange return values. You should probably steer clear of this calling style, unless you actually *need* to use it.

Summary

Now you know all about services, the second main communication mechanism in ROS. Services are really just synchronous remote procedure calls and allow explicit two-way communication between nodes. You should now be able to use services provided by other packages in ROS, and also to implement your own services.

Once again, we didn't cover all of the details of services. To get more information on more sophisticated uses of services, you should look at the services API documentation (*http://wiki.ros.org/Services?distro=indigo*).

You should use services for things that you only need to do occasionally, or when you need a synchronous reply. The computations in a service callback should take a short, bounded amount of time to complete. If they're going to take a long time, or the time is going to be highly variable, you should think about using an *action*, which we describe in the next chapter.

## CHAPTER 5

Actions

The previous chapter described ROS services, which are useful for synchronous request/response interactions—that is, for those cases where asynchronous ROS topics don't seem like the best fit. However, services aren't always the best fit, either, in particular when the request that's being made is more than a simple instruction of the form "get (or set) the value of X."

While services are handy for simple get/set interactions like querying status and managing configuration, they don't work well when you need to initiate a long-running task. For example, imagine commanding a robot to drive to some distant location; call it `goto_position`. The robot will require significant time (seconds, minutes, perhaps longer) to do so, with the exact amount of time impossible to know in advance, since obstacles may arise that result in a longer path.

Imagine what a service interface to `goto_position` might look like to the caller: you send a request containing the goal location, then you wait for an indeterminate amount of time to receive the response that tells you what happened. While waiting, your calling program is forced to block, you have no information about the robot's progress toward the goal, and you can't cancel or change the goal. To address these shortcomings, ROS provides *actions*.

ROS *actions* are the best way to implement interfaces to time-extended, goal-oriented behaviors like `goto_position`. While services are synchronous, actions are asynchronous. Similar to the request and response of a service, an action uses a *goal* to initiate a behavior and sends a *result* when the behavior is complete. But the action further uses *feedback* to provide updates on the behavior's progress toward the goal and also allows for goals to be canceled. Actions are themselves implemented using topics. An action is essentially a higher-level protocol that specifies how a set of topics (goal, result, feedback, etc.) should be used in combination.

Using an action interface to goto_position, you send a goal, then move on to other tasks while the robot is driving. Along the way, you receive periodic progress updates (distance traveled, estimated time to goal, etc.), culminating in a result message (did the robot make it to the goal or was it forced to give up?). And if something more important comes up, you can at any time cancel the goal and send the robot somewhere else.

Actions require only a little more effort to define and use than do services, and they provide a lot more power and flexibility. Let's see how they work.

Defining an Action

The first step in creating a new action is to define the *goal, result,* and *feedback* message formats in an *action definition file*, which by convention has the suffix *.action.* The *.action* file format is similar to the *.srv* format used to define services, just with an additional field. And, as with services, each field within an *.action* file will become its own message.

As a simple example, let's define an action that acts like a timer (we'll come back to the more useful goto_position behavior in Chapter 10). We want this timer to count down, signaling us when the specified time has elapsed. Along the way, it should tell us periodically how much time is left. When it's done, it should tell us how much time actually elapsed.

 We're building a timer because it's a simple example of an action. In a real robot system, you would use the time support that is built into ROS client libraries, such as rospy.sleep().

Shown in Example 5-1 is an action definition that will satisfy these requirements.

Example 5-1. Timer.action

```
# This is an action definition file, which has three parts: the goal, the
# result, and the feedback.
#
# Part 1: the goal, to be sent by the client
#
# The amount of time we want to wait
duration time_to_wait
---
# Part 2: the result, to be sent by the server upon completion
#
# How much time we waited
duration time_elapsed
# How many updates we provided along the way
```

```
uint32 updates_sent
---
# Part 3: the feedback, to be sent periodically by the server during
# execution.
#
# The amount of time that has elapsed from the start
duration time_elapsed
# The amount of time remaining until we're done
duration time_remaining
```

Just like with service-definition files, we use three dashes (---) as the separator between the parts of the definition. While service definitions have two parts (request and response), action definitions have three parts (goal, result, and feedback).

The action file *Timer.action* should be placed in a directory called *action* within a ROS package. As with our previous examples, this file is already present in the basics package.

With the definition file in the right place, we need to run catkin_make to create the code and class definitions that we will actually use when interacting with the action, just like we did for new services. To get catkin_make to generate this code, we need to add some lines to the *CMakeLists.txt* file. First, add actionlib_msgs to the () call (in addition to any other packages that are already there):

```
find_package(catkin REQUIRED COMPONENTS
  # other packages are already listed here
  actionlib_msgs
)
```

Then, use the add_action_files() call to tell catkin about the action files you want to compile:

```
add_action_files(
  DIRECTORY action
  FILES Timer.action
)
```

Make sure you list the dependencies for your actions. You also need to explicitly list actionlib_msgs as a dependency in order for actions to compile properly:

```
generate_messages(
  DEPENDENCIES
  actionlib_msgs
  std_msgs
)
```

Finally, add actionlib_msgs as a dependency for catkin:

```
catkin_package(
  CATKIN_DEPENDS
  actionlib_msgs
)
```

With all of this information in place, running `catkin_make` in the top level of our `catkin` workspace does quite a bit of extra work for us. Our *Timer.action* file is processed to produce several message-definition files: *TimerAction.msg*, *TimerAction-Feedback.msg*, *TimerActionGoal.msg*, *TimerActionResult.msg*, *TimerFeedback.msg*, *TimerGoal.msg*, and *TimerResult.msg*. These messages are used to implement the action client/server protocol, which, as mentioned previously, is built on top of ROS topics. The generated message definitions are in turn processed by the message generator to produce corresponding class definitions. Most of the time, you'll use only a few of those classes, as you'll see in the following examples.

Implementing a Basic Action Server

Now that we have a definition of the goal, result, and feedback for the timer action, we're ready to write the code that implements it. Like topics and services, actions are a callback-based mechanism, with your code being invoked as a result of receiving messages from another node.

The easiest way to build an action server is to use the `SimpleActionServer` class from the `actionlib` package. We'll start by defining only the callback that will be invoked when a new goal is sent by an action client. In that callback, we'll do the work of the timer, then return a result when we're done. We'll add feedback reporting in the next step. Example 5-2 shows the code for our first action server.

Example 5-2. simple_action_server.py

```python
#! /usr/bin/env python
import rospy

import time
import actionlib
from basics.msg import TimerAction, TimerGoal, TimerResult

def do_timer(goal):
    start_time = time.time()
    time.sleep(goal.time_to_wait.to_sec())
    result = TimerResult()
    result.time_elapsed = rospy.Duration.from_sec(time.time() - start_time)
    result.updates_sent = 0
    server.set_succeeded(result)

rospy.init_node('timer_action_server')
server = actionlib.SimpleActionServer('timer', TimerAction, do_timer, False)
server.start()
rospy.spin()
```

Let's step through the key parts of the code. First we import the standard Python `time` package, which we'll use for the timer functionality of our server. We also import the

ROS `actionlib` package that provides the `SimpleActionServer` class that we'll be using. Finally, we import some of the message classes that were autogenerated from our *Timer.action* file:

```
import time
import actionlib
from basics.msg import TimerAction, TimerGoal, TimerResult
```

Next, we define `do_timer()`, the function that will be invoked when we receive a new goal. In this function, we handle the new goal in-place and set a result before returning. The type of the `goal` argument that is passed to `do_timer()` is `TimerGoal`, which corresponds to the goal part of *Timer.action*. We save the current time, using the standard Python `time.time()` function, then sleep for the time requested in the goal, converting the `time_to_wait` field from a ROS duration to seconds:

```
def do_timer(goal):
    start_time = time.time()
    time.sleep(goal.time_to_wait.to_sec())
```

The next step is to build up the result message, which will be of type `TimerResult`; this corresponds to the result part of *Timer.action*. We fill in the `time_elapsed` field by subtracting our saved start time from the current time, and converting the result to a ROS duration. We set `updates_sent` to zero, because we didn't send any updates along the way (we'll add that part shortly):

```
result = TimerResult()
result.time_elapsed = rospy.Duration.from_sec(time.time() - start_time)
result.updates_sent = 0
```

Our final step in the callback is to tell the `SimpleActionServer` that we successfully achieved the goal by calling `set_succeeded()` and passing it the result. For this simple server, we always succeed; we'll address failure cases later in this chapter:

```
server.set_succeeded(result)
```

Back in the global scope, we initialize and name our node as usual, then create a `SimpleActionServer`. The first constructor argument for `SimpleActionServer` is the server's name, which will determine the namespace into which its constituent topics will be advertised; we'll use `timer`. The second argument is the type of the action that the server will be handling, which in our case is `TimerAction`. The third argument is the goal callback, which is the function `do_timer()` that we defined earlier. Finally, we pass `False` to disable autostarting the server. Having created the action server, we explicitly `start()` it, then go into the usual ROS `spin()` loop to wait for goals to arrive:

```
rospy.init_node('timer_action_server')
server = actionlib.SimpleActionServer('timer', TimerAction, do_timer, False)
server.start()
rospy.spin()
```

Autostarting should *always* be disabled on action servers, because it can allow a race condition that leads to puzzling bugs. It was an oversight in the implementation of actionlib to make autostarting the default, but by the time the problem was discovered, there was too much existing code that relied on that default behavior to change it.

Checking That Everything Works as Expected

Now that we have implemented the action server, we can do a couple of checks to ensure that it's working as expected. Start up a roscore and then run the action server:

```
user@hostname$ rosrun basics simple_action_server.py
```

Let's check that the expected topics are present:

```
user@hostname$ rostopic list
/rosout
/rosout_agg
/timer/cancel
/timer/feedback
/timer/goal
/timer/result
/timer/status
```

That looks good: we can see the five topics in the timer namespace that are used under the hood to manage the action. Let's take a closer look at the /timer/goal topic, using rostopic:

```
user@hostname$ rostopic info /timer/goal
Type: basics/TimerActionGoal

Publishers: None

Subscribers:
 * /timer_action_server (http://localhost:63174/)
```

What's a TimerActionGoal? Let's dig in further, now with rosmsg:

```
user@hostname$ rosmsg show TimerActionGoal
[basics/TimerActionGoal]:
std_msgs/Header header
  uint32 seq
  time stamp
  string frame_id
actionlib_msgs/GoalID goal_id
  time stamp
  string id
basics/TimerGoal goal
  duration time_to_wait
```

Interesting; we can see our goal definition in there, as the `goal.time_to_wait` field, but there are also some extra fields that we didn't specify. Those extra fields are used by the action server and client code to keep track of what's happening. Fortunately, that bookkeeping information is automatically stripped away before our server code sees a goal message. While a `TimerActionGoal` message is sent over the wire, what we see in our goal execution is a bare `TimerGoal` message, which is just what we defined in our *.action* file:

```
user@hostname$ rosmsg show TimerGoal
[basics/TimerGoal]:
duration time_to_wait
```

In general, if you're using the libraries in the `actionlib` package, you should not need to access the autogenerated messages with `Action` in their type name. The bare `Goal`, `Result`, and `Feedback` messages should suffice.

If you like, you can publish and subscribe directly to an action server's topics using the autogenerated `Action` message types. This is a nice feature of ROS actions: they are just a higher-level protocol built on top of ROS messages. But for most applications (including everything that we'll cover in this book), the `actionlib` libraries will do the job, handling the underlying messages for you behind the scenes.

Using an Action

The easiest way to use an action is via the `SimpleActionClient` class from the `actionlib` package. Example 5-3 shows a simple client that sends a goal to our action server and waits for the result.

Example 5-3. simple_action_client.py

```python
#! /usr/bin/env python
import rospy

import actionlib
from basics.msg import TimerAction, TimerGoal, TimerResult

rospy.init_node('timer_action_client')
client = actionlib.SimpleActionClient('timer', TimerAction)
client.wait_for_server()
goal = TimerGoal()
goal.time_to_wait = rospy.Duration.from_sec(5.0)
client.send_goal(goal)
client.wait_for_result()
print('Time elapsed: %f'%(client.get_result().time_elapsed.to_sec()))
```

Let's step through the key parts of the code. Following the usual imports and initialization of our ROS node, we create a `SimpleActionClient`. The first constructor argument is the name of the action server, which the client will use to determine the topics that it will use when communicating with the server. This name must match the one that we used in creating the server, which is timer. The second argument is the type of the action, which must also match the server: TimerAction.

Having created the client, we tell it to wait for the action server to come up, which it does by checking for the five advertised topics that we saw earlier when testing the server. Similar to rospy.wait_for_service(), which we used to wait for a service to be ready, SimpleActionClient.wait_for_server() will block until the server is ready:

```
client = actionlib.SimpleActionClient('timer', TimerAction)
client.wait_for_server()
```

Now we create a goal of type TimerGoal and fill in the amount of time we want the timer to wait, which is five seconds. Then we send the goal, which causes the transmission of the goal message to the server:

```
goal = TimerGoal()
goal.time_to_wait = rospy.Duration.from_sec(5.0)
client.send_goal(goal)
```

Next, we wait for a result from the server. If things are working properly, we expect to block here for about five seconds. After the result comes in, we use get_result() to retrieve it from within the client object and print out the time_elapsed field that was reported by the server:

```
client.wait_for_result()
print('Time elapsed: %f'%(client.get_result().time_elapsed.to_sec()))
```

Checking That Everything Works as Expected

Now that we have implemented the action client, we can get to work. Make sure that your roscore and action server are still running, then run the action client:

```
user@hostname$ rosrun basics simple_action_client.py
Time elapsed: 5.001044
```

Between the invocation of the client and the printing of the result data, you should see a delay of approximately five seconds, as requested. The time elapsed should be slightly more than five seconds, because a call to time.sleep() will usually take a little longer than requested.

Implementing a More Sophisticated Action Server

508.450So far, actions look a lot like services, just with more configuration and setup. Now it's time to exercise the asynchronous aspects of actions that set them apart from services. We'll start on the server side, making some changes that demonstrate how to abort a goal, how to handle a goal preemption request, and how to provide feedback while pursuing a goal. Example 5-4 shows the code for our improved action server.

Example 5-4. fancy_action_server.py

```python
#! /usr/bin/env python
import rospy

import time
import actionlib
from basics.msg import TimerAction, TimerGoal, TimerResult, TimerFeedback

def do_timer(goal):
    start_time = time.time()
    update_count = 0

    if goal.time_to_wait.to_sec() > 60.0:
        result = TimerResult()
        result.time_elapsed = rospy.Duration.from_sec(time.time() - start_time)
        result.updates_sent = update_count
        server.set_aborted(result, "Timer aborted due to too-long wait")
        return

    while (time.time() - start_time) < goal.time_to_wait.to_sec():

        if server.is_preempt_requested():
            result = TimerResult()
            result.time_elapsed = \
                rospy.Duration.from_sec(time.time() - start_time)
            result.updates_sent = update_count
            server.set_preempted(result, "Timer preempted")
            return

        feedback = TimerFeedback()
        feedback.time_elapsed = rospy.Duration.from_sec(time.time() - start_time)
        feedback.time_remaining = goal.time_to_wait - feedback.time_elapsed
        server.publish_feedback(feedback)
        update_count += 1

        time.sleep(1.0)

    result = TimerResult()
    result.time_elapsed = rospy.Duration.from_sec(time.time() - start_time)
    result.updates_sent = update_count
    server.set_succeeded(result, "Timer completed successfully")

rospy.init_node('timer_action_server')
server = actionlib.SimpleActionServer('timer', TimerAction, do_timer, False)
server.start()
rospy.spin()
```

Let's step through the changes with respect to Example 5-2. Because we will be providing feedback, we add TimerFeedback to the list of message types that we import:

```
from basics.msg import TimerAction, TimerGoal, TimerResult, TimerFeedback
```

Stepping inside our do_timer() callback, we add a variable that will keep track of how many times we publish feedback:

```
update_count = 0
```

Next, we add some error checking. We don't want this timer to be used for long waits, so we check whether the requested time_to_wait is greater than 60 seconds, and if so, we explicitly abort the goal by calling set_aborted(). This call sends a message to the client notifying it that the goal has been aborted. Like with set_succeeded(), we include a result; doing this is optional, but a good idea if possible. We also include a status string to help the client understand what happened; in this case, we aborted because the requested wait was too long. Finally, we return from the callback because we're done with this goal:

```
if goal.time_to_wait.to_sec() > 60.0:
    result = TimerResult()
    result.time_elapsed = rospy.Duration.from_sec(time.time() - start_time)
    result.updates_sent = update_count
    server.set_aborted(result, "Timer aborted due to too-long wait")
    return
```

Now that we're past the error check, instead of just sleeping for the requested time in one shot, we're going to loop, sleeping in increments. This allows us to do things while we're working toward the goal, such as checking for preemption and providing feedback:

```
while (time.time() - start_time) < goal.time_to_wait.to_sec():
```

In the loop, we first check for preemption by asking the server is_preempt_reques ted(). This function will return True if the client has requested that we stop pursuing the goal (this could also happen if a second client sends us a new goal). If so, similar to the abort case, we fill in a result and provide a status string, this time calling set_preempted():

```
if server.is_preempt_requested():
    result = TimerResult()
    result.time_elapsed = \
        rospy.Duration.from_sec(time.time() - start_time)
    result.updates_sent = update_count
    server.set_preempted(result, "Timer preempted")
    return
```

Next we send feedback, using the type TimerFeedback, which corresponds to the feedback part of *Timer.action*. We fill in the time_elapsed and time_remaining fields, then call `publish_feedback()` to send it to the client. We also increment `update_count` to reflect the fact that we sent another update:

```
feedback = TimerFeedback()
feedback.time_elapsed = rospy.Duration.from_sec(time.time() - start_time)
feedback.time_remaining = goal.time_to_wait - feedback.time_elapsed
server.publish_feedback(feedback)
update_count += 1
```

Then we sleep a little and loop. Sleeping for a fixed amount of time here is not the right way to implement a timer, as we could easily end up sleeping longer than requested, but it makes for a simpler example:

```
time.sleep(1.0)
```

Exiting the loop means that we've successfully slept for the requested duration, so it's time to notify the client that we're done. This step is very similar to the simple action server, except that we fill in the `updates_sent` field and add a status string:

```
result = TimerResult()
result.time_elapsed = rospy.Duration.from_sec(time.time() - start_time)
result.updates_sent = update_count
server.set_succeeded(result, "Timer completed successfully")
```

The rest of the code is unchanged from Example 5-2: initialize the node, create and start the action server, then wait for goals.

Using the More Sophisticated Action

Now we'll modify the action client to try out the new capabilities that we added to the action server: we'll process feedback, preempt a goal, and trigger an abort. Example 5-5 shows the code for our improved action client.

Example 5-5. fancy_action_client.py

```
#! /usr/bin/env python
import rospy

import time
import actionlib
from basics.msg import TimerAction, TimerGoal, TimerResult, TimerFeedback

def feedback_cb(feedback):
    print('[Feedback] Time elapsed: %f'%(feedback.time_elapsed.to_sec()))
    print('[Feedback] Time remaining: %f'%(feedback.time_remaining.to_sec()))

rospy.init_node('timer_action_client')
client = actionlib.SimpleActionClient('timer', TimerAction)
client.wait_for_server()
```

```
goal = TimerGoal()
goal.time_to_wait = rospy.Duration.from_sec(5.0)
# Uncomment this line to test server-side abort:
#goal.time_to_wait = rospy.Duration.from_sec(500.0)
client.send_goal(goal, feedback_cb=feedback_cb)

# Uncomment these lines to test goal preemption:
#time.sleep(3.0)
#client.cancel_goal()

client.wait_for_result()
print('[Result] State: %d'%(client.get_state()))
print('[Result] Status: %s'%(client.get_goal_status_text()))
print('[Result] Time elapsed: %f'%(client.get_result().time_elapsed.to_sec()))
print('[Result] Updates sent: %d'%(client.get_result().updates_sent))
```

Let's step through the changes with respect to Example 5-3. We define a callback, feedback_cb(), that will be invoked when we receive a feedback message. In this callback we just print the contents of the feedback:

```
def feedback_cb(feedback):
    print('[Feedback] Time elapsed: %f'%(feedback.time_elapsed.to_sec()))
    print('[Feedback] Time remaining: %f'%(feedback.time_remaining.to_sec()))
```

We register our feedback callback by passing it as the feedback_cb keyword argument when calling send_goal():

```
client.send_goal(goal, feedback_cb=feedback_cb)
```

After receiving the result, we print a little more information to show what happened. The get_state() function returns the state of the goal, which is an enumeration that is defined in actionlib_msgs/GoalStatus. While there are 10 possible states, in this example we'll encounter only three: PREEMPTED=2, SUCCEEDED=3, and ABORTED=4. We also print the status text that was included by the server with the result:

```
print('[Result] State: %d'%(client.get_state()))
print('[Result] Status: %s'%(client.get_goal_status_text()))
print('[Result] Time elapsed: %f'%(client.get_result().time_elapsed.to_sec()))
print('[Result] Updates sent: %d'%(client.get_result().updates_sent))
```

Checking That Everything Works as Expected

Let's try out our new server and client. As before, start up a roscore, then run the server:

```
user@hostname$ rosrun basics fancy_action_server.py
```

In another terminal, run the client:

```
user@hostname$ rosrun basics fancy_action_client.py
[Feedback] Time elapsed: 0.000044
[Feedback] Time remaining: 4.999956
```

```
[Feedback] Time elapsed: 1.001626
[Feedback] Time remaining: 3.998374
[Feedback] Time elapsed: 2.003189
[Feedback] Time remaining: 2.996811
[Feedback] Time elapsed: 3.004825
[Feedback] Time remaining: 1.995175
[Feedback] Time elapsed: 4.006477
[Feedback] Time remaining: 0.993523
[Result] State: 3
[Result] Status: Timer completed successfully
[Result] Time elapsed: 5.008076
[Result] Updates sent: 5
```

Everything works as expected: while waiting, we receive one feedback update per second, then we receive a successful result (SUCCEEDED=3).

Now let's try preempting a goal. In the client, following the call to send_goal(), uncomment these two lines, which will cause the client to sleep briefly, then request that the server preempt the goal:

```
# Uncomment these lines to test goal preemption:
#time.sleep(3.0)
#client.cancel_goal()
```

Run the client again:

```
user@hostname$ rosrun basics fancy_action_client.py
[Feedback] Time elapsed: 0.000044
[Feedback] Time remaining: 4.999956
[Feedback] Time elapsed: 1.001651
[Feedback] Time remaining: 3.998349
[Feedback] Time elapsed: 2.003297
[Feedback] Time remaining: 2.996703
[Result] State: 2
[Result] Status: Timer preempted
[Result] Time elapsed: 3.004926
[Result] Updates sent: 3
```

That's the behavior we expect: the server pursues the goal, providing feedback, until we send the cancellation request, after which we receive the result confirming the preemption (PREEMPTED=2).

Now let's trigger a server-side abort. In the client, uncomment this line to change the requested wait time from 5 seconds to 500 seconds:

```
# Uncomment this line to test server-side abort:
#goal.time_to_wait = rospy.Duration.from_sec(500.0)
```

Run the client again:

```
user@hostname$ rosrun basics fancy_action_client.py
[Result] State: 4
[Result] Status: Timer aborted due to too-long wait
```

```
[Result] Time elapsed: 0.000012
[Result] Updates sent: 0
```

As expected, the server immediately aborted the goal (ABORTED=4).

Summary

In this chapter, we covered *actions*, a powerful communications tool that is commonly used in ROS systems. Table 5-1 compares actions to *topics* and *services*, which we covered in earlier chapters. Similar to services, actions allow you to make a request (for actions, a *goal*) and receive a response (for actions, a *result*). But actions offer much more control to both the client and the server than do services. The server can provide feedback along the way while it's servicing the request: the client can cancel a previously issued request; and, because they're built atop ROS *messages*, actions are asynchronous, allowing for nonblocking programming on both sides.

Table 5-1. Comparison of topics, services, and actions

Type	Best used for
Topic	One-way communication, especially if there might be multiple nodes listening (e.g., streams of sensor data)
Service	Simple request/response interactions, such as asking a question about a node's current state
Action	Most request/response interactions, especially when servicing the request is not instantaneous (e.g., navigating to a goal location)

Taken together, these features of actions make them well suited to many aspects of robot programming. It's common in a robotics application to implement time-extended, goal-seeking behaviors, whether it's goto_position or clean_the_house. Any time you need to be able to trigger a behavior, actions are probably the right tool for the job. In fact, any time that you're using a service, it's worth considering replacing it with an action; actions require a bit more code to use, but in return they're much more powerful and extensible than services. We'll see many examples in future chapters where actions provide rich but easy-to-use interfaces to some pretty complex behaviors.

As usual, we did not cover the entire API in this chapter. There are more sophisticated uses of actions that can be useful in situations where you need more control over how the system behaves, such as what to do when there are multiple clients and/or multiple simultaneous goals. For full details, consult the actionlib API documentation (*http://wiki.ros.org/actionlib?distro=indigo*).

At this point, you know all of the basics of ROS: how nodes are organized into a graph, how to use the basic command-line tools, how to write simple nodes, and how to get these nodes to communicate with each other. Before we look at our first complete robot application in Chapter 7, let's take a moment to talk about the various parts of a robot system, for both real and simulated robots, and how they relate to ROS.

## CHAPTER 6

Robots and Simulators

The previous chapters discussed many fundamental concepts of ROS. They may have seemed rather vague and abstract, but those concepts were necessary to describe how data moves around in ROS and how its software systems are organized. In this chapter, we will introduce common robot subsystems and describe how the ROS architecture handles them. Then, we will introduce the robots that we will use throughout the remainder of the book and describe the simulators in which we can most easily experiment with them.

Subsystems

Like all complex machines, robots are most easily designed and analyzed by considering one subsystem at a time. In this section, we will introduce the main subsystems commonly found on the types of robots considered in this book. Broadly speaking, they can be divided into three categories: *actuation*, *sensing*, and *computing*. In the ROS context, actuation subsystems are the subsystems that interact directly with how the robot's wheels or arms move. Sensing subsystems interact directly with sensor hardware, such as cameras or laser scanners. Finally, the computational subsystems are what tie actuators and sensing together, with (ideally) some relatively intelligent processing that allows the robot to perform useful tasks. We will introduce these subsystems in the next few sections. Note that we are not attempting to provide an exhaustive discussion; rather, we are trying to describe these subsystems just deeply enough to convey the issues typically faced when interacting with them from a software development standpoint.

Actuation: Mobile Platform

The ability to move around, or *locomote*, is a fundamental capability of many robots. It is surprisingly nuanced: there are many books written entirely on this subject!

However, broadly speaking, a mobile base is a collection of actuators that allow a robot to move around. They come in an astonishingly wide variety of shapes and sizes.

Although legged locomotion is popular in some domains in the research community, and camera-friendly walking robots have seen great progress in recent years, most robots drive around on wheels. This is because of two main reasons. First, wheeled platforms are often simpler to design and manufacture. Second, for the very smooth surfaces that are common in artificial environments, such as indoor floors or outdoor pavement, wheels are the most energy-efficient way to move around.

The simplest possible configuration of a wheeled mobile robot is called *differential drive*. It consists of two independently actuated wheels, often located on the centerline of a round robot. In this configuration, the robot moves forward when both wheels turn forward, and spins in place when one wheel drives forward and one drives backward. Differential-drive robots often have one or more *casters*, which are unpowered wheels that spin freely to support the front and back of the robot, just like the wheels on the bottom of a typical office chair. This is an example of a *statically stable* robot, which means that, when viewed from above, the center of mass of the robot is inside a polygon formed by the points of contact between the wheels and the ground. Statically stable robots are simple to model and control, and among their virtues is the fact that power can be shut off to the robot at any time, and it will not fall over.

However, *dynamically stable* or *balancing* wheeled mobile robots are also possible, with the term *dynamic* implying that the actuators must constantly be in motion (however slight) to preserve stability. The simplest dynamically stable wheeled robots look like (and often are literally built upon) Segway platforms, with a pair of large differential-drive wheels supporting a tall robot above. Among the benefits of balancing wheeled mobile bases is that the wheels contacting the ground can have very large diameters, which allows the robot to smoothly drive over small obstacles: imagine the difference between running over a pebble with an office-chair wheel versus a bicycle wheel (this is, in fact, precisely the reason why bicycle wheels are large). Another advantage of balancing wheeled mobile robots is that the footprint of the robot can be kept small, which can be useful in tight quarters.

The differential-drive scheme can be extended to more than two wheels and is often called *skid steering*. Four-wheel and six-wheel skid-steering schemes are common, in which all of the wheels on the left side of the robot actuate together, and all of the wheels on the right side actuate together. As the number of wheels extends beyond six, typically the wheels are connected by external *tracks*, as exemplified by excavators or tanks.

As is typically the case in engineering, there are trade-offs with the skid-steering scheme, and it makes sense for some applications, but not all. One advantage is that skid steering provides maximum traction while preserving mechanical simplicity (and thus controlling cost), since all contact points between the vehicle and the ground are being actively driven. However, skid steering is, as its name states, constantly skidding when it is not driving exactly forward or backward.

In some situations, traction and the ability to surmount large obstacles are valued so highly that skid steering platforms are used extensively. However, all this traction comes at a cost: the constant skidding is tremendously inefficient, since massive energy is spent tearing up the dirt (or heating up the wheels) whenever the robot turns at low speeds. In the most extreme case, when trying to turn in place with one set of wheels turning forwards and the other turning backward, the wheels are skidding dramatically, which can tear up gentle surfaces and wear tires quickly. This is why excavators are typically towed to a construction site on a trailer!

The inefficiencies and wear and tear of skid steering are among the reasons why passenger cars use more complex (and expensive) schemes to get around. They are often called *Ackerman* platforms, in which the rear wheels are always pointed straight ahead, and the front wheels turn together. Placing the wheels at the extreme corners of the vehicle maximizes the area of the supporting polygon, which is why cars can turn sharp corners without tipping over and (when not driven in action movies) car wheels do not have to skid when turning. However, the downside of Ackerman platforms is that they cannot drive sideways, since the rear wheels are always facing forward. This is why parallel parking is a dreaded portion of any driver's license examination: elaborate planning and sequential actuator maneuvers are required to move an Ackerman platform sideways.

All of the platforms described thus far can be summarized as being *non-holonomic*, which means that they cannot move in *any* direction at any given time. For example, neither differential-drive platforms nor Ackerman platforms can move sideways. To do this, a *holonomic* platform is required, which can be built using *steered casters*. Each steered caster actuator has two motors: one motor rotates the wheel forward and backward, and another motor steers the wheel about its vertical axis. This allows the platform to move in any direction while spinning arbitrarily. Although significantly more complex to build and maintain, these platforms simplify motion planning. Imagine the ease of parallel parking if you could drive sideways into a parking spot!

As a special case, when the robot only needs to move on very smooth surfaces, a low-cost holonomic platform can be built using *Mecanum* wheels. These are clever contraptions in which each wheel has a series of rollers on its rim, angled at 45 degrees to the plane of the wheel. Using this scheme, motion in any direction (with any rate of rotation) is possible at all times, using only four actuators, without skidding. However, due to the small diameter of the roller wheels, it is only suitable for very smooth surfaces such as hard flooring or extremely short-pile carpets.

Because one of the design goals of ROS is to allow software reuse across a variety of robots, ROS software that interacts with mobile platforms virtually always uses a Twist message. A *twist* is a way to express general linear and angular velocities in three dimensions. Although it may seem easier to express mobile base motions simply by expressing wheel velocities, using the linear and angular velocities of the center of the vehicle allows the software to abstract away the kinematics of the vehicle.

For example, high-level software can command the vehicle to drive forward at 0.5 meters/second while rotating clockwise at 0.1 radians/second. From the standpoint of the high-level software, whether the mobile platform's actuators are arranged as differential-drive, Ackerman steering, or Mecanum wheels is irrelevant, just as the transmission ratios and wheel diameters are irrelevant to high-level behaviors.

The robots described in this book will only be navigating on flat, two-dimensional surfaces and are commonly called *planar robots*. However, expressing velocities in three dimensions allows path planning or obstacle avoidance software to be used by vehicles capable of more general motions, such as aerial, underwater, or space vehicles. It is important to recognize that even for vehicles designed for two-dimensional navigation, the general three-dimensional twist methodology is necessary to express desired or actual motions of many types of actuators, such as grippers, since they are often capable of three-dimensional motions when flying on the end of a manipulator arm even when the mobile base is constrained to the floor plane. Manipulators, in fact, comprise the other main application domain for robot actuators and will be discussed in the next section.

Actuation: Manipulator Arm

Many robots need to *manipulate* objects in their environment. For example, packing or palletizing robots sit on the end of a production line, grab items coming down the line, and place them into boxes or stacks. There is an entire domain of robot manipulation tasks called *pick and place*, in which manipulator arms grasp items and place them somewhere else. Security robot tasks include handling suspicious items, for which a strong manipulator arm is often required. An emerging class of *personal robots* hope to be useful in home and office applications, performing manipulation tasks including cleaning, delivering items, preparing meals, and so on.

As with mobile bases, there's astonishing variety in manipulator-arm subsystems across robots, with many trade-offs made to support particular application domains and price points.

Although there are exceptions, the majority of manipulator arms are formed by a *chain* of rigid *links* connected by *joints*. The simplest kinds of joints are single-axis revolute joints (also called "pin" joints), where one link has a shaft that serves as the axis around which the next link rotates, in the same way that a typical residential door rotates around its hinge pins. However, *linear* joints (also called *prismatic* joints) are also common, in which one link has a *slide* or tube along which the next link travels, just as a sliding door runs sideways back and forth along its track.

A fundamental characteristic of a robot manipulator is the number of *degrees of freedom* (DOF) of its design. Often, the number of joints is equal to the number of actuators; when those numbers differ, typically the DOF is taken to be the lower of the two numbers. Regardless, the number of degrees of freedom is one of the most significant drivers of manipulator size, mass, dexterity, cost, and reliability. Adding DOF to the *distal* (far) end of a robot arm typically increases its mass, which requires larger actuators on the *proximal* (near) joints, which further increases the mass of the manipulator.

In general, six DOF are required to position the wrist of the manipulator arm in any location and orientation within its *workspace*, providing that each joint has full range of motion. In this context, *workspace* has a precise meaning: it is the space that a robot manipulator can reach. A subset of the robot's workspace, called the *dextrous workspace*, is the region in which a robot can achieve all positions and orientations of the end effector. Generally speaking, having a larger dextrous workspace is a good thing for robots, but unfortunately full (360-degree) range of motion on six joints of a robot is often extremely difficult to achieve at reasonable cost, due to constraints of mechanical structures, electrical wiring, and so on. As a result, seven-DOF arms are often used. The seventh DOF provides an extra degree of freedom that can be used to move the links of the arm while maintaining the position and orientation of the wrist, much as a human arm can move its elbow through an arc segment while maintaining the wrist in the same position. This "extra" DOF can help contribute to a relatively large dextrous workspace even when each individual joint has a restricted range of motion.

Research robots intended for manipulation tasks in human environments often have human-scale, seven-DOF arms, quite simply because the desired workspaces are human-scale surfaces, such as tables or countertops in home and office environments. In contrast, robots intended for industrial applications have wildly varying dimensions and joint configurations depending on the tasks they are to perform, since each additional DOF introduces additional cost and reliability concerns.

So far, we have discussed the two main classes of robot actuators: those used for locomotion, and those used for manipulation. The next major class of robot hardware is its sensors. We'll start with the sensor head, a common mounting scheme, and then describe the subcomponents found in many robot sensor heads.

Sensors

Robots must sense the world around them in order to react to variations in tasks and environments. The sensors can range from minimalist setups designed for quick installation to highly elaborate and tremendously expensive sensor rigs.

Many successful industrial deployments use surprisingly little sensing. A remarkable number of complex and intricate industrial manipulation tasks can be performed through a combination of clever mechanical engineering and *limit switches*, which close or open an electrical circuit when a mechanical lever or plunger is pressed, in order to start execution of a preprogrammed robotic manipulation sequence. Through careful mechanical setup and tuning, these systems can achieve amazing levels of throughput and reliability. It is important, then, to consider these *binary* sensors when enumerating the world of robotic sensing. These sensors are typically either "on" or "off." In addition to mechanical limit switches, other binary sensors include *optical limit switches*, which use a mechanical "flag" to interrupt a light beam, and *bump sensors*, which channel mechanical pressure along a relatively large distance to a single mechanical switch. These relatively simple sensors are a key part of modern industrial automation equipment, and their importance can hardly be overstated.

Another class of sensors return *scalar* readings. For example, a pressure sensor can estimate the mechanical or barometric pressure and will typically output a scalar value along some range of sensitivity chosen at time of manufacture. Range sensors can be constructed from many physical phenomena (sound, light, etc.) and will also typically return a scalar value in some range, which seldom includes zero or infinity!

Each sensor class has its own quirks that distort its view of reality and must be accommodated by sensor-processing algorithms. These quirks can often be surprisingly severe. For example, a range sensor may have a "minimum distance" restriction: if an object is closer than that minimum distance, it will not be sensed. As a result of these quirks, it is often advantageous to combine several different types of sensors in a robotic system.

However, many of the applications we will describe in this book are reliant on "rich" sensor data, which is a vague term that generally means that the robot's perception algorithms consider something more than a small number of binary or scalar sensors. Any configuration of sensing hardware is possible (and has likely been tried), but for convenience, aesthetics, and to preserve line-of-sight with the center of the workspace, it is common for robots to have a *sensor head* on top of the platform that integrates several sensors in the same physical enclosure. Often, sensor heads sit atop a *pan/tilt* assembly, so that they can rotate to a bearing of interest and look up or down as needed. The following several sections will describe sensors commonly found in robot sensor heads and on other parts of their bodies.

Visual cameras

Higher-order animals tends to rely on visual data to react to the world around them. If only robots were as smart as animals! Unfortunately, using camera data intelligently is surprisingly difficult, as we will describe in later chapters of this book. However,

---

cameras are cheap and often useful for teleoperation, so it is common to see them on robot sensor heads.

Interestingly, it is often more mathematically robust to describe robot tasks and environments in three dimensions (3D) than it is to work with 2D camera images. This is because the 3D shapes of tasks and environments are *invariant* to changes in scene lighting, shadows, occlusions, and so on. In fact, in a surprising number of application domains, the visual data is largely ignored; the algorithms are interested in 3D data. As a result, intense research efforts have been expended on producing 3D data of the scene in front of the robot.

When two cameras are rigidly mounted to a common mechanical structure, they form a *stereo camera*. Each camera sees a slightly different view of the world, and these slight differences can be used to estimate the distances to various features in the image. This sounds simple, but as always, the devil is in the details. The performance of a stereo camera depends on a large number of factors, such as the quality of the camera's mechanical design, its resolution, its lens type and quality, and so on. Equally important are the qualities of the scene being imaged: a stereo camera can only estimate the distances to mathematically discernable *features* in the scene, such as sharp, high-contrast corners. A stereo camera cannot, for example, estimate the distance to a featureless wall, although it can most likely estimate the distance to the corners and edges of the wall, if they intersect a floor, ceiling, or other wall of a different color. Many natural outdoor scenes possess sufficient texture that stereo vision can be made to work quite well for depth estimation. Uncluttered indoor scenes, however, can often be quite difficult.

Several conventions have emerged in the ROS community for handling cameras. The canonical ROS message type for images is sensor_msgs/Image, and it contains little more than the size of the image, its pixel encoding scheme, and the pixels themselves. To describe the *intrinsic distortion* of the camera resulting from its lens and sensor alignment, the sensor_msgs/CameraInfo message is used. Often, these ROS images need to be sent to and from OpenCV, a popular computer vision library. The cv_bridge package is intended to simplify this operation and will be used throughout the book.

Depth cameras

As discussed in the previous section, even though visual camera data is intuitively appealing, and seems like it should be useful somehow, many perception algorithms work much better with 3D data. Fortunately, the past few years have seen massive progress in low-cost *depth cameras*. Unlike the passive stereo cameras described in the previous section, depth cameras are *active* devices. They illuminate the scene in various ways, which greatly improves the system performance. For example, a completely featureless indoor wall or surface is essentially impossible to detect using passive stereo vision. However, many depth cameras will shine a texture pattern on the surface, which is subsequently imaged by its camera. The texture pattern and camera are typically set to operate in near-infrared wavelengths to reduce the system's sensitivity to the colors of objects, as well as to not be distracting to people nearby.

Some common depth cameras, such as the Microsoft Kinect, project a *structured light* image. The device projects a precisely known pattern into the scene, its camera observes how this pattern is deformed as it lands on the various objects and surfaces of the scene, and finally a *reconstruction algorithm* estimates the 3D structure of the scene from this data. It's hard to overstate the impact that the Kinect has had on modern robotics! It was designed for the gaming market, which is orders of magnitude larger than the robotics sensor market, and could justify massive expenditures for the development and production of the sensor. The launch price of $150 was incredibly cheap for a sensor capable of outputting so much useful data. Many robots were quickly retrofitted to hold Kinects, and the sensor continues to be used across research and industry.

Although the Kinect is the most famous (and certainly the most widely used) depth camera in robotics, many other depth-sensing schemes are possible. For example, *unstructured light* depth cameras employ "standard" stereo-vision algorithms with random texture injected into the scene by some sort of projector. This scheme has been shown to work far better than passive stereo systems in feature-scarce environments, such as many indoor scenes.

A different approach is used by *time-of-flight* depth cameras. These imagers rapidly blink an infrared LED or laser illuminator, while using specially designed pixel structures in their image sensors to estimate the time required for these light pulses to fly into the scene and bounce back to the depth camera. Once this "time of flight" is estimated, the (constant) speed of light can be used to convert the estimates into a *depth image*.

Intense research and development is occurring in this domain, due to the enormous existing and potential markets for depth cameras in video games and other mass-market user-interaction scenarios. It is not yet clear which (if any) of the schemes discussed previously will end up being best suited for robotics applications. At the time of writing, cameras using all of the previous modalities are in common usage in robotics experiments.

Just like visual cameras, depth cameras produce an enormous amount of data. This data is typically in the form of *point clouds*, which are the 3D points estimated to lie on the surfaces facing the camera. The fundamental point cloud message is `sensor_msgs/PointCloud2` (so named purely for historical reasons). This message allows for unstructured point cloud data, which is often advantageous, since depth cameras often cannot return valid depth estimates for each pixel in their images. As such, depth images often have substantial "holes," which processing algorithms must handle gracefully.

Laser scanners

Although depth cameras have greatly changed the depth-sensing market in the last few years due to their simplicity and low cost, there are still some applications in which *laser scanners* are widely used due to their superior accuracy and longer sensing range. There are many types of laser scanners, but one of the most common schemes used in robotics involves shining a laser beam on a rotating mirror spinning around 10 to 80 times per second (typically 600 to 4,800 RPM). As the mirror rotates, the laser light is pulsed rapidly, and the reflected waveforms are correlated with the outgoing waveform to estimate the time of flight of the laser pulse for a series of angles around the scanner.

Laser scanners used for autonomous vehicles are considerably different from those used for indoor or slow-moving robots. Vehicle laser scanners made by companies such as Velodyne must deal with the significant aerodynamic forces, vibrations, and temperature swings common to the automotive environment. Since vehicles typically move much faster than smaller robots, vehicle sensors must also have considerably longer range so that sufficient reaction time is possible. Additionally, many software tasks for autonomous driving, such as detecting vehicles and obstacles, work much better when multiple laser *scanlines* are received each time the device rotates, rather than just one. These extra scanlines can be extremely useful when distinguishing between classes of objects, such as between trees and pedestrians. To produce multiple scanlines, automotive laser scanners often have multiple lasers mounted together in a rotating structure, rather than simply rotating a mirror. All of these additional features naturally add to the complexity, weight, size, and thus the cost of the laser scanner.

The complex signal processing steps required to produce range estimates are virtually always handled by the firmware of the laser scanner itself. The devices typically output a vector of ranges several dozen times per second, along with the starting and stopping angles of each measurement vector. In ROS, laser scans are stored in `sensor_msgs/LaserScan` messages, which map directly from the output of the laser scanner. Each manufacturer, of course, has their own raw message formats, but ROS drivers exist to translate between the raw output of many popular laser scanner manufacturers and the `sensor_msgs/LaserScan` message format.

Shaft encoders

Estimating the motions of the robot is a critical component of virtually all robotic systems, with solutions ranging from low-level control schemes to high-level mapping, localization, and manipulation algorithms. Although estimates can be derived from many sources, the simplest and often most accurate estimates are produced simply by counting how many times the motors or wheels have turned.

Many different types of *shaft encoders* are designed expressly for this purpose. Shaft encoders are typically constructed by attaching a marker to the shaft and measuring its motion relative to another frame of reference, such as the chassis of the robot or the previous link on a manipulator arm. The implementation may be done with magnets, optical discs, variable resistors, or variable capacitors, among many other options, with trade-offs including size, cost, accuracy, maximum speed, and whether the measurement is *absolute* or *relative* to the position at power-up. Regardless, the principle remains the same: the angular position of a marker on a shaft is measured relative to an adjacent *frame of reference*.

Just like automobile speedometers and odometers, shaft encoders are used to count the precise number of rotations of the robot's wheels, and thereby estimate how far the vehicle has traveled and how much it has turned. Note that *odometry* is simply a count of how many times the drive wheels have turned, and is also known as *dead reckoning* in some domains. It is *not* a direct measurement of the vehicle position. Minute differences in wheel diameters, tire pressures, carpet weave direction (really!), axle misalignments, minor skidding, and countless other sources of error are cumulative over time. As a result, the raw odometry estimates of *any* robot will drift; the longer the robot drives, the more error accumulates in the estimate. For example, a robot traveling down the middle of a long, straight corridor will *always* have odometry that is a gradual curve. Put another way, if both tires of a differential-drive robot are turned in the same direction at the exact same wheel velocity, the robot will never drive in a truly straight line. This is why mobile robots need additional sensors and clever algorithms to build maps and navigate.

Shaft encoders are also used extensively in robot manipulators. The vast majority of manipulator arms have at least one shaft encoder for every rotary joint, and the vector of shaft encoder readings is often called the *manipulator configuration*. When combined with a geometric model of each link of a manipulator arm, the shaft encoders allow higher-level collision-avoidance, planning, and trajectory-following algorithms to control the robot.

Because the mobility and manipulation uses of shaft encoders are quite different, the ROS conventions for each use are also quite different. Although the raw encoder counts may also be reported by some mobile-base device drivers, odometry estimates are most useful when reported as a *spatial transformation* represented by a `geometry_msgs/Transform` message. This concept will be discussed at great length throughout the book, but in general, a spatial transform describes one frame of reference relative to another frame of reference. In this case, the odometry transform typically describes the shaft encoder's odometric estimate relative to the position of the robot at power-up, or where its encoders were last reset.

In contrast, the encoder readings for manipulator arms are typically broadcast by ROS manipulator device drivers as `sensor_msgs/JointState` messages. The `JointState` message contains vectors of angles in radians, and angular velocities in radians per second. Since typical shaft encoders have thousands of discrete states per revolution, the ROS device drivers for manipulator arms are required to scale the encoders as needed, accounting for transmissions and linkages, to produce a `JointState` vector with standard units. These messages are used extensively by ROS software packages, as they provide the minimal complete description of the state of a manipulator.

That about covers it for the physical parts of a robot system. We now turn our attention to the "brains," where the robot interprets sensor data and determines how to move its body, and where we'll be spending most of our time in this book.

Computation

Impressive robotic systems have been implemented on computing resources ranging from large racks of servers down to extremely small and efficient 8-bit microcontrollers. Fierce debates have raged throughout the history of robotics as to exactly how much computer processing is required to produce robust, useful robot behavior. Insect brains, for example, are extremely small and power-efficient, yet insects are arguably the most successful life forms on the planet. Biological brains process data very differently from "mainstream" systems-engineering approaches of human technology, which has led to large and sustained research projects that study and try to replicate the success of bio-inspired computational architectures.

ROS takes a more traditional software-engineering approach to robotic computational architecture; as described in the first few chapters of this book, ROS uses a dynamic message-passing graph to pass data between software nodes, which are typically isolated by the POSIX process model. This does not come for free. It certainly requires additional CPU cycles to serialize a message from one node, send it over some interprocess or network communications method to another node, and deserialize it for another node. However, it is our opinion that the rapid prototyping and software integration benefits of this architecture outweigh its computational overhead.

Because of this messaging overhead and the emphasis on module isolation, ROS is not currently intended to run on extremely small microcontrollers. ROS can be (and has been) used to emulate and rapid-prototype minimalist processing paradigms. Typically, however, ROS is used to build systems that include considerable perceptual input and complex processing algorithms, where its modular and dynamically extensible architecture can simplify system design and operation.

ROS currently must run on top of a full-featured operating system such as Linux or Mac OS X. Fortunately, the continuing advance of Moore's law and mass-market demand for battery-powered devices has led to ever-smaller and more power-efficient platforms capable of running full operating systems. ROS can run on small-form-factor embedded computer systems such as Gumstix, Raspberry Pi, or BeagleBone, among many others. Going up the performance and power curve, ROS has been widely used on a large range of laptops, desktops, and servers. Human-scale robots often carry one or more standard PC motherboards running Linux headless, which are accessed over a network link.

Complete Robots

The previous section described subsystems commonly found on many types of robots running ROS. Many of these robots used in research settings are custom built to investigate a particular research problem. However, there are a growing number of standard products that can be purchased and used "out of the box" for research, development, and operations in many domains of robotics. This section will describe several of these platforms, which will be used for examples throughout the rest of the book.

PR2

The PR2 robot was one of the original ROS target platforms. In many ways, it was the "ultimate" research platform for service-robotics software at the time of its release in 2010. Its mobile base is actuated by four steerable casters and has a laser scanner for navigation. Atop this mobile base, the robot has a telescoping torso that carries two human-scale seven-DOF arms. The arms have a unique passive mechanical counter-balance, which permits the use of surprisingly low-power motors for human-scale arms.

The PR2 has a pan/tilt head equipped with a wide range of sensors, including a "nodding" laser scanner that can tilt up and down independently of the head, a pair of stereo cameras for short and long distances, and a Kinect depth camera. Additionally, each forearm of the robot has a camera, and the gripper fingertips have tactile sensors. All told, the PR2 has two laser scanners, six cameras, a depth camera, four tactile arrays, and 1 kHz encoder feedback. All of this data is handled by a pair of computers in the base of the robot, with an onboard gigabit network connecting them to a pair of WiFi radios.

All of this functionality came at a price, since the PR2 was not designed for low cost. When it was commercially available, the PR2 listed for about $400,000.[1] Despite this financial hurdle, its fully integrated "out-of-the-box" experience was a landmark for research robots and is why PR2 robots are being actively used in dozens of research

---

1 All prices are approximate, as of the time of writing, and quoted in US dollars.

labs around the world. Figure 6-1 shows a PR2 running in the Gazebo simulator. Simulators will be discussed later in this chapter.

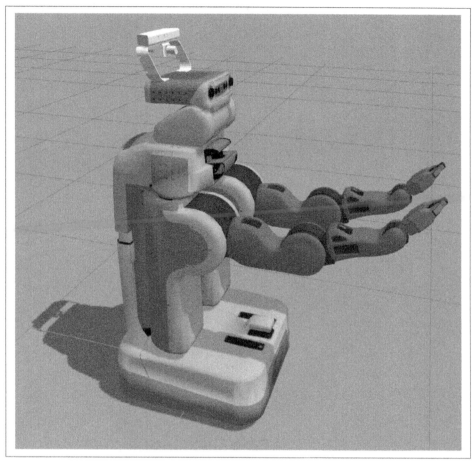

Figure 6-1. The PR2 robot running in the Gazebo simulator

Fetch

Fetch is a mobile manipulation robot intended for warehouse applications. The design team at Fetch Robotics, Inc. includes many of those who designed the PR2 robot, and in some ways the Fetch robot can be seen as a smaller, more practical and cost-effective "spiritual successor" of the PR2. The single-arm robot, shown in Figure 6-2 is fully ROS-based and has a compact sensor head built around a depth camera. The differential-drive mobile base has a laser scanner intended for navigation purposes and a telescoping torso. At the time of writing, the price of the robot has not been publicly released, but it is expected to be much more affordable than the PR2.

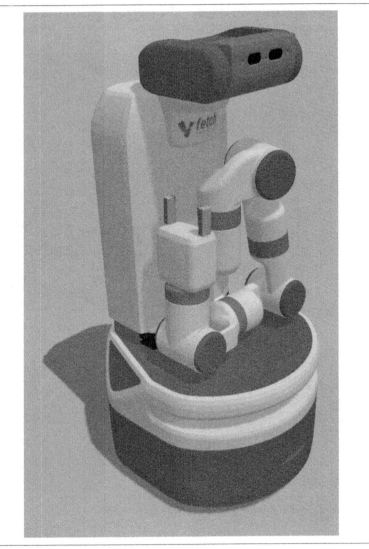

Figure 6-2. The Fetch robot running in the Gazebo simulator

Robonaut 2

The NASA/GM Robonaut 2 (Figure 6-3 is a human-scale robot designed with the extreme reliability and safety systems necessary for operation aboard the International Space Station. At the time of writing, the Robonaut 2 (a.k.a R2) aboard the space station is running ROS for high-level task control. Much more information is available at *http://robonaut.jsc.nasa.gov*.

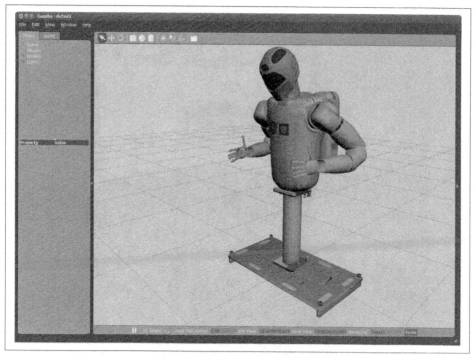

Figure 6-3. The NASA R2 robot running in the Gazebo simulator

TurtleBot

The TurtleBot was designed in 2011 as a minimalist platform for ROS-based mobile robotics education and prototyping. It has a small differential-drive mobile base with an internal battery, power regulators, and charging contacts. Atop this base is a stack of laser-cut "shelves" that provide space to hold a netbook computer and depth camera, and lots of open space for prototyping. To control cost, the TurtleBot relies on a depth camera for range sensing; it does not have a laser scanner. Despite this, mapping and navigation can work quite well for indoor spaces. TurtleBots are available from several manufacturers for less than $2,000. More information is available at *http://turtlebot.org*.

Because the shelves of the TurtleBot (pictured in Figure 6-4) are covered with mounting holes, many owners have added additional subsystems to their TurtleBots, such as small manipulator arms, additional sensors, or upgraded computers. However, the "stock" TurtleBot is an excellent starting point for indoor mobile robotics. Many similar systems exist from other vendors, such as the Pioneer and Erratic robots and thousands of custom-built mobile robots around the world. The examples in this book will use the TurtleBot, but any other small differential-drive platform could easily be substituted.

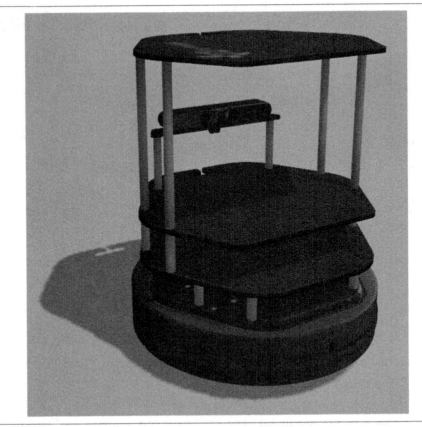

Figure 6-4. The TurtleBot robot running in the Gazebo simulator

Simulators

Although the preceding list of robots includes platforms that we consider to be remarkably low-cost compared to prior robots of similar capabilities, they are still significant investments. In addition, real robots require logistics including lab space, recharging of batteries, and operational quirks that often become part of the institutional knowledge of the organization operating the robot. Sadly, even the best robots break periodically due to various combinations of operator error, environmental conditions, manufacturing or design defects, and so on.

Many of these headaches can be avoided by using *simulated* robots. At first glance, this seems to defeat the whole purpose of robotics; after all, the very definition of a robot involves perceiving and/or manipulating the environment. Software robots, however, are extraordinarily useful. In simulation, we can model as much or as little of reality as we desire. Sensors and actuators can be modeled as ideal devices, or they can incorporate various levels of distortion, errors, and unexpected faults. Although data logs can be used in automated test suites to verify that sensing algorithms produce expected results, automated testing of control algorithms typically requires simulated robots, since the algorithms under test need to be able to experience the consequences of their actions.

Simulated robots are the ultimate low-cost platforms. They are free! They do not require complex operating procedures; you simply spawn a `roslaunch` script and wait a few seconds, and a shiny new robot is created. At the end of the experimental run, a quick Ctrl-C and the robot vaporizes. For those of us who have spent many long nights with the pain and suffering caused by operating real robots, the benefits of simulated robots are simply magical.

Due to the isolation provided by the messaging interfaces of ROS, a vast majority of the robot's software graph can be run identically whether it is controlling a real robot or a simulated robot. At runtime, as the various nodes are launched, they simply find one another and connect. Simulation input and output streams connect to the graph in the place of the device drivers of the real robot. Although some parameter tuning is often required, ideally the *structure* of the software will be the same, and often the simulation can be modified to reduce the amount of parameter tweaks required when transitioning between simulation and reality.

As alluded to in the previous paragraphs, there are many use cases for simulated robots, ranging from algorithm development to automated software verification. This has led to the creation of a large number of robot simulators, many of which integrate nicely with ROS. The following sections describe two simulators that will be used in this book.

Stage

For many years, the two-dimensional *simultaneous localization and mapping* (SLAM) problem was one of the most heavily researched topics in the robotics community. A number of 2D simulators were developed in response to the need for repeatable experiments, as well as the many practical annoyances of gathering long datasets of robots driving down endless office corridors. Canonical laser range-finders and differential-drive robots were modeled, often using simple *kinematic* models that enforce that, for example, the robot stays plastered to a 2D surface and its range sensors only interact with vertical walls, creating worlds that vaguely resemble that of *Pac-Man* (see Figure 6-5). Although limited in scope, these 2D simulators are very fast computationally, and they are generally quite simple to interact with.

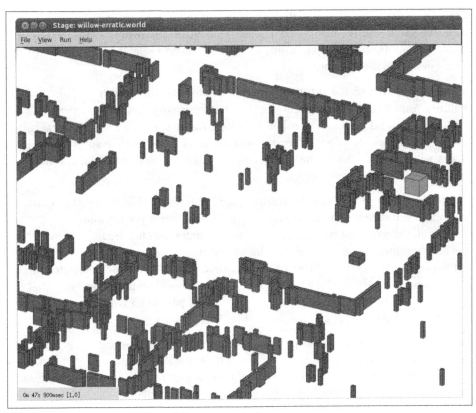

Figure 6-5. Typical screenshot of the Stage simulator

Stage is an excellent example of this type of 2D simulator. It has a relatively simple modeling language that allows the creation of planar worlds with simple types of objects. Stage was designed from the outset to support multiple robots simultaneously interacting with the same world. It has been wrapped with a ROS integration package that accepts velocity commands from ROS and outputs an odometric transformation as well as the simulated laser range-finders from the robot(s) in the simulation.

Gazebo

Although Stage and other 2D simulators are computationally efficient and excel at simulating planar navigation in office-like environments, it is important to note that planar navigation is only one aspect of robotics. Even when only considering robot navigation, a vast array of environments require nonplanar motion, ranging from outdoor ground vehicles to aerial, underwater, and space robotics. Three-dimensional simulation is necessary for software development in these environments.

In general, robot motions can be divided into *mobility* and *manipulation*. The mobility aspects can be handled by two- or three-dimensional simulators in which the environment around the robot is *static*. Simulating manipulation, however, requires a significant increase in the complexity of the simulator to handle the dynamics of not just the robot, but also the *dynamic* models in the scene. For example, at the moment that a simulated household robot is picking up a handheld object, contact forces must be computed between the robot, the object, and the surface the object was previously resting upon.

Simulators often use *rigid-body* dynamics, in which all objects are assumed to be incompressible, as if the world were a giant pinball machine. This assumption drastically improves the computational performance of the simulator, but often requires clever tricks to remain stable and realistic, since many rigid-body interactions become *point contacts* that do not accurately model the true physical phenomena. The art and science of managing the tension between computational performance and physical realism are highly nontrivial. There are many approaches to this trade-off, with many well suited to some domains but ill suited to others.

Like all simulators, Gazebo (Figure 6-6) is the product of a variety of trade-offs in its design and implementation. Historically, Gazebo has used the Open Dynamics Engine for rigid-body physics, but recently it has gained the ability to choose between physics engines at startup. For the purposes of this book, we will be using Gazebo with either the Open Dynamics Engine or with the Bullet Physics library, both of which are capable of real-time simulation with relatively simple worlds and robots and, with some care, can produce physically plausible behavior.

Figure 6-6. Typical screenshot of the Gazebo simulator

ROS integrates closely with Gazebo through the `gazebo_ros` package. This package provides a Gazebo *plugin* module that allows bidirectional communication between Gazebo and ROS. Simulated sensor and physics data can stream from Gazebo to ROS, and actuator commands can stream from ROS back to Gazebo. In fact, by choosing consistent names and data types for these data streams, it is possible for Gazebo to *exactly* match the ROS API of a robot. When this is achieved, all of the robot software above the device-driver level can be run identically both on the real robot, and (after parameter tuning) in the simulator. This is an enormously powerful concept and will be used extensively throughout this book.

Other Simulators

There are many other simulators that can be used with ROS, such as MORSE and V-REP. Each simulator, whether it be Gazebo, Stage, MORSE, V-REP, turtlesim, or any other, has a different set of trade-offs. These include trade-offs in speed, accuracy, graphics quality, dimensionality (2D versus 3D), types of sensors supported, usability, platform support, and so on. No simulator of which we are aware is capable of maximizing all of those attributes simultaneously, so the choice of the "right" simulator for a particular task will be dependent on many factors.

Summary

In this chapter, we've looked at the subsystems of a typical robot, focusing on the types of robots that ROS is most concerned with: mobile manipulation platforms. By now, you should have a pretty good idea of what a robot looks like, and you should be starting to figure out how ROS might be used to control one, reading data from the sensors, figuring out how to interpret that data and what to do, and sending commands to the acutators to make it move.

The next chapter ties together all of the material you've already read and shows you how to write code that will make a robot wander around. As discussed in this chapter, all of the code we will write in this book can be targeted either at real robots or at simulated robots. Onward!

## CHAPTER 7

Wander-bot

The first chapters of this book introduced many of the abstract ROS concepts used for communication between modules, such as topics, services, and actions. Then, the previous chapter introduced many of the sensing and actuation subsystems commonly found in modern robots. In this chapter, we will put these concepts together to create a robot that can wander around its environment. This might not sound terribly earth-shattering, but such a robot is actually capable of doing meaningful work: there is an entire class of tasks that are accomplished by driving across the environment. For example, many vacuuming or other floor-cleaning tasks can be accomplished by cleverly designed and carefully tuned algorithms where the robot, carrying its cleaning tool, traverses its environment somewhat randomly. The robot will eventually drive over all parts of the environment, completing its task.

In this chapter, we will go step by step through the process of writing minimalist ROS-based robot control software, including creating a ROS package and testing it in simulation.

Creating a Package

First, let's create the workspace directory tree, which we will place in ~/*wanderbot_ws*:

```
user@hostname$ mkdir -p ~/wanderbot_ws/src
user@hostname$ cd ~/wanderbot_ws/src
user@hostname$ catkin_init_workspace
```

That's it! Next, it's just one more command to create a package in the new workspace. To create a package called wanderbot that uses rospy (the Python client for ROS) and a few standard ROS message packages, we will use the catkin_create_pkg command:

```
user@hostname$ cd ~/wanderbot_ws/src
user@hostname$ catkin_create_pkg wanderbot rospy geometry_msgs sensor_msgs
```

The first argument, wanderbot, is the name of the new package we want to create. The following arguments are the names of packages that the new package depends on. W must include these because the ROS build system needs to know the package dependencies in order to efficiently keep the builds up to date when source files change, and to generate any required installation dependencies when packages are released.

After running the catkin_create_pkg command, there will be a package directory called *wanderbot* inside the workspace, including the following files:

- *~/wanderbot_ws/src/wanderbot/CMakeLists.txt*, a starting point for the build script for this package
- *package.xml*, a machine-readable description of the package, including details such as its name, description, author, license, and which other packages it depends on to build and run

Now that we've created our wanderbot package , we can create a minimal ROS node inside of it. In the previous chapters, we were just sending generic messages between nodes, such as strings or integers. Now, we can send something robot-specific. The following code will send a stream of motion commands 10 times per second, alternating every 3 seconds between driving and stopping. When driving, the program will send forward velocity commands of 0.5 meters per second. When stopped, it will send commands of 0 meters per second. This program is shown in Example 7-1.

Example 7-1. Red light! Green light!

```
#!/usr/bin/env python
import rospy
from geometry_msgs.msg import Twist

cmd_vel_pub = rospy.Publisher('cmd_vel', Twist, queue_size=1) ❶
rospy.init_node('red_light_green_light')

red_light_twist = Twist() ❷
green_light_twist = Twist()
green_light_twist.linear.x = 0.5 ❸

driving_forward = False
light_change_time = rospy.Time.now()
rate = rospy.Rate(10)

while not rospy.is_shutdown():
  if driving_forward:
    cmd_vel_pub.publish(green_light_twist) ❹
```

```
    else:
      cmd_vel_pub.publish(red_light_twist)
    if light_change_time > rospy.Time.now(): ❺
      driving_forward = not driving_forward
      light_change_time = rospy.Time.now() + rospy.Duration(3)
    rate.sleep() ❻
```

❶ The `queue_size=1` argument tells `rospy` to only buffer a single outbound message. In case the node sending the messages is transmitting at a higher rate than the receiving node(s) can receive them, `rospy` will simply drop any messages beyond the `queue_size`.

❷ The message constructors set all fields to zero. Therefore, the `red_light_twist` message tells a robot to stop, since all of its velocity subcomponents are zero.

❸ The `x` component of the linear velocity in a `Twist` message is, by convention, aligned in the direction the robot is facing, so this line means "drive straight ahead at 0.5 meters per second."

❹ We need to continually publish a stream of velocity command messages, since most mobile base drivers will time out and stop the robot if they don't receive at least several messages per second.

❺ This branch checks the system time and toggles the red/green light periodically.

❻ Without this call to `rospy.sleep()` the code would still run, but it would send far too many messages, and take up an entire CPU core!

A lot of Example 7-1 is just setting up the system and its data structures. The most important function of this program is to change behavior every 3 seconds from driving to stopping. This is performed by the three-line block reproduced here, which uses `rospy.Time` to measure the duration since the last change of behavior:

```
    if light_change_time > rospy.Time.now():
      driving_forward = not driving_forward
      light_change_time = rospy.Time.now() + rospy.Duration(3)
```

Like all Python scripts, it is convenient to make it an executable so that we can invoke the script directly on the command line:

```
user@hostname$ chmod +x red_light_green_light.py
```

Now, we can use our program to control a simulated robot. But first, we need to make sure that the Turtlebot simulation stack is installed:

```
user@hostname$ sudo apt-get install ros-indigo-turtlebot-gazebo
```

We are now ready to instantiate a Turtlebot in the simulator. We'll use a simple world to start, by typing this in a new terminal window (remember to hit the Tab key often when typing ROS shell commands for autocompletion):

```
user@hostname$ roslaunch turtlebot_gazebo turtlebot_world.launch
```

Figure 7-1 shows the initial TurtleBot world, in which a few obstacles are strewn about.

Figure 7-1. The initial Turtlebot world in Gazebo

Now, in a different terminal window, let's fire up our control node:

```
user@hostname$ ./red_light_green_light.py cmd_vel:=cmd_vel_mux/input/teleop
```

The cmd_vel remapping is necessary so that we are publishing our Twist messages to the topic that the Turtlebot software stack is expecting. Although we could have declared our cmd_vel_pub to publish to this topic in the *red_light_green_light.py* source code, our usual goal is to write ROS nodes that are as generic as possible, and in this case, we can easily remap cmd_vel to whatever is required by any robot's software stack.

When red_light_green_light.py is running, you should now see a Turtlebot alternating every second between driving forward and stopping. Progress! When you are bored with it, just give a Ctrl-C to the newly created node as well as the TurtleBot simulation.

Reading Sensor Data

Blindly driving around is fun, but we typically want robots to use sensor data. Fortunately, streaming sensor data into ROS nodes is quite easy. Whenever we want to receive a topic in ROS, it's often helpful to first just echo it to the console, to make sure that it is actually being published under the topic name we expect and to confirm that we understand the data type.

In the case of Turtlebot, we want to see something like a laser scan: a linear vector of ranges from the robot to the nearest obstacles in various directions. To save on cost, sadly, the Turtlebot does not have a real laser scanner. It does, however, have a Kinect depth camera, and the Turtlebot software stack extracts the middle few rows of the Kinect's depth image, does a bit of filtering, and then publishes the data as sensor_msgs/LaserScan messages on the scan topic. This means that from the standpoint of the high-level software, the data shows up exactly like "real" laser scans on more expensive robots. The only difference is that the field of view is just narrower, and the maximum detectable range is quite a bit shorter than with typical laser scanners. To illustrate this difference in field of view, compare the Gazebo simulation rendering shown in Figure 7-2 to the actual simulated laser-scanner stream shown in Figure 7-3. Although the Turtlebot is able to perceive the obstacle directly in front of it, the obstacle on its right side is mostly out of view. Such are the trade-offs involved with using low-cost depth cameras as navigation sensors!

To start using the sensor data, we can just dump the scan topic to the console to verify that the simulated laser scanner is working. First, fire up a Turtlebot simulation, if one isn't already running:

```
user@hostname$ roslaunch turtlebot_gazebo turtlebot_world.launch
```

Then, in another console, use rostopic to echo the topic:

```
user@hostname$ rostopic echo scan
```

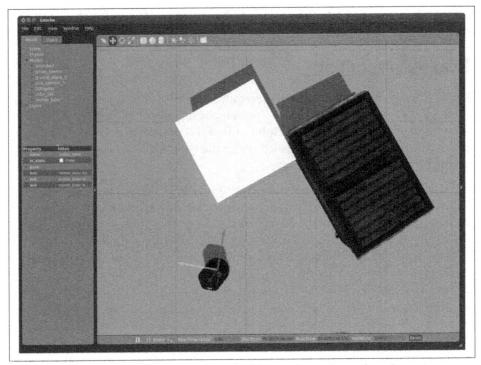

Figure 7-2. A bird's-eye Gazebo view of a Turtlebot in front of two obstacles

This will print a continuous stream of text representing the LaserScan messages. When you're bored, press Ctrl-C to stop it. Most of the text is the ranges member of the LaserScan message, which is exactly what we are interested in: the ranges array contains the range from the Turtlebot to the nearest object at bearings easily computed from the ranges array index. Specifically, if the message instance is named msg, we can compute the bearing for a particular range estimate as follows, where i is the index into the ranges array:

```
bearing = msg.angle_min + i * msg.angle_max / len(msg.ranges)
```

To retrieve the range to the nearest obstacle directly in front of the robot, we will select the middle element of the ranges array:

```
range_ahead = msg.ranges[len(msg.ranges)/2]
```

Or, to return the range of the closest obstacle detected by the scanner:

```
closest_range = min(msg.ranges)
```

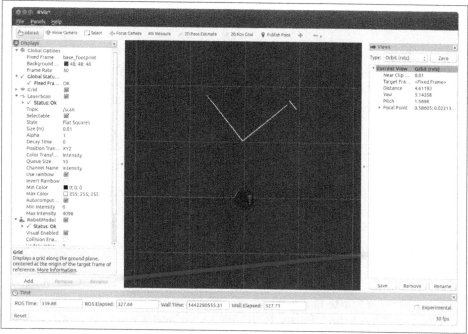

Figure 7-3. A bird's-eye view of the same scene as Figure 7-2, rendering the simulated laser scan extracted from the simulated Kinect data of the Turtlebot—the object directly in front of the robot is visible, but the object to its right is mostly out of view

This signal chain is deceptively complex: we are picking out elements of an *emulated* laser scan, which is itself produced by picking out a few of the middle rows of the Turtlebot's Kinect depth camera, which is itself generated in Gazebo by backprojecting rays into a simulated environment! It's hard to overemphasize the utility of simulation for robot software development.

Example 7-2 is a complete ROS node that prints the distance to an obstacle directly in front of the robot.

Example 7-2. range_ahead.py

```python
#!/usr/bin/env python
import rospy
from sensor_msgs.msg import LaserScan

def scan_callback(msg):
  range_ahead = msg.ranges[len(msg.ranges)/2]
  print "range ahead: %0.1f" % range_ahead

rospy.init_node('range_ahead')
```

```
scan_sub = rospy.Subscriber('scan', LaserScan, scan_callback)
rospy.spin()
```

This little program shows how easy it is to connect to data streams in ROS and process them in Python. The scan_callback() function is called each time a new message arrives on the scan topic. This callback function then prints the range measured to the object directly in front of the robot by picking the middle element of the ranges field of the LaserScan message:

```
def scan_callback(msg):
    range_ahead = msg.ranges[len(msg.ranges)/2]
    print "range ahead: %0.1f" % range_ahead
```

We can experiment with this program in Gazebo by dragging and rotating the Turtlebot around in the world. Click the Move icon in the Gazebo toolbar to enter Move mode, and then click and drag the Turtlebot around the scene. The terminal running range_ahead.py will print a continually changing stream of numbers indicating the range (in meters) from the Turtlebot to the nearest obstacle (if any) directly in front of it.

Gazebo also has a Rotate tool that will (by default) rotate a model about its vertical axis. Both the Move and Rotate tools will immediately affect the output of the *range_ahead.py* program, since the simulation (by default) stays running while models are being dragged and rotated.

Sensing and Actuation: Wander-bot!

We have now written *red_light_green_light.py*, which causes Turtlebot to drive *open-loop*, and *range_ahead.py*, which uses the Turtlebot's sensors to estimate the range to the nearest object directly in front of the Turtlebot. We can put these two capabilities together and write *wander.py*, shown in Example 7-3, which will cause the Turtlebot to drive straight ahead until it sees an obstacle within 0.8 meters or times out after 30 seconds. Then, the Turtlebot will stop and spin to a new heading. It will continue doing those two things until the end of time or Ctrl-C, whichever comes first.

Example 7-3. wander.py

```
#!/usr/bin/env python
import rospy
from geometry_msgs.msg import Twist
from sensor_msgs.msg import LaserScan

def scan_callback(msg):
  global g_range_ahead
  g_range_ahead = min(msg.ranges)

g_range_ahead = 1 # anything to start
```

```
scan_sub = rospy.Subscriber('scan', LaserScan, scan_callback)
cmd_vel_pub = rospy.Publisher('cmd_vel', Twist, queue_size=1)
rospy.init_node('wander')
state_change_time = rospy.Time.now()
driving_forward = True
rate = rospy.Rate(10)

while not rospy.is_shutdown():
  if driving_forward:
    if (g_range_ahead < 0.8 or rospy.Time.now() > state_change_time):
      driving_forward = False
      state_change_time = rospy.Time.now() + rospy.Duration(5)
  else: # we're not driving_forward
    if rospy.Time.now() > state_change_time:
      driving_forward = True # we're done spinning, time to go forward!
      state_change_time = rospy.Time.now() + rospy.Duration(30)
  twist = Twist()
  if driving_forward:
    twist.linear.x = 1
  else:
    twist.angular.z = 1
  cmd_vel_pub.publish(twist)

  rate.sleep()
```

As will always be the case with ROS Python programs, we start by importing rospy and the ROS message types we'll need: the Twist and LaserScan messages. Since this program is so simple, we'll just use a global variable called g_range_ahead to store the minimum range that our (simulated) laser scanner detects in front of the robot. This makes the scan_callback() function very simple; it just copies out the range to our global variable. And yes, this is horrible programming practice in complex programs, but for this small example, we'll pretend it's OK.

We start the actual program by creating a subscriber to scan and a publisher to cmd_vel, as we did previously. We also set up two variables that we'll use in our controller logic: state_change_time and driving_forward. The rate variable is a helpful construct in rospy: it helps create loops that run at a fixed frequency. In this case, we'd like to run our controller at 10 Hz, so we construct a rospy.Rate object by passing 10 to its constructor. Then, we call rate.sleep() at the end of our main loop; each time through, rospy will adjust the amount of actual sleeping time so that we run at something close to 10 Hz on average. The actual amount of sleeping time will depend on what else is being done in the control loop and the speed of the computer; we can just call rospy.Rate.sleep() and not worry about it.

The actual control loop is kept as simple as possible. The robot is in one of two states: driving_forward or not driving_forward. When in the driving_forward state, the robot keeps driving until it either sees an obstacle within 0.8 meters or times out after 30 seconds, after which it transitions to the not driving_forward state:

```
if (g_range_ahead < 0.8 or rospy.Time.now() > state_change_time):
    driving_forward = False
    state_change_time = rospy.Time.now() + rospy.Duration(5)
```

When the robot is in the not driving_forward state, it simply spins in place for five seconds, then transitions back to the driving_forward state:

```
if rospy.Time.now() > state_change_time:
    driving_forward = True # we're done spinning, time to go forward!
    state_change_time = rospy.Time.now() + rospy.Duration(30)
```

As before, we can quickly test our program in a Turtlebot simulation. Let's start one up:

```
user@hostname$ roslaunch turtlebot_gazebo turtlebot_world.launch
```

Then, in a separate console, we can make wander.py executable and run it:

```
user@hostname$ chmod +x red_light_green_light.py
user@hostname$ ./wander.py cmd_vel:=cmd_vel_mux/input/teleop
```

The TurtleBot will wander around aimlessly, while avoiding collisions with obstacles it can see. Hooray!

Summary

In this chapter, we first created an open-loop control system in *red_light_green_light.py* that started and stopped the Turtlebot based on a simple timer. Then, we saw how to read the information from the Turtlebot's depth camera. Finally, we closed the loop between sensing and actuation by creating Wander-bot, a program that causes the Turtlebot to avoid obstacles and randomly wander around its environment. This brought together all of the aspects of the book thus far: the streaming data transport mechanisms of ROS, the discussion of robot sensors and actuators, and the simulation framework of Gazebo. In the next chapter, we will start making things more complex by listening to user input, as we create Teleop-bot.

## PART II

Moving Around Using ROS

## CHAPTER 8

Teleop-bot

The previous section covered fundamental concepts in ROS, provided a brief overview of subsystems common to many robots, and finished with Wander-bot, a program that drove a Turtlebot around aimlessly. In this section of the book, we will show how to build a series of robots that become more and more sophisticated in their motions, culminating with a state-of-the-art 2D navigation system. We will then conclude this section by showing how to move manipulator arms using common ROS packages.

This chapter will describe how to drive a robot around via *teleoperation*. Although the term "robot" often brings up images of *fully autonomous* robots that are able to make their own decisions in all situations, there are many domains in which close human guidance is standard practice due to a variety of factors. Since teleoperated systems are, generally speaking, simpler than autonomous systems, they make a natural starting point. In this chapter, we will construct progressively more complex teleoperation systems.

As discussed in the previous chapter, we drive a Turtlebot by publishing a stream of `Twist` messages. Although the `Twist` message has the ability to describe full 3D motion, when operating differential-drive planar robots, we only need to populate two members: the linear (forward/backward) velocity, and the angular velocity about the vertical axis, which can also be called *yaw rate* and is simply the measure of how quickly the robot is spinning. From those two fields, it is then an exercise in trigonometry to compute the required wheel velocities of the robot as a function of the spacing of the wheels and their diameter. This calculation is usually done at low levels in the software stack, either in the robot's device driver or in the firmware of a microcontroller onboard the robot. From the teleoperation software's perspective, we simply command the linear and angular velocities in meters per second and radians per second, respectively.

Given that we need to produce a stream of velocity commands to move the robot, the next question is, how can we elicit these commands from the robot operator? There are a wide variety of approaches to this problem, and naturally we should start with the simplest approach to program: keyboard input.

Development Pattern

Throughout the remainder of the book, we will encourage a development pattern that makes use of the ROS debugging tools wherever possible. Since ROS is a distributed system with topic-based communications, we can quickly create testing environments to help our debugging, so that we are only starting and stopping a single piece of the system every time we need to tweak a bit of code. Structuring our software as a collection of very small message-passing programs makes it easier and more productive to insert ROS debugging tools into these message flows.

In the specific case of producing Teleop-bot velocity commands, we will write two programs: one that listens for keystrokes and then broadcasts them as ROS messages, and one that listens for those keystroke ROS messages and outputs Twist messages in response. This extra layer of indirection helps isolate the two functional pieces of this system, as well as making it easier for us, or anyone else in the open source community, to reuse the individual pieces in a completely different system. Creating a constellation of small ROS nodes often will simplify the creation of manual and (especially) automated software tests. For example, we can feed a canned sequence of keystroke messages to the node that translates between keystrokes and motion commands, comparing the output motion command with the previously defined "correct" response. Then, we can set up automated testing to verify the correct behavior as the software evolves over time.

Once we have decided the highest-level breakdown of how a task should be split into ROS nodes, the next task is to write them! As is often the case with software design, sometimes it helps to create a *skeleton* of the desired system that prints console messages or just publishes dummy messages to other nodes in the system. However, our preferred approach is to build the required collection of new ROS nodes incrementally, with a strong preference for writing *small* nodes.

Keyboard Driver

The first node we need to write for keyboard-Teleop-bot is a keyboard driver that listens for keystrokes and publishes them as std_msgs/String messages on the keys topic. There are many ways to perform this task. Example 8-1 uses the Python termios and tty libraries to place the terminal in raw mode and capture keystrokes, which are then published as std_msgs/String messages.

Example 8-1. key_publisher.py

```
#!/usr/bin/env python
import sys, select, tty, termios
import rospy
from std_msgs.msg import String

if __name__ == '__main__':
  key_pub = rospy.Publisher('keys', String, queue_size=1)
  rospy.init_node("keyboard_driver")
  rate = rospy.Rate(100)
  old_attr = termios.tcgetattr(sys.stdin)
  tty.setcbreak(sys.stdin.fileno())
  print "Publishing keystrokes. Press Ctrl-C to exit..."
  while not rospy.is_shutdown():
    if select.select([sys.stdin], [], [], 0)[0] == [sys.stdin]:
      key_pub.publish(sys.stdin.read(1))
    rate.sleep()
  termios.tcsetattr(sys.stdin, termios.TCSADRAIN, old_attr)
```

This program uses the `termios` library to capture raw keystrokes, which requires working around some quirks of how Unix consoles operate. Typically, consoles buffer an entire line of text, only sending it to programs when the user presses Enter. In our case, we want to receive the keys on our program's standard input stream as soon as they are pressed. To alter this behavior of the console, we first need to save the attributes:

```
old_attr = termios.tcgetattr(sys.stdin)
tty.setcbreak(sys.stdin.fileno())
```

Now, we can continually poll the `stdin` stream to see if any characters are ready. Although we could simply block on `stdin`, that would cause our process to not fire any ROS callbacks, should we add any in the future. Thus, it is good practice to instead call `select()` with a timeout of zero, which will return immediately. We will then spend the rest of our loop time inside `rate.sleep()`, as shown in this snippet:

```
if select.select([sys.stdin], [], [], 0)[0] == [sys.stdin]:
  key_pub.publish(sys.stdin.read(1))
rate.sleep()
```

Finally, we need to put the console back into standard mode before our program exits:

```
termios.tcsetattr(sys.stdin, termios.TCSADRAIN, old_attr)
```

To test if the keyboard driver node is operating as expected, three terminals are needed. In the first terminal, run `roscore`. In the second terminal, run the `key_publisher.py` node. In the third terminal, run `rostopic echo keys`, which will print any and all messages that it receives on the `keys` topic to the console. Then, set focus back to the second terminal by clicking on it or using window manager shortcuts such as Alt-Tab to switch between terminals. Keystrokes in the second terminal should cause std_msgs/String messages to print to the console of the third terminal. Progress! When you're finished testing, press Ctrl-C in all terminals to shut everything down.

You'll notice that "normal" keys, such as letters, numerals, and simple punctuation, work as expected. However, "extended" keys, such as the arrow keys, result in std_msgs/String messages that are either weird symbols or multiple messages (or both). That is expected, since our minimalist key_publisher.py node is just pulling characters one at a time from stdin—and improving key_publisher.py is an exercise left to the motivated reader! For the remainder of this chapter, we will use just alphabetic characters.

Motion Generator

In this section, we will use the common keyboard mapping of *w, x, a, d, s* to express, respectively, that we want the robot to go forward, go backward, turn left, turn right, and stop.

As a first attempt at this problem, we'll make a ROS node that outputs a Twist message every time it receives a std_msgs/String message that starts with a character it understands, as shown in Example 8-2.

Example 8-2. keys_to_twist.py

```python
#!/usr/bin/env python
import rospy
from std_msgs.msg import String
from geometry_msgs.msg import Twist

key_mapping = { 'w': [ 0, 1], 'x': [0, -1],
                'a': [-1, 0], 'd': [1,  0],
                's': [ 0, 0] }

def keys_cb(msg, twist_pub):
  if len(msg.data) == 0 or not key_mapping.has_key(msg.data[0]):
    return # unknown key
  vels = key_mapping[msg.data[0]]
  t = Twist()
  t.angular.z = vels[0]
  t.linear.x  = vels[1]
  twist_pub.publish(t)

if __name__ == '__main__':
  rospy.init_node('keys_to_twist')
  twist_pub = rospy.Publisher('cmd_vel', Twist, queue_size=1)
  rospy.Subscriber('keys', String, keys_cb, twist_pub)
  rospy.spin()
```

This program uses a Python dictionary to store the mapping between keystrokes and the target velocities:

```
key_mapping = { 'w': [ 0, 1], 'x': [0, -1],
                'a': [-1, 0], 'd': [1,  0],
                's': [ 0, 0] }
```

In the callback function for the keys topic, incoming keys are looked up in this dictionary. If a key is found, the target velocities are extracted from the dictionary:

```
if len(msg.data) == 0 or not key_mapping.has_key(msg.data[0]):
   return # unknown key
vels = key_mapping[msg.data[0]]
```

In an effort to prevent runaway robots, most robot device drivers will automatically stop the robot if no messages are received in a few hundred milliseconds. The program in the previous listing would work, but only if it had a continual stream of key-presses to continually generate Twist messages for the robot driver. That would be exciting for a few seconds, but once the euphoria of "Hey, the robot is moving!" wears off, we'll be searching for improvements!

Issues such as robot firmware timeouts can be tricky to debug. As with everything in ROS (and complex systems in general), the key for debugging is to find ways to divide the system into smaller pieces and discover where the problem lies. The rostopic tool can help in several ways. As in the previous section, start three terminals: one with roscore, one with key_publisher.py, and one with keys_to_twist.py. Then, we can start a fourth terminal for various incantations of rostopic.

First, we can see what topics are available:

```
user@hostname$ rostopic list
```

This provides the following output:

```
/cmd_vel
/keys
/rosout
/rosout_agg
```

The last two items, /rosout and /rosout_agg, are part of the general-purpose ROS logging scheme and are always there. The other two, cmd_vel and keys, are what our programs are publishing. Now, let's dump the cmd_vel data stream to the console:

```
user@hostname$ rostopic echo cmd_vel
```

Each time a valid key is pressed in the console with key_publisher.py, the rostopic console should print the contents of the resulting Twist message published by keys_to_twist.py. Progress! As always with ROS console tools, simply press Ctrl-C to exit. Next, let's use rostopic hz to compute the average rate of messages:

```
user@hostname$ rostopic hz cmd_vel
```

The rostopic hz command will compute an average of the rate of messages on a topic every second and print those estimates to the console. With keys_to_twist.py, this estimate will almost always be zero, with minor bumps up and down each time a key is pressed in the keyboard driver console.

 The rostopic tools are your friends! Virtually every ROS programming and (especially) debugging session includes some usage of rostopic to rapidly introspect the system and verify that data is flowing as expected.

To make this node useful for robots that require a steady stream of velocity commands, we will output a Twist message every 100 milliseconds, or at a rate of 10 Hz, by simply repeating the last motion command if a new key was not pressed. Although we could do something like this by using a sleep(0.1) call in the while loop, this would only ensure that the loop runs *no faster* than 10 Hz; the timing results would likely have quite a bit of variance since the scheduling and execution time of the loop itself are not taken into account. Because computers have widely varying clock speeds and overall computational performance, the exact amount of CPU time that a loop would need to sleep to maintain a particular update rate is not knowable ahead of time. Looping tasks are thus better accomplished with the ROS *rate* construct, which continually estimates the time spent processing the loop to obtain more consistent results, as shown in Example 8-3.

Example 8-3. keys_to_twist_using_rate.py

```python
#!/usr/bin/env python
import rospy
from std_msgs.msg import String
from geometry_msgs.msg import Twist

key_mapping = { 'w': [ 0, 1], 'x': [0, -1],
                'a': [-1, 0], 'd': [1,  0],
                's': [ 0, 0] }
g_last_twist = None

def keys_cb(msg, twist_pub):
  global g_last_twist
  if len(msg.data) == 0 or not key_mapping.has_key(msg.data[0]):
    return # unknown key
  vels = key_mapping[msg.data[0]]
  g_last_twist.angular.z = vels[0]
  g_last_twist.linear.x  = vels[1]
  twist_pub.publish(g_last_twist)
```

```
if __name__ == '__main__':
  rospy.init_node('keys_to_twist')
  twist_pub = rospy.Publisher('cmd_vel', Twist, queue_size=1)
  rospy.Subscriber('keys', String, keys_cb, twist_pub)
  rate = rospy.Rate(10)
  g_last_twist = Twist() # initializes to zero
  while not rospy.is_shutdown():
    twist_pub.publish(g_last_twist)
    rate.sleep()
```

Now, when the keys_to_twist_using_rate.py node is running, we will see a quite
consistent 10 Hz message stream when we run rostopic hz cmd_vel. This can be
seen using a separate console running rostopic echo cmd_vel, as in the previous
section. The key difference between this program and the previous one is the use of
rospy.Rate():

```
rate = rospy.Rate(10)
g_last_twist = Twist() # initializes to zero
while not rospy.is_shutdown():
  twist_pub.publish(g_last_twist)
  rate.sleep()
```

When debugging low-dimensional data, such as the velocity commands sent to a
robot, it is often useful to plot the data stream as a time series. ROS provides a
command-line tool called rqt_plot that can accept *any* numerical data message
stream and plot it graphically in real time.

To create an rqt_plot visualization, we need to send rqt_plot the exact message
field that we want to see plotted. To find this field name, we can use several methods.
The simplest is to look at the output of rostopic echo. This is always printed in
YAML, a simple whitespace-based markup format. For example, rostopic echo
cmd_vel will print a series of records of this format:

```
linear:
  x: 0.0
  y: 0.0
  z: 0.0
angular:
  x: 0.0
  y: 0.0
  z: 0.0
```

Nested structures are indicated by whitespace: first, the linear field structure has
field names x, y, z; this is followed by the angular field structure, with the same
members.

Alternatively, we can discover the topic data type using rostopic:

```
user@hostname$ rostopic info cmd_vel
```

This will print quite a bit of information about the topic publishers and subscribers, as well as stating that the cmd_vel topic is of type geometry_msgs/Twist. With this data type name, we can use the rosmsg command to print the structure:

```
user@hostname$ rosmsg show geometry_msgs/Twist
geometry_msgs/Vector3 linear
  float64 x
  float64 y
  float64 z
geometry_msgs/Vector3 angular
  float64 x
  float64 y
  float64 z
```

This console output shows us that the linear and angular members of the Twist message are of type geometry_msgs/Vector3, which has fields named x, y, and z. Granted, we already knew that from the rostopic echo output, but rosmsg show is sometimes a useful way of obtaining this information when we don't have a data stream available to print to the console.

Now that we know the topic name and the names of the fields, we can generate streaming plots of the linear velocity that we are publishing by using slashes to descend into the message structure and select the fields of interest. As mentioned previously, for planar differential-drive robots, the only nonzero fields in the Twist message will be the x-axis linear (forward/backward) velocity and the z-axis (yaw) angular velocity. We can start streaming those fields to a plot with a single command:

```
user@hostname$ rqt_plot cmd_vel/linear/x cmd_vel/angular/z
```

This plot will look something like Figure 8-1 as keys are pressed and the stream of velocity commands changes.

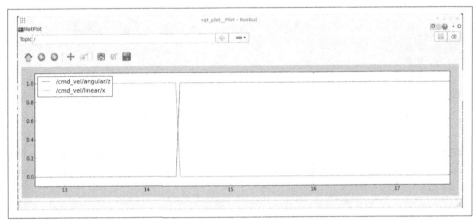

Figure 8-1. A live plot rendered by rqt_plot that shows the linear and angular velocity commands over time

---

We now have a pipeline built where pressing letters on the keyboard will send velocity commands to a robot, and we can view those velocities in a live plot. That's great! But there's a lot of room for improvement. First, notice in the previous plot that our velocities are always either 0, −1, or +1. ROS uses SI units throughout, which means that we are asking our robot to drive forward and backward at one meter per second and turn at one radian per second. Unfortunately, robots run at greatly varying speeds in different applications: for a robotic car, one meter per second is very slow; however, for a small indoor robot navigating a corridor, one meter per second is actually quite fast. We need a way to *parameterize* this program, so that it can be used with multiple robots. We'll do that in the next section.

Parameter Server

We can improve the *keys_to_twist_using_rate.py* program by using ROS *parameters* to specify the linear and angular velocity scales. Of course, there are countless ways that we can give parameters to programs. When developing robotic systems, it is often useful to set parameters in a variety of ways: at the command line when debugging, in roslaunch files, from graphical interfaces, from other ROS nodes, or even in separate parameter files to cleanly define behavior for multiple platforms or environments. The ROS master, often called roscore, includes a *parameter server* that can be read or written by all ROS nodes and command-line tools. The parameter server can support quite sophisticated interactions, but for our purposes in this chapter, we will only be setting parameters at the command line when running our teleoperation nodes.

The parameter server is a generic key/value store. There are many strategies for how to name parameters, but for our teleoperation node, we want a *private* parameter name. In ROS, a private parameter name is still publicly accessible; the notion of "private" simply means that its full name is formed by appending the parameter name to the node's name. This ensures that no name clashes can occur, because node names are always unique (see "Names, Namespaces, and Remapping" on page 22). For example, if our node name is keys_to_twist, we can have private parameters named keys_to_twist/linear_scale and keys_to_twist/angular_scale.

To set private parameters on the command line at the time the node is launched, prepend the parameter name with an underscore and set its value using := syntax, as follows:

```
./keys_to_twist_parameterized.py _linear_scale:=0.5 _angular_scale:=0.4
```

This would set the keys_to_twist/linear_scale parameter to 0.5 and the keys_to_twist/angular_scale parameter to 0.4, immediately before the node is launched. These parameter values are then returned by the has_param() and get_param() calls, as shown in Example 8-4.

Example 8-4. keys_to_twist_parameterized.py

```python
#!/usr/bin/env python
import rospy
from std_msgs.msg import String
from geometry_msgs.msg import Twist

key_mapping = { 'w': [ 0, 1], 'x': [0, -1],
                'a': [-1, 0], 'd': [1,  0],
                's': [ 0, 0] }
g_last_twist = None
g_vel_scales = [0.1, 0.1] # default to very slow

def keys_cb(msg, twist_pub):
  global g_last_twist, g_vel_scales
  if len(msg.data) == 0 or not key_mapping.has_key(msg.data[0]):
    return # unknown key
  vels = key_mapping[msg.data[0]]
  g_last_twist.angular.z = vels[0] * g_vel_scales[0]
  g_last_twist.linear.x  = vels[1] * g_vel_scales[1]
  twist_pub.publish(g_last_twist)

if __name__ == '__main__':
  rospy.init_node('keys_to_twist')
  twist_pub = rospy.Publisher('cmd_vel', Twist, queue_size=1)
  rospy.Subscriber('keys', String, keys_cb, twist_pub)
  g_last_twist = Twist() # initializes to zero
  if rospy.has_param('~linear_scale'):
    g_vel_scales[1] = rospy.get_param('~linear_scale')
  else:
    rospy.logwarn("linear scale not provided; using %.1f" %\
                  g_vel_scales[1])

  if rospy.has_param('~angular_scale'):
    g_vel_scales[0] = rospy.get_param('~angular_scale')
  else:
    rospy.logwarn("angular scale not provided; using %.1f" %\
                  g_vel_scales[0])

  rate = rospy.Rate(10)
  while not rospy.is_shutdown():
    twist_pub.publish(g_last_twist)
    rate.sleep()
```

At startup, this program queries the parameter server using `rospy.has_param()` and `rospy.get_param()`, and outputs a warning if the specified parameter was not set:

```python
    if rospy.has_param('~linear_scale'):
      g_vel_scales[1] = rospy.get_param('~linear_scale')
    else:
      rospy.logwarn("linear scale not provided; using %.1f" %\
                    g_vel_scales[1])
```

This warning is printed using the ROS logging system, which has a few benefits over a standard Python print() call. First, the ROS logging calls, such as logwarn(), logi nfo(), and logerror(), print colorized text to the console. That may sound inconsequential, but it actually can be quite useful when watching or scrolling for warnings or errors in a noisy console stream. The ROS logging calls can also (optionally) be routed to a centralized console of warnings and errors, so that the warning and error streams from large, complex collections of nodes can be monitored more easily.

The warning text produced by rospy.logwarn() also prepends a timestamp:

```
[WARN] [WallTime: 1429164125.989] linear scale not provided. Defaulting to 0.1
[WARN] [WallTime: 1429164125.989] angular scale not provided. Defaulting to 0.1
```

The get_param() function optionally accepts a second parameter, serving as a default parameter when the parameter key is not available on the parameter server. In many cases, using this optional second parameter can shorten code and provides an appropriate level of functionality. For general-purpose nodes such as keys_to_twist.py that want a parameter to be explicitly defined, however, using has_param() to determine the existence of an explicit parameter definition can be useful.

The syntax to use keys_to_twist_parameterized.py with explicit command-line parameters is as follows:

```
./keys_to_twist_parameterized.py _linear_scale:=0.5 _angular_scale:=0.4
```

The resulting stream of Twist messages is scaled as expected: for example, pressing *w* (move forward) in the console running key_publisher.py will result in a stream of these messages appearing in the rostopic echo cmd_vel output:

```
linear:
  x: 0.5
  y: 0.0
  z: 0.0
angular:
  x: 0.0
  y: 0.0
  z: 0.0
```

Each time we launch keys_to_twist_parameterized.py, we can specify the desired maximum velocities for our robot. Even more conveniently, we can put these parameters into launch files so that we don't have to remember them! But first, we need to deal with the physics problem of finite acceleration, which we will address in the next section.

Velocity Ramps

Unfortunately, like all objects with mass, robots cannot start and stop instantaneously. Physics dictates that robots accelerate gradually over time. As a result, when a robot's wheel motors try to instantly jump to a wildly different velocity, typically something bad happens, such as skidding, belts slipping, "shuddering" as the robot repeatedly hits electrical current limits, or possibly even something breaking in the mechanical driveline. To avoid these problems, we should *ramp* our motion commands up and down over a finite amount of time. Often lower levels of robot firmware will enforce this, but in general, it's considered good practice not to send impossible commands to robots. Example 8-5 applies ramps to the outgoing velocity stream, to limit the instantaneous accelerations that we are asking of the motors.

Example 8-5. keys_to_twist_with_ramps.py

```python
#!/usr/bin/env python
import rospy
import math
from std_msgs.msg import String
from geometry_msgs.msg import Twist

key_mapping = { 'w': [ 0, 1], 'x': [ 0, -1],
                'a': [ 1, 0], 'd': [-1,  0],
                's': [ 0, 0] }
g_twist_pub = None
g_target_twist = None
g_last_twist = None
g_last_send_time = None
g_vel_scales = [0.1, 0.1] # default to very slow
g_vel_ramps = [1, 1] # units: meters per second^2

def ramped_vel(v_prev, v_target, t_prev, t_now, ramp_rate):
  # compute maximum velocity step
  step = ramp_rate * (t_now - t_prev).to_sec()
  sign = 1.0 if (v_target > v_prev) else -1.0
  error = math.fabs(v_target - v_prev)
  if error < step: # we can get there within this timestep-we're done.
    return v_target
  else:
    return v_prev + sign * step  # take a step toward the target

def ramped_twist(prev, target, t_prev, t_now, ramps):
  tw = Twist()
  tw.angular.z = ramped_vel(prev.angular.z, target.angular.z, t_prev,
                            t_now, ramps[0])
  tw.linear.x = ramped_vel(prev.linear.x, target.linear.x, t_prev,
                           t_now, ramps[1])
  return tw
```

```python
def send_twist():
  global g_last_twist_send_time, g_target_twist, g_last_twist,\
         g_vel_scales, g_vel_ramps, g_twist_pub
  t_now = rospy.Time.now()
  g_last_twist = ramped_twist(g_last_twist, g_target_twist,
                              g_last_twist_send_time, t_now, g_vel_ramps)
  g_last_twist_send_time = t_now
  g_twist_pub.publish(g_last_twist)

def keys_cb(msg):
  global g_target_twist, g_last_twist, g_vel_scales
  if len(msg.data) == 0 or not key_mapping.has_key(msg.data[0]):
    return # unknown key
  vels = key_mapping[msg.data[0]]
  g_target_twist.angular.z = vels[0] * g_vel_scales[0]
  g_target_twist.linear.x  = vels[1] * g_vel_scales[1]

def fetch_param(name, default):
  if rospy.has_param(name):
    return rospy.get_param(name)
  else:
    print "parameter [%s] not defined. Defaulting to %.3f" % (name, default)
    return default

if __name__ == '__main__':
  rospy.init_node('keys_to_twist')
  g_last_twist_send_time = rospy.Time.now()
  g_twist_pub = rospy.Publisher('cmd_vel', Twist, queue_size=1)
  rospy.Subscriber('keys', String, keys_cb)
  g_target_twist = Twist() # initializes to zero
  g_last_twist = Twist()
  g_vel_scales[0] = fetch_param('~angular_scale', 0.1)
  g_vel_scales[1] = fetch_param('~linear_scale', 0.1)
  g_vel_ramps[0] = fetch_param('~angular_accel', 1.0)
  g_vel_ramps[1] = fetch_param('~linear_accel', 1.0)

  rate = rospy.Rate(20)
  while not rospy.is_shutdown():
    send_twist()
    rate.sleep()
```

The code is a bit more complex, but the main lines of interest are in the `ram ped_vel()` function, where the velocity is computed under the acceleration constraint provided as a parameter. Each time it is called, this function takes a step toward the target velocity, or, if the target velocity is within one step away, it goes directly to it:

```
def ramped_vel(v_prev, v_target, t_prev, t_now, ramp_rate):
    # compute maximum velocity step
    step = ramp_rate * (t_now - t_prev).to_sec()
    sign = 1.0 if (v_target > v_prev) else -1.0
    error = math.fabs(v_target - v_prev)
    if error < step: # we can get there within this timestep-we're done.
      return v_target
    else:
        return v_prev + sign * step  # take a step toward the target
```

At the command line, the following incantation of our teleop program will produce reasonable behavior for the Turtlebot:

```
user@hostname$ ./keys_to_twist_with_ramps.py _linear_scale:=0.5\
    _angular_scale:=1.0_linear_accel:=1.0 _angular_accel:=1.0
```

The motion commands we are sending the Turtlebot are now physically possible to achieve, as shown in Figure 8-2, since they take nonzero time to ramp up and down. Using the `rqt_plot` program as shown previously, we can generate a live plot of the system:

```
user@hostname$ rqt_plot cmd_vel/linear/x cmd_vel/angular/z
```

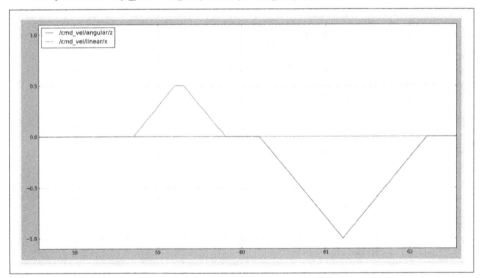

Figure 8-2. The velocity commands in this plot ramp up and down over finite time, allowing this trajectory to be physically achievable

To reiterate: even if we were to give instantaneously changing or "step" commands to the Turtlebot, somewhere in the signal path, or in the physics of the mechanical system, the step commands would be slowed into ramps. The advantage to doing this in higher-level software is that there is simply more visibility into what is happening, and hence a better understanding of the behavior of the system.

Let's Drive!

Now that we have reasonable `Twist` messages streaming from our teleop program over the `cmd_vel` topic, we can drive some robots. Let's start by driving a Turtlebot. Thanks to the magic of robot simulation, we can get a Turtlebot up and running with a single command:

```
user@hostname$ roslaunch turtlebot_gazebo turtlebot_world.launch
```

This will launch a Gazebo instance with a world similar to that shown in Figure 8-3, as well as emulating the software and firmware of the Turtlebot behind the scenes.

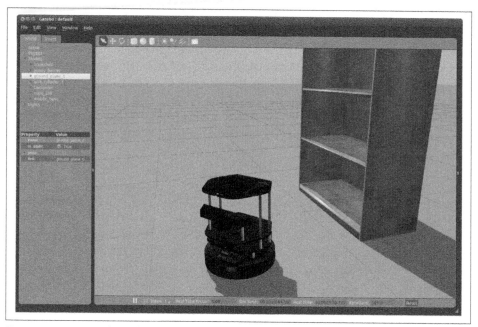

Figure 8-3. A snapshot of a simulated Turtlebot in front of a bookcase in the Gazebo simulator

Next, we want to run our teleop program, which broadcasts `Twist` messages on the `cmd_vel` topic:

```
user@hostname$ ./keys_to_twist_with_ramps.py
```

However, if we do this, it won't work! Why? Because the Turtlebot looks for its `Twist` motion messages on a different topic. This is an extremely common problem to debug in distributed robotic software systems, or in any large software system, for that matter. We will describe a variety of tools for debugging these types of problems in a later chapter. For now, however, to make the Turtlebot simulator work, we need to publish `Twist` messages to a topic named `cmd_vel_mux/input/teleop`. That is, we need to *remap* our `cmd_vel` message so that they are published on that topic instead. We can use the ROS remapping syntax to do this on the command line, without changing our source code:

```
user@hostname$ ./keys_to_twist_with_ramps.py cmd_vel:=cmd_vel_mux/input/teleop
```

We can now drive the Turtlebot around in Gazebo using the *w*, *a*, *s*, *d*, *x* buttons on the keyboard. Hooray!

This style of teleoperation is similar to how remote-controlled cars work: the teleoperator maintains line-of-sight with the robot, sends motion commands, observes how they affect the robot and its environment, and reacts accordingly. However, it is often impossible or undesirable to maintain line-of-sight contact with the robot. This requires the teleoperator to visualize the robot's sensors and see the world through the "eyes" of the robot. ROS provides several tools to simplify development of such systems, including `rviz`, which will be described in the following section.

rviz

`rviz` stands for *ROS visualization*. It is a general-purpose 3D visualization environment for robots, sensors, and algorithms. Like most ROS tools, it can be used for any robot and rapidly configured for a particular application. For teleoperation, we want to be able to see the camera feed of the robot. First, we will start from the configuration described in the previous section, where we have four terminals open: one for `roscore`, one for the keyboard driver, one for `keys_to_teleop_with_rates.py`, and one that ran a `roslaunch` script to bring up Gazebo and a simulated TurtleBot. Now, we'll need a fifth console to run `rviz`, which is in its own package, also called `rviz` :

```
user@hostname$ rosrun rviz rviz
```

`rviz` can plot a variety of data types streaming through a typical ROS system, with heavy emphasis on the three-dimensional nature of the data. In ROS, all forms of data are attached to a *frame of reference*. For example, the camera on a Turtlebot is attached to a reference frame defined relative to the center of the Turtlebot's mobile base. The *odometry* reference frame, often called `odom`, is taken by convention to have its origin at the location where the robot was powered on, or where its odometers were most recently reset. Each of these frames can be useful for teleoperation, but it is often desirable to have a "chase" perspective, which is immediately behind the robot and looking over its "shoulders." This is because simply viewing the robot's camera frame can be deceiving—the field of view of a camera is often much narrower than we are used to as humans, and thus it is easy for teleoperators to bonk the robot's shoulders when turning corners. A sample view of rviz configured to generate a chase perspective is shown in Figure 8-4. Observing the sensor data in the same 3D view as a rendering of the robot's geometry can make teleoperation more intuitive.

Like many complex graphical user interfaces (GUIs), rviz has a number of *panels* and *plugins* that can be configured as needed for a given task. Configuring rviz can take some time and effort, so the *state* of the visualization can be saved to configuration files for later reuse. Additionally, when closing rviz, by default the program will save its configuration to a special local file; the next time rviz is run, it will then instantiate and configure the same panels and plugins.

The default, unconfigured rviz window will appear as shown in Figure 8-5. It can be disconcerting at first, since there is nothing there! In the next few pages, we will show how to add various streams to rviz to end up with the visualization shown in Figure 8-4.

The first task is to choose the frame of reference for the visualization. In our case, we want a visualization perspective that is attached to the robot, so we can follow the robot as it drives around. On any given robot, there are many possible frames of reference, such as the center of the mobile base, various links of the robot's structure, or even a wheel (note that this frame would continually flip around and around, making it rather dizzying as a vantage point for rviz). For the purposes of teleoperation, we will select a frame of reference attached to the optical center of the Kinect depth camera on the Turtlebot. To do this, click in the table cell to the right of the "Fixed Frame" row in the upper-left panel of rviz. This will pop up the menu shown in the following screenshot, which contains all transform frames currently broadcasting in this ROS system. For now, select camera_depth_frame in the pop-up menu, as shown in Figure 8-6. Selecting the fixed frame for visualization is one of the most important configuration steps of rviz.

Figure 8-4. rviz configured to render the Turtlebot geometry as well as its depth camera and 2D image data

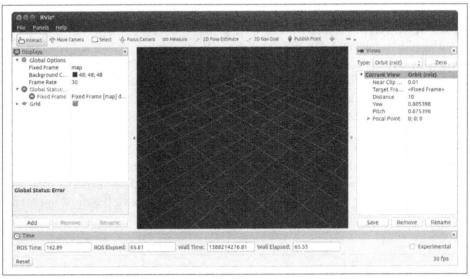

Figure 8-5. The initial state of rviz, before any visualization panels have been added to the configuration

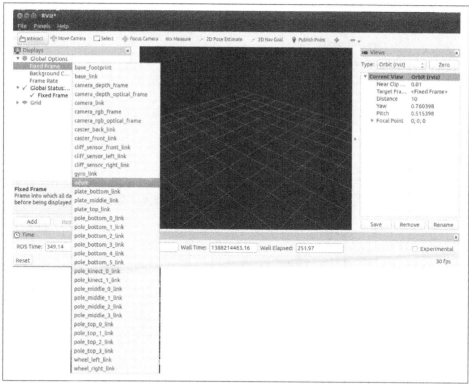

Figure 8-6. The fixed frame pop-up menu

Next, we want to view the 3D model of the robot. To accomplish this, we will insert an instance of the *robot model* plugin. Although the Turtlebot has no moving parts (other than its wheels) that we need to visualize, it is still useful to see a rendering of the robot to improve situational awareness and a get sense of scale for teleoperation. To add the robot model to the rviz scene, click the "Add" button on the lefthand side of the rviz window, approximately halfway down. This will bring up a dialog box, shown in Figure 8-7, that contains all of the available rviz plugins for various data types.

Figure 8-7. rviz dialog box used to select the data type that is currently being added to the visualization

From this dialog box, select "RobotModel" and then click "OK". Plugin instances appear in the tree-view control at the left of the `rviz` window. To configure a plugin, ensure it is expanded in the tree view. Its configurable parameters can then be edited. For the Robot Model plugin, the only configuration typically required is to enter the name of the robot model on the parameter server. However, since the ROS convention is for this to be called `robot_description`, this is autofilled and typically "just works" for single-robot applications. This will produce an `rviz` visualization similar to that shown in Figure 8-8, which is centered on a model of the Turtlebot.

Figure 8-8. A Turtlebot model added to rviz

In order to teleoperate the Turtlebot reasonably, we need to plot its sensors. To plot the depth image from the Kinect camera on the Turtlebot, click "Add" and then select "PointCloud2" from the plugin dialog box, near the lower-left corner of rviz. The PointCloud2 plugin has quite a few options to configure in the tree-view control in the left pane of rviz. Most importantly, we need to tell the plugin which topic should be plotted. Click the space to the right of the "Topic" label, and a drop-down box will appear, showing the PointCloud2 topics currently visible on the system. Select /camera/depth/points, and the Turtlebot's point cloud should be visible, as shown in Figure 8-9.

The Kinect camera on the Turtlebot also produces a color image output, in addition to its depth image. Sometimes it can be useful for teleoperation to render both the image and the point cloud. rviz provides a plugin for this. Click "Add" near the lower-left corner of rviz, and then select "Image" from the plugin dialog box. As usual, this will instantiate the plugin, and now we need to configure it. Click on the whitespace to the right of the "Image Topic" label of the Image plugin property tree, and then select /camera/rgb/image_raw. The camera stream from the Turtlebot should then be plotted in the left pane of rviz, as shown in Figure 8-10.

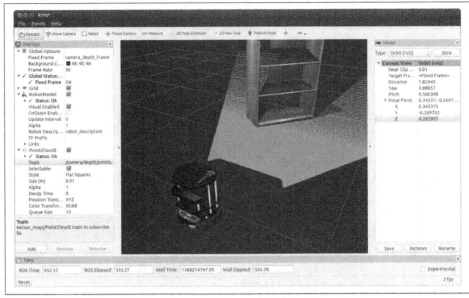

Figure 8-9. The Turtlebot's depth camera data has been added to the visualization

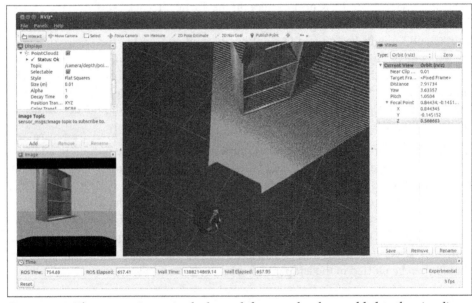

Figure 8-10. The camera image in the lower-left corner has been added to the visualization, allowing teleoperators to see the first-person perspective as well as the third-person perspective of the main window

The rviz interface is panelized and thus can be easily modified to suit the needs of the application. For example, we can drag the Image panel to the righthand column of the rviz window and resize it so that the depth image and camera image are similarly sized. We can then rotate the 3D visualization so that it is looking at the point cloud data from the side, which could be useful in some situations. An example panel configuration is shown in Figure 8-11.

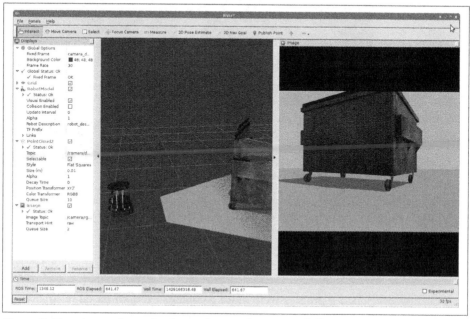

Figure 8-11. rviz panels can be dragged around to create different arrangements—here, the left panel has the third-person renderings of the depth camera data, and the visual camera is shown in the right panel

Alternatively, we can rotate the 3D scene so that it has a top-down perspective, which can be useful for driving in tight quarters. An example of this "bird's-eye" perspective is shown in Figure 8-12.

These examples just scratch the surface of what rviz can do! It is an extremely flexible tool that we will use throughout the remainder of the book.

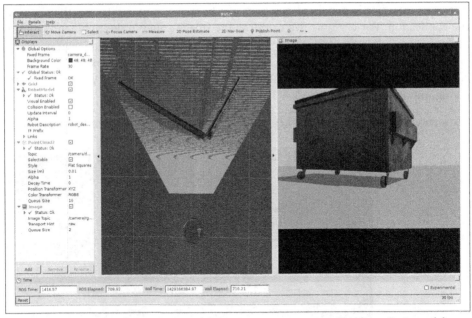

Figure 8-12. Rotating the perspective of the 3D view to create a "bird's eye" view of the environment

Summary

This chapter developed a progressively more complex keyboard-based teleoperation scheme and then showed how to connect the resulting motion commands to a Turtlebot. Finally, this chapter introduced `rviz` and showed how to quickly configure `rviz` to render point cloud and camera data, to create a teleoperation interface for a mobile robot.

Although teleoperated robots have many important applications, it is often more convenient or economical for robots to drive themselves. In the next chapter, we will describe one approach for building 2D maps, which is a necessary step for robots to start driving themselves.

## CHAPTER 9

Building Maps of the World

Now that you know how ROS works and have moved your robot around a bit, it's time to start looking at how to get it to navigate around the world on its own. In order to do this, the robot needs to know where it is, and where you want it to go to. Typically, this means that it needs to have a map of the world and to know where it is in this map. In this chapter, we're going to see how to build a high-quality map of the world, using data from your robot's sensors. We'll then use these maps in the next chapter when we talk about how to make the robot move about in the world.

If your robot had perfect sensors and knew exactly how it was moving, then building a map would be simple: you could take the objects detected by the sensors, transform them into some global coordinate frame (using the robot's position and some geometry), and then record them in a map (in this global coordinate frame). Unfortunately, in the real world, it's not quite that easy. The robot doesn't know exactly how it's moving, since it's interacting with an uncertain world. No sensor is perfect, and you'll have to deal with noisy measurements. How can you combine all this error-laden information together to produce a usable map?

Luckily, ROS has a set of tools that will do this for you. The tools are based on some quite advanced mathematics, but, luckily, you don't have to understand everything that's going on under the hood in order to use them. We'll describe these tools in this chapter, but first let's talk a bit about exactly what we mean by "map."

Maps in ROS

Navigation maps in ROS are represented by a 2D grid, where each grid cell contains a value that corresponds to how likely it is to be occupied. Figure 9-1 shows an example of a map learned directly from the sensor data on a robot. White is open space, black is occupied, and the grayish color is unknown.

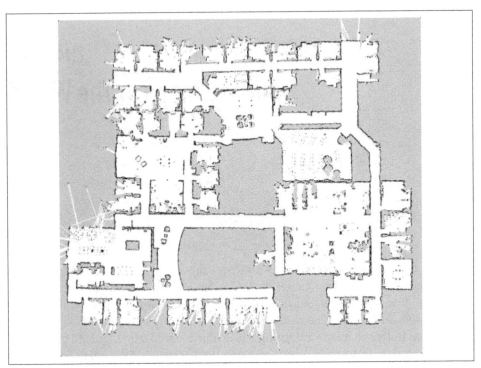

Figure 9-1. An example of a map used by ROS

Map files are stored as images, with a variety of common formats being supported (such as PNG, JPG, and PGM). Although color images can be used, they are converted to grayscale images before being interpreted by ROS. This means that maps can be displayed with any image display program. Associated with each map is a YAML file that holds additional information, such as the resolution (the length of each grid cell in meters), where the origin of the map is, and thresholds for deciding if a cell is occupied or unoccupied. Example 9-1 shows an example of a map YAML file.

Example 9-1. map.yaml

```
image: map.pgm
resolution: 0.1
origin: [0.0, 0.0, 0.0]
occupied_thresh: 0.65
free_thresh: 0.196
negate: 1
```

It's worth pointing out that images and maps have different coordinate frames and conventions associated with them. Images are indexed from the top left, with the y-axis going down the image, and store integer values, often from 0 to 255. High values (such as 255) correspond to white, and low values (such as 0) correspond to black. Maps, on the other hand, can have an arbitrary origin, specified in the YAML file. Since maps are probabilistic representations of the world, high values correspond to something being there, and low values correspond to empty space. Since we're used to using paper, most people associate black with something there and white with nothing there when using a map.

As with many things in ROS, most of the time, you won't need to think about this. However, if you're going to be directly editing your maps in an image editor, then it really helps to understand the differences between the image file format and the map that it represents.

This map is stored in the file *map.png*, has cells that represent 10 cm squares of the world, and has an origin at (0, 0, 0). A cell is considered to be occupied if the value in it is more than 65% of the total range allowed by the image format. A cell is unoccupied if it has a value less than 19.6% of the allowable range. This means that occupied cells will have a large value and will appear lighter in color in the image. Unoccupied cells will have a lower value and would appear darker. Since it is more intuitive for open space to be represented by white and occupied space by black, the `negate` flag allows for the values in the cells to be inverted before being used by ROS. So, for Example 9-1, if we assume that each cell holds a single unsigned byte (an integer from 0 to 255), each of the values will first be inverted by subtracting the original value from 255. Then, all cells with a value less that 49 (255 * 0.196 = 49.98) will be considered free, and all those with a value greater than 165 (255 * 0.65 = 165.75) will be considered to be occupied. All other cells will be classified as "unknown." These classifications will be used by ROS when we try to plan a path through this map for the robot to follow.

Since maps are represented as image files, you can edit them in your favorite image editor. This allows you to tidy up any maps that you create from sensor data, removing things that shouldn't be there, or adding in fake obstacles to influence path planning. A common use of this is to stop the robot from planning paths through certain areas of the map by, for example, drawing a line across a corridor you don't want to the robot to drive through, as you can see in Figure 9-2. The navigation system (which we'll talk about in the next chapter) will not be able to plan a path through these lines. This allows you to control where the robot can and cannot go as it wanders around the world.

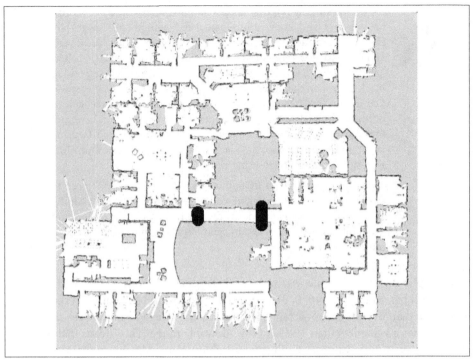

Figure 9-2. A hand-modified map—black lines were added to stop the robot from planning paths down the corridor in the middle of the map

Before we start to talk about how we're going to build maps in ROS, we're going to take a short detour to talk about `rosbag`. This is a tool that allows you to record and replay published messages and is especially useful when building large maps of the world.

Recording Data with rosbag

`rosbag` is a tool that lets us record messages and replay them later. This is really useful when debugging new algorithms, since it lets you present the same data to the algorithm over and over, which will help you isolate and fix bugs. It also allows you to develop algorithms without having to use a robot all the time. You can record some sensor data from the robot with `rosbag`, then use this recorded data to work on your code. `rosbag` can do more than record and play back data, but that's what we're going to focus on for now.

To record messages, we use the record functionality and a list of topic names. For example, to record all the messages sent over the scan and tf topics, you would run:

```
user@hostname$ rosbag record scan tf
```

This will save all of the messages in a file with a name in the format *YYYY-MM-DD-HH-mm-ss.bag*, corresponding to the time that rosbag was run. This should give each bag file a unique name, assuming you don't run rosbag more than once a second. You can change the name of the output file using the -O or --output-name flags, and add a prefix with the -o and --output-prefix flags. For example, these commands:

```
user@hostname$ rosbag record -O foo.bag scan tf
user@hostname$ rosbag record -o foo scan tf
```

would create bags named *foo.bag* and *foo_2015-10-05-14-29-30.bag*, respectively (obviously, with appropriate values for the current date and time). We can also record *all* of the topics that are currently publishing with the -a flag:

```
user@hostname$ rosbag record -a
```

While this is often useful, it can also record *a lot* of data, especially on robots with a lot of sensors, like the PR2. There are also flags that let you record topics that match a regular expression, which are described in detail on the rosbag wiki page (*http://wiki.ros.org/rosbag?distro=indigo*). rosbag will record data until you stop it with a Ctrl-C.

You can play back a pre-recorded bag file with the play functionality. There are a number of command-line parameters that allow you to manipulate how fast you play back the bag, where you start in the file, and other things (all of which are documented on the wiki), but the basic usage is straightforward:

```
user@hostname$ rosbag play --clock foo.bag
```

This will replay the messages recorded in the bag file *foo.bag*, as if they were being generated live from ROS nodes. Giving more than one bag file name will result in the bag files being played sequentially. The --clock flag causes rosbag to publish the clock time, which will be important when we come to build our maps.

 The --clock flag will cause rosbag to publish the clock time from when the bag was recorded. If something else is also publishing time, such as the Gazebo simulator, this can cause a lot of problems. If two sources are publishing (different) times, then time will appear to jump around, and this will confuse the mapping algorithm (and possibly many other nodes). When you're using rosbag with the --clock-- argument, make sure that nothing else is publishing a time. The easiest way to do this is to stop any simulators you have running.

You can find out information about a bag file with the `info` functionality:

```
user@hostname$ rosbag info laser.bag
path:         laser.bag
version:      2.0
duration:     1:44s (104s)
start:        Jul 07 2011 10:04:13.44 (1310058253.44)
end:          Jul 07 2011 10:05:58.04 (1310058358.04)
size:         8.2 MB
messages:     2004
compression:  none [11/11 chunks]
types:        sensor_msgs/LaserScan [90c7ef2dc6895d81024acba2ac42f369]
topics:       base_scan    2004 msgs    : sensor_msgs/LaserScan
```

This gives you details about how much time the bag covers, when it started and stopped recording, how large it is, how many messages it has in it, and what those messages (and topics) are. This is useful for you to verify that a bag that you just recorded has the right information in it.

 rosbag is also a great tool to use when debugging new algorithms for your robot. Instead of feeding live sensor data to your algorithm as you try to debug it, you can record a representative set of data with rosbag and then play it back. This means that your algorithm is seeing exactly the same data every time you run it. This repeatability will speed up your debugging, since you can guarantee that any changes in behavior are caused by changes in your code, and not by some new sensor input that you've never seen before. Even if the world does not change and your sensor does not move, measurement errors mean that you'll never see the same stream of sensor data twice. This will slow down your debugging, especially for complex algorithms.

Building Maps

Now we're going to look at how you can build a map like the one shown in Figure 9-1 using the tools in ROS. One thing to note about that map in Figure 9-1 is that it's quite "messy." Since it was created from sensor data taken from a robot, it includes some things you might not expect. Along the bottom edge of the map, the wall seems to have holes in it. These are caused by bad sensor readings, possibly the result of clutter under the desks in those rooms. The strange blob in the largish room toward the top in the middle is a pool table. The gray spots in the larger room going diagonally down and right are chair legs (this was a conference room). The walls are not always perfectly straight, and there are sometimes "unknown" areas in the middle of rooms if the sensors never made measurements there. When you start to make maps of your own with your robot, you should be prepared for them to look like this. Generally speaking, using more data to create the map will result in a better map. However, no map will be perfect. Even though the maps might not look all that great to you, they're still perfectly useful to the robot, as we will see.

You can build maps with the `slam_gmapping` node from the `gmapping` package. The `slam_gmapping` node uses an implementation of the GMapping algorithm, written by Giorgio Grisstti, Cyrill Stachniss, and Wolfram Burgard. GMapping uses a Rao-Blackwellized particle filter to keep track of the likely positions of the robot, based on its sensor data and the parts of the map that have already been built. If you're interested in the details of the algorithm, they're described in these two papers:

- Giorgio Grisetti, Cyrill Stachniss, and Wolfram Burgard, "Improved Techniques for Grid Mapping with Rao-Blackwellized Particle Filters," *IEEE Transactions on Robotics* 23 (2007): 34–46.
- Giorgio Grisetti, Cyrill Stachniss, and Wolfram Burgard, "Improving Grid-based SLAM with Rao-Blackwellized Particle Filters by Adaptive Proposals and Selective Resampling," *Proceedings of the IEEE International Conference on Robotics and Automation* (2005): 2432–2437.

First, we're going to generate some data to build the map from. Although you can build a map using live sensor data, as the robot moves about the world, we're going to take another approach. We're going to drive the robot around and save the sensor data to a file using `rosbag`. We're then going to replay this sensor data and use `slam_gmapping` to build a map for us. Collecting data in a bag file is often a good idea when building a map, since it lets you play around with the parameters of the `slam_gmapping` node to get a good map, without having to go and run the robot through the world again. This can be a real time-saver, especially if you need to tweak the mapping node parameters a lot.

First, let's record some data.Start up a simulator with a Turtlebot in it:

```
user@hostname$ roslaunch turtlebot_stage turtlebot_in_stage.launch
```

This launch file starts up the Stage robot simulator and an instance of `rviz`. Zoom out a bit in the simulator (using the mouse wheel), and you should see something like Figure 9-3.

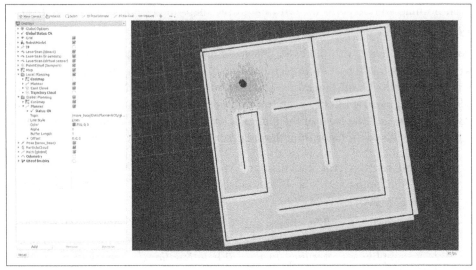

Figure 9-3. The rviz visualizer showing a simple world with a Turtlebot in it

Now, start up the the keyboard_teleop node from the turtlebot_teleop package:

```
user@hostname$ roslaunch turtlebot_teleop keyboard_teleop.launch
```

This will let you drive the robot around in the simulated world using the keys shown by the node when it started:

```
Control Your Turtlebot!
//--------------------------
Moving around:
   u    i    o
   j    k    l
   m    ,    .

q/z : increase/decrease max speeds by 10%
w/x : increase/decrease only linear speed by 10%
e/c : increase/decrease only angular speed by 10%
space key, k : force stop
anything else : stop smoothly

CTRL-C to quit

currently:     speed 0.2     turn 1
```

Practice driving the robot around for a bit. Once you've got the hang of it, we can get started collecting some data. `slam_gmapping` builds maps from data from the laser range-finder and the odometry system, as reported by `tf`. Although the Turtlebot doesn't actually have a laser range-finder, it creates `LaserScan` messages from its Kinect data and sends them over the `scan` topic. With the simulator still running, in a new terminal window, start recording some data:

```
user@hostname$ rosbag record -O data.bag /scan /tf
```

Now, drive the robot around the world for a while. Try to cover as much of the map as possible, and make sure you visit the same locations a couple of times. Doing this will result in a better final map. If you get to the end of this section and your map doesn't look very good, try recording some new data and drive the robot around the simulated world for longer, or a bit more slowly.

Once you've driven around for a while, use Ctrl-C to stop `rosbag`. Verify that you have a data bag called *data.bag*. You can find out what's in this bag by using the `ros bag info` command:

```
user@hostname$ rosbag info data.bag
path:         data.bag
version:      2.0
duration:     3:15s (195s)
start:        Dec 31 1969 16:00:23.80 (23.80)
end:          Dec 31 1969 16:03:39.60 (219.60)
size:         14.4 MB
messages:     11749
compression:  none [19/19 chunks]
types:        sensor_msgs/LaserScan [90c7ef2dc6895d81024acba2ac42f369]
              tf2_msgs/TFMessage    [94810edda583a504dfda3829e70d7eec]
topics:       /scan   1959 msgs   : sensor_msgs/LaserScan
              /tf     9790 msgs   : tf2_msgs/TFMessage    (3 connections)
```

Once you have a bag that seems to have enough data in it, stop the simulator with a Ctrl-C in the terminal you ran `roslaunch` in. It's important to stop the simulator before starting the mapping process, because it will be publishing `LaserScan` messages that will conflict with those that are being replayed by `rosbag`. Now it's time to build a map. Start `roscore` in one of the terminals. In another terminal, we're going to tell ROS to use the timestamps recorded in the bag file, and start the `slam_gmapping` node:

```
user@hostname$ rosparam set use_sim_time true
user@hostname$ rosrun gmapping slam_gmapping
```

If your robot's laser scan topic is not called scan, you will need to tell slam_gmapping what it is by adding *scan:=laser_scan_topic* when you start the node. The mapper should now be running, waiting to see some data.

We're going to use rosbag play to replay the data that we recorded from the simulated robot:

```
user@hostname$ rosbag play --clock data.bag
```

When it starts receiving data, slam_gmapping should start printing out diagnostic information. Sit back and wait until rosbag finishes replaying the data and slam_gmapping has stopped printing diagnostics. At this point, your map has been built, but it hasn't been saved to disk. Tell slam_gmapping to do this by using the map_saver node from the map_server package. Without stopping slam_gmapping, run the map_saver node in another terminal:

```
user@hostname$ rosrun map_server map_saver
```

This will save two files to disk: *map.pgm*, which contains the map, and *map.yaml*, which contains the map metadata. Take a look, and make sure you can see these files. You can view the map file using any standard image viewer, such as eog.

The map shown in Figure 9-4 was generated by slowly rotating the TurtleBot in place for a little more than one revolution, without moving from its starting position in the simulator. The first thing to notice about this map is that the actual mapped part of the world is tiny compared to the rest of the map. This is because the default size of ROS maps is 200 m × 200 m, with a cell size of 5 cm (that means that the image size is 2,000 x 2,000 pixels). Figure 9-5 shows a zoomed-in version of the interesting part of the map. This map isn't very good: the walls are not at right angles to each other, the open space extends beyond one of the walls, and there are notable gaps in several of the walls. As Figure 9-5 shows, getting a good map is not just a simple matter of running slam_gmapping on any old set of data. Building a good map is hard and can be time-consuming, but it's worth the investment—a good map will make navigating around the world and knowing where you are a lot easier, as we'll see in the next chapter.

Figure 9-4. A map generated from a Turtlebot spinning in place

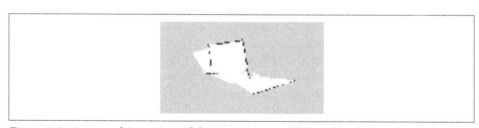

Figure 9-5. A zoomed-in section of the map generated from a Turtlebot spinning in place

The YAML file generated by slam_gmapping looks like this:

```
image: map.pgm
resolution: 0.050000
origin: [-100.000000, -100.000000, 0.000000]
negate: 0
occupied_thresh: 0.65
free_thresh: 0.196
```

Why is the map *so* bad? One of the reasons is that the sensors on the Turtlebot are not great for creating maps. slam_gmapping expects LaserScan messages, and as mentioned earlier, the Turtlebot doesn't have a laser range-finder; instead, it uses the data from a Microsoft Kinect sensor to synthesize LaserScan messages, which can be used by slam_gmapping. The problem is that this fake laser range-finder has a shorter range and a narrower field of view than a typical laser sensor does. slam_gmapping uses the laser data to estimate how the robot is moving, and this estimation is better with long-range data over a wide field of view.

We can improve mapping quality by setting some of the gmapping parameters to different values:

```
user@hostname$ rosparam set /slam_gmapping/angularUpdate 0.1
user@hostname$ rosparam set /slam_gmapping/linearUpdate 0.1
user@hostname$ rosparam set /slam_gmapping/lskip 10
user@hostname$ rosparam set /slam_gmapping/xmax 10
user@hostname$ rosparam set /slam_gmapping/xmin -10
user@hostname$ rosparam set /slam_gmapping/ymax 10
user@hostname$ rosparam set /slam_gmapping/ymin -10
```

These change how far the robot has to rotate (angularUpdate) and move (linearUpdate) before a new scan is considered for inclusion in the map, how many beams to skip when processing each LaserScan message (lskip), and the extent of the map (xmin, xmax, ymin, ymax).

We can also improve the quality of the maps by driving around slowly, especially when turning the robot. Make the parameter changes listed here and collect a new bag of data by driving your robot around slowly, and you'll get a map that looks more like Figure 9-6. It's still not perfect (no map built from sensor data ever is), but it's certainly better than the previous one. Note that the parameter changes only affect slam_gmapping, so you could use them with the original data bag you collected, without driving the robot around again. As we noted earlier, this is one of the advantages of using recorded data when building maps.

 When building a map with slam_gmapping, record the information you need with rosbag. This will let you experiment with different values of the slam_gmapping parameters to get a better map.

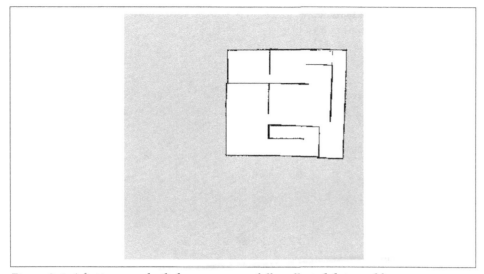

Figure 9-6. A better map, built from more carefully collected data and better parameter settings

You can also build your maps directly from published messages, without saving them to a bag file first. To do this, you just need to start the slam_gmapping node while you're driving your robot around. We prefer to record the data first, since there's less computational load on the robot when you're driving it around that way. In the end, however, you should end up with similar maps, regardless of whether or not you saved the data with rosbag first.

Starting a Map Server and Looking at a Map

Once you have a map, you need to make it available to ROS. You do this by running the map_server node from the map_server package, and pointing it at the YAML file for a map you have already made. As explained earlier, this YAML file contains the filename for the image that represents the map and additional information about it, like the resolution (meters per pixel), where the origin is, what the thresholds for occupied and open space are, and whether the image uses white for open space or occupied space. With roscore running, you can start a map server like this:

```
user@hostname$ rosrun map_server map_server map.yaml
```

where map.yaml is the map YAML file. Running the map server will result in two topics being published. map contains messages of type nav_msgs/OccupancyGrid, corresponding to the map itself. map_metadata contains messages of type nav_msgs/MapMetaData, corresponding to the data in the YAML file:

```
user@hostname$ rostopic list
/map
/map_metadata
/rosout
/rosout_agg

user@hostname$ rostopic echo map_metadata
map_load_time:
  secs: 1427308667
  nsecs: 991178307
resolution: 0.0250000003725
width: 2265
height: 2435
origin:
  position:
    x: 0.0
    y: 0.0
    z: 0.0
  orientation:
    x: 0.0
    y: 0.0
    z: 0.0
    w: 1.0
```

This shows that the map contains 2,265 x 2,435 cells, with a resolution of 2.5 cm per cell. The origin of the world coordinate frame is the origin of the map, with the same orientation. We can take a look at the map in rviz, to see what's actually in it. Start up a map server like this:

```
user@hostname$ roscd mapping/maps
user@hostname$ rosrun map_server map_server willow.yaml
```

Now, in another terminal, start up an instance of rviz:

```
user@hostname$ rosrun rviz rviz
```

Add a display of type Map, and set the topic name to /map. Make sure that the fixed frame is also set to /map. You should see something like Figure 9-7.

This map was built using a PR2 robot with a laser range-finder and slam_gmapping, and it illustrates a number of things you often see in maps built from sensor data. First, it is not axis-aligned. When the robot was collecting data to build the map, the odometry data coordinate frame was aligned with the starting position of the robot, which means that the final map is rotated a bit. We can fix this in the YAML file if we want to, although it doesn't affect the robot's ability to navigate.

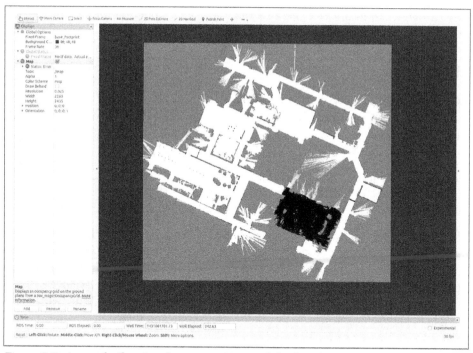

Figure 9-7. A map built using slam_gmapping and displayed in rviz

Second, the map is quite messy. Although the corridors and open spaces are fairly clean, there seem to be a lot of long, skinny open spaces coming off these open spaces. These are actually rooms that the robot did not drive into. As the robot drove past these rooms, the laser range-finder made some measurements into them, but there wasn't enough data to reconstruct a decent map of each room. Again, this won't affect the ability of the robot to localize itself, but it does mean that we might not be able to get the robot to navigate into these rooms autonomously, since they're technically not in the map.

Finally, there's a big black blob in the lower-right corner of the map. This is a room that the robot should not go into, even though it's on the map. After the map was made, someone loaded the image file into a graphics program like `gimp` and painted the pixels in the room black. When the robot tries to plan a path in the map, these areas will be considered to be occupied, and it will not plan a path through them. This change will affect the robot's ability to localize itself a bit, especially when it is near the doorway to this space. Localization involves comparing the current sensor readings to the map, to make sure the robot is seeing what it expects to in a given location. Since there's an obstacle in the map (the big black blob) that doesn't match up with something in the real world, the robot's confidence in where it is will be lower. However, as long as it can see enough of the world that *does* match up with its map (which it can in this case, because the laser range-finder on the PR2 has a wide field of view), the localization algorithm is robust enough to cope.

Summary

In this chapter, we looked at how to use the slam_gmapping package to create a high-quality map of the robot's environment. We also introduced you to rosbag, which can let you save published messages to a file and replay them later. We'll be seeing rosbag again later on in this book, since it's a useful tool.

One of the important things to remember about building maps is that, although many roboticists consider it to be a "solved problem," it is often tricky to do in practice, especially with cheaper robots and less capable sensors.

We've really just scratched the surface of the ROS mapping system. There are a huge number of parameters you can set to alter the mapping behavior. These are all documented at the gmapping wiki page (*http://wiki.ros.org/gmapping?distro=indigo*) and described in the papers mentioned earlier. However, unless you know what the effects of changing these parameters are, we'd recommend that you don't fiddle with them too much. Find some settings that work for your robot, and then don't change them.

Once you've built maps a few times, and you have a feel for it, it shouldn't take too long to make a new one when you find yourself in a new environment. Once you have a map, then you're ready to have your robot start to autonomously navigate about, which is the subject of the next chapter.

## CHAPTER 10

Navigating About the World

One of the most basic things that a robot can do is to move around the world. To do this effectively, the robot needs to know where it is and where it should be going. This is usually acheived by giving the robot a map of the world, a starting location, and a goal location. In the previous chapter, we saw how to build a map of the world from sensor data. Now, we'll look at how to make your robot autonomously navigate from one part of the world to another, using this map and the ROS navigation packages. We'll start by helping the robot to figure out where it is.

Localizing the Robot in a Map

In this section, we'll see how we can use the ROS `amcl` package to localize the robot in a map. The `amcl` node implements a set of probabilistic localization algorithms, collectively known as *Adaptive Monte Carlo Localization*, which are described in the book *Probabilistic Robotics* by Sebsastian Thrun, Wolfram Burgard, and Dieter Fox (MIT Press). In particular, it uses the algorithms `sample_motion_model_odometry`, `beam_range_finder_model`, `likelihood_field_range_finder_model`, `Augmented_MCL`, and `KLD_Sampling_MCL`. While you don't need to know all of the technical details of how these algorithms work in order to use the localization package, understanding some of the high-level details will make your life easier when you're trying to make localization work.[1]

The location of the robot, also known as its *pose*, is represented by a position and orientation in the *map coordinate frame* (sometimes also called the *world coordinate*

---

[1] This is true of many things in ROS. While it's possible to use them without understanding the underlying algorithms, knowing what's going on under the hood will be invaluable if you ever need to debug strange robot behavior.

frame). `amcl` maintains a set of these poses, representing where it thinks the robot might be. Each of these *candidate poses* has associated with it a probability; higher-probability poses are more likely to be where the robot actually is. As the robot moves around the world, the sensor readings are compared to the readings that would be expected for each of the poses, according to the map. For each candidate pose, if the readings are consistent with the map, then the probability of that pose increases. If the readings are inconsistent, then the probability decreases. Over time, candidate poses with very low probability (i.e., where the robot is most likely not really in that pose) go away, while those with high probability stick around. As the robot moves around the world, the candidate poses move with it, following the odometry estimates that the robot generates.

So, `amcl` starts off with a set of candidate poses centered around where we think that the robot is. Over time, as the robot moves around and takes sensor measurements of the world, this set of poses should converge to the actual pose of the robot. At any given time, the most likely pose of the robot, which is used for path planning, is the candidate pose with the highest probability. It's important to note, however, that this might not be the actual pose of the robot. It's likely to be *close* to the actual pose, but it's very unlikely to be *exactly* the actual pose. In practice, this means that when you use the navigation system to move the robot to a particular place in the world, it's likely to get close, but it will never end up in exactly the right place, even if the localization system claims that it's there. This is one of the trade-offs of using probabilistic algorithms; they're really robust and work well most of the time, but you can't guarantee that they're completely accurate. However, they're usually accurate enough for path planning and, when combined with a sensor-based local path-following algorithm, for navigation.

Now that you understand a bit about how the localization system works, let's take a look at it in action. First, let's make sure that any map server you might be running is stopped. Once you've done that run this launch file:

```
user@hostname$ roslaunch turtlebot_stage turtlebot_in_stage.launch
```

This will start up a simulation of a simple maze world with a Turtlebot robot in it, launch a map server with a map made from this world, start the `amcl` node, and launch an instance of `rviz` so that you can see what's going on. Your `rviz` window should look similar to Figure 10-1, and you should also see a few other windows appear (for the simulator and some other things; we'll ignore them for now).

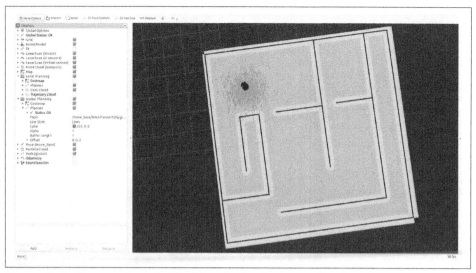

Figure 10-1. The rviz view of a Turtlebot 2 robot being simulated in Stage

Uncheck all of the displays in `rviz` except RobotModel, Map, and ParticleCloud. We'll get back to the other displays later, when we talk about how the navigation system in ROS works. For now, you should be able to see the robot, a map (which has been hand-drawn, rather than learned from sensor data), and a set of green arrows, like in Figure 10-2. The green arrows are the pose estimates from `amcl`; that is, the places where the localization algorithm thinks that the robot might be. With this launch file they're automatically generated, but in some situations, you might have to provide an initial position estimate yourself. You can do this by clicking on the "2D Pose Estimate" button, then clicking, holding, and dragging in the `rviz` window. The arrow that you see is your estimate of where the robot should be in the map, and it's passed on to the `amcl` algorithm. The algorithm then probabilistically generates possible poses around this initial estimate. Try this now. You can set the initial pose of the robot to anywhere in the map, even if it's really not there. Once you set the estimate, notice how the visualization of the robot jumps to that location. This is because `rviz` relies on the pose estimate to place the robot in the map, while stage (the simulator) actually *knows* where the robot is.

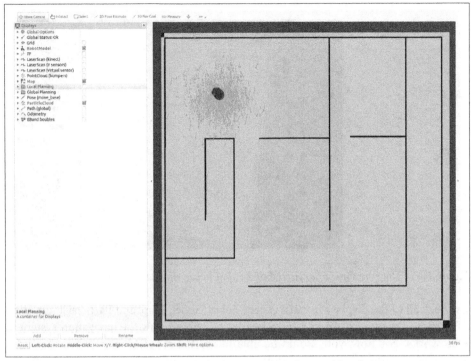

Figure 10-2. rviz showing just the robot, the map, and the amcl localization estimates

Getting a Good Initial Localization

How do you get a good initial localization for the robot? After you have the hang of giving pose estimates using rviz, try to give a pose estimate that reflects the actual position of the robot. You can see this in the stage simulation window. It's quite easy to get a rough estimate, but how can you tell how good it actually is?

One way to improve the estimate is to compare it to the robot's sensor data. Turn on the "LaserScan (kinect)" display, and you should see the data from the simulated laser range-finder on the Turtlebot. If the robot is well localized, then this data should line up well with the map. Figure 10-3 shows a poor initial estimate: the laser contact points don't line up with the walls at all.

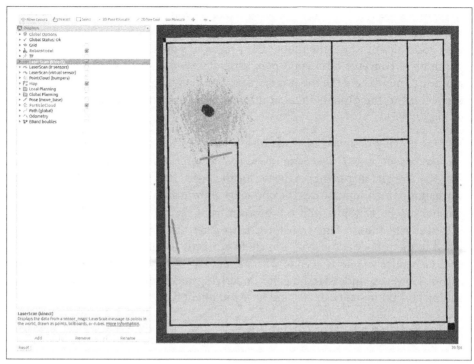

Figure 10-3. A poor initial localization, where the sensor data does not line up with the map

Try giving some more initial pose estimates, and see if you can get the sensor data to agree with the map. Remember that `rviz` is rendering things in 3D, with perspective, and that the laser data is being shown slightly above the floor. This means that even a perfectly located robot might result in laser data looking like it's not quite on top of the walls in the map. Once you have the robot well localized again, you can get it to drive around the world. Don't worry if you're not in exactly the right place. As long as you're roughly localized, ROS can deal with it.

What's Going on Behind the Scenes

You've seen how to localize the robot using `rviz`, but what's actually happening behind the scenes? As with everything in ROS, it's all about messages sent over topics.

`rviz` subscribes to a topic called `initialpose`, of type `geometry_msgs/PoseWith CovarianceStamped`. When it gets a message on this topic, it resets the set of candidate poses that it's keeping, randomly generating them from a normal distribution, centered on the pose in the message. All `rviz` is doing when you use it to set an initial pose is publishing a message on this topic.

Instead of using a normally distributed initial pose, you can get `amcl` to use a uniform set of candidate poses, scattered all over the map. You might do this if you really don't have a good idea of where the robot is. However, this makes it (much) harder for the algorithms to converge on a good pose estimate, so you should only do this if you *really* don't know where the robot is starting. You can enable this behavior by making a service call to the `global_localization` service, using an empty request (of type `std_srvs/Empty`).

`amcl` was initially designed to work with robots that have a laser range-finder that generates `sensor_msgs/LaserScan` messages. It subscribes to the topics `scan` (for the laser), `map` (for the map), `initialpose` (for the pose estimate), and `tf` (for transform information, which summarizes the odometry information published by the robot). It publishes on the `tf` topic, with a transform from the `odom` coordinate frame to the `map` coordinate frame. This transform represents the correction that needs to be applied to the robot's odometry estimate to correctly locate it in the map coordinate frame. Generally, you don't need to worry about any of this, since ROS takes care of it for you. However, understanding the underlying mechanisms is helpful in understanding how the system can fail, and how you might fix it.

Tips for Setting a Better Initial Pose

Good navigation relies on a good localization of the robot. One way to improve the initial pose of the robot is to look at its sensor readings in `rviz` and make sure that they match the map well, like we did earlier. This works particularly well if you have a laser range-finder, since the data from it is like a local map. Move the initial pose estimate around until the laser readings correspond well to the map, and you should have a good pose estimate.

To make the pose estimate even better, you can drive the robot around a bit before doing any autonomous navigation. This will let the set of candidate particles in the `amcl` node converge onto the actual position of the robot, and give a more reliable estimate of where it is. With a bit of practice, you can learn the sorts of movements that will make this happen quickly for your particular robot and sensors.

Using the ROS Navigation Stack

Now that we've got a (more-or-less) localized robot, let's get it to drive around a bit. We're going to start by interacting with the navigation system, often called the *nav stack* by ROS old-timers, through `rviz`. First, though, let's talk a bit about what the nav stack actually is and how it works.

The ROS Navigation Stack

The ROS navigation system is pretty complex, and we're only going to scratch the surface of it here. Full details of what it can do and how it can be configured are available on the navigation wiki page (*http://wiki.ros.org/navigation?distro=indigo*). For now, we're going to assume that the nav stack has been configured for your robot and is working as it should. If this isn't the case, you're going to need to go to the wiki and follow the instructions there (or jump ahead to Chapter 17).

At its heart, the nav stack is a system that allows a ROS-enabled robot to move about the world to a specified goal position efficiently, and without hitting things along the way. It integrates information from the map, localization system, sensors, and odometry to plan a good path from the current position to the goal position, and then follows it to the best of the robot's ability. If the robot gets stuck, usually because of some unmapped obstacles, it can replan and recover. The nav stack is one of the most heavily used parts of ROS, since almost every robot that moves uses it.

At a high level, the nav stack works like this:

1. A *navigation goal* is sent to the nav stack. This is done using an action call with a goal of type MoveBaseGoal, which specifies a goal pose (position and orientation) in some coordinate frame (commonly the map frame).

2. The nav stack uses a path-planning algorithm in the *global planner* to plan the shortest path from the current location to the goal, using the map.

3. This path is passed to the *local planner*, which tries to drive the robot along the path. The local planner uses information from the sensors in order to avoid obstacles that appear in front of the robot but that are not in the map, such as people. If the local planner gets stuck and cannot make progress, it can ask the global planner to make a new plan and then attempt to follow that.

4. When the robot gets close to the goal pose, the action terminates and we're done.

We'll start by looking at how to do this in rviz.

Navigating in rviz

Assuming that your robot is well localized, getting it to navigate around the world is easy. Click on the "2D Nav Goal" button, and then click and drag in the rviz window to give the robot a target position, known as a *goal pose*. The robot should drive to the goal pose on its own, not hitting anything along the way. Congratulations! You've just used the nav stack in ROS.

Before we show you what's actually going on under the hood, take a look at the set of possible poses maintained by amcl. As the robot was moving, amcl was comparing the readings from the laser range-finder to what it expected to see, given the possible poses and the map. If the readings and the predictions were similar in a particular candidate pose, `amcl` gave it a higher probability of being the real pose. If the readings and the predictions were very different, `amcl` lowered the probability of the pose. Poses with very low probabilities were deleted and replaced with new ones close to the existing ones with higher probability. Over time, the cloud of poses converged onto the actual position of the robot.

This convergence of the `amcl` localization happens even if the pose is slightly off. Give the robot a new pose estimate a little bit away from its actual location, and notice how the set of candidate poses spreads out again. Now, give it a nav goal a small distance away, and watch what happens to the set of candidate poses. Either the navigation stack failed because the pose estimate was just too far off to recover from, or the pose estimate converged on the robot's position. If navigation failed, then try again, making the pose estimate a little closer to the robot's actual position than the last time. Keep trying it until you can get the localization estimate to converge, so that you can get a sense of how far off you can be and still recover.

Once you're done confusing the robot, make sure it's well-localized again. Now, we're going to take a look at what's actually going on inside the nav stack. You don't, strictly speaking, need to know this to use the nav stack, but it's often useful when it comes to understanding situations where there's a navigation failure.

Seeing What's Going On

There are a lot of moving parts in the nav stack, and you can see what many of them are doing using `rviz`. In this section, we're going to get the robot to navigate around the world, looking at how the various functions of the nav stack interact.

The first thing that the nav stack does is to create the *global costmap*. This is a data structure that says how good or bad it is for the robot to be in a particular place in the map. Being in collision with a wall is really bad. Being in open space is good. Getting close to a wall is worse than being in open space, but not as bad as hitting it. Click the checkbox for the Global Planning display, expand it, then click the Costmap checkbox. This will show you the global costmap, as in Figure 10-4.

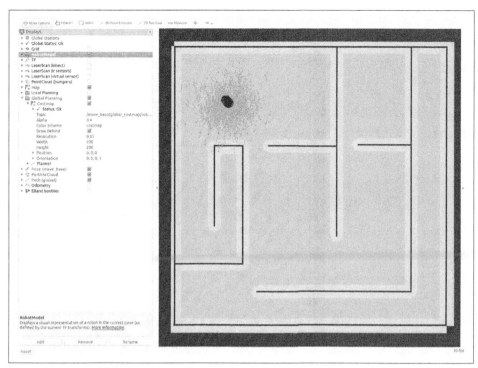

Figure 10-4. The global costmap, showing more expensive areas close to the walls

As with most things in ROS, the costmap is available on a topic. In this case, the topic is `/move_base/global_costmap/costmap`, which has a type of `nav_msgs/Occupancy Grid`. In general, it's a good idea to make internal data structures in your nodes visible in this way, since it lets you look at them in `rviz`, which can be invaluable for debugging and figuring out why your robot isn't doing what you expect it to.

Enable the "Path (global)" display to see the global path that ROS calculates, the "Pose (move_base)" display to see the goal pose, and the "Planner" display to see the near-term path. Now give the robot a navigation goal and see what happens. Once it starts moving, you should see something like Figure 10-5.

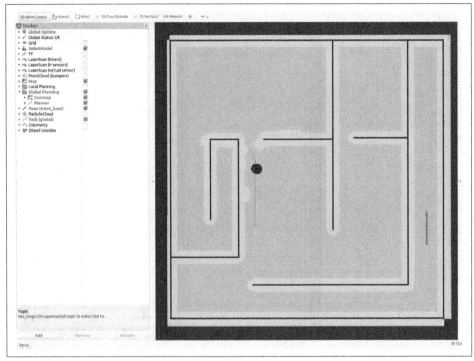

Figure 10-5. The robot in motion, showing the global path that it has calculated

The goal pose is shown by the red arrow in the lower right of the map. The path that ROS has decided on is shown as the green line. Notice how this line stays in areas of low cost, away from the walls. The part of the path that is closest to the robot is shown by the red line.

The global path is the one that the robot wants to follow, but the *actual* path that it moves along is determined by the local planner. The local planner balances following the global path with avoiding local obstacles that are detected by the robot's sensors, but are not in the map. Enable the "Local Planning" display (and make sure that the "Costmap", "Planner", and "Cost Cloud" displays are enabled) to see the local costmap and planning information (see Figure 10-6). The local planner balances following the path and not hitting things, and shows good places to move through as "hot" colors and bad places as "cold" colors. The local costmap shows how good or bad it thinks cells are, with hot colors being bad and cold colors being good (confusingly). Give the robot a few navigation goals, and see how the local path mostly stays within the red regions of the planner visualization. Also notice how the planner and the local costmap are attached to the robot's coordinate frame, and follow it around.

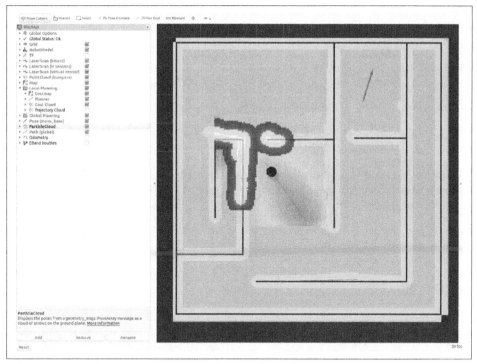

Figure 10-6. A Turtlebot driving to a navigation goal, with all displays enabled

Now that you know how to get your robot to navigate around the world using `rviz`, let's look at how to do the same thing in a program.

Navigating in Code

It's just as easy to move your robot around using code as it is to move it with `rviz`. All you have to do is make the action calls yourself. You can send the robot on a patrol with our example `patrol` node:

```
user@hostname$ rosrun navigation patrol.py
```

This node, shown in Example 10-1, has a list of goal poses that it cycles through in order, calling the `move_base` action repeatedly and then waiting for it to terminate.

Example 10-1. patrol.py

```
#!/usr/bin/env python

import rospy
import actionlib
```

```
from move_base_msgs.msg import MoveBaseAction, MoveBaseGoal


waypoints = [   ❶
    [(2.1, 2.2, 0.0), (0.0, 0.0, 0.0, 1.0)],
    [(6.5, 4.43, 0.0), (0.0, 0.0, -0.984047240305, 0.177907360295)]
]


def goal_pose(pose):   ❷
    goal_pose = MoveBaseGoal()
    goal_pose.target_pose.header.frame_id = 'map'
    goal_pose.target_pose.pose.position.x = pose[0][0]
    goal_pose.target_pose.pose.position.y = pose[0][1]
    goal_pose.target_pose.pose.position.z = pose[0][2]
    goal_pose.target_pose.pose.orientation.x = pose[1][0]
    goal_pose.target_pose.pose.orientation.y = pose[1][1]
    goal_pose.target_pose.pose.orientation.z = pose[1][2]
    goal_pose.target_pose.pose.orientation.w = pose[1][3]

    return goal_pose


if __name__ == '__main__':
    rospy.init_node('patrol')

    client = actionlib.SimpleActionClient('move_base', MoveBaseAction)   ❸
    client.wait_for_server()

    while True:
        for pose in waypoints:      ❹
            goal = goal_pose(pose)
            client.send_goal(goal)
            client.wait_for_result()
```

❶ A list of the waypoints for the robot to patrol.

❷ A helper function to turn a waypoint into a MoveBaseGoal.

❸ Create a simple action client, and wait for the server to be ready.

❹ Loop through the waypoints, sending each as an action goal.

This code just repeatedly sends action goals to the move_base action and waits for them to complete. The waypoints are specified by position and a quaternion that represents rotation. You can specify the frame that these coordinates are in as part of the MoveBaseGoal argument. In our case, we're using the map frame. However, if you wanted to go to an object, and that object had its own coordinate frame that ROS knew about, you could just as easily use that. We'll talk more about coordinate frames later on in this book.

Summary

In this chapter, we saw how to get a robot to move about in the world and how to issue high-level commands that harness the power of the ROS nav stack. We saw how to localize the robot in a map and how to give it navigation commands both with rviz and through an action call in our own code. We also talked a little about how the navigation system in ROS works and how to see it working through rviz.

The nav stack in ROS is a complicated and highly configurable thing, and we've barely scratched the surface of it in this chapter. The navigation wiki page (*http:// wiki.ros.org/navigation?distro=indigo*) has a lot more detail, both on how to use the nav stack and on how to adapt it to work better for your particular use case. In particular, the move_base wiki page (*http://wiki.ros.org/move_base?distro=indigo*) lists all of the parameters you can set to tune the performance of the nav stack.

If you're interested in how the navigation system works in detail, it's described in David Lu's ROSCon 2014 talk (*http://bit.ly/lu_roscon2014*) and in this paper:

- David V. Lu, Dave Hershberger, and William D. Smart, "Layered Costmaps for Context-Sensitive Navigation." Proceedings of the IEEE/RSJ International Conference on Robots and Systems (2014): 709–715.

We'll return to navigating a robot around the world later in the book, when we look at how to get the robot to do some something useful as it patrols your building. Next, however, we're going to look at how to move your robot's arms and how to manipulate things in the world.

## CHAPTER 11

Chess-bot

Thus far, this book has focused on driving mobile robots in office-like environments. This was because planar robot navigation can be explored using relatively low-cost hardware, and the topic is sufficiently valuable, complex, and nuanced to use it as a practical introduction to controlling robots using ROS. However, the field of robotics is far larger than planar mobile robots! In this chapter, we will enter an entirely different domain: *manipulation*. Unfortunately, robot manipulators are often complex and expensive machines, making them less commonly found in academic and hobbyist laboratories. Fortunately, it's possible, and strongly encouraged, to develop robot-manipulation software entirely using the free and open source Gazebo simulator! In this chapter, we will use Gazebo extensively to demonstrate how to develop software for the Robonaut 2 (also known as R2), a stunning state-of-the-art robot developed by NASA and GM. One copy of Robonaut 2 is actually on the International Space Station, and the software you will write in this chapter will run just as well in the Gazebo simulator on your personal computer as it would run on the actual R2 on the space station!

Robotic manipulators come in an astonishingly wide variety of shapes and sizes. Industrial robotic manipulators are famous for performing tasks like welding, painting, and stacking with superhuman power, speed, and endurance. It is important to note, however, that despite how things may appear at first glance, many industrial robot installations are "blind." That is, the robotic spot welder or painter will perform *exactly* the same operation whenever an object enters its environment, typically called a *workcell*. A major effort when designing a workcell is thus to ensure that the workpiece—for example, a partially finished car body—always arrives in precisely the same location before the robotic manipulator starts its preplanned motion. This is the type of functionality that we will develop in this chapter; we won't use perceptual data until later in the book.

The goal of this chapter is to describe the fundamentals of understanding and programming robot manipulators, and to demonstrate how to move robot manipulators through prespecified environments using the toolchains of ROS and related open source projects. We will absolutely not present a complete theoretical derivation of robotic manipulation! That deserves an entire book (or bookshelf) of its own. In this book, we will cover just enough of the principles to help explain the complexity of the tools.

Joints, Links, and Kinematic Chains

Robotic manipulators are a collection of *joints* held together by a structure of some sort. In classical robotics, there are two major classes of manipulator joints: *revolute* and *prismatic*. Revolute joints (also known as *rotary* or *pin* joints) rotate about an *axis of rotation*. For example, your elbow behaves like a revolute joint. In contrast, *prismatic* joints (also known as *linear* joints) move linearly along an axis of motion, like a sliding door or a telescoping car radio antenna.

Prismatic joints are often used where extreme precision is required, such as in robots that place tiny electrical components on circuit boards, robotic imaging systems for microscopy, or "3D printers," which are typically prismatic robots that precisely move a plastic extruder. Many robots include a combination of revolute and prismatic joints. However, to reduce the size, weight, and cost of the robot while maximizing the workspace size, many manipulators include only revolute joints. As a result, for the remainder of this chapter, we will exclusively discuss revolute joints.

In manipulator terminology, a *link* is a section of a robot arm connected by a *joint*. For example, your upper arm is a link, as is your lower arm. Typically, robotic links are made from a relatively rigid material, such as aluminum or hard plastic. In this book, we will assume that links are truly rigid. In many domains, this assumption is not always correct, because the links are heavily loaded, they are moving very quickly, or both, which requires complex analysis to ensure stable control. We won't go there. For the purposes of the following discussion, links are rigid sections of material that connect joints. These fundamental terms are illustrated by the sketch in Figure 11-1.

A series of connected links and joints is known as a *kinematic chain*. Knowing the geometry of a kinematic chain is a fundamental requirement of controlling a robotic manipulator. Usually, one side of a kinematic chain is considered to be *grounded*, meaning that it is fixed with respect to some other coordinate frame, such as a factory floor or the torso of a robot. An *open* kinematic chain is one in which the non-grounded side of the chain is free to move around the workspace. The free-floating side of a manipulator is usually fitted with some sort of *end effector*, such as a welding iron, a paint gun, a grinding wheel, or a general-purpose gripper or suction cup.

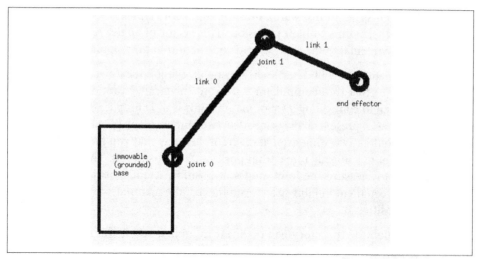

Figure 11-1. The fundamental components of robot manipulators: joints and links

From a programming perspective, we want to be able to position the end effector of a robot manipulator in any position and orientation within its workspace. In an ideal world, this would be easy. Sadly, the real world complicates things, for several reasons. First, in many robots, each joint has a limited *range of motion*. Wires, hoses, mechanical structures, and other constraints often prevent manipulator joints from being able to spin endlessly. Second, the workspace usually has some *obstacles*, such as fixed objects the manipulator must avoid. Third, real-world robotic joints can only accelerate and decelerate at limited rates. *Motion planning* is the field of study that addresses these issues (and more). To appreciate them, we will first dive into a bit of theory.

Joint Space

When we were considering planar mobile robots, there were only two major coordinate frames to keep in mind: the *map frame*, which is fixed relative to the environment and never moves; and the *robot frame*, which is attached to the robot and moves with it. As described in the previous chapter, mobile robot *localization* algorithms seek to describe the relationship between the map frame and the robot frame.

In manipulation, we typically have many more coordinate frames to deal with: each link of a robot manipulator has a coordinate frame that needs to be described relative to the link before it. Fortunately, the relationships between these frames are usually known to a high degree of precision, thanks to sensors called *joint encoders*, which are typically fitted to each joint of a manipulator and directly measure the rotational positions. The exact mechanism varies: joint encoders can measure magnetic, optical, resistive, or capacitive phenomena. However, after low-level processing (typically performed at high speed in firmware), most manipulators typically know the angular positions of all their joints to high precision. This vector of angles is called the *joint state*, and is fundamental to the analysis and control of robot manipulators.

For the manipulators we will describe in this book, the joint state vector is simply a list of joint angles that the manipulator hardware "magically" produces for us. The simplest approach to controlling a robot manipulator is in *joint space*. For purposes of illustration, we will present a diagram of a two-dimensional planar arm, since it projects nicely onto a two-dimensional diagram. Let's say that you have a task where you want the arm to endlessly move from position A to position B. The simplest control strategy is to measure the joint angles at position A and position B, and then interpolate between them in joint space. And indeed, the manipulator will travel from position A to position B.

However, although the trajectory will be linear in joint space, it will not be linear in the "real world," or the *task space* of the end effector. Sometimes, the task space is called *Cartesian space* to emphasize that the end effector is moving through a Cartesian world, not joint space. Most of the time, we want to control an end effector in task space, not joint space. That is, we want the end effector to move in straight lines in task space, not straight lines in joint space. To illustrate this, let's assume that we are programming a robot to clean a window that is in front of it, on a vertical wall. The robot needs to gently wipe the window with its end effector. If we place the starting position at the top of the window and the ending position at the bottom of the window, a straightforward joint-space interpolation will result in the end effector crashing through the window, as pictured in Figure 11-2. Whoops!

To explain what's happening, we need to use *forward kinematics*. This is how we convert from joint space to task space; we apply transformations that use our knowledge of the geometry, or *kinematics*, of the robot arm. This geometry includes how long each link is, the angles between the axes of rotation, and the joint angles. The math can get messy to write longhand, but after some simplification it always reduces to a few matrix multiplications, which computers are really good at doing. The forward kinematics function thus transforms the joint state of the manipulator into the task space position of its end effector. The forward kinematics function is fast and unambiguous: you put in a joint state, you get out a position. ROS provides many tools for this, most notably the `tf` package, which will be used later in this chapter.

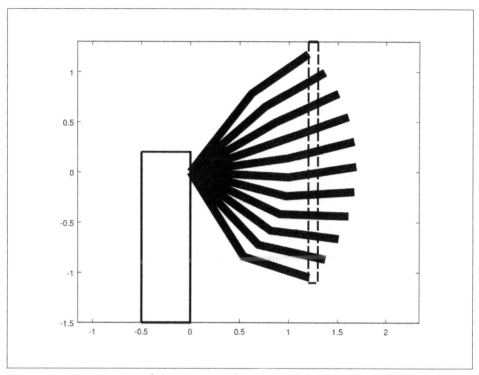

Figure 11-2. Poor motion planning causes the robot at left, attempting to clean the window at right, to break it instead

Forward kinematics tells us where the end of the arm is, relative to the rest of the robot. That is useful, but really what we want is the opposite operation: given a desired point in the world (say, the top of the window we are trying to clean), what should the arm's joint angles be? This is called *inverse kinematics*.

Inverse Kinematics

Let's say that we have a task space position A (the top of the window) and a task space position B (the bottom of the window). We want to compute the joint states for each of those position, which we can feed to joint-space controllers to move the arm.

Although we can relatively quickly derive the inverse kinematics equations for the two-dimensional arm shown in these diagrams, things will get nasty really quickly when we move up to arms with more joints. Once the arm has more than six joints, it gets even more interesting: there is no longer a unique inverse kinematics solution! Instead, there can be a *set* or *manifold* of solutions, all of which achieve the desired end-effector position. For example, you can hold your hand in the same position in front of you and move your elbow in an arc. That is the one-dimensional subspace of inverse kinematic solutions for that particular location and orientation of your hand. Because we're lazy and our arms are heavy, we usually choose the solution where our elbow is hanging down. But that is just one out of many possible arm configurations that result in our hands staying in the same place.

It gets still more complex: things that are "out of reach" of the robot have no inverse kinematics solution. There is also a nasty region right on the edge of what the robot can reach, where it can achieve *some* end effector orientations, but not all. To illustrate this, imagine reaching out for something that is *just* within your reach. You'll find that you can only grab it in one way. But once you bring that object a few inches closer, you can pick it up in any direction by reorienting your wrist and elbow.

To reiterate: the inverse kinematics problem is really hard. For any given position and orientation of the end effector, there can be infinite, finite, or zero joint-state solutions.

Fortunately, there are some good inverse kinematics software packages out there, including several that operate nicely with ROS. You can describe the arm geometry to these packages using ROS parameters and then call ROS services to ask for joint-state solutions for desired end effector positions. Using such a package, we could improve our window-cleaning robot: we could calculate a series of "waypoints" along the trajectory from position A to position B, all of which lie on the task space straight line between A and B.

If we calculate enough of these intermediate points, we may even be able to get the robot to wipe the window without breaking it. But this approach is still a bit nasty, due to several concerns we haven't addressed yet, including singularities (when a joint is fully extended), limited ranges of motion, limited joint velocities and accelerations, and obstacles in the environment. Dealing with these issues in a general fashion is really hard. This is why there are complex software packages called *motion planners*, which take all of these factors into account. You simply tell them where the manipulator is, where you want it to be, and provide a description of the robot and its environment. The motion planner then performs some impressive mathematics and responds with a *trajectory* of joint states that you can feed to the manipulator's joint controllers. If all goes well, the manipulator end effector will then smoothly follow the calculated path in the task space while not crashing into anything.

The Key to Success

Robot manipulators are complex beasts: they have many motors and mechanical moving parts, they are filled with flexing cables and electronics, and they have delicate sensors throughout to measure joint angles and forces. In other words, they are expensive and prone to failure. Indeed, working with manipulators offers wonderful glimpses of an advanced technological future, contrasted with the sad, broken reality of the present when a robot stops working. Just like for any robotics domain, the key to success when developing software for robot manipulation is *simulation*. For planar mobile robots, we were championing simulation from an operational standpoint: simulated robot batteries can be "recharged" instantly, you don't have to chase down the hallway after them when debugging, you can simulate faster than reality to cover many kilometers of experiments very quickly, and so on.

For manipulation, this rationale is even more convincing, since robot manipulators are far more complex and expensive. They often have a relatively delicate end effector attached to the very end of the manipulator, which is of course the part of the manipulator that experiences the highest velocities and is most likely to crash into something.

So, like a broken record, we will repeat it again: the key to success in robot manipulation, as in all areas in robotics, is *simulation*. Throughout this book, we are using simulated robots as development targets. For this chapter, we will take advantage of the fact that simulation is free in order to program a stunningly beautiful state-of-the-art robot: the NASA/GM Robonaut 2. This is a fun robot to use in simulation, since one copy of the R2 is actually on the International Space Station (see Figure 11-3).

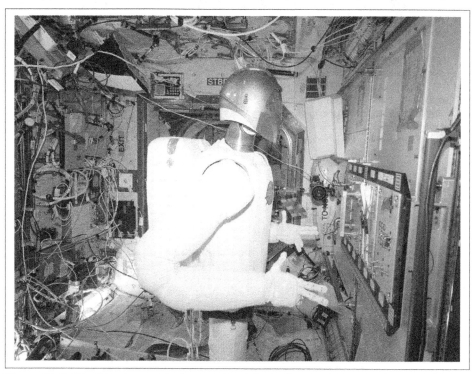

Figure 11-3. The R2 robot on the International Space Station (image credit: NASA)

As you'd expect for a machine rated for operation in space, the R2 is extraordinarily reliable and was designed for high performance and predictability. As a consequence, it is very expensive and is not the type of platform you'd want to use when carelessly experimenting with some new code you've hacked together. Fortunately, NASA has released a Gazebo model of an R2, which we can easily install. Then, we can instantiate R2 in Gazebo and aggressively prototype our software, risking none of the guilt associated with wrecking millions of dollars' worth of equipment!

Since the code we will write is generally robot-agnostic, everything we learn about controlling an R2 in Gazebo can be applied to other robots (it just looks cooler on an R2). So, let's get started.

Installing and Running a Simulated R2

The following commands will check out the latest version of the R2 simulation model for Gazebo and the R2 controllers, as well as installing some more ROS packages from the build farm:

```
user@hostname$ sudo apt-get install ros-indigo-ros-control \
  ros-indigo-gazebo-ros-control ros-indigo-joint-state-controller \
  ros-indigo-effort-controllers ros-indigo-joint-trajectory-controller \
  ros-indigo-moveit* ros-indigo-octomap* ros-indigo-object-recognition-*
user@hostname$ mkdir -p ~/chessbot/src
user@hostname$ cd ~/chessbot/src
user@hostname$ git clone -b indigo \
  https://bitbucket.org/nasa_ros_pkg/nasa_r2_simulator.git
user@hostname$ git clone -b indigo \
  https://bitbucket.org/nasa_ros_pkg/nasa_r2_common.git
user@hostname$ cd ..
user@hostname$ catkin_make
```

Now, we can load our newly built R2 simulation workspace and start up an R2 in Gazebo:

```
cd ~/chessbot
source devel/setup.bash
roslaunch r2_gazebo r2_gazebo.launch
```

This will launch Gazebo with a world file that includes an R2 and looks something like Figure 11-4.

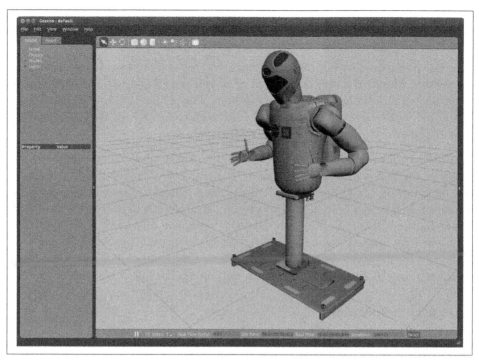

Figure 11-4. The starting configuration of the R2 simulation

Thanks to the wonders of robot simulation and the abstraction layers of ROS, we can now write software for the R2 that will run identically either on this simulation or on a real robot. To start, let's make the R2 wave its arms around randomly. To do this, we will use MoveIt, a comprehensive motion planning package that interacts nicely with ROS. Fortunately for us, MoveIt already includes all of the configuration details for the R2, such as the geometries of all its links, the joint positions and orientations, and so on. We can simply tell MoveIt where we want the end effectors to be positioned, and MoveIt will perform the necessary high-dimensional computational geometry to produce a collision-free path to the goal.

First, we need to run a `robot_state_publisher` node, which will use the geometric descriptions of the R2 and its joint state vector to continually calculate all of the coordinate frames of the robot (i.e., it computes forward kinematics). The standard ROS implementation of this operation is robot-neutral, so we can just start it up, and it will do the right thing for the R2:

```
user@hostname$ rosrun robot_state_publisher robot_state_publisher
```

Now, we have a console that has spawned the R2 simulator (`r2_gazebo`), a console that is running `robot_state_publisher`, and a graphical window showing the R2 simulation. We can now get a new terminal and start MoveIt, configured for the R2:

```
*cd* ~/chessbot
source devel/setup.bash
roslaunch r2_moveit_config move_group.launch
```

This will start a number of programs, topics, and services, and set a large number of parameters. MoveIt is a very complex piece of software, and a full explanation of its inner workings is beyond the scope of this book. For the purposes of this chapter, we can give MoveIt target positions for the R2 hands, and it will find and follow a smooth trajectory to get there.

The program shown in Example 11-1 will continually generate random poses for the hands of the Robonaut 2, so it will wave its arms around endlessly. Note, however, that the behavior is not purely random: the planner will seek to keep the elbows in the middle of their ranges of motion. This prevents the robot from nearing the singularities or collisions that can occur if the elbow gets jammed up against the torso or flies up toward the vertical. You'll also notice that the joint velocities smoothly ramp up and down during acceleration and deceleration of the arms. All of this is critical to producing smooth, reliable trajectories on real robots. The full source code follows.

Example 11-1. r2_mime.py

```
#!/usr/bin/env python
import sys, rospy, tf, moveit_commander, random
from geometry_msgs.msg import Pose, Point, Quaternion
from math import pi

orient = [Quaternion(*tf.transformations.quaternion_from_euler(pi, -pi/2, -pi/2)),
          Quaternion(*tf.transformations.quaternion_from_euler(pi, -pi/2, -pi/2))] ❶
pose = [Pose(Point( 0.5, -0.5, 1.3), orient[0]),
        Pose(Point(-0.5, -0.5, 1.3), orient[1])] ❷
moveit_commander.roscpp_initialize(sys.argv) ❸
rospy.init_node('r2_wave_arm',anonymous=True)
group = [moveit_commander.MoveGroupCommander("left_arm"),
         moveit_commander.MoveGroupCommander("right_arm")]
# now, wave arms around randomly
while not rospy.is_shutdown():
  pose[0].position.x =  0.5 + random.uniform(-0.1, 0.1)
  pose[1].position.x = -0.5 + random.uniform(-0.1, 0.1)
  for side in [0,1]:
    pose[side].position.z =  1.5 + random.uniform(-0.1, 0.1)
    group[side].set_pose_target(pose[side])
    group[side].go(True)

moveit_commander.roscpp_shutdown()
```

❶ The quaternion_from_euler() function converts orientations between the Euler-angle representation (roll/pitch/yaw), which is relatively intuitive, and the quaternion representation, which is used by most computational geometry packages because of its numerical stability but unfortunately is very difficult to intuitively understand.

❷ The orientations created by the previous lines are used to stuff the Pose messages.

❸ moveit_commander is the Python interface to the MoveIt motion planning system.

The robot moves! Hooray! That little program will choose random positions for the R2's palms that lie on a vertical plane just in front of the robot. Every second or so, it will choose a new point on that plane and then move the robot's palms to lie flat on the plane for each arm, as shown in Figure 11-5.

Figure 11-5. A simulated R2 mime

The benefits of MoveIt are clearly apparent in this simple little program. Notice how we didn't need to know anything about the joint limits, link lengths, acceleration/deceleration capabilities, or really anything about the R2? We simply told MoveIt where we wanted the hands to go, and it figured out everything else.

Moving R2 from the Command Line

Now, let's create a simple interface where we can type in arm poses and have the R2 nicely move its arms to those positions using MoveIt. Example 11-2 is just a refactoring of the previous code snippet, wrapping it up into something that will be a bit easier to reuse.

Example 11-2. r2_cli.py

```python
#!/usr/bin/env python
import sys, rospy, tf, moveit_commander, random
from geometry_msgs.msg import Pose, Point, Quaternion

class R2Wrapper:
  def __init__(self):
    self.group = {'left': moveit_commander.MoveGroupCommander("left_arm"),
                  'right': moveit_commander.MoveGroupCommander("right_arm")}
  def setPose(self, arm, x, y, z, phi, theta, psi):
    if arm != 'left' and arm != 'right':
      raise ValueError("unknown arm: '%s'" % arm)
    orient = \
      Quaternion(*tf.transformations.quaternion_from_euler(phi, theta, psi)) ❶
    pose = Pose(Point(x, y, z), orient)
    self.group[arm].set_pose_target(pose)
    self.group[arm].go(True)

if __name__ == '__main__':
  moveit_commander.roscpp_initialize(sys.argv)
  rospy.init_node('r2_cli',anonymous=True)
  argv = rospy.myargv(argv=sys.argv) # filter out any arguments used by ROS
  if len(argv) != 8:
    print "usage: r2_cli.py arm X Y Z phi theta psi"
    sys.exit(1)
  r2w = R2Wrapper()
  r2w.setPose(argv[1], *[float(num) for num in sys.argv[2:]])
  moveit_commander.roscpp_shutdown()
```

❶ The quaternion_from_euler() function does the trigonometry required to convert between the Euler-angle and quaternion representations of an orientation.

With this little wrapper program, we can type commands at the shell to move the arms around, like these few examples:

```
user@hostname$ ./r2_cli.py left   0.5 -0.5 1.3 3.14 -1.5 -1.57
user@hostname$ ./r2_cli.py right -0.4 -0.6 1.4 3.14 -1.5 -1.57
user@hostname$ ./r2_cli.py left   0.4 -0.4 1.2 3.14 -1.5 -1.57
```

Now, at first glance, it might seem like typing random six-dimensional coordinates at the command line isn't a particularly elegant user interface. It is, indeed, rather terrible. However, we can use this building block to create some command-line aliases, so that our shell becomes more useful for running the R2. We can put these aliases into a simple text file that the command shell (bash) can read, named *r2.bash*, as shown in Example 11-3.

Example 11-3. r2.bash

```bash
#!/bin/bash
alias r2lhome="./r2_cli.py left   0.5 -0.5 1  1.57 0 -1.57"
alias r2rhome="./r2_cli.py right -0.5 -0.5 1 -1.57 0 -1.57"
alias r2home="r2lhome;r2rhome"
```

To load these aliases into the current shell, type `source ./r2.bash` at the command line. You can then simply type `r2home`, and the robot will plan a safe path to its home position and smoothly execute it.

For most robots, there are typically a few postures that are useful for many tasks, or even just for daily operation and maintenance. A small command-line program and a few bash aliases like this can make life much more convenient.

Moving R2 Around a Chessboard

The previous `R2Wrapper` class accepted six-dimensional coordinates for its pose targets: the three-dimensional Cartesian (x, y, z) coordinates, and a description of the desired rotation of the hand using Euler angles (roll, pitch, and yaw). For example, we could ask the R2 robot to position its hand 30 centimeters above, 20 centimeters to the right, and 10 centimeters in front of its torso, with its palm facing outward (0 degrees roll, 90 degrees pitch, 0 degrees yaw), to prepare for a *high-five* maneuver. Specifying commands in six dimensions is a useful way to express the desired manipulator behavior of a robot when we must be as general-purpose as possible. It's fun for the first few times to type 6D coordinates at the command line, but it gets old quickly. Often, it is much more convenient to describe the robot's postures in terms of the task the robot is supposed to be doing.

As an example of this type of task, we will build a Chess-bot. It will thus be convenient to describe the positions of the arms in chessboard coordinates. The standard way of describing a chessboard is to use a letter for a row (also known as a "rank" in chess) and a number for a column (called a "file" in chess)—for example, g2, a3, f1, a8, and so on.

Example 11-4 builds upon our previous example, showing one way to accept command-line instructions for commanding the R2's left arm to move to the designated chessboard rank and file, and also specifying the desired height above the chessboard.

Example 11-4. r2_chessboard_cli.py

```python
#!/usr/bin/env python
import sys, rospy, tf, moveit_commander, random
from geometry_msgs.msg import Pose, Point, Quaternion

class R2ChessboardWrapper:
  def __init__(self):
    self.left_arm = moveit_commander.MoveGroupCommander("left_arm")

  def setPose(self, x, y, z, phi, theta, psi):
    orient = \
      Quaternion(*tf.transformations.quaternion_from_euler(phi, theta, psi))
    pose = Pose(Point(x, y, z), orient)
    self.left_arm.set_pose_target(pose)
    self.left_arm.go(True)

  def setSquare(self, square, height_above_board):
    if len(square) != 2 or not square[1].isdigit():
      raise ValueError(
        "expected a chess rank and file like 'b3' but found %s instead" %
        square)
    rank_y = -0.3 - 0.05 * (ord(square[0]) - ord('a'))
    file_x =  0.5 - 0.05 * int(square[1])
    z = float(height_above_board) + 1.0
    self.setPose(file_x, rank_y, z, 3.14, 0.3, -1.57)

if __name__ == '__main__':
  moveit_commander.roscpp_initialize(sys.argv)
  rospy.init_node('r2_chessboard_cli')
  argv = rospy.myargv(argv=sys.argv) # filter out any arguments used by ROS
  if len(argv) != 3:
    print "usage: r2_chessboard.py square height"
    sys.exit(1)
  r2w = R2ChessboardWrapper()
  r2w.setSquare(*argv[1:])
  moveit_commander.roscpp_shutdown()
```

With this program, we can now command the R2 to move its arm around in chess coordinates, like this:

```
user@hostname$ ./r2_chessboard_cli.py a2 0.04
```

This commands the arm to a pose that is 4 cm above square a2. Progress!

We must now stop and come to terms with something: this approach of hardcoding a bunch of constants into the control code is exceedingly brittle. How did we know that the chessboard is 1 meter above the floor and 30 cm in front of the R2? What if our robot were in a boisterous chess club where the chessboard could be bumped and moved a few centimeters? The robot would have no idea. When it tried to move a piece, it would miss, which would be embarrassing. It would lose the chess match.

And yet, many successful robots are programmed precisely like this. Most "classical" industrial robots, for example, operate conceptually in the same manner as the previous script: various important poses are "taught" to the robot by skilled operators using a "teach pendant" that allows them to fly the robot arm to various key positions and record them. So long as the environment and task never change, as is the case in many industrial applications, this works perfectly well. Just don't try it in a rowdy chess club!

In later chapters in this book, we will introduce various perception algorithms and libraries that allow robots to respond to changes in their environment or task. But for the remainder of this chapter, we will assume that the world is perfectly known ahead of time.

Operating the Hand

Now that we can move the R2's palm above the chess squares, we need to be able to open and close the fingers. We will use MoveIt again, but this time we will just be sending the target joint vectors to MoveIt. For our Chess-bot, we will only need two states for the hand: a "pinch" grasp of some sort, and a pose that we will use just before pinching, which we'll call "pre-pinch." We can hardcode those postures and send them to MoveIt, which will then ensure that acceleration/deceleration limits are observed and that self-collisions do not occur—since we don't want to have the fingers crash into each other. Although there are more sophisticated approaches, this strategy of hardcoding a few useful postures is common in robotics, especially in domains where the environment is perfectly known ahead of time. We will take this approach in Example 11-5, where two predefined joint vectors will be used to create "open" and "closed" hand positions to grasp the chess pieces.

Example 11-5. r2_hand.py

```python
#!/usr/bin/env python
import sys, rospy, tf, moveit_commander, random
from geometry_msgs.msg import Pose, Point, Quaternion

class R2Hand:
  def __init__(self):
    self.left_hand = moveit_commander.MoveGroupCommander("left_hand")

  def setGrasp(self, state):
    if state == "pre-pinch":
      vec = [ 0.3, 0, 1.57, 0,  # index
              -0.1, 0, 1.57, 0, # middle
              0, 0, 0,          # ring
              0, 0, 0,          # pinkie
              0, 1.1, 0, 0]     # thumb
    elif state == "pinch":
      vec = [ -0.1, 0, 1.57, 0,
              0, 0, 1.57, 0,
              0, 0, 0,
              0, 0, 0,
              0, 1.1, 0, 0]
    elif state == "open":
      vec = [0] * 18
    else:
      raise ValueError("unknown hand state: %s" % state)
    self.left_hand.set_joint_value_target(vec)
    self.left_hand.go(True)

if __name__ == '__main__':
  moveit_commander.roscpp_initialize(sys.argv)
  rospy.init_node('r2_hand')
  argv = rospy.myargv(argv=sys.argv) # filter out any arguments used by ROS
  if len(argv) != 2:
    print "usage: r2_hand.py STATE"
    sys.exit(1)
  r2w = R2Hand()
  r2w.setGrasp(argv[1])
```

The program in Example 11-5 will let us type on the command line to command three hand postures to R2: open, pre-pinch, and pinch. Because of a joint limit on the thumb travel, we will be doing a pinch grasp between the sides of the index and middle fingers. It looks a little unusual, but it works! Using r2_hand.py, we can produce the two postures shown in Figure 11-6 and Example 11-7:

```
user@hostname$ ./r2_hand.py pre-pinch
user@hostname$ ./r2_hand.py pinch
```

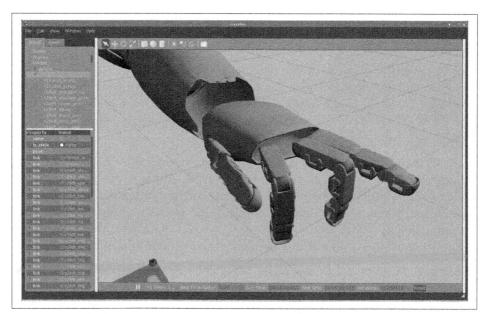

Figure 11-6. The pre-pinch hand posture

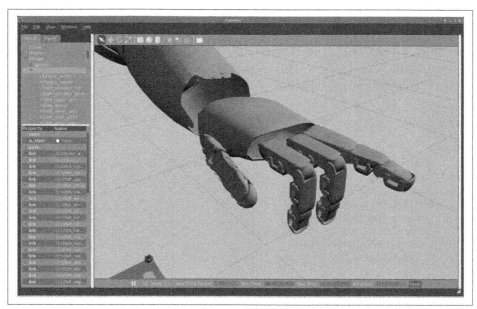

Figure 11-7. The pinch hand posture

Now, it's time to make a chessboard!

Modeling a Chessboard

A large part of the effort in robot simulation is spent in modeling the environment of interest. At first, this can seem like time not particularly well spent. After all, we're trying to control a robot, not stare at a computer! But developing the model quickly pays huge dividends: unlike in the real world, you can click a button and instantly reset the world to the *exact* same configuration. This is incredibly useful. But, back to chess!

There are many ways to create simulation models and worlds in ROS, but in this case, we are using the Robonaut 2 world released by NASA. Although we could copy their world and launch files and modify them, it is easier to instantiate the chessboard and pieces from Python by spawning the models inside an existing running simulation. This approach also allows us to reset the game board as necessary, without having to restart the simulation. This will be convenient as we are tuning the motion sequences.

The first step is to model a chess piece. This can be an arbitrarily complex process, depending on the desired level of fidelity. Right now, we want to keep it as simple as possible, so we are modeling chess pieces just as identical blocks. Models in Gazebo can be represented in several XML formats, but the currently recommended format for new models is the Simulation Description Format (SDF). Our rectangular chess-piece model is represented in the SDF XML shown in Example 11-6. This listing is rather long and can appear tedious, but we wanted to provide a full example that shows how to model a simple object in Gazebo because when important SDF tags are omitted (for example, `inertia`, or `collision`, or `contact`), the simulation can behave in confusing or counterintuitive ways.

Example 11-6. chess_piece.sdf

```
<?xml version='1.0'?>
<sdf version ='1.4'>
  <model name ='piece'>
    <link name ='link'>
      <inertial>
        <mass>0.001</mass>
        <inertia>
          <ixx>0.0000001667</ixx>
          <ixy>0</ixy>
          <ixz>0</ixz>
          <iyy>0.0000000667</iyy>
          <iyz>0</iyz>
          <izz>0.0000001667</izz>
        </inertia>
      </inertial>
      <collision name="collision">
        <geometry>
          <box><size>0.02 0.02 0.04</size></box>
```

```
        </geometry>
        <surface>
          <friction>
            <ode>
              <mu>0.4</mu>
              <mu2>0.4</mu2>
            </ode>
          </friction>
          <contact>
            <ode>
              <max_vel>0.1</max_vel>
              <min_depth>0.0001</min_depth>
            </ode>
          </contact>
        </surface>
      </collision>
      <visual name="visual">
        <geometry>
          <box><size>0.02 0.02 0.04</size></box>
        </geometry>
      </visual>
    </link>
  </model>
</sdf>
```

We will also represent the chessboard as a very wide, flat box in SDF, as shown in Example 11-7. This SDF listing is simpler, because the chessboard will be treated as an immovable object in the simulation and thus does not need its inertial properties to be defined.

Example 11-7. chess_board.sdf

```
<?xml version='1.0'?>
<sdf version ='1.4'>
  <model name ='box'>
    <static>true</static>
    <link name ='link'>
      <collision name="collision">
        <geometry>
          <box><size>0.5 0.5 0.02</size></box>
        </geometry>
        <surface>
          <friction>
            <ode>
              <mu>0.1</mu>
              <mu2>0.1</mu2>
            </ode>
          </friction>
          <contact>
            <ode>
              <max_vel>0.1</max_vel>
```

```
        <min_depth>0.001</min_depth>
      </ode>
    </contact>
  </surface>
</collision>
<visual name="visual">
  <geometry>
    <box><size>0.5 0.5 0.02</size></box>
  </geometry>
</visual>
        </link>
      </model>
    </sdf>
```

Now, we need a script that can spawn and place these models in a running simulation, since we will be knocking over a lot of chess pieces. As before, there are many
ways to do this. In this case, we'll demonstrate how to spawn models in Python. Gazebo provides ROS services for deleting and spawning models (among other tasks),
which we will use to set up the board. Because the board may already exist in the simulation, Example 11-8 first tries to delete the pieces before spawning new ones.

Example 11-8. spawn_chessboard.py

```python
#!/usr/bin/env python
import sys, rospy, tf
from gazebo_msgs.srv import *
from geometry_msgs.msg import *
from copy import deepcopy

if __name__ == '__main__':
  rospy.init_node("spawn_chessboard")
  rospy.wait_for_service("gazebo/delete_model")
  rospy.wait_for_service("gazebo/spawn_sdf_model")
  delete_model = rospy.ServiceProxy("gazebo/delete_model", DeleteModel)
  delete_model("chessboard")
  s = rospy.ServiceProxy("gazebo/spawn_sdf_model", SpawnModel)
  orient = Quaternion(*tf.transformations.quaternion_from_euler(0, 0, 0))
  board_pose = Pose(Point(0.25,1.39,0.90), orient)
  unit = 0.05
  with open("chessboard.sdf", "r") as f:
    board_xml = f.read()
  with open("chess_piece.sdf", "r") as f:
    piece_xml = f.read()

  print s("chessboard", board_xml, "", board_pose, "world")

  for row in [0,1,6,7]:
    for col in xrange(0,8):
      piece_name = "piece_%d_%d" % (row, col)
      delete_model(piece_name)
```

```
pose = deepcopy(board_pose)
pose.position.x = board_pose.position.x - 3.5 * unit + col * unit
pose.position.y = board_pose.position.y - 3.5 * unit + row * unit
pose.position.z += 0.02
s(piece_name, piece_xml, "", pose, "world")
```

That's it! Now, whenever we want to reset the chessboard in our running R2 simulation, we can just run the *spawn_chessboard.py* script. The resulting setup looks like Figure 11-8.

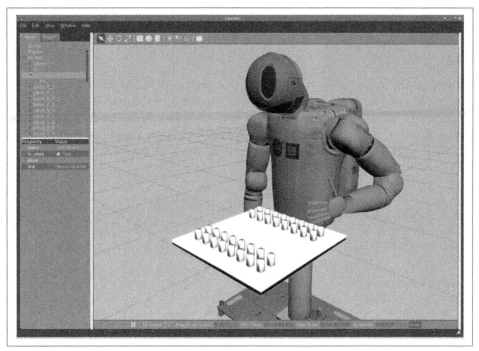

Figure 11-8. A Gazebo screenshot of the R2 chess simulation

Playing Back a Famous Chess Game

Now we will put all the elements of this chapter together. We have written scripts that can smoothly navigate the arm to the (predefined) locations of chess squares, open and close the fingers, and set up the chessboard. Now, we can put all of this together to "play back" chess game descriptions. But where do we find the game logs? Fortunately, that is not a problem with chess. It is one of the most well-documented games in existence. There are several textfile formats for chess games, including one called Portable Game Notation (PGN). Fortunately, there is already an open source Python parser for PGN files. We can install it like so:

```
sudo apt-get install python-pip
sudo pip install pgnparser
```

Your authors are not great chess players. In fact, we are quite terrible. We played a quick game against the computer and were soundly defeated. For the benefit of science, we recorded our inglorious defeat to PGN format and used `pgn-extract` to convert it to standard chess long algebraic notation. Our defeat is thus completely described in the following descriptions of chess moves, each one taking us closer to checkmate:

> 1. e2e4 c7c5 2. d2d4 c5d4 3. d1d4 b8c6 4. c2c4 c6d4 5. b1c3 d4c2+ 6. e1d1 c2a1 7. a2a4 e7e5 8. c1g5 d8g5 9. c3d5 g5d8 10. f2f4 e5f4 11. g1f3 g8f6 12. d5f6+ d8f6 13. f1d3 f6b2 14. h1e1 b2g2 15. e1e2 g2f3 16. d1c1 f3d3 17. e2e1 d3c2# 0-1

We can use the `pgnparser` library to parse that block of text into something easier to feed to our command-line parser, written in the previous section. The `pgn.loads()` function will read the game description into a Python list of well-defined move strings. We then parse these strings in `playGame()` to create simple scripted motions to pick up pieces and move them to their landing places, as shown in Example 11-9.

Example 11-9. r2_chess_pgn.py

```python
#!/usr/bin/env python
import sys, rospy, tf, moveit_commander, random
from geometry_msgs.msg import Pose, Point, Quaternion
import pgn

class R2ChessboardPGN:
  def __init__(self):
    self.left_arm = moveit_commander.MoveGroupCommander("left_arm")
    self.left_hand = moveit_commander.MoveGroupCommander("left_hand")

  def setGrasp(self, state):
    if state == "pre-pinch":
      vec = [ 0.3, 0, 1.57, 0,  # index
              -0.1, 0, 1.57, 0, # middle
              0, 0, 0,          # ring
              0, 0, 0,          # pinkie
              0, 1.1, 0, 0]     # thumb
    elif state == "pinch":
      vec = [ 0, 0, 1.57, 0,
              0, 0, 1.57, 0,
              0, 0, 0,
              0, 0, 0,
              0, 1.1, 0, 0]
    elif state == "open":
      vec = [0] * 18
    else:
      raise ValueError("unknown hand state: %s" % state)
```

```
    self.left_hand.set_joint_value_target(vec)
    self.left_hand.go(True)

  def setPose(self, x, y, z, phi, theta, psi):
    orient = \
      Quaternion(*tf.transformations.quaternion_from_euler(phi, theta, psi))
    pose = Pose(Point(x, y, z), orient)
    self.left_arm.set_pose_target(pose)
    self.left_arm.go(True)

  def setSquare(self, square, height_above_board):
    if len(square) != 2 or not square[1].isdigit():
      raise ValueError(
        "expected a chess rank and file like 'b3' but found %s instead" %
        square)
    print "going to %s" % square
    rank_y = -0.24 - 0.05 * int(square[1])
    file_x =  0.5 - 0.05 * (ord(square[0]) - ord('a'))
    z = float(height_above_board) + 1.0
    self.setPose(file_x, rank_y, z, 3.14, 0.3, -1.57)

  def playGame(self, pgn_filename):
    game = pgn.loads(open(pgn_filename).read())[0]
    self.setGrasp("pre-pinch")
    self.setSquare("a1", 0.15)
    for move in game.moves:
      self.setSquare(move[0:2], 0.10)
      self.setSquare(move[0:2], 0.015)
      self.setGrasp("pinch")
      self.setSquare(move[0:2], 0.10)
      self.setSquare(move[2:4], 0.10)
      self.setSquare(move[2:4], 0.015)
      self.setGrasp("pre-pinch")
      self.setSquare(move[2:4], 0.10)

if __name__ == '__main__':
  moveit_commander.roscpp_initialize(sys.argv)
  rospy.init_node('r2_chess_pgn',anonymous=True)
  argv = rospy.myargv(argv=sys.argv) # filter out any arguments used by ROS
  if len(argv) != 2:
    print "usage: r2_chess_pgn.py PGNFILE"
    sys.exit(1)
  print "playing %s" % argv[1]
  r2pgn = R2ChessboardPGN()
  r2pgn.playGame(argv[1])
  moveit_commander.roscpp_shutdown()
```

That's it! We can now play back any famous (or not so famous) chess game stored in PGN format on our simulated R2, as seen in Figure 11-9. However, you will soon notice that eventually some pieces get knocked over (Figure 11-10) and that we have intentionally left out some crucial components of a world-class Chess-bot. For example, we have not coded up what should happen when R2 captures a piece. The script will try to smash the captured piece with the capturing piece, so one of them will go flying across the simulator. We leave these details as an exercise to the motivated reader!

Summary

Of course, this chapter was not just about building Chess-bots, awesome though they are. It was intended to demonstrate how we can use MoveIt to quickly build applications where we pick and place items between predefined locations. Pick-and-place tasks have enormous economic impact in the world of industrial robotics. At their core, these tasks are not that different from those performed by a Chess-bot!

Thus far, we have primarily been building robotic systems without sensory input. Although a surprisingly large (and valuable) number of tasks can be done without sensor processing, many exciting new robotics applications rely on extensive perceptual systems. In the next chapter, we will start adding sensors to our simulated robots.

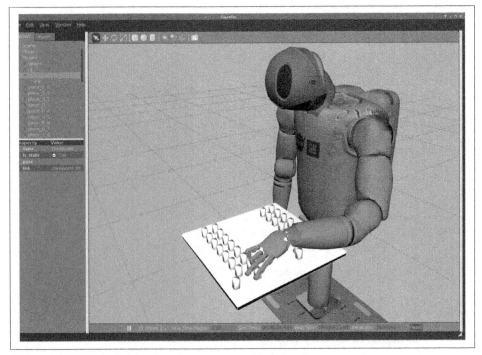

Figure 11-9. R2 playing back a chess game

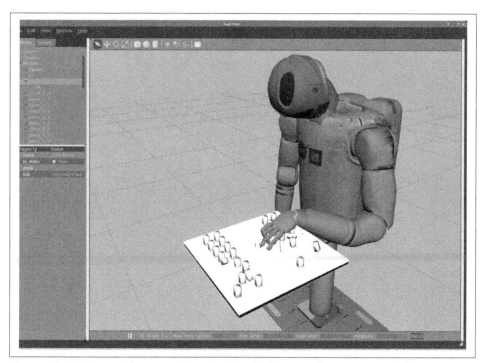

Figure 11-10. Eventually, some pieces get knocked over—it happens to all of us!

## PART III

Perception and Behavior

## CHAPTER 12

Follow-bot

The previous several chapters were mostly concerned with getting robots to move around: either moving the robot base for locomotion or moving a robot arm for manipulation. Most of the systems we've built thus far would be considered *open-loop* systems, meaning that they have no feedback loop. That is, these systems do not use sensor data to correct for errors that accumulate over time. In this chapter, we will start working with sensors to create *closed-loop* systems that compute errors and feed them back into the control system, with the goal of reducing errors of various sorts.

Let's start by creating a robot that can follow lines on the ground using a camera. We will do this using OpenCV, a popular open source computer vision library. To build this system, we will need to do the following steps:

- Acquire images from a camera and pass them to OpenCV.
- Filter the images to identify the center of the line we are to follow.
- Steer the robot so that the center of the robot stays on the center of the line.

This will be a closed-loop system: the robot will sense the steering error as it drifts off the line and then steer back toward the center of the line. As we have always been doing in this book, we will develop this entire application in simulation. First, we will show how to subscribe to images in ROS.

Acquiring Images

Images in ROS are sent around the system using the sensor_msgs/Image message type. To have images stream into our nodes, we need to subscribe to a topic where they are being published. Each robot will have its own method for doing this, and names may vary. We will explore how to find the topic names using a Turtlebot simulation. To get started, start three terminals: one for `roscore`, one for the Turtle-Bot simulation in Gazebo, and one for interactive commands.

Start `roscore` in the first terminal:

```
user@hostname$ roscore
```

In the second terminal, start a Turtlebot simulation:

```
user@hostname$ roslaunch turtlebot_gazebo turtlebot_world.launch
```

Now, in the third terminal, we'll run some interactive shell commands. If this is our first time using this particular robot, we may not know what topics will contain the robot's camera data. So, let's sniff around a bit:

```
user@hostname$ rostopic list
```

This prints out a few dozen topics, some of which sound image-related:

```
/camera/depth/camera_info
/camera/depth/image_raw
/camera/depth/points
/camera/parameter_descriptions
/camera/parameter_updates
/camera/rgb/camera_info
/camera/rgb/image_raw
/camera/rgb/image_raw/compressed
/camera/rgb/image_raw/compressed/parameter_descriptions
/camera/rgb/image_raw/compressed/parameter_updates
/camera/rgb/image_raw/compressedDepth
/camera/rgb/image_raw/compressedDepth/parameter_descriptions
/camera/rgb/image_raw/compressedDepth/parameter_updates
/camera/rgb/image_raw/theora
/camera/rgb/image_raw/theora/parameter_descriptions
/camera/rgb/image_raw/theora/parameter_updates
```

This is a standard ROS interface for a modern depth camera like the Microsoft Kinect or Asus Xtion Pro. The first three topics start with `camera/depth` and, indeed, they deal with the calibration data and depth-sensor data. We'll get to the depth data later in this chapter, but first, let's deal with the visual images. The visual images streaming from the Turtlebot's camera appear on the `camera/rgb/image_raw` topic. The controller we will write is intended to run directly on the Turtlebot, so we should subscribe directly to the `image_raw` topic. If we were operating over a bandwidth-limited connection, such as a WiFi link, we might want to subscribe to the `image_raw/compressed` topic, which will run each frame through an image-compression library before sending it over the wire. The `theora` topic applies even more compression by creating a compressed video stream, rather than compressing the images one at a time. In typical camera streams, this results in considerable network bandwidth savings, at the expense of compression artifacts, potentially increased processor usage, and latency. In general, compressed video streams make sense when the goal is to support human teleoperators; however, whenever possible, uncompressed images work best for computer vision algorithms.

Now that we know that the image data is available on the camera/rgb/image_raw topic, we can write a minimal rospy node that will subscribe to this data, as shown in Example 12-1.

Example 12-1. follower.py

```python
#!/usr/bin/env python
import rospy
from sensor_msgs.msg import Image

def image_callback(msg):
  pass

rospy.init_node('follower')
image_sub = rospy.Subscriber('camera/rgb/image_raw', Image, image_callback)
rospy.spin()
```

This program is the minimal code required to subscribe to image messages. But it doesn't really do anything. The image callback doesn't do anything at all:

```python
def image_callback(msg):
    pass
```

on the camera/rgb/image_raw topic—however—the program does at least subscribe to messages. To verify this, first let's make *follower.py* an executable:

```
user@hostname$ chmod +x follower.py
```

And run it:

```
user@hostname$ ./follower.py
```

> Many of the examples in the book change the permissions of a Python source file and then run it as an executable on the command line. This is simply a matter of personal preference. It is equally valid to explicitly invoke the Python interpreter and pass the Python script as an argument:
>
> ```
> user@hostname$ python follower.py
> ```

The program will not produce any output. So, how can we know if it really subscribed to the image stream? Let's leave follower.py running, start another terminal, and interrogate the system:

```
user@hostname$ rosnode list
```

This will print a list of all currently running nodes. All but one of them are started by the Turtlebot simulation launch file:

```
/bumper2pointcloud
/cmd_vel_mux
/depthimage_to_laserscan
/follower
/gazebo
/laserscan_nodelet_manager
/mobile_base_nodelet_manager
/robot_state_publisher
/rosout
```

We can see that our `follower` node is indeed on the list of running nodes. Now, we can ask `roscore` to give us some details about its connections by typing the following:

```
user@hostname$ rosnode info follower
```

This prints lots of interesting output:

```
Node [/follower]
Publications:
 * /rosout [rosgraph_msgs/Log]

Subscriptions:
 * /camera/rgb/image_raw [sensor_msgs/Image]
 * /clock [rosgraph_msgs/Clock]

Services:
 * /follower/set_logger_level
 * /follower/get_loggers


contacting node http://qbox-home:59300/ ...
Pid: 5896
Connections:
 * topic: /rosout
    * to: /rosout
    * direction: outbound
    * transport: TCPROS
 * topic: /clock
    * to: /gazebo (http://qbox-home:37981/)
    * direction: inbound
    * transport: TCPROS
 * topic: /camera/rgb/image_raw
    * to: /gazebo (http://qbox-home:37981/)
    * direction: inbound
    * transport: TCPROS
```

The first block of that output lists the publications, subscriptions, and services that the node instantiated. Most were autogenerated by `rospy`, but we can see the `camera/rgb/image_raw` subscription that was part of the minimal program of

Example 12-1. The second section is often more interesting. To produce that section, the rosnode command-line program contacted the follower.py node and received a list of its current connections. The last element in that list shows that the /camera/rgb/image_raw subscription is indeed receiving inbound messages from the /gazebo node. Often, it is useful to understand how quickly messages are arriving. Fortunately, a simple shell command can estimate this for us:

```
user@hostname$ rostopic hz /camera/rgb/image_raw
```

The rostopic hz command will run forever; press Ctrl-C to make it stop. A few seconds of that command will print the output similar to the following:

```
subscribed to [/camera/rgb/image_raw]
average rate: 19.780
    min: 0.040s max: 0.060s std dev: 0.00524s window: 19
average rate: 19.895
    min: 0.040s max: 0.060s std dev: 0.00428s window: 39
average rate: 20.000
    min: 0.040s max: 0.060s std dev: 0.00487s window: 60
average rate: 20.000
    min: 0.040s max: 0.060s std dev: 0.00531s window: 79
average rate: 19.959
    min: 0.040s max: 0.060s std dev: 0.00544s window: 99
average rate: 20.000
    min: 0.040s max: 0.060s std dev: 0.00557s window: 104
```

From this output, we can gather that the camera/rgb/image_raw messages are arriving at 20 frames per second. Good!

Now that we know that the program in Example 12-1 is indeed receiving images, we need to do something with them! There are many different ways to proceed, but one of the most popular is to pass the images to the OpenCV library. OpenCV contains efficient, well-tested implementations of many popular computer vision algorithms. To pass data between the ROS and OpenCV image formats, we can use the cv_bridge package, which contains functions to convert between ROS sensor_msgs/Image messages and the objects used by OpenCV.

Example 12-2 instantiates a CvBridge object and uses it to convert the incoming sensor_msgs/Image stream to OpenCV messages and display them on the screen using the OpenCV imshow() function.

Example 12-2. follower_opencv.py

```
#!/usr/bin/env python
import rospy
from sensor_msgs.msg import Image
import cv2, cv_bridge

class Follower:
```

```
def __init__(self):
    self.bridge = cv_bridge.CvBridge()
    cv2.namedWindow("window", 1)
    self.image_sub = rospy.Subscriber('camera/rgb/image_raw',
                                       Image, self.image_callback)
def image_callback(self, msg):
    image = self.bridge.imgmsg_to_cv2(msg,desired_encoding='bgr8')
    cv2.imshow("window", image)
    cv2.waitKey(3)

rospy.init_node('follower')
follower = Follower()
rospy.spin()
```

As an example, the Turtlebot was moved and rotated within the default simulation world so that it was oriented facing a dumpster, as shown in Figure 12-1.

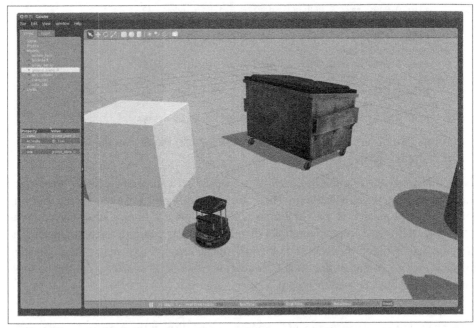

Figure 12-1. A Gazebo perspective of a Turtlebot facing a dumpster

Meanwhile, Gazebo is dutifully generating simulated camera images and streaming them to our program, which is using the OpenCV imshow() and waitKey() functions to render them to a GUI window (see Figure 12-2).

Figure 12-2. A dumpster, from the TurtleBot's perspective

That's it! We are now streaming simulated camera images through Gazebo, ROS, and OpenCV!

Although it's fun to look at dumpsters, let's look at something else. Let's load a Gazebo world with a nice bright line in it:

```
user@hostname$ roslaunch followbot course.launch
```

That Gazebo world file will start a Turtlebot on a yellow line that we want to follow, as shown in Figure 12-3. Why would we want to follow a line? Because lines are often used to mark routes, whether inside a controlled environment like a warehouse or a factory, or on roadways. Although each country has a particular scheme of colors and stripe patterns, broadly speaking, being able to detect and follow lines is one of the (many) skills required for autonomous driving.

In the next section, we will manipulate the images coming from the Turtlebot's camera to detect the center of the line in the camera frames.

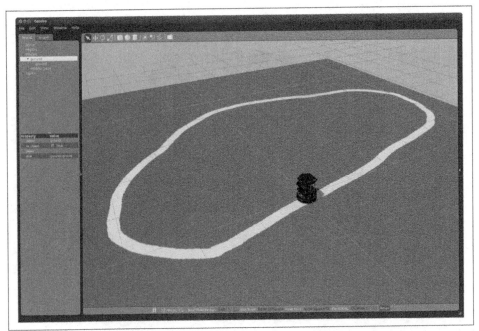

Figure 12-3. A Gazebo screenshot showing a Turtlebot on the course we want to follow

Detecting the Line

In this section, we will use OpenCV in Python to process the images coming through ROS from a simulated Turtlebot in the world shown in Figure 12-3. The goal is to detect the location of the target line in the Turtlebot's camera and follow it around the course. A typical image from the Turtlebot's camera is shown in Figure 12-4.

There are many strategies that can be used to detect and follow lines in various situations. Many PhD dissertations have been granted for this topic, which becomes arbitrarily complex when considering the variability and noise associated with, for example, roadway striping. Fortunately, in our case we are just going to consider an optimally painted, optimally illuminated bright yellow line. Our strategy will be to filter a block of rows of the image by color and drive the robot toward the center of the pixels that pass the color filter. The first step, then, is to filter the image by color. The purpose of this exercise is not just to show how to follow lines, but to demonstrate how to subscribe to an image stream in ROS and push it though the OpenCV library in Python. This general pipeline could then be used in other application problems by tapping into the wide variety of excellent computer vision algorithms implemented in OpenCV.

Figure 12-4. A typical view from the Turtlebot's camera when following a line

The task at hand is to find the yellow line in the Turtlebot's image stream. The most obvious approach is to find the red, green, blue (RGB) value of a yellow image pixel and filter for nearby RGB values. Unfortunately, filtering on RGB values turns out to be a surprisingly poor way to find a particular color in an image, since the raw RGB values are a function of the overall brightness as well as the color of the object. Slightly different lighting conditions would result in the filter failing to perform as intended. Instead, a better technique for filtering by color is to transform RGB images into hue, saturation, value (HSV) images. The HSV image separates the RGB components into hue (color), saturation (color intensity), and value (brightness). Once the image is in this form, we can then apply a threshold for hues near yellow to obtain a *binary image* in which pixels are either true (meaning they pass the filter) or false (they do not pass the filter). The following code snippets and examples images will illustrate this process.

In Example 12-3, we implement this using OpenCV, which makes this task quite easy in Python.

Example 12-3. follower_color_filter.py

```python
#!/usr/bin/env python
import rospy, cv2, cv_bridge, numpy
from sensor_msgs.msg import Image

class Follower:
  def __init__(self):
    self.bridge = cv_bridge.CvBridge()
    cv2.namedWindow("window", 1)
    self.image_sub = rospy.Subscriber('camera/rgb/image_raw',
                                      Image, self.image_callback)
  def image_callback(self, msg):
    image = self.bridge.imgmsg_to_cv2(msg)
    hsv = cv2.cvtColor(image, cv2.COLOR_BGR2HSV)
    lower_yellow = numpy.array([ 50,  50, 170])
    upper_yellow = numpy.array([255, 255, 190])
    mask = cv2.inRange(hsv, lower_yellow, upper_yellow)
    masked = cv2.bitwise_and(image, image, mask=mask)
    cv2.imshow("window", mask )
    cv2.waitKey(3)

rospy.init_node('follower')
follower = Follower()
rospy.spin()
```

As before, the CvBridge module converts ROS sensor_msgs/Image messages into the OpenCV image format:

```python
image = self.bridge.imgmsg_to_cv2(msg)
```

We can then pass the OpenCV image to the cvtColor() function to convert between the RGB representation and its equivalent representation in the HSV space:

```python
hsv = cv2.cvtColor(image, cv2.COLOR_BGR2HSV)
```

The cvtColor() function will produce the HSV image shown in Figure 12-5 when presented with the RGB image shown previously in Figure 12-4.

Then, in the HSV space, we can create lower and upper bounds for the desired hues using numpy and then pass those bounds to OpenCV's inRange() function to produce a binary image:

```python
lower_yellow = numpy.array([ 50,  50, 170])
upper_yellow = numpy.array([255, 255, 190])
mask = cv2.inRange(hsv, lower_yellow, upper_yellow)
```

The resulting binary image is shown in Figure 12-6.

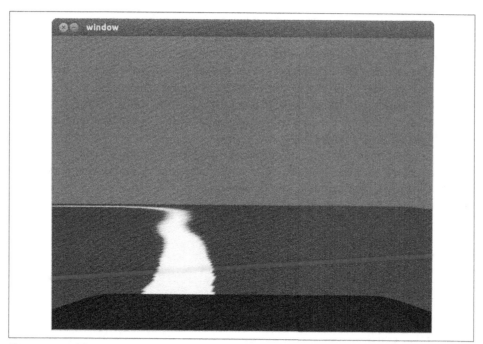

Figure 12-5. The HSV representation of a Turtlebot camera image when following a line

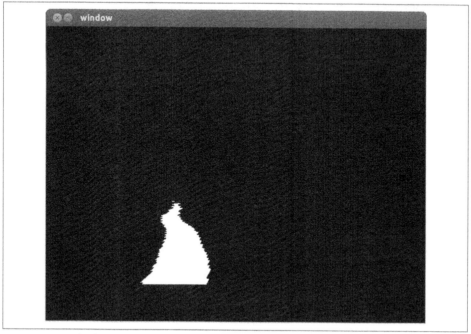

Figure 12-6. The binary image obtained by a hue filter on the HSV image

Obtaining a binary image of the line is a key first step in the image-processing pipe-line. However, our goal is to follow the line, not just to take interesting pictures of it! To follow the line, we will use a simple strategy: we will only look at a 20-row portion of the image, starting three-quarters of the way down the image. The rationale behind this approach is that, from a controls perspective, we are really only concerned with the portion of the line that is immediately in front of the robot. With this strategy, what happens to the line five meters in front of the robot is irrelevant; our controller will only be concerned with what is in the field of view of the camera approximately one meter in front of the robot. To debug our implementation, we will first write a program, shown in Example 12-4, that implements this image processing strategy and draws a dot where it thinks the center of the line is within the portion of the image corresponding to roughly one meter in front of the robot.

Example 12-4. follower_line_finder.py

```python
#!/usr/bin/env python
import rospy, cv2, cv_bridge, numpy
from sensor_msgs.msg import Image

class Follower:
  def __init__(self):
    self.bridge = cv_bridge.CvBridge()
    cv2.namedWindow("window", 1)
    self.image_sub = rospy.Subscriber('camera/rgb/image_raw',
                                      Image, self.image_callback)
    self.twist = Twist()
  def image_callback(self, msg):
    image = self.bridge.imgmsg_to_cv2(msg,desired_encoding='bgr8')
    hsv = cv2.cvtColor(image, cv2.COLOR_BGR2HSV)
    lower_yellow = numpy.array([ 10,  10,  10])
    upper_yellow = numpy.array([255, 255, 250])
    mask = cv2.inRange(hsv, lower_yellow, upper_yellow)

    h, w, d = image.shape
    search_top = 3*h/4
    search_bot = search_top + 20
    mask[0:search_top, 0:w] = 0
    mask[search_bot:h, 0:w] = 0
    M = cv2.moments(mask)
    if M['m00'] > 0:
      cx = int(M['m10']/M['m00'])
      cy = int(M['m01']/M['m00'])
      cv2.circle(image, (cx, cy), 20, (0,0,255), -1)

    cv2.imshow("window", image)
    cv2.waitKey(3)

rospy.init_node('follower')
```

```
follower = Follower()
rospy.spin()
```

To restrict our search to the 20-row portion of the image corresponding to the one-meter distance in front of the Turtlebot, we will use the OpenCV and numpy libraries to zero out (i.e., erase any filter hits of) pixels outside the desired region. This code snippet uses the Python *slice notation* to express pixel regions in a compact syntax:

```
h, w, d = image.shape
search_top = 3*h/4
search_bot = search_top + 20
mask[0:search_top, 0:w] = 0
mask[search_bot:h, 0:w] = 0
```

Then, we will use the OpenCV moments() function to calculate the *centroid*, or arithmetic center, of the blob of the binary image that passes our filter:

```
M = cv2.moments(mask)
if M['m00'] > 0:
    cx = int(M['m10']/M['m00'])
    cy = int(M['m01']/M['m00'])
```

Finally, to help in debugging, it is often useful to draw calculations and estimates on top of the original camera image. In Example 12-4 we draw a solid red circle on the original RGB image to indicate the algorithm's estimate of the center of the line in the target image portion:

```
cv2.circle(image, (cx, cy), 20, (0,0,255), -1)
```

This will produce output similar to Figure 12-7.

It is important to note that Example 12-4 is written to handle not just still images, but continual image streams. To better understand the strengths and weaknesses, leave follower_line_finder.py up and running, and use the Move and Rotate tools in Gazebo to observe the behavior of follower_line_finder.py as the position and bearing change in simulation. Next, we will use the line-centroid estimation as our control input.

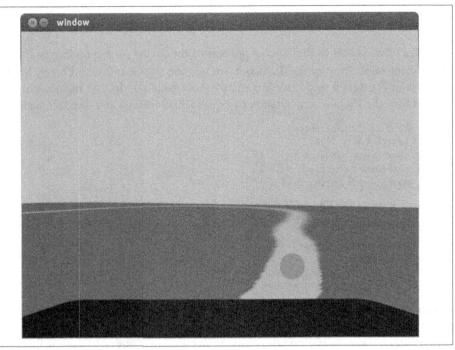

Figure 12-7. The original image with the red circle overlay, which shows the algorithm's estimate of the center of the line

Following the Line

In the previous section, we worked up to a line detection algorithm. Now that we have a line detection scheme up and running, we can move on to the task of driving the robot such that the line stays near the center of the camera frame. In Example 12-5, we demonstrate one approach to this problem: a P-controller. The P in this controller's name stands for *proportional* and simply means that a linear scaling of an error drives the control output. In our case, the error signal is the distance between the centerline of the image and the center of the line we are trying to follow.

Example 12-5. follower_p.py

```python
#!/usr/bin/env python
import rospy, cv2, cv_bridge, numpy
from sensor_msgs.msg import Image
from geometry_msgs.msg import Twist

class Follower:
  def __init__(self):
    self.bridge = cv_bridge.CvBridge()
    cv2.namedWindow("window", 1)
```

```
    self.image_sub = rospy.Subscriber('camera/rgb/image_raw',
                                       Image, self.image_callback)
    self.cmd_vel_pub = rospy.Publisher('cmd_vel_mux/input/teleop',
                                        Twist, queue_size=1)
    self.twist = Twist()
  def image_callback(self, msg):
    image = self.bridge.imgmsg_to_cv2(msg,desired_encoding='bgr8')
    hsv = cv2.cvtColor(image, cv2.COLOR_BGR2HSV)
    lower_yellow = numpy.array([ 10,  10,  10])
    upper_yellow = numpy.array([255, 255, 250])
    mask = cv2.inRange(hsv, lower_yellow, upper_yellow)

    h, w, d = image.shape
    search_top = 3*h/4
    search_bot = 3*h/4 + 20
    mask[0:search_top, 0:w] = 0
    mask[search_bot:h, 0:w] = 0
    M = cv2.moments(mask)
    if M['m00'] > 0:
      cx = int(M['m10']/M['m00'])
      cy = int(M['m01']/M['m00'])
      cv2.circle(image, (cx, cy), 20, (0,0,255), -1)
      err = cx - w/2
      self.twist.linear.x = 0.2
      self.twist.angular.z = -float(err) / 100
      self.cmd_vel_pub.publish(self.twist)
    cv2.imshow("window", image)
    cv2.waitKey(3)

rospy.init_node('follower')
follower = Follower()
rospy.spin()
```

The P-controller is implemented in the following four lines:

```
err = cx - w/2
self.twist.linear.x = 0.2
self.twist.angular.z = -float(err) / 100
self.cmd_vel_pub.publish(self.twist)
```

The first line calculates the error signal: the distance between the center column of the image and the estimated center of the line. The following two lines calculate the values to be used for the Turtlebot's cmd_vel stream and scale it to something physically achievable by a Turtlebot. Finally, the last line publishes the sensor_msgs/Twist message to its peer nodes (in this case, is simply the Turtlebot base).

Although the code is surprisingly short, this system is actually doing some reasonable behavior and is able to follow lines in Gazebo.

Summary

In this chapter, we showed how to use OpenCV with ROS in Python. Specifically, we showed how to filter and threshold a ROS image stream by hue, and how to generate an error signal and drive a minimalist feedback controller. The result is a program that will drive a simulated Turtlebot to follow lines around a Gazebo simulation.

Even though line following has many useful applications, such as following road signage or factory floor markings, it is often not quite enough by itself. A common requirement for higher-level robot navigation is to travel between specific points on a map. In the next chapter, we will describe an approach to this problem using the ROS navigation stack and tools for creating and managing state machines.

## CHAPTER 13

On Patrol

In Chapter 10, you saw how to use the ROS nav stack to get your robot to a specific place in the world. In this chapter, we'll build on these basic navigation capabilities and look at how to get your robot to patrol around the world, collecting interesting information as it goes. We'll also use this application as an excuse to learn about task-level control of robots, where we sequence entire behaviors rather than single actions.

Simple Patrolling

As with most things in ROS, there are several ways to implement a patrol system. In fact, the code we saw in Example 10-1 is all we need. This code, shown again in Example 13-1, moves the robot from one pose in the world to another. All we need to do is to put the places in the world that we want the patrol to cover in the list of way-points, and we're all set.

Example 13-1. patrol.py

```python
#!/usr/bin/env python

import rospy
import actionlib

from move_base_msgs.msg import MoveBaseAction, MoveBaseGoal


waypoints = [   ❶
    [(2.1, 2.2, 0.0), (0.0, 0.0, 0.0, 1.0)],
    [(6.5, 4.43, 0.0), (0.0, 0.0, -0.984047240305, 0.177907360295)]
]
```

```
def goal_pose(pose):    ❷
    goal_pose = MoveBaseGoal()
    goal_pose.target_pose.header.frame_id = 'map'
    goal_pose.target_pose.pose.position.x = pose[0][0]
    goal_pose.target_pose.pose.position.y = pose[0][1]
    goal_pose.target_pose.pose.position.z = pose[0][2]
    goal_pose.target_pose.pose.orientation.x = pose[1][0]
    goal_pose.target_pose.pose.orientation.y = pose[1][1]
    goal_pose.target_pose.pose.orientation.z = pose[1][2]
    goal_pose.target_pose.pose.orientation.w = pose[1][3]

    return goal_pose


if __name__ == '__main__':
    rospy.init_node('patrol')

    client = actionlib.SimpleActionClient('move_base', MoveBaseAction)    ❸
    client.wait_for_server()

    while True:
        for pose in waypoints:    ❹
            goal = goal_pose(pose)
            client.send_goal(goal)
            client.wait_for_result()
```

❶ A list of the waypoints for the robot to patrol.

❷ A helper function to turn a waypoint into a MoveBaseGoal.

❸ Create a simple action client, and wait for the server to be ready.

❹ Loop through the waypoints, sending each as an action goal.

If all we wanted to do was to implement a simple patrol system, then this code would probably be just fine. It does everything that we need to move the robot from one waypoint to the next by making repeated action calls to the nav stack. However, if we also want the robot to do something else while it's navigating or when it reaches a waypoint, we have to write code that synchronizes with the navigation behavior. To make this easier to implement and debug, it makes sense to encapsulate it in some way. In the next section, we're going to see one way of doing this encapsulating, using the idea of state machines and the smach task-level coordination library.

State Machines

The idea of a state machine is a fundamental one in computer science. The basic idea is that your robot can be in one of a finite number of states, such as "waiting," "moving," and "recharging," each of which maps to a behavior. When one state ends, the system immediately moves into another state (for example, changing from "waiting" to "moving" as the robot starts to navigate around the world). The robot must always be in one and only one of these states, and there must be a finite number of them. Which state the robot transitions to can depend on the outcome of the just-finished state. For example, if the robot just moved to its charging station, it might transition from "moving" to "charging," rather than to "waiting." Once it is charged, then it might transition from "charging" to "waiting." The behaviors that correspond to the states "waiting," "moving," and "charging" can be encapsulated in the states, and the transitions between them are specified by the structure of the state machine.

While this sounds pretty simple, state machines can be used to control quite complex behaviors. Figure 13-1 shows the state machine for the plugging-in behavior of the PR2 robot. The robot can drive up to a socket, pick up its own charging cable, and plug it into the outlet autonomously. Obviously, there are many things that can go wrong; a state machine is a good tool to understand the task-level behavior of a system like this and to make sure that we have all of our bases covered.

Each ellipse or box in Figure 13-1 is a state, and the arrows are the transitions between them, labeled by the conditions under which they are followed. The boxes with a gray background are state machines in their own right (we'll discuss this shortly, but you can just think of them as states for now), while the boxes at the very bottom (preempted, aborted, plugged_in, and unplugged) are the outcomes of the whole state machine. When the DETECT_OUTLET state ends, for example, it reports that it succeeded, aborted, or was preempted. If it succeeded, then the system transitions to the FETCH_PLUG state. If it aborted, the next state is FAIL_STILL_UNPLUGGED. If it was preempted (i.e., something interrupted it unexpectedly), the whole system returns preempted.

Notice that some states have a single transition condition (such as FAIL_ STILL_ UNPLUGGED), while others have several. Typically, this will mean that the states with a single transition condition cannot fail and only do one thing.

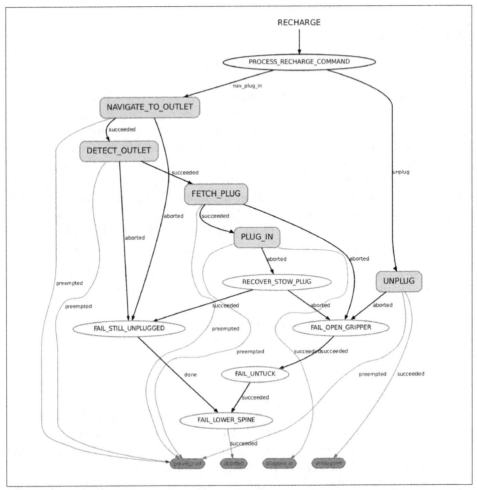

Figure 13-1. State machine for the PR2 robot to plug into an electrical outlet, generated by the smach_viewer *node*

The states have meaningful names, such as DETECT_OUTLET and PLUG_IN, and so do the transition conditions (succeeded, aborted, etc.). The convention in ROS is to name states with ALL_CAPS and transition conditions with all lowercase. Let's look at how we can specify state machines like this in ROS.

State Machines in ROS

State machines in ROS are built using the smach package and its ROS-specific extensions in smach_ros. smach contains a lot more than just state machines, but that's the part we're going to focus on for now. You should think about using smach when you have a complex robot behavior that you can break up into a set of subbehaviors that happen in a fixed structure. Basically, if you can draw the behavior of your system using a diagram like Figure 13-1, then it's probably a good candidate for smach. However, if you need blazing-fast state transitions to control a low-level aspect of your robot, then smach is not a good choice, mostly because it was written in Python. There is very little overhead in smach, though and it's likely to be a good choice for most of the state machines you write.

So, now that we know what a state machine is, and what it's good for, let's look at how we define a simple state machine with smach.

Defining State Machines with smach

State machines in smach are defined procedurally, using Python code, rather than through some sort of definition file. This allows for a lot of flexibility in the way that state machines are put together, as we'll see later in this chapter. First, though, we're going to look at a toy example of a very simple state machine, to get you used to some of the basic concepts used by smach.

Example 13-2 shows the code to define and run a very simple two-state state machine in smach. State ONE prints the word "one" and then transitions to state TWO. State TWO prints "two" and transitions to state ONE. Not very exciting, we admit, but it's got all of the pieces that we want to show you.

Example 13-2. simple_fsm.py

```
#!/usr/bin/env python

import rospy
from smach import State,StateMachine

from time import sleep


class One(State):
    def __init__(self):
        State.__init__(self, outcomes=['success'])

    def execute(self, userdata):
        print 'one'
        sleep(1)
        return 'success'

class Two(State):
    def __init__(self):
        State.__init__(self, outcomes=['success'])

    def execute(self, userdata):
        print 'two'
```

```
        sleep(1)
        return 'success'


if __name__ == '__main__':
    sm = StateMachine(outcomes=['success'])
    with sm:
        StateMachine.add('ONE', One(), transitions={'success':'TWO'})
        StateMachine.add('TWO', Two(), transitions={'success':'ONE'})

    sm.execute()
```

The first thing that we need to do is to import the stuff we'll need from smach. In this simple example, we're going to use the classes State and StateMachine:

```
from smach import State,StateMachine
```

In addition to this, you're going to need to add smach as a dependency in your *package.xml* file, to make sure ROS knows where to find things.

Next, we define some states for our state machine. States in smach are instances of Python classes that inherit from the State class:

```
class One(State):
    def __init__(self):
        State.__init__(self, outcomes=['success'])

    def execute(self, userdata):
        print 'one'
        sleep(1)
        return 'success'
```

This code defines a state class for our state machine. It inherits from the smach State class. In our class constructor, we explicitly call the parent class constructor, passing in a list of all the possible outcomes from our state. Outcomes are the labels on the arrows in Figure 13-1 and are simple strings in our code. They should mean something in the context of the behavior that the state implements. In this case, there is only a single outcome, success.

Each state also needs to implement an execute(self, userdata) function, which is where all the work of the state happens. When the state machine transitions to a particular state, that state's execute() function is called. The function takes a userdata argument, which we're going to ignore for now, that allows data to be passed in on the fly from the previous state. The function *must* return one of the outcomes listed in the base class constructor call. Since we only have one outcome, success, that's what we return.

After defining another (very similar) state class, it's time to actually construct the state machine itself:

```
sm = StateMachine(outcomes=['success'])
with sm:
    StateMachine.add('ONE', One(), transitions={'success':'TWO'})
    StateMachine.add('TWO', Two(), transitions={'success':'ONE'})

sm.execute()
```

We start by creating an instance of a StateMachine called sm, passing it a list of possible outcomes. These are different from the lists of outcomes of the states we're going to build our state machine out of, although they could have the same names. Since smach allows for hierarchical state machines, we can use sm as the state in *another* state machine. This is what happened in the gray boxes in Figure 13-1.

Once we have our (empty) state machine, we can open it with a with statement, and start to populate it with states. Each state is added with the add() function and has a name, an instance of the state, and a dictionary of transitions. The first call to add() adds a state called ONE, with an instance of the class One. On an outcome of success, it transitions to a state called TWO. Similarly, TWO is implemented with an instance of Two and transitions back to ONE on an outcome of success.

What this simple state machine does, then, is just repeatedly print "one" and "two" to the screen. Let's test it to make sure that it's doing the right thing. When we run the code, the sm.execute() call is what starts things rolling:

```
user@hostname$ rosrun patrol simple_fsm.py
[ DEBUG ] : Adding state (ONE, <__main__.One object at 0x7fa64a818190>, \
    {'success': 'TWO'})
[ DEBUG ] : Adding state 'ONE' to the state machine.
[ DEBUG ] : State 'ONE' is missing transitions: {}
[ DEBUG ] : TRANSITIONS FOR ONE: {'success': 'TWO'}
[ DEBUG ] : Adding state (TWO, <__main__.Two object at 0x7fa64a818210>, \
    {'success': 'ONE'})
[ DEBUG ] : Adding state 'TWO' to the state machine.
[ DEBUG ] : State 'TWO' is missing transitions: {}
[ DEBUG ] : TRANSITIONS FOR TWO: {'success': 'ONE'}
[  INFO ] : State machine starting in initial state 'ONE' with userdata:
        []
one
[  INFO ] : State machine transitioning 'ONE':'success'-->'TWO'
two
[  INFO ] : State machine transitioning 'TWO':'success'-->'ONE'
one
[  INFO ] : State machine transitioning 'ONE':'success'-->'TWO'
two
[  INFO ] : State machine transitioning 'TWO':'success'-->'ONE'
one
[  INFO ] : State machine transitioning 'ONE':'success'-->'TWO'
two
[  INFO ] : State machine transitioning 'TWO':'success'-->'ONE'
one
```

```
[ INFO ] : State machine transitioning 'ONE':'success'-->'TWO'
two
[ INFO ] : State machine transitioning 'TWO':'success'-->'ONE'
one
```

smach provides a lot of debugging information using the logging system. If you look at the DEBUG-level messages, you can see that we've successfully added two states and the correct transitions. smach does a static check on the state machine once it is assembled, to make sure that everything is wired up legally and that all outcomes are connected to states. The state machine then starts to run, and we can see the output ("one" and "two") interspersed with informational messages about the state transitions.

Congratulations! You've run your first smach state machine. Now, let's look at something slightly more relevant to moving a robot around the world.

A Slightly More Relevant Example

Example 13-3 shows a more advanced use of smach. The idea here is that we have two things that our robot can do: drive in a straight line and turn in place. We're going to implement each of these behaviors in a separate smach state and then connect them together to get the robot to drive along polygonal paths.

Example 13-3. shapes.py

```python
#!/usr/bin/env python

import rospy
from smach import State,StateMachine

from time import sleep


class Drive(State):
    def __init__(self, distance):
        State.__init__(self, outcomes=['success'])
        self.distance = distance

    def execute(self, userdata):
        print 'Driving', self.distance
        sleep(1)
        return 'success'

class Turn(State):
    def __init__(self, angle):
        State.__init__(self, outcomes=['success'])
        self.angle = angle

    def execute(self, userdata):
```

```
            print 'Turning', self.angle
            sleep(1)
            return 'success'


if __name__ == '__main__':
    triangle = StateMachine(outcomes=['success'])
    with triangle:
        StateMachine.add('SIDE1', Drive(1), transitions={'success':'TURN1'})
        StateMachine.add('TURN1', Turn(120), transitions={'success':'SIDE2'})
        StateMachine.add('SIDE2', Drive(1), transitions={'success':'TURN2'})
        StateMachine.add('TURN2', Turn(120), transitions={'success':'SIDE3'})
        StateMachine.add('SIDE3', Drive(1), transitions={'success':'success'})

    square = StateMachine(outcomes=['success'])
    with square:
        StateMachine.add('SIDE1', Drive(1), transitions={'success':'TURN1'})
        StateMachine.add('TURN1', Turn(90), transitions={'success':'SIDE2'})
        StateMachine.add('SIDE2', Drive(1), transitions={'success':'TURN2'})
        StateMachine.add('TURN2', Turn(90), transitions={'success':'SIDE3'})
        StateMachine.add('SIDE3', Drive(1), transitions={'success':'TURN3'})
        StateMachine.add('TURN3', Turn(90), transitions={'success':'SIDE4'})
        StateMachine.add('SIDE4', Drive(1), transitions={'success':'success'})

    shapes = StateMachine(outcomes=['success'])
    with shapes:
        StateMachine.add('TRIANGLE', triangle, transitions={'success':'SQUARE'})
        StateMachine.add('SQUARE', square, transitions={'success':'success'})

    shapes.execute()
```

We start as before, by including the bits of smach we need and defining our states. For this example, we have two classes corresponding to states, Drive and Turn. The constructors for these classes each take a single argument corresponding to the distance to drive (in meters) and the angle to turn through (in degrees), respectively. Both only have a single outcome, success. If this code actually controlled a real robot, the execute() function would have code in it to move the robot (and probably to verify that things had gone as expected).

Things get a bit more interesting when we start to define the state machines. We can define a triangular path by driving, turning, driving, turning, and driving again. This is similar to the original example:

```
        triangle = StateMachine(outcomes=['success'])
        with triangle:
            StateMachine.add('SIDE1', Drive(1), transitions={'success':'TURN1'})
            StateMachine.add('TURN1', Turn(120), transitions={'success':'SIDE2'})
            StateMachine.add('SIDE2', Drive(1), transitions={'success':'TURN2'})
            StateMachine.add('TURN2', Turn(120), transitions={'success':'SIDE3'})
            StateMachine.add('SIDE3', Drive(1), transitions={'success':'success'})
```

In the code, we also define a state machine that drives the robot in a square. Then, we can chain these two state machines together.

```
shapes = StateMachine(outcomes=['success'])
with shapes:
    StateMachine.add('TRIANGLE', triangle, transitions={'success':'SQUARE'})
    StateMachine.add('SQUARE', square, transitions={'success':'success'})

shapes.execute()
```

The third state machine, shapes, will first run the triangle state machine, and then the square one. This is an example of how we can build hierarchical state machines with smach. Notice that the states have the same names in both triangle and square. This is fine, since the states are owned by different machines, and there's no ambiguity.

We can run this code to verify that it works as expected:

```
user@hostname$ rosrun patrol shapes.py

...

[ INFO ] : State machine starting in initial state 'TRIANGLE' with userdata:
           []
[ INFO ] : State machine starting in initial state 'SIDE1' with userdata:
           []
Driving 1
[ INFO ] : State machine transitioning 'SIDE1':'success'-->'TURN1'
Turning 120
[ INFO ] : State machine transitioning 'TURN1':'success'-->'SIDE2'
Driving 1
[ INFO ] : State machine transitioning 'SIDE2':'success'-->'TURN2'
Turning 120
[ INFO ] : State machine transitioning 'TURN2':'success'-->'SIDE3'
Driving 1
[ INFO ] : State machine terminating 'SIDE3':'success':'success'
[ INFO ] : State machine transitioning 'TRIANGLE':'success'-->'SQUARE'
[ INFO ] : State machine starting in initial state 'SIDE1' with userdata:
           []
Driving 1
[ INFO ] : State machine transitioning 'SIDE1':'success'-->'TURN1'
Turning 90
[ INFO ] : State machine transitioning 'TURN1':'success'-->'SIDE2'
Driving 1
[ INFO ] : State machine transitioning 'SIDE2':'success'-->'TURN2'
Turning 90
[ INFO ] : State machine transitioning 'TURN2':'success'-->'SIDE3'
Driving 1
[ INFO ] : State machine transitioning 'SIDE3':'success'-->'TURN3'
Turning 90
[ INFO ] : State machine transitioning 'TURN3':'success'-->'SIDE4'
Driving 1
```

```
[  INFO ] : State machine terminating 'SIDE4':'success':'success'
[  INFO ] : State machine terminating 'SQUARE':'success':'success'
```

Note that the state machine construction messages have been removed to save space.

Defining State Machines Procedurally

While the previous example worked as expected, the way in which we constructed the state machines was a bit clunky, listing each move in the polygon explicitly. Since we're defining the state machines procedurally, we can do better, as you can see in Example 13-4.

Example 13-4. shapes2.py

```python
#!/usr/bin/env python

import rospy
from smach import State,StateMachine

from time import sleep


class Drive(State):
    def __init__(self, distance):
        State.__init__(self, outcomes=['success'])
        self.distance = distance

    def execute(self, userdata):
        print 'Driving', self.distance
        sleep(1)
        return 'success'

class Turn(State):
    def __init__(self, angle):
        State.__init__(self, outcomes=['success'])
        self.angle = angle

    def execute(self, userdata):
        print 'Turning', self.angle
        sleep(1)
        return 'success'

def polygon(sides):
    polygon = StateMachine(outcomes=['success'])
    with polygon:
        # Add all but the final side
        for i in xrange(sides - 1):
            StateMachine.add('SIDE_{0}'.format(i + 1),
                             Drive(1),
                             transitions={'success':'TURN_{0}'.format(i + 1)})
```

```
        # Add all the turns
        for i in xrange(sides - 1):
            StateMachine.add('TURN_{0}'.format(i + 1),
                             Turn(360.0 / sides),
                             transitions={'success':'SIDE_{0}'.format(i + 2)})

        # Add the final side
        StateMachine.add('SIDE_{0}'.format(sides),
                         Drive(1),
                         transitions={'success':'success'})

    return polygon


if __name__ == '__main__':
    triangle = polygon(3)
    square = polygon(4)

    shapes = StateMachine(outcomes=['success'])
    with shapes:
        StateMachine.add('TRIANGLE', triangle, transitions={'success':'SQUARE'})
        StateMachine.add('SQUARE', square, transitions={'success':'success'})

    shapes.execute()
```

The main improvement here is that we define a function that, given the number of sides in a polygon, will define a state machine to draw it:

```
def polygon(sides):
    polygon = StateMachine(outcomes=['success'])
    with polygon:
        # Add all but the final side
        for i in xrange(sides - 1):
            StateMachine.add('SIDE_{0}'.format(i + 1),
                             Drive(1),
                             transitions={'success':'TURN_{0}'.format(i + 1)})

        # Add all the turns
        for i in xrange(sides - 1):
            StateMachine.add('TURN_{0}'.format(i + 1),
                             Turn(360.0 / sides),
                             transitions={'success':'SIDE_{0}'.format(i + 2)})

        # Add the final side
        StateMachine.add('SIDE_{0}'.format(sides),
                         Drive(1),
                         transitions={'success':'success'})

    return polygon
```

This function creates a StateMachine instance, then adds the states. First it adds all but the last movement, then all of the turns, and finally it adds the last movement.

This last movement is special, since it's the last one in the state machine. The state names are generated procedurally, as are the transition targets. We added all of the driving states first and then all the turning states to emphasize that we don't need to add states in any particular order, as long as they are all wired up correctly.

The addition of the `polygon()` function simplifies the creation of the `triangle` and `square` state machines:

```
triangle = polygon(3)
square = polygon(4)
```

Running this example gives the same output as Example 13-3, as we would expect.

Patrolling with State Machines

Now that we've seen how to construct state machines with smach, it's time to get back to our robot and see how we can set up our patrol with a simple state machine. It actually turns out to be remarkably straightforward: we only need to implement a single state, corresponding to driving to a particular waypoint, and then chain these states together to get the patrol. Example 13-5 shows the code.

Example 13-5. patrol_fsm.py

```python
#!/usr/bin/env python

import rospy
import actionlib
from smach import State,StateMachine
from move_base_msgs.msg import MoveBaseAction, MoveBaseGoal

waypoints = [
    ['one', (2.1, 2.2), (0.0, 0.0, 0.0, 1.0)],
    ['two', (6.5, 4.43), (0.0, 0.0, -0.984047240305, 0.177907360295)]
]

class Waypoint(State):
    def __init__(self, position, orientation):
        State.__init__(self, outcomes=['success'])

        # Get an action client
        self.client = actionlib.SimpleActionClient('move_base', MoveBaseAction)
        self.client.wait_for_server()

        # Define the goal
        self.goal = MoveBaseGoal()
        self.goal.target_pose.header.frame_id = 'map'
        self.goal.target_pose.pose.position.x = position[0]
        self.goal.target_pose.pose.position.y = position[1]
        self.goal.target_pose.pose.position.z = 0.0
```

```
                self.goal.target_pose.pose.orientation.x = orientation[0]
                self.goal.target_pose.pose.orientation.y = orientation[1]
                self.goal.target_pose.pose.orientation.z = orientation[2]
                self.goal.target_pose.pose.orientation.w = orientation[3]

        def execute(self, userdata):
            self.client.send_goal(self.goal)
            self.client.wait_for_result()
            return 'success'


if __name__ == '__main__':
    rospy.init_node('patrol')

    patrol = StateMachine('success')
    with patrol:
        for i,w in enumerate(waypoints):
            StateMachine.add(w[0],
                             Waypoint(w[1], w[2]),
                             transitions={'success':waypoints[(i + 1) % \
                             len(waypoints)][0]})

    patrol.execute()
```

Each instance of the Waypoint state has its own action client and a single goal point. When the execute() function is called, it sends this goal to the nav stack and waits for it to terminate. Notice that the action client is created and waited for when the instance is created, which means that by the time the state machine is executed all states have a running action client, and none of them have to wait. We also precompute MoveBaseGoal in the constructor, since it's not going to ever change.

Creating the state machine is just a case of getting one Waypoint instance for each element in the waypoints list and setting up the transitions correctly. The last waypoint transitions back to the first one.

Running this code will give exactly the same behavior as running Example 10-1 from the chapter about navigating around the world. However, the new version of the code is better encapsulated and more extensible (as we will see later on in the book).

A Better Way to Patrol

Using states to issue action requests is a common design pattern in ROS. So much so, in fact, that there's a special-purpose mechanism that helps us to do it more efficiently than in Example 13-5. The smach_ros package contains a number of ROS-specific states that can simplify state machine construction, as we can see in Example 13-6.

Example 13-6. better_patrol_fsm.py

```python
#!/usr/bin/env python

import rospy
from smach import StateMachine       ❶
from smach_ros import SimpleActionState   ❷
from move_base_msgs.msg import MoveBaseAction, MoveBaseGoal

waypoints = [
    ['one', (2.1, 2.2), (0.0, 0.0, 0.0, 1.0)],
    ['two', (6.5, 4.43), (0.0, 0.0, -0.984047240305, 0.177907360295)]
]

if __name__ == '__main__':
    rospy.init_node('patrol')

    patrol = StateMachine(['succeeded','aborted','preempted'])
    with patrol:
        for i,w in enumerate(waypoints):
            goal_pose = MoveBaseGoal()
            goal_pose.target_pose.header.frame_id = 'map'

            goal_pose.target_pose.pose.position.x = w[1][0]
            goal_pose.target_pose.pose.position.y = w[1][1]
            goal_pose.target_pose.pose.position.z = 0.0

            goal_pose.target_pose.pose.orientation.x = w[2][0]
            goal_pose.target_pose.pose.orientation.y = w[2][1]
            goal_pose.target_pose.pose.orientation.z = w[2][2]
            goal_pose.target_pose.pose.orientation.w = w[2][3]

            StateMachine.add(w[0],
                             SimpleActionState('move_base',
                                               MoveBaseAction,
                                               goal=goal_pose),
                             transitions={'succeeded':waypoints[(i + 1) % \
                                 len(waypoints)][0]})
    patrol.execute()
```

❶ We don't need to import State any more, since we're not using it now.

❷ We do need to import SimpleActionState from smach_ros, though.

In this code, we've replaced our Waypoint state class with a SimpleActionState instance. This takes the name of the action (move_base), the type of the action (Move BaseAction), and the action goal (constructed from the waypoint list). Notice how this greatly simplifies our code; the largest single part is now setting the fields in the goal state.

Summary

In this chapter, we've seen how to build simple state machines in ROS using smach and how these machines can be used to control a robot at the task level. In particular, we've seen how to rewrite the simple patrol code from Chapter 10 to use a state machine under the hood. It turns out that a lot of robot control code has this sort of structure, where mostly independent behaviors are chained together. The Wanderbot example discussed in Chapter 7 is a great example. Take a look at the code in Example 7-3 again; an alternative smach implementation should jump out at you now.

 smach has a *lot* more functionality than we've covered in this chapter. As always, more details are available at the smach wiki page (*http://wiki.ros.org/smach?distro=indigo*) and the smach_ros wiki page (*http://wiki.ros.org/smach_ros?distro=indigo*).

Up to this point, we've mostly looked as how to get your robot to do a set of fairly specific tasks wiht ROS. In the next chapter, we're going to combine these ideas (and more) to build a complete application: a robot that works in a stockroom.

## CHAPTER 14

Stockroom-bot

In this chapter, we will combine some of the techniques introduced in previous chapters to program a robot to move items around in a stockroom. This type of task is common in many industries where goods are stored with controlled access, from the relatively small "cage" rooms in retail stores where high-value items are stored, to the chemical and medical supply rooms in hospitals, and all the way up through the massive, highly controlled warehouses used to fulfill ecommerce orders and handle the supply chains of large manufacturing corporations. Despite the varied applications, many tasks in these stockrooms are quite similar: items are precisely organized in a restricted-access area, and they need to be gathered in response to incoming requests.

As we have emphasized throughout this book, it is all but impossible to write robust, complex robot software without a simulation environment. Accordingly, we will spend the first portion of this chapter creating a simulated stockroom. As always, the time spent creating a good simulation model pays huge dividends in robot software development!

Stockroom Simulation

Let's get started by creating a workspace called ws for our stockroom_bot package:

```
user@hostname$ mkdir -p ~/ws/src/stockroom_bot
user@hostname$ cd ~/ws/src/stockroom_bot
```

Next, we'll create a minimal *package.xml* file in this directory, shown in Example 14-1, that will allow the ROS package management system to find the files we'll create during this chapter.

Example 14-1. package.xml for stockroom_bot

```xml
<?xml version="1.0"?>
<package>
  <name>stockroom_bot</name>
  <version>0.0.0</version>
  <description>The stockroom_bot package</description>
  <maintainer email="maintainer@example.com">Name of Maintainer</maintainer>
  <license>BSD</license>
  <author email="author@example.com">Name of Author</author>
  <buildtool_depend>catkin</buildtool_depend>
  <build_depend>rospy</build_depend>
  <run_depend>rospy</run_depend>
</package>
```

Then, `catkin` will create our terminal initialization scripts in *~/ws/devel* on the initial invocation of `catkin_make`:

```
user@hostname$ cd ~/ws
user@hostname$ catkin_make
```

As usual in ROS- and Gazebo-based software development, we'll be using many terminal windows. It will save us a lot of typing if we set up a `bash` alias so that we can quickly set up our terminal environments. We can create an alias called `sb`, as an abbreviation for `stockroom_bot`, by placing this line at the end of *~/.bashrc*:

```
user@hostname$ alias sb='source ~/ws/devel/setup.bash; \
    export GAZEBO_MODEL_PATH=${HOME}/ws/src/stockroom_bot'
```

Once we have reloaded the *~/.bashrc* file or started a new terminal, whenever we start to configure a terminal for `stockroom_bot` development or testing, we can just type `sb` at the command line. This will make your life much easier and helps you to manage environment configurations when you have multiple development projects on your machine at the same time.

 Whenever you find yourself typing something more than once or twice in a terminal window, setting up a quick `bash` alias will often make your life at the terminal more pleasant.

Now, let's get started on simulating a stockroom with our newly configured workspace. Many stockrooms are organized by placing smaller items into a uniform set of bins, which are then labeled with the names of the items they contain. To get started with our stockroom simulation, we will first model a bin. Of course, bins come in all shapes and sizes, depending on the application. In our case, we want to model bins that can hold items that a hand-sized robot gripper can easily pick up, so we'll make our bins 40 cm square and 20 cm tall.

As usual in ROS and Gazebo, there are many ways that one could accomplish this task. It is possible, for example, to make an intricate model in a 3D modeling or CAD program and export the geometry into a format that Gazebo can understand. However, since we may want to have a large number of bins in our simulated stockroom, we will opt to manually create the bin out of the minimum number of primitive shapes in Gazebo, to make the simulation as fast as possible.

First, let's make directories in our package for the local Gazebo storage and for our bin model:

```
user@hostname$ mkdir -p ~/ws/src/stockroom_bot/models/bin
```

Because the *models* directory is referenced by the GAZEBO_MODEL_PATH environment variable that we configured earlier, it will be crawled by Gazebo at startup. As such, the *models* directory must adhere to a specific structure, where all subdirectories have a "magic" file called *model.config* that describes the version of the model format and links to the other files that contain the actual model. In our case, the minimal *model.config* file we can place in *models/bin* is shown in Example 14-2, which simply provides a name and tells Gazebo that the actual bin model will be in a file called *model.sdf*.

Example 14-2. Bin model.config

```
<?xml version="1.0"?>
<model>
  <name>Bin</name>
  <sdf version="1.4">model.sdf</sdf>
</model>
```

The actual modeling happens in the *model.sdf* file. Here, we will model our bin as having five sides, each of which is a rectangular prism, or a box, in the terminology of the Simulation Description File (SDF) format that can be parsed by Gazebo.

To make this easier to show on a printed page, we have only included the bottom and left sides of the bin in Example 14-3. The remaining three sides are similar, and as for other the examples in the book, the full source code can be downloaded from the Web; it is only shown here for explanatory purposes.

Example 14-3. Bin model.sdf

```
<?xml version='1.0'?>
<sdf version ='1.4'>
  <model name ='box'> ❶
    <static>true</static> ❷
    <link name='bottom'> ❸
      <collision name="collision_bottom">
        <geometry>
```

```
      <box>
        <size>0.4 0.4 0.02</size> ❹
      </box>
    </geometry>
  </collision>
  <collision name="collision_left"> ❺
    <pose>-0.2 0 0.1 0 0 0</pose> ❻
    <geometry><box><size>0.02 0.4 0.2</size></box></geometry>
  </collision>
  <visual name="visual_bottom">
    <geometry><box><size>0.4 0.4 0.02</size></box></geometry>
    <material><script><name>Gazebo/Blue</name></script></material> ❼
  </visual>
  <visual name="visual_left">
    <pose>-0.2 0 0.1 0 0 0</pose>
    <geometry><box><size>0.02 0.4 0.2</size></box></geometry>
    <material><script><name>Gazebo/Blue</name></script></material>
  </visual>
</link>
  </model>
</sdf>
```

❶ The `<model>` tag's name attribute must agree with the name in the *model.config* file.

❷ The `<static>` tag means that Gazebo won't have to compute dynamics on this model. This saves considerable CPU time.

❸ The `<link>` tag can include multiple `<collision>` and `<visual>` tags that describe the geometries used for physics and rendering, respectively. In this model, they are the same, but often the `collision` shapes are much simpler than the `visual` shapes.

❹ This nesting of `<geometry><box><size>` tags will create a 40 cm x 40 cm x 2 cm box. In the rest of the file, these tags are combined on the same line, for simplicity.

❺ Each `collision` and `visual` object must have a unique `name` attribute!

❻ The `<pose>` tag will move the `geometry` objects in this tag away from the origin by the specified 6D (*x y z roll pitch yaw*) transformation.

❼ This `<material>` tag refers to a built-in Gazebo material to set the shape's color.

The bin model is shown rendered in Gazebo in Figure 14-1.

Figure 14-1. The bin described in Example 14-3 rendered Gazebo

Our next task will be to create a label for each of the bins. In a human-operated stock-room, this is typically done by printing characters on labels that are attached to the bins. However, machine vision often works better with different forms of labels that are easier for algorithms to parse. The retail bar-code system is one well-known example of machine-friendly labeling. There are several newer forms of labeling that extend this concept into two dimensions, such as QR codes, which have impressive information density. However, in robotics, we are often interested not just in extracting text from a label, but also in calculating the orientation and distance of the label relative to the robot. Although there are several options available, in this chapter we will use the ALVAR marker system because it is already integrated with ROS and works quite well "out of the box." ALVAR marker tags are two-dimensional binary images, such as those in Figure 14-2.

Figure 14-2. Example ALVAR marker tags that encode the numbers 0, 1, and 2

The encoding of these tags is carefully computed to reduce reading errors and to permit accurate calculation of the orientation and distance of the tag relative to a camera that images it. Some care is required to use them appropriately, such as solidly securing the tag's paper printout to a flat surface, and ensuring that the tag is printed at the correct scale; however by and large, ALVAR marker tags can work surprisingly well in a variety of application environments. Happily, there is a ready-made ROS package for recognizing ALVAR tags in ROS sensor_msgs/Image messages. It can be installed the usual way on Ubuntu:

```
user@hostname$ sudo apt-get install ros-indigo-ar-track-alvar* imagemagick
```

That package also provides a program that can create the ALVAR marker tags. Our simulated stockroom will have 12 bins, so we'll want to automatically create 12 ALVAR tag image, and 12 "material script" files, which are used by Gazebo and its underlying graphics engine (OGRE) to describe the visual properties of objects in the simulation, such as texture images that can be "plastered" on objects. Later on, we will reference these material scripts in a Gazebo world file.

Like any repetitive task, we want to script the creation of the ALVAR tag images and the material script files, so that we can easily tweak the parameters and regenerate them as needed. Although any scripting language could be used, for consistency, we used Python to create a script for this purpose; it is listed in Example 14-4.

Example 14-4. generate_codes_and_materials.py

```
#!/usr/bin/env python
import os
for i in xrange(0,12):
    os.system("rosrun ar_track_alvar createMarker {0}".format(i))  ❶
    fn = "MarkerData_{0}.png".format(i)
    os.system("convert {0} -bordercolor white -border 100x100 {0}".format(fn))  ❷
    with open("product_{0}.material".format(i), 'w') as f:  ❸
      f.write("""
material product_%d {
```

```
      receive_shadows on
      technique {
        pass {
          ambient 1.0 1.0 1.0 1.0
          diffuse 1.0 1.0 1.0 1.0
          specular 0.5 0.5 0.5 1.0
          lighting on
          shading gouraud
          texture_unit { texture MarkerData_%d.png }
        }
      }
    }
    """ % (i, i))
```

❶ Runs the createMarker program in the ar_track_alvar package, which creates a PNG image that encodes the specified number. Although a more sophisticated program could use subprocess.call() and check error codes, etc., this example is just trying to be as concise as possible.

❷ Runs the ImageMagick utility to add a thick white border around the ALVAR marker tag, to help improve recognition.

❸ Generates material scripts that include a reference (toward the end) to the ALVAR texture image.

The Eye-of-GNOME program, invoked using eog, is a handy way to quickly view images on the command line, such as the ALVAR marker images produced by the ar_track_alvar createMarker command.

Now that we have the ALVAR marker tag images and material scripts to label each bin, we're ready to make an entire stockroom full of them. Yet again, we are faced with a choice among an innumerable number of ways that we can do this. We could write a single massive XML file by hand that instantiates the bin model as many times as needed. That would work, but it would be painful if we decided we wanted a slightly different bin spacing in our simulated stockroom, which would require hand-editing many constants in the XML. We could also spawn the bin models program-matically, like we did for the chessboard. That would incur a bit of startup time, but it could work. Or we could use the xacro (XML Macros) language, but unfortunately that system doesn't allow for loops, which means we'd still have quite a few constants repeated throughout the file. In this chapter, we'll show another way to create Gazebo worlds full of repetitive models: using a Python template engine.

A Python template engine will let us mix Python with our XML in the Gazebo world file. This will allow us, for example, to quickly create for loops in the XML, which the

Python template engine will process and expand into repeated blocks of XML code. We can also use "normal" programming constructs like functions and variables, which we'll use to shorten the code wherever possible.

There are many Python template engines available, but we'll use the EmPy engine in this example. Modeling a world with various types of repeating features is a complex task, and we will go through the templated world file in several sections.

First, we need to install EmPy, if it isn't already installed on the system:

```
user@hostname$ sudo apt-get install python-empy
```

The start of the file to generate the XML Gazebo would for the stockroom simulatio-nis shown in Example 14-5.

Example 14-5. Header of the EmPy template to generate the Gazebo world

```
<?xml version="1.0" ?>
<sdf version="1.4">
<world name="stockroom">
<gui>
  <camera name="camera"> ❶
    <pose>3 -2 3.5 0.0 .85 2.4</pose>
    <view_controller>orbit</view_controller>
  </camera>
</gui>
<include><uri>model://sun</uri></include>
<include><uri>model://ground_plane</uri></include>
```

❶ The <camera> tag specifies a camera location, so that you don't have to manually move the camera to a useful vantage point every time you start the simulation.

So far, so good. But now things get a bit unusual: the EmPy templating engine can "interleave" Python with XML, using the at sign (@) symbol as a delimiter. Anything within curly braces following an at sight (@{})will execute as "normal" Python code. Anything within parentheses (@()) will be evaluated as a Python expression, and the evaluation of the expression will be pasted into the XML document in the place of the @() expression. Finally, anything within square brackets (@[]) is considered a Python control structure to be used by EmPy: for loops, if/else blocks, and so on. EmPy, of course, is a large system with its own manual, but those three rules are enough to be able to understand the code. Keeping that EmPy syntax in mind, the EmPy XML template used to generate an aisle of bins is shown in Example 14-6.

Example 14-6. Section of EmPy XML template used to generate two rows of bins

```
@{from numpy import arange} ❶
@{bin_count = 0}
@[for side in ['left','right']] ❷
  @[if side == 'left']
    @{y = -1.5} ❸
    @{yaw = 3.1415}
  @[else]
    @{y = 1.5}
    @{yaw = 0}
  @[end if]
  @[for x in arange(-1.5, 1.5, 0.5)] ❹
    <include>
      <name>bin_@(bin_count)</name> ❺
      <pose>@(x) @(y) 0.5 0 0 @(yaw)</pose> ❻
      <uri>model://bin</uri> ❼
    </include>
    <model name="bin_@(bin_count)_tag"> ❽
      <static>true</static>
      <pose>@(x) @(y*1.125) 0.63 0 0 @(yaw)</pose> ❾
      <link name="link">
        <visual name="visual">
          <geometry><box><size>0.2 0.01 0.2</size></box></geometry>
          <material>
            <script>
              <uri>model://bin/tags</uri> ❿
              <name>product_@(bin_count)</name> ⓫
            </script>
          </material>
        </visual>
      </link>
    </model>
    @{bin_count += 1}
  @[end for]
@[end for]
```

❶ This is "normal" Python: we can import packages as usual.

❷ Despite the funny escape brackets, this is again just "normal" Python.

❸ The *y* and *yaw* variables differ depending on whether we're on the left or right side of the aisle of bins.

❹ The numpy arange() function lets us increment a for loop using a floating-point step, which, in this case, we will use to position the bins.

❺ The @(bin_count) expression is used to generate unique model names for the bins in Gazebo.

❻ The position variables are used to space the bins appropriately. Note that by varying the *y* and the step of the *x* variable, we can easily change the layout of the bin spacing.

❼ This refers to the bin model that we made earlier in this chapter, thanks to the GAZEBO_MODEL_PATH variable we have set in our environment.

❽ Next, we will create thin boxes that will be "painted" with the ALVAR markers, to label the bins.

❾ The tags will be positioned on the back walls of the bins.

❿ The uri> tag tells Gazebo where we have placed the material scripts.

⓫ This expression references the material scripts that we made previously, which, in turn, reference the actual ALVAR marker images.

The EmPy XML in Example 14-6 is enough to create the bins, but we also need some walls in our stockroom so that the robot's laser scanner can have something to localize against. Again, there are many ways to model walls, but since we were already evaluating the Gazebo world file with the EmPy template engine, we opted to define the walls using Python functions in EmPy, as shown in Example 14-7.

Example 14-7. Section of EmPy XML template used to generate the stockroom walls

```
@[def wall(p1, p2, height)] ❶
  @{wall.count += 1}
  @[if abs(p1[0]-p2[0]) < 0.01] ❷
    @{thickness_x = 0.1}
    @{thickness_y = abs(p1[1]-p2[1])}
  @[else]
    @{thickness_x = abs(p1[0]-p2[0])}
    @{thickness_y = 0.1}
  @[end if]
  <model name="wall_@(wall.count)"> ❸
    <static>true</static>
    <pose>@((p1[0]+p2[0])/2.) @((p1[1]+p2[1])/2.) @(height/2.) 0 0 0</pose>
    <link name="link">
      <collision name='visual'> ❹
        <geometry>
          <box>
            <size>@(thickness_x) @(thickness_y) @(height)</size>
          </box>
```

```
          </geometry>
        </collision>
        <visual name='visual'>
          <geometry>
            <box>
              <size>@(thickness_x) @(thickness_y) @(height)</size>
            </box>
          </geometry>
        </visual>
      </link>
    </model>
@[end def]
@{wall.count = 0}
@( wall((-1.75, -1.75), ( 6.00 , -1.75), 1) ) ❺
@( wall((-1.75, -1.75), (-1.75,  1.75), 1) )
@( wall((-1.75,  1.75), ( 6.00,  1.75), 1) )
@( wall(( 3.00,  0.75), ( 3.00,  1.75), 1) )
@( wall(( 3.00, -0.75), ( 3.00, -1.75), 1) )
@( wall(( 6.00, -1.75), ( 6.00, -1.00), 1) )
@( wall(( 6.00,  0.00), ( 6.00,  1.75), 1) )
@( wall(( 5.00, -1.75), ( 5.00,  1.75), 0.7) )
  <model name="counter_top">
    <static>true</static>
    <pose>4.9 0 0.7 0 0 0</pose>
    <link name="link">
      <visual name="collision">
        <geometry><box><size>0.4 3.5 0.05</size></box></geometry>
      </visual>
      <visual name="visual">
        <geometry><box><size>0.4 3.5 0.05</size></box></geometry>
      </visual>
    </link>
  </model>
</world>
</sdf>
```

❶ Even though it looks a bit strange with the brackets, this is a normal Python
    function declaration using EmPy escaping syntax.

❷ This simplistic code assumes that walls are aligned along the x-axis or the y-axis,
    which is often the case in traditional commercial buildings.

❸ As before, we are using a Python counter variable to generate unique model
    names as the template engine cycles through the for loop.

❹ The collision and visual objects are identical in this case, since they are both
    as simple as possible.

❺ These EmPy evaluation expressions use the `wall()` function defined earlier to create the stockroom walls in a way that makes it relatively quick to modify the dimensions later.

Whew! That was a lot of XML. Using EmPy helped to simplify the task: the template expansion of the EmPy input shown in Example 14-5, Example 14-6, and Example 14-7 comes out to well over 500 lines of XML. To generate the output of the EmPy expansion, we use shell redirection:

```
user@hostname$ empy aisle.world.em > aisle.world
```

The resulting *aisle.world* file can be loaded directly by Gazebo:

```
user@hostname$ gazebo aisle.world
```

All this work has paid off: we now have a stockroom simulation that we can use for software development and testing, with all of the numerous strategic benefits this provides (enumerated in prior chapters). An overview screenshot of the world is shown in Figure 14-3, and a close-up showing a row of storage bins with ALVAR markers is shown in Figure 14-4.

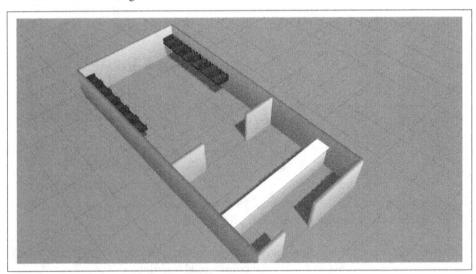

Figure 14-3. The stockroom simulation

Finally, let's put some items in our stockroom. For now, we'll just drop an identical small box into each bin. Since we may want to randomize the box position and orientation in the future, we'll place these models programmatically, just like we did in Chapter 11. Example 14-8 shows a Python script that will spawn models for the items in our stockroom and place them in their storage bins.

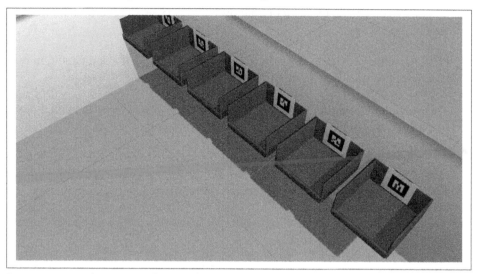

Figure 14-4. A close-up rendering of the simulated storage bin arrangement, showing their ALVAR markers

Example 14-8. stock_products.py

```python
#!/usr/bin/env python
import rospy, tf
from gazebo_msgs.srv import *
from geometry_msgs.msg import *

if __name__ == '__main__':
  rospy.init_node("stock_products")
  rospy.wait_for_service("gazebo/delete_model") ❶
  rospy.wait_for_service("gazebo/spawn_sdf_model")
  delete_model = rospy.ServiceProxy("gazebo/delete_model", DeleteModel)
  s = rospy.ServiceProxy("gazebo/spawn_sdf_model", SpawnModel)
  orient = Quaternion(*tf.transformations.quaternion_from_euler(0, 0, 0))
  with open("models/product_0/model.sdf", "r") as f:
    product_xml = f.read() ❷
  for product_num in xrange(0, 12):
    item_name = "product_{0}_0".format(product_num)
    delete_model(item_name) ❸
  for product_num in xrange(0, 12):
    bin_y = 2.8 * (product_num / 6) - 1.4 ❹
    bin_x = 0.5 * (product_num % 6) - 1.5
```

```
item_name = "product_{0}_0".format(product_num)
item_pose = Pose(Point(x=bin_x, y=bin_y, z=2), orient) ❺
s(item_name, product_xml, "", item_pose, "world") ❻
```

❶ `wait_for_service()` is used to ensure Gazebo is ready for our script.

❷ We'll be sending the item's model file over the ROS service, so first we need to load it into a string.

❸ First, we will try to delete any prior model of this name in the simulation, in case this script has already been run before on the same instance of Gazebo.

❹ This version of the script will always place the items in the same location, but we could later add some randomization to evaluate system robustness.

❺ The z coordinate is intentionally quite a bit higher than the bins. This lets us modify the bin height in the other files without worrying about matching it here, since the items will just fall in the simulator until they come to rest in the bin.

❻ This is the actual call to the Gazebo spawner service proxy, which will instantiate our item models one at a time.

Now that we have our stockroom ready, we can start using it to develop our robot software! Although creating the simulation environment may have seemed tedious, its utility will quickly become apparent as we use it extensively throughout the remainder of the chapter.

Driving to Bins

The simulated stockroom allows us to try out a number of different ideas relatively quickly and easily. We can even try to drop various robot models into the stockroom to see how they fit. For example, Figure 14-5 shows a PR2 robot dropped into the stockroom.

Although the PR2 could definitely accomplish this task, for the remainder of this chapter, we will use the Fetch robot, manufactured by Fetch Robotics. A model of Fetch is freely available and can be easily installed on Ubuntu:

```
user@hostname$ sudo apt-get install ros-indigo-fetch*
```

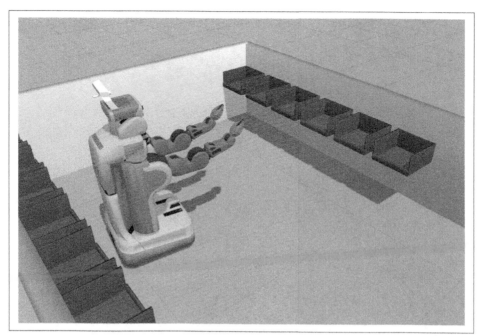

Figure 14-5. A PR2 robot dropped into the simulated stockroom

The Fetch robot is designed specifically for the domain of warehouse automation, and its one-arm design and relatively compact footprint are a good match to the stockroom system that we are developing in this chapter. We can start Gazebo with our stockroom world and spawn a Fetch robot in the middle of it using *stockroom.launch*, shown in Example 14-9. This will produce the scene shown in Figure 14-6.

Example 14-9. stockroom.launch

```
<launch>
  <include file="$(find gazebo_ros)/launch/empty_world.launch">
    <arg name="world_name" value="$(find stockroom_bot)/worlds/aisle.world"/>
  </include>
  <include file="$(find fetch_gazebo)/launch/include/fetch.launch.xml"/>
</launch>
```

As described in Chapters 9 and 13, the first thing we need to do for autonomous navigation is to create a map. To do this, just like in the previous chapters, we teleoperate the robot while recording its laser scanner readings and odometry, which are broadcast on the /base_scan and /tf topics, respectively:

```
user@hostname$ rosbag record -O stockroom_bot.bag /base_scan /tf
```

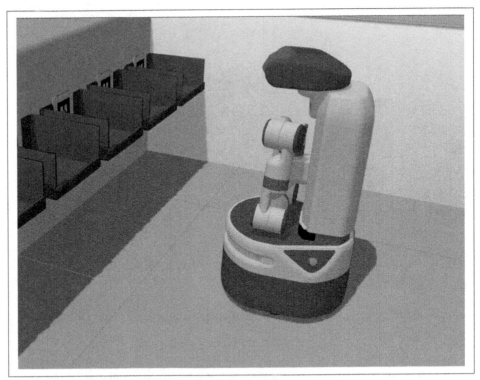

Figure 14-6. A Fetch robot dropped into the simulated stockroom

After driving around the world so that the laser scanner has seen all of the corners to build its map, just Ctrl-C the logger, teleoperation, and simulation. This is necessary because, when playing back the bag file, the ROS clock will skip backward in time, which would confuse unsuspecting programs.

First, in a fresh terminal, we'll explicitly tell ROS to source its clock from the logged simulation time:

```
user@hostname$ rosparam set use_time_time true
```

Next, we'll start the SLAM system:

```
user@hostname$ rosrun gmapping slam_gmapping scan:=base_scan \
  _odom_frame:=odom_combined
```

and then start playing back the log file:

```
user@hostname$ rosbag play --clock stockroom_bot.bag
```

The slam_gmapping terminal will print status messages as it processes the laser scans and robot odometry data. After the log has finished playing, just as in Chapter 9, we'll need to save the map to an image file. Start up a new terminal and run the map_saver command:

```
user@hostname$ rosrun map_server map_saver
```

This will create *map.pgm* in your current working directory. Since the robot has a laser scanner and reasonable odometry, the map will look very nice, as shown in Figure 14-7.

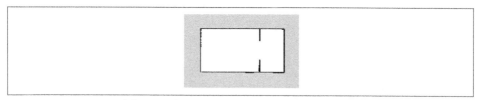

Figure 14-7. A map of the simulation stockroom, which will be used for robot navigation.

Because the stockroom is so much smaller than the maps shown in the preceding chapters, the *map.yaml* file will be different, since we only need a 20 × 20 meter map, as shown in Example 14-10.

Example 14-10. map.yaml

```
image: map.pgm
resolution: 0.050000
origin: [-10.000000, -10.000000, 0.000000]
negate: 0
occupied_thresh: 0.65
free_thresh: 0.196
```

Now that we have built a map of the stockroom, we can feed it to the Fetch navigation subsystem, which, like in the PR2 and many other robots, is built on the ROS move_base navigation stack. The launch file listed in Example 14-11 shows how to feed the map into the navigation stack.

Example 14-11. nav.launch

```
<launch>
  <include file="$(find fetch_navigation)/launch/fetch_nav.launch">
    <arg name="map_file" value="$(find stockroom_bot)/map.yaml"/>
  </include>
  <node pkg="stockroom_bot" name="initial_localization"
        type="initial_localization.py"/>
</launch>
```

Now that the Fetch navigation system is up, we can feed navigation goals to it using the same move_base action interface described in the previous chapter. Because we know the structure of our stockroom, we can incorporate the bin spacing in a Python script and refer to the bins by their numeric indices on the command line, rather than their 2D spatial coordinates. Example 14-12 shows how we can take a bin-number command, calculate the 2D coordinate of the bin, and feed that as a target to the robot's navigation stack.

Example 14-12. go_to_bin.py

```python
#!/usr/bin/env python
import sys, rospy, tf, actionlib
from geometry_msgs.msg import *
from move_base_msgs.msg import MoveBaseAction, MoveBaseGoal
from tf.transformations import quaternion_from_euler
from std_srvs.srv import Empty
from look_at_bin import look_at_bin

if __name__ == '__main__':
  rospy.init_node('go_to_bin')
  rospy.wait_for_service("/move_base/clear_costmaps")
  rospy.ServiceProxy("/move_base/clear_costmaps", Empty)()
  args = rospy.myargv(argv=sys.argv)
  if len(args) != 2:
    print "usage: go_to_bin.py BIN_NUMBER"
    sys.exit(1)
  bin_number = int(args[1])
  move_base = actionlib.SimpleActionClient('move_base', MoveBaseAction)
  move_base.wait_for_server()
  goal = MoveBaseGoal()
  goal.target_pose.header.frame_id = 'map'
  goal.target_pose.pose.position.x = 0.5 * (bin_number % 6) - 1.5;
  goal.target_pose.pose.position.y = 1.1 * (bin_number / 6) - 0.55;
  if bin_number >= 6:
    yaw = 1.57
  else:
    yaw = -1.57
  orient = Quaternion(*quaternion_from_euler(0, 0, yaw))
  goal.target_pose.pose.orientation = orient
  move_base.send_goal(goal)
  move_base.wait_for_result()
  look_at_bin()
```

Picking Up the Item

Once the robot has arrived in front of a bin, the next step is to point the robot's head so that it is aiming at the bin. There are many ways to do this, and the best choice will be somewhat dependent on the ROS API of the robot in question. The Fetch robot provides an action server called head_controller/point_head, which we can call from Python to aim the head in the correct direction. Example 14-13 shows a minimalist program that uses this action interface to command the Fetch robot's head to point down, toward the bin in front of it.

Example 14-13. look_at_bin.py

```python
#!/usr/bin/env python
import sys, rospy, actionlib
from control_msgs.msg import PointHeadAction, PointHeadGoal

def look_at_bin():
  head_client = actionlib.SimpleActionClient("head_controller/point_head",
    PointHeadAction)
  head_client.wait_for_server()
  goal = PointHeadGoal()
  goal.target.header.stamp = rospy.Time.now()
  goal.target.header.frame_id = "base_link"
  goal.target.point.x = 0.7
  goal.target.point.y = 0
  goal.target.point.z = 0.4
  goal.min_duration = rospy.Duration(1.0)
  head_client.send_goal(goal)
  head_client.wait_for_result()

if __name__ == '__main__':
  rospy.init_node('look_at_bin')
  look_at_bin()
```

Even though Example 14-12 will send the perfectly correct position of where we want the robot to park so that it can reach an item in the bin, often the robot won't end up exactly where we asked. This is due to many factors, including localization noise and the navigation system's goal tolerance, since, especially on differential-drive robots like the Fetch, the navigation system doesn't want the robot to have to do many "parallel-park" maneuvers to budge sideways a few centimeters. All navigation systems have a nonzero goal tolerance, within which the navigation system just declares victory and stops trying to reposition the robot. All of these parameters will vary depending on the robot and environment, but in our simulated Fetch system, we can expect position errors of plus or minus 10 centimeters. This produces the situation shown in Figure 14-8, where the robot is in approximately the right position but is certainly not exactly aligned with the target bin.

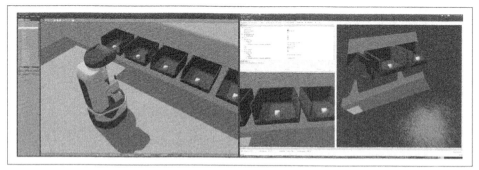

Figure 14-8. Laser-only navigation can result in not-quite perfect alignment

Fortunately, our bins are labeled with ALVAR markers! We can program the robot to use the estimated ALVAR marker range and relative orientation so that it can derive manipulation targets from the visual marker, rather than relying on extraordinary precision from the navigation system. This will typically be considerably more accurate than what the laser-based navigation system can achieve.

First, we need to fire up the ALVAR detector node. Example 14-14 shows a launch file that will start an ALVAR tracker node from the ar_track_alvar package. This launch file also creates a static transform broadcaster for each of the ALVAR frames, to rotate the frames returned by the ALVAR detector node such that the z-axes point up, which is necessary in order to feed those transforms to the navigation stack. Although it would be much more elegant and scalable to create these relative transformations on the fly as ALVAR markers were detected, for the sake of brevity and simplicity, and because our environment only has 12 bins with ALVAR markers, we will opt for the minimalist solution of repeatedly instantiating static_transformation_publisher nodes to create the transformations we need.

Example 14-14. markers.launch

```
<launch>
  <arg name="marker_size" default="12.3"/> ❶
  <arg name="max_new_marker_error" default="0.2"/>
  <arg name="max_track_error" default="0.8"/>
  <arg name="cam_image_topic" default="/head_camera/rgb/image_raw"/>
  <arg name="cam_info_topic" default="/head_camera/rgb/camera_info"/>
  <arg name="output_frame" default="/base_link"/>
  <node name="ar_track_alvar" pkg="ar_track_alvar"
        type="individualMarkersNoKinect" respawn="false" output="screen"
        args="$(arg marker_size) $(arg max_new_marker_error) \
              $(arg max_track_error) $(arg cam_image_topic) \
              $(arg cam_info_topic) $(arg output_frame)" /> ❷
  <arg name="tag_rot" default="0 0 0 0 0 -1.57"> ❸
  <arg name="tag_trans" default="0 -0.28 -0.1 0 0 0">

❹
  <node pkg="tf" type="static_transform_publisher" name="ar_0_up"
        args="$(arg tag_rot) ar_marker_0 ar_0_up 100"/>
  <node pkg="tf" type="static_transform_publisher" name="ar_1_up"
        args="$(arg tag_rot)  ar_marker_1 ar_1_up 100"/>
  <node pkg="tf" type="static_transform_publisher" name="ar_2_up"
        args="$(arg tag_rot) ar_marker_2 ar_2_up 100"/>
  <node pkg="tf" type="static_transform_publisher" name="ar_3_up"
        args="$(arg tag_rot) ar_marker_3 ar_3_up 100"/>
  <node pkg="tf" type="static_transform_publisher" name="ar_4_up"
        args="$(arg tag_rot) ar_marker_4 ar_4_up 100"/>
  <node pkg="tf" type="static_transform_publisher" name="ar_5_up"
        args="$(arg tag_rot) ar_marker_5 ar_5_up 100"/>
  <node pkg="tf" type="static_transform_publisher" name="ar_6_up"
        args="$(arg tag_rot) ar_marker_6 ar_6_up 100"/>
```

```
    <node pkg="tf" type="static_transform_publisher" name="ar_7_up"
        args="$(arg tag_rot) ar_marker_7 ar_7_up 100"/>
    <node pkg="tf" type="static_transform_publisher" name="ar_8_up"
        args="$(arg tag_rot) ar_marker_8 ar_8_up 100"/>
    <node pkg="tf" type="static_transform_publisher" name="ar_9_up"
        args="$(arg tag_rot) ar_marker_9 ar_9_up 100"/>
    <node pkg="tf" type="static_transform_publisher" name="ar_10_up"
        args="$(arg tag_rot) ar_marker_10 ar_10_up 100"/>
    <node pkg="tf" type="static_transform_publisher" name="ar_11_up"
        args="$(arg tag_rot) ar_marker_11 ar_11_up 100"/>
```

❺
```
    <node pkg="tf" type="static_transform_publisher" name="item_0"
        args="$(arg tag_trans) ar_0_up item_0 100"/>
    <node pkg="tf" type="static_transform_publisher" name="item_1"
        args="$(arg tag_trans) ar_1_up item_1 100"/>
    <node pkg="tf" type="static_transform_publisher" name="item_2"
        args="$(arg tag_trans) ar_2_up item_2 100"/>
    <node pkg="tf" type="static_transform_publisher" name="item_3"
        args="$(arg tag_trans) ar_3_up item_3 100"/>
    <node pkg="tf" type="static_transform_publisher" name="item_4"
        args="$(arg tag_trans) ar_4_up item_4 100"/>
    <node pkg="tf" type="static_transform_publisher" name="item_5"
        args="$(arg tag_trans) ar_5_up item_5 100"/>
    <node pkg="tf" type="static_transform_publisher" name="item_6"
        args="$(arg tag_trans) ar_6_up item_6 100"/>
    <node pkg="tf" type="static_transform_publisher" name="item_7"
        args="$(arg tag_trans) ar_7_up item_7 100"/>
    <node pkg="tf" type="static_transform_publisher" name="item_8"
        args="$(arg tag_trans) ar_8_up item_8 100"/>
    <node pkg="tf" type="static_transform_publisher" name="item_9"
        args="$(arg tag_trans) ar_9_up item_9 100"/>
    <node pkg="tf" type="static_transform_publisher" name="item_10"
        args="$(arg tag_trans) ar_10_up item_10 100"/>
    <node pkg="tf" type="static_transform_publisher" name="item_11"
        args="$(arg tag_trans) ar_11_up item_11 100"/>
</launch>
```

❶ The <arg> tags define configurable parameters for this launch file that will be passed to ar_track_alvar. Spelling out the parameters as top-level <arg> tags allows them to be overridden if other roslaunch files include this file, as well as making the file a bit easier to read.

❷ The <node> tag will actually spawn ar_track_alvar with the forwarded parameters.

❸ The tag_rot and tag_trans strings will be passed to the static_transform_ publisher nodes; they are consolidated here to eliminate redundant typing and simplify tweaking the values as needed.

❹ The following sequence of 12 `static_transform_publisher` nodes creates relative rotation poses for the detected ALVAR tag pose(s).

❺ Similarly, the following sequence of `static_transform_publisher` nodes creates relative translation poses for the rotated ALVAR tag pose(s).

The ROS transform system is quite helpful in cases like this: we can express our manipulation goal as a static transformation from the frame of the detected ALVAR marker. The transformation chain is actually quite complex in this case: working backward, we know we want the robot to grasp (for example) 28 cm directly in front and 10 cm below the ALVAR marker of the bin we are interested in. Since we have seen the ALVAR marker in the camera frame, we can estimate the distance and orientation of the ALVAR marker relative to the camera. From there, we can use the joint encoders of the head and torso joints of the Fetch robot to derive the transformation between the camera and the base of the robot, which we can then feed as a goal state to the arm's motion planner.

When debugging these complex transformation chains, it is often helpful to see the transformation dependency chain in graphical form. Fortunately, the `tf` package provides a utility for this, called `view_frames`. At any time when a ROS system is running, the following command will produce a PDF rendering of the transformation tree:

```
user@hostname$ rosrun tf view_frames.py
```

Figure 14-9 shows the result of running this program when ALVAR markers were being detected by the Fetch robot. It is far too complex to read without being able to zoom in and out, but suffice it to say that the fixed (map) frame is at the top of the tree, and the ALVAR marker frames are at the lower-left of the tree!

The *view_frames.py* program provided by `tf` is a way to get a schematic view of the transform tree of a ROS system. Zooming and rotating the transform tree in `rviz` can also be illuminating and helpful for rendering transforms coherently with spatial sensor data and other intermediate data sets. However, for just making sure that the various branches of the transform tree are properly connected to each other, it's hard to beat the topological view of *view_frames.py*.

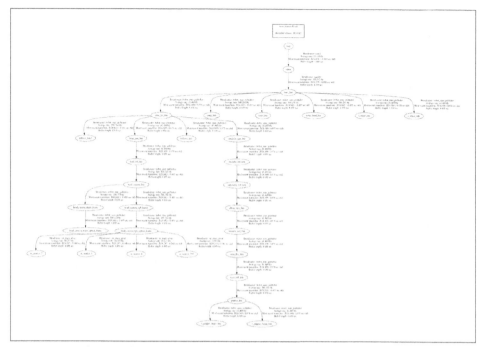

Figure 14-9. The transformation graph of the scene shown in Figure 14-10

In many situations, however, a live, interactive, spatially accurate 3D view of the transformation graph can be extremely helpful during software development and debugging. As we have shown in prior chapters, `rviz` is a highly configurable visualization system for ROS. Among the many other data types that it can handle, `rviz` can be configured to render the ROS transformation graph in real time. Figure 14-10 shows a screenshot in which both Gazebo and `rviz` windows are visible, showing both the state of the simulation and the generated camera images, the laser localization cloud, and the transformation graph showing some ALVAR marker detections.

Figure 14-10. Viewing the Gazebo (left) and rviz (right) windows simultaneously—the rendering perspectives are approximately equal

Using the transforms generated by the ALVAR marker detection system, we can command the robot to reach out and grasp an item that is in a known position relative to the ALVAR marker at the back of the bin. Example 14-15 is intended to run once the robot is close enough to a bin to detect its ALVAR marker, after which it will generate an arm motion planner goal that is relative to the bin, not the robot. Of course, actually achieving that goal is up to the navigation system, but at least one source of error (localization noise) has been greatly reduced.

In Chapter 11, we introduced MoveIt, a popular motion planning framework for ROS-based robots. Fortunately, the Fetch robot also has a MoveIt configuration available, and we can call it in exactly the same way as we did with the Robonaut 2 in Chapter 11. Example 14-15 will command the arm to grasp the item in front of the robot and lift it up. The script uses ALVAR marker detections to generate precise motion planner targets for MoveIt.

Example 14-15. pick_up_item.py

```python
#!/usr/bin/env python
import sys, rospy, tf, actionlib, moveit_commander
from control_msgs.msg import (GripperCommandAction, GripperCommandGoal)
from geometry_msgs.msg import *
from tf.transformations import quaternion_from_euler
from look_at_bin import look_at_bin
from std_srvs.srv import Empty
from moveit_msgs.msg import CollisionObject
from moveit_python import PlanningSceneInterface

if __name__ == '__main__':
  moveit_commander.roscpp_initialize(sys.argv)
  rospy.init_node('pick_up_item')
  args = rospy.myargv(argv = sys.argv)
  if len(args) != 2:
    print("usage: pick_up_item.py BIN_NUMBER")
    sys.exit(1)
  item_frame = "item_%d" % int(args[1])

  rospy.wait_for_service("/clear_octomap")
  clear_octomap = rospy.ServiceProxy("/clear_octomap", Empty)

  gripper = actionlib.SimpleActionClient("gripper_controller/gripper_action",
    GripperCommandAction)
  gripper.wait_for_server() ❶

  arm = moveit_commander.MoveGroupCommander("arm") ❷
  arm.allow_replanning(True)
  tf_listener = tf.TransformListener() ❸
  rate = rospy.Rate(10)

  gripper_goal = GripperCommandGoal() ❹
```

```
gripper_goal.command.max_effort = 10.0

scene = PlanningSceneInterface("base_link")

p = Pose()
p.position.x = 0.4 + 0.15
p.position.y = -0.4
p.position.z = 0.7 + 0.15
p.orientation = Quaternion(*quaternion_from_euler(0, 1, 1))
arm.set_pose_target(p) ❺

while True:
  if arm.go(True):
    break
  clear_octomap()
  scene.clear()

look_at_bin()
while not rospy.is_shutdown():
  rate.sleep()
  try:
    t = tf_listener.getLatestCommonTime('/base_link', item_frame) ❻
    if (rospy.Time.now() - t).to_sec() > 0.2:
      rospy.sleep(0.1)
      continue

    (item_translation, item_orientation) = \
      tf_listener.lookupTransform('/base_link', item_frame, t) ❼
  except(tf.Exception, tf.LookupException,
         tf.ConnectivityException, tf.ExtrapolationException):
    continue

  gripper_goal.command.position = 0.15
  gripper.send_goal(gripper_goal) ❽
  gripper.wait_for_result(rospy.Duration(1.0))

  print "item: " + str(item_translation)
  scene.addCube(
      "item", 0.05,
      item_translation[0], item_translation[1], item_translation[2])

  p.position.x = item_translation[0] - 0.01 - 0.06
  p.position.y = item_translation[1]
  p.position.z = item_translation[2] + 0.04 + 0.14
  p.orientation = Quaternion(*quaternion_from_euler(0, 1.2, 0))
  arm.set_pose_target(p)
  arm.go(True) ❾

  #os.system("rosservice call clear_octomap")

  gripper_goal.command.position = 0
  gripper.send_goal(gripper_goal)
```

```
gripper.wait_for_result(rospy.Duration(2.0))

scene.removeAttachedObject("item")

clear_octomap()

p.position.x = 0.00
p.position.y = -0.25
p.position.z = 0.75 - .1
p.orientation = Quaternion(*quaternion_from_euler(0, -1.5, -1.5))
arm.set_pose_target(p)
arm.go(True)  ❿
break  ⓫
```

❶ Since we will need a connection to the gripper action server later to grab the target object, there's no sense proceeding further until it's up. We'll wait here for the gripper server (and, by implication, the rest of the Fetch robot controller) to start.

❷ As in previous chapters, we'll use MoveGroupCommander as a Python interface to the MoveIt motion planning system.

❸ The TransformListener instance is how we will subscribe to the transformations (both static and dynamic) being broadcasted by the rest of our system, including the robot joint states, the move_base navigation subsystem, and the ALVAR marker subsystem.

❹ We'll need a gripper goal object later on to send to the gripper action server. We'll initialize it here to save space later, but this is just a stylistic choice.

❺ This pose of the arm is chosen so that the gripper is out of the way of the depth camera, yet still in a "high" posture to make life a bit easier on the motion planner. Many robots have postures such as this, sometimes called "ready," "pregrasp," or something similar.

❻ By default, the tf transform system will "remember" transforms for several seconds. However, since our robot is moving around, we want to ensure that we only use transform data that is quite recent. We're using 200 ms as a threshold for "recent enough," but that threshold will be application-dependent.

❼ This line will actually extract the requested transformation from the tf library's local representation of the transform tree.

❽ This command will fully open the gripper of the Fetch robot.

❾ Here is where the magic happens! We are asking MoveIt to plan and execute a collision-free path to the item's location.

---

⑩ This command instructs the arm to lift up the object and bring it back closer to the robot's torso.

⑪ If we've made it this far, we have now picked up the object, and we can exit the outer `while` loop that was originally searching for detections of the target object.

This bin-filled stockroom scene is considerably more complex than the Chess-bot world. As a result, we will use the built-in MoveIt collision mapping system. This uses a package called `octomap` to build and maintain a 3D volumetric pixel (*voxel*) map of occupied and free cells in the workspace. Voxel maps are complex structures, but fortunately, the behavior is transparent from the MoveIt user's perspective: the arm simply won't crash into things that the depth camera can see. Figure 14-11 shows a typical OctoMap rendering of the stockroom scene in `rviz`. The "boxy" appearance is OctoMap's data structure: the world is represented as a series of small cubes. The task of MoveIt's planning subsystem is to generate arm paths that avoid the obstacles represented in the OctoMap rendering, while still arriving at the goal state. This task is processor-intensive, which is why motion planning often takes a few seconds to complete.

Note that activating OctoMap's collision-avoidance system was purely a configuration task. The high-level usage of MoveIt remains the same; it just takes a bit longer to run when MoveIt has to consider all of those obstacles.

The amazing thing about a high-dimensional motion planning system like MoveIt is that it gracefully uses all the joints on the robot to achieve the commanded gripper positions and orientations. As discussed previously, the robot's navigation system will deliver the robot in front of the bin, but with a typical positioning error on the order of +/- 10 cm due to map discretization, sensor noise, and a host of other factors. The arm motion planner can use all of the joints of the arm (and on the Fetch robot, the torso-lift joint) to deliver the gripper to a precise location relative to the fiducial marker on the back of the bin. So long as the arm doesn't crash into anything, the motion planner is free to be "creative" in what arm postures and trajectories it uses.

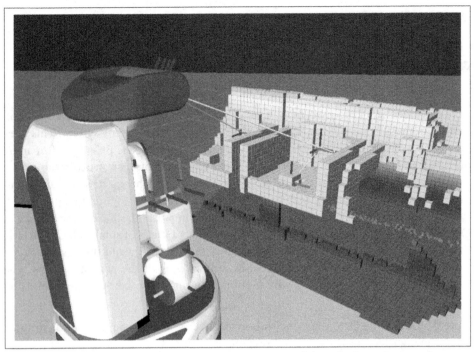

Figure 14-11. The OctoMap system generates 3D maps of the robot's workspace, for use by the arm path planner

In practice, the planning problem is so difficult that algorithms often make use of random "guesses" for trajectories and iteratively refine them during the planning process. This means that there will be considerable variation in the solutions the planner comes up with. We asked Stockroom-bot to pick up an object from the same bin several times and assembled the grasp configurations into several renderings in Figure 14-12. Although the gripper was always in the same orientation relative to the green "target" item, the positioning of the rest of the arm and torso varied considerably.

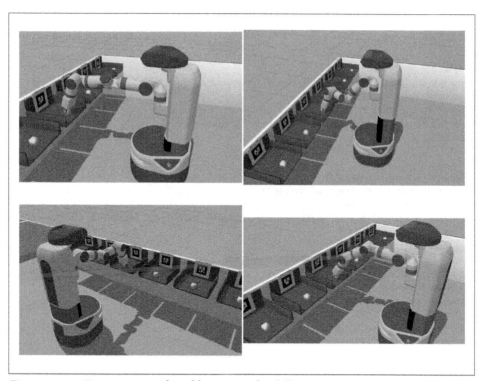

Figure 14-12. Various grasps found by MoveIt for different alignments of the robot with respect to the bin

Now that we can pick up the item, the final process is to deliver it to the "customer counter" outside the stockroom. This process requires the robot to navigate to a position behind the counter, extend the arm, open the gripper to drop the object, and then retract the arm and return to the stockroom. These steps are accomplished by the script in Example 14-16, which implements a minimalist approach to these problems, and illustrated in Figure 14-13 and Figure 14-14.

Example 14-16. deliver_to_counter.py

```python
#!/usr/bin/env python
import sys, rospy, tf, actionlib, moveit_commander
from geometry_msgs.msg import *
from move_base_msgs.msg import MoveBaseAction, MoveBaseGoal
from tf.transformations import quaternion_from_euler
from control_msgs.msg import (GripperCommandAction, GripperCommandGoal)

if __name__ == '__main__':
  moveit_commander.roscpp_initialize(sys.argv)
  rospy.init_node('deliver_to_counter')
  args = rospy.myargv(argv=sys.argv)
  gripper = actionlib.SimpleActionClient("gripper_controller/gripper_action",
    GripperCommandAction)
  gripper.wait_for_server()
  move_base = actionlib.SimpleActionClient('move_base', MoveBaseAction)
  move_base.wait_for_server()
  goal = MoveBaseGoal()
  goal.target_pose.header.frame_id = 'map'
  goal.target_pose.pose.position.x = 4
  orient = Quaternion(*quaternion_from_euler(0, 0, 0))
  goal.target_pose.pose.orientation = orient
  move_base.send_goal(goal)
  move_base.wait_for_result()

  arm = moveit_commander.MoveGroupCommander("arm")
  arm.allow_replanning(True)
  p = Pose()
  p.position.x = 0.9
  p.position.z = 0.95
  p.orientation = Quaternion(*quaternion_from_euler(0, 0.5, 0))
  arm.set_pose_target(p)
  arm.go(True)
  gripper_goal = GripperCommandGoal()
  gripper_goal.command.max_effort = 10.0
  gripper_goal.command.position = 0.15
  gripper.send_goal(gripper_goal)
  gripper.wait_for_result(rospy.Duration(1.0))

  p.position.x = 0.05
  p.position.y = -0.15
  p.position.z = 0.75
  p.orientation = Quaternion(*quaternion_from_euler(0, -1.5, -1.5))
  arm.set_pose_target(p)
  arm.go(True)

  goal.target_pose.pose.position.x = 0
  move_base.send_goal(goal)
  move_base.wait_for_result()
```

Figure 14-13. The Fetch robot reaching out to deliver an item onto the "customer counter" in the front of the stockroom

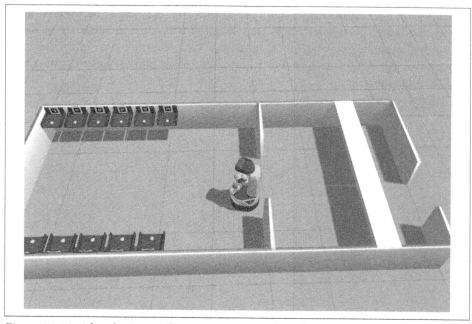

Figure 14-14. After the item-delivery phase is complete, the Fetch robot returns to its "ready position" in the center of the bins

Summary

This chapter described a useful robotic application: stockroom automation. Various tools in the ROS and Gazebo ecosystem were utilized to develop an approach to the problem. First, we developed a Gazebo model of the environment. Next, we mapped this simulated environment and created scripts to drive the robot to the various storage bins. Then, we developed a script for the robot to use visual fiducial markers to precisely determine locations within the storage bins and grasp objects from known locations relative to the bins. The final code example showed how to drive the robot to the customer counter, drop the item, and return the robot to the stockroom.

These code examples provide building blocks that could be used to create a real-world robot application. Of course, in the interest of simplifying the examples, we did not provide robust error handling or a notification system so that the robot can "call a friend" when it gets stuck. We also did not describe a user interface. All of these additional aspects can be developed with existing or modified ROS tools: the Robot Web Tools system can be used to interface user-facing web interfaces to ROS systems, for example. The simulation environment and building-block scripts developed in this chapter could then be used to allow user experience (UX) designers to develop the user-facing interface purely in simulation, which would permit huge time savings and automated interface testing.

Up until this point in the book, we have been using existing robot platforms, such as the Turtlebot, Robonaut 2, and Fetch robots. However, the field of robotics is full of custom hardware! Fortunately, ROS was designed with custom hardware in mind, since it had multiple evolving robots in its user base from day one. In the next few chapters, we will demonstrate how to add custom robots into various components of the ROS ecosystem.

## PART IV

Bringing Your Own Stuff into ROS

## CHAPTER 15

Your Own Sensors and Actuators

Up until now, we've looked at how you can use ROS to interact with existing sensor and actuator hardware. Although ROS covers a wide variety of popular sensors and actuators, it doesn't cover all of them. As new hardware becomes available, we'll have to bring it into ROS, so that it can be used by the community.

In this chapter, we'll see how you can integrate new sensors and actuators into the ROS ecosystem. This process is, for the most part, relatively painless; it involves writing ROS wrappers around the APIs that you're already using to access these devices. We'll start off with adding your own sensors.

Adding Your Own Sensors

How do you add a new sensor to ROS? We're going to assume that the sensor already has a Python API that you can call to get measurements from it, and that you know how to use this API. We're also going to assume that everything is wired up correctly and that you've been able to use this API to successfully read the sensor. Although this seems like common sense, you should always verify that things are working as expected before you start to wrap up a sensor in ROS. If you know that the sensor is working, then anything that goes wrong will be a problem with the ROS wrapper, which will make things easier to debug.

A (Fake) Sensor

For this chapter, we're going to use a fake sensor (called FakeSensor) with a simple API. This Python class is going to simulate a real sensor, allowing us to show you how to wrap up a sensor in ROS without you having to buy any additional hardware. Although it's not a real sensor, it has the types of API commonly found on real sensors.

Our fake sensor brings up a simple graphical interface using the PySide graphical library (which you need to have installed on your computer), shown in Figure 15-1 with a dial in it. Turning the dial causes the sensor to output different measurements (integers from 0 to 99).

Figure 15-1. The graphical interface for our fake sensor

The measurements from this sensor can be accessed in two ways: by explicitly calling the class's value() function, or by registering a callback that gets called whenever the values change. We'll see some code for both of these shortly.

Designing the ROS Wrapper

Before we look at how to implement a ROS wrapper for our sensor, we need to make a couple of design decisions. The first is whether the ROS wrapper should stream the values of the sensor over a topic or only give measurements when asked, using a service or action call. This really depends on how you're going to use the data from the sensor, so we're going to cover both approaches here.

The second decision to make is how you're going to access data from the sensor. Some sensors will have only one way to get data from them, but some (like our Fake Sensor) will have multiple ways. Again, you should make this decision based on how you're going to use the sensor and how costly it is to make measurements using your sensor's API. Sometimes it may only make sense to implement one option, but in other cases you may want to implement more than one.

Finally, you need to decide what type of ROS messages your wrapper will produce. As a general rule, you should try to use message types that are already defined in ROS, so that your newly wrapped sensor is as broadly useful as possible. For our FakeSensor, we've decided to interpret the measurements as angles and to use a Quaternion (*http://docs.ros.org/api/geometry_msgs/html/msg/Quaternion.html*) from the geometry_msgs (*http://wiki.ros.org/geometry_msgs?distro=indigo*) package.

Why not have the wrapper just provide angles in radians and use Float32 (*http://docs.ros.org/api/std_msgs/html/msg/Float32.html*) messages from std_msgs (*http://wiki.ros.org/std_msgs?distro=indigo*)? This would be simpler, since we wouldn't have to convert the output of the sensor (an integer from 0 to 99) into a quaternion. We could certainly do that, but it would be less useful, in the long run, than using a qua-ternion. Angles can be represented in a variety of ways, and ROS has settled on qua-ternions as the standard. If we have a sensor that returns angles, we should follow the standard and stick to quaternions, even if it's (slightly) more work or we don't think it's necessarily the right decision. The more of the ROS ecosystem (including code that we write ourselves) that sticks to the accepted conventions, the more interopera-ble everything will be, and the more likely it is that other people will use our code.

Design 1: Periodic Measurements over a Topic

The first wrapper that we will look at will send out measurements periodically over a topic. Example 15-1 shows the code that does this.

Example 15-1. topic_sensor.py

```python
#!/usr/bin/env python

from math import pi

from fake_sensor import FakeSensor    ❶

import rospy
import tf

from geometry_msgs.msg import Quaternion    ❷


def make_quaternion(angle):    ❸
    q = tf.transformations.quaternion_from_euler(0, 0, angle)
    return Quaternion(*q)


if __name__ == '__main__':
    sensor = FakeSensor()    ❹

    rospy.init_node('fake_sensor')

    pub = rospy.Publisher('angle', Quaternion, queue_size=10)

    rate = rospy.Rate(10.0)    ❺
    while not rospy.is_shutdown():    ❻
        angle = sensor.value() * 2 * pi / 100.0

        q = make_quaternion(angle)

        pub.publish(q)

        rate.sleep()
```

❶ Import the code to access the sensor measurements.

❷ Since we're using a `Quaternion`, we need to import that, too.

❸ A convenience function to convert from yaw (in radians) to a `Quaternion`.

❹ Set up access to the sensor.

❺ Set a publishing rate.

❻ Loop until the node is shut down.

The interesting part of the core is the loop where we read the sensor, translate the returned measurement into something useful, and then publish it out on a topic. In this example, we take the measurement, an integer between 0 and 99, and turn that into an angle in radians. We then take that angle—which we're going to interpret as a rotation around the z-axis (a yaw)—and turn that into a `Quaternion`. We've encapsulated this translation into a helper function to make things cleaner. Then, we publish the calculated `Quaternion` on the topic and sleep for a while.

Something new here is the quaternion translation code. Quaternions are a representation of rotation that uses four real-valued numbers. Intuitively, these correspond to a vector (three values) and a rotation around that vector (fourth value). There are several ways to represent quaternions, and it's always best to use the built-in functions in ROS to do the translation. If you do it by hand, you might get the wrong representation by accident and create a bug that's hard to find.

We can verify that the node is publishing what we expect it to using `rostopic`:

```
user@hostname$ rostopic list
/angle
/rosout
/rosout_agg

user@hostname$ rostopic hz angle
average rate: 9.999
        min: 0.100s max: 0.100s std dev: 0.00006s window: 10
average rate: 10.000
        min: 0.100s max: 0.100s std dev: 0.00005s window: 20
average rate: 10.000
        min: 0.100s max: 0.100s std dev: 0.00007s window: 30
average rate: 10.000
        min: 0.100s max: 0.100s std dev: 0.00006s window: 40
average rate: 10.000
        min: 0.100s max: 0.100s std dev: 0.00007s window: 46

user@hostname$ rostopic echo -n 1 angle
x: 0.0
```

```
  y: 0.0
  z: 0.0
  w: 1.0
  ---
```

That looks about right. We see the `angle` topic with `rostopic list`, and it seems to be publishing at the right rate, according to `rostopic hz`. Finally, `rostopic echo` shows that the data is reasonable. Note that we stopped `rostopic hz` with a Ctrl-C; otherwise, it would run forever.

So, it's as simple as that: read the sensor, translate the readings into something useful, publish them out, wait a bit, and repeat. Now, we're going to look at what to do for sensors that stream their information to you.

 When publishing data from a sensor, it's often a good idea to use a ROS message type with a `Header`, so that you can add a timestamp to the data that you send. While this isn't strictly necessary, it lets you coordinate data from multiple sensors in time (by correlating their timestamps using the `message_filters` package (*http://wiki.ros.org/message_filters?distro=indigo*)).

Design 2: Streaming Measurements over a Topic

Now, let's assume that the sensor returns measurements automatically, in a stream, using a callback mechanism. The ROS wrapper code in this case is very similar to that shown in Example 15-1, except that we put all of the translation and publishing code in the callback that we pass to the sensor. Example 15-2 shows the details.

Example 15-2. topic_sensor2.py

```python
#!/usr/bin/env python

from math import pi

from fake_sensor import FakeSensor

import rospy
import tf

from geometry_msgs.msg import Quaternion


def make_quaternion(angle):
    q = tf.transformations.quaternion_from_euler(0, 0, angle)
    return Quaternion(*q)

def publish_value(value):
    angle = value * 2 * pi / 100.0
```

```
    q = make_quaternion(angle)
    pub.publish(q)


if __name__ == '__main__':
    rospy.init_node('fake_sensor')

    pub = rospy.Publisher('angle', Quaternion, queue_size=10)

    sensor = FakeSensor()
    sensor.register_callback(publish_value)
```

The key difference in this code is that we register a callback function, `pub` `lish_value()` with the sensor handler to deal with the measurements returned by the sensor. This is a common design pattern with sensors and one that is widely used in ROS. In the callback function, which is passed the measurement value, we again do the translation, build a `Quaternion`, and publish it out to the topic. In this case, we will only publish at the rate the sensor produces measurements. If this only happens infrequently, and getting an old measurement is better than waiting (potentially a long time) for a new one, then you might consider making this a latched topic (see "Latched Topics" on page 38).

Design 3: Streaming Measurements Published at a Fixed Rate

Suppose your sensor API uses callbacks and delivers measurements every now and then, but you want to publish these measurements at a fixed rate. This is a combination of the first two designs and is illustrated by Example 15-3.

Example 15-3. topic_sensor3.py

```
#!/usr/bin/env python

from math import pi
from threading import Lock

from fake_sensor import FakeSensor

import rospy
import tf

from geometry_msgs.msg import Quaternion


def make_quaternion(angle):
    q = tf.transformations.quaternion_from_euler(0, 0, angle)
    return Quaternion(*q)

def save_value(value):
    with lock: ❶
```

```
        angle = value * 2 * pi / 100.0  ❷


if __name__ == '__main__':
    lock = Lock()  ❸

    sensor = FakeSensor()
    sensor.register_callback(save_value)

    rospy.init_node('fake_sensor')

    pub = rospy.Publisher('angle', Quaternion, queue_size=10)

    angle = None  ❹
    rate = rospy.Rate(10.0)
    while not rospy.is_shutdown():
        with lock:
            if angle:  ❺
                q = make_quaternion(angle)
                pub.publish(q)

        rate.sleep()
```

❶   Get the lock on `angle`.

❷   Update the value of `angle`, based on the sensor measurement.

❸   Create a lock for `angle`, to prevent simultaneous access.

❹   Initially set `angle` to None. This will be overwritten in the first execution of the callback function.

❺   If the callback has assigned a value to `angle`, this will evaluate; then the `if` clause will evaluate `True`, and a new message will be published on the topic. If the callback hasn't run yet, no message will be published.

This code contains both a callback, to deal with the sensor measurements, and a publishing loop, to deal with publishing messages on the topic. We have also added a concurrency lock, to avoid the `angle` variable being accessed in the callback and in the publishing loop at the same time. The callback function simply stores the current value of the angle, based on the sensor measurement. This value is published periodically by the publishing loop.

Design 4: Sensor Measurements on Demand

The final design we will look at deals with the case where you only want to report a sensor measurement on demand, when some node asks for it. If the process of getting a measurement from the sensor is quick, then you should use a service call for this. If it is slower, then you should probably use an action call. We will illustrate the basic approach with a service call; the action interface will be structured similarly.

Our service call will take no arguments, and return a Quaternion. Example 15-4 shows the service-definition file.

Example 15-4. FakeSensor.srv

```
std_msgs/Empty
---
geometry_msgs/Quaternion quaternion
```

We could omit the std_msgs/Empty definition, and ROS would interpret this as defining a service call with no inputs. However, we've chosen to use the Empty message type here, to explicitly show that we're not expecting any inputs.

Example 15-5 shows the code for a service-based ROS wrapper for our sensor. The structure of a service node should be familiar from the discussion in Chapter 4.

Example 15-5. service_sensor.py

```python
#!/usr/bin/env python

from math import pi

from fake_sensor import FakeSensor

import rospy
import tf

from geometry_msgs.msg import Quaternion
from stuff.srv import FakeSensor,FakeSensorResponse


def make_quaternion(angle):
    q = tf.transformations.quaternion_from_euler(0, 0, angle)
    return Quaternion(*q)

def callback(request):    ❶
    angle = sensor.value() * 2 * pi / 100.0
    q = make_quaternion(angle)

    return FakeSensorResponse(q)
```

```
if __name__ == '__main__':
    sensor = FakeSensor()

    rospy.init_node('fake_sensor')

    service = rospy.Service('angle', FakeSensor, callback) ❷
```

❶   Callback function to deal with the service request.

❷   Set up the service handler.

If your sensor returns measurements through a callback mechanism, then you'll have to store these values using a method similar to the one in "Design 3: Streaming Measurements Published at a Fixed Rate" on page 264, and then return them in the service callback.

Adding Your Own Actuators

Now that we've seen how to add your own sensors to ROS, let's take a look at how you can add in your own actuators. The general approach is going to be similar: decide how you're going to send commands to the actuator, decide on what data types to use, and then encapsulate the existing API in a ROS wrapper.

A (Fake) Actuator

Just like in the sensor example, we're going to use a fake actuator (called FakeActuator) to illustrate how you might write a ROS wrapper for a real actuator. As before, our fake actuator, shown in Figure 15-2, brings up a PySide GUI. The elements of this GUI represent a light (top), a volume control (middle), and a rotational element (bottom). Think of it as representing a searchlight and speaker on a swiveling base. Although it's not a real actuator, it does have some of the properties that you might see in a real actuator API. You can toggle the light on and off with a call to the toggle_light() function, you can set a volume with the set_volume() function, and you can set a rotational position with the set_position() function. Each of these three parts of the actuator also has a function that tells you what state it's currently in (light_on(), volume(), and position(), respectively). More importantly for the rest of this section, these three parts of the actuator are representative of the types of interactions we have with real actuators.

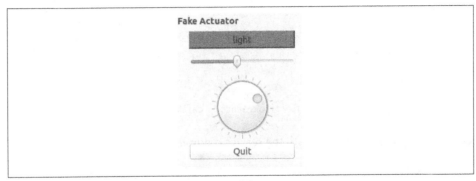

Figure 15-2. The graphical interface for our fake actuator

Designing the ROS Wrapper

When designing the ROS wrapper, there are two main things to consider: what type of interaction to have with the actuator hardware and what data types you should be using. For our fake sensor, there are three parts to the device: the volume control, the light, and the rotational position. We'll deal with each of these separately.

The type of interaction that you have with the actuator will determine the ROS mechanism that you use to control it. If you're going to be constantly sending commands to the hardware, then you should use a topic. If you are occasionally sending commands that get implemented quickly by the hardware, then you should use a service call. Finally, if you're occasionally sending commands that take a long time (or a highly variable amount of time) to complete, then you should use an action. We'll expand on this in the following sections. For now, though, the code for the ROS wrapper around our fake actuator is shown in Example 15-6.

Example 15-6. actuator.py

```python
#!/usr/bin/env python

from fake_actuator import FakeActuator

import rospy
import actionlib
from std_msgs.msg import Float32

from sensors.srv import Light,LightResponse
from sensors.msg import RotationAction,RotationFeedback,RotationResult


def volume_callback(msg):
    actuator.set_volume(min(100, max(0, int(msg.data * 100))))
```

```
def light_callback(request):
    actuator.toggle_light(request.on)
    return LightResponse(actuator.light_on())


def rotation_callback(goal):
    feedback = RotationFeedback()
    result = RotationResult()

    actuator.set_position(goal.orientation)
    success = True

    rate = rospy.Rate(10)
    while fabs(goal.orientation - actuator.position()) > 0.01:
        if a.is_preempt_requested():
            success = False
            break;

        feedback.current_orientation = actuator.position()
        a.publish_feedback(feedback)
        rate.sleep()

    result.final_orientation = actuator.position()
    if success:
        a.set_succeeded(result)
    else:
        a.set_preempted(result)


if __name__ == '__main__':
    actuator = FakeActuator() ❶

    # Initialize the node
    rospy.init_node('fake')

    # Topic for the volume
    t = rospy.Subscriber('fake/volume', Float32, volume_callback) ❷

    # Service for the light
    s = rospy.Service('fake/light', Light, light_callback) ❸

    # Action for the position
    a = actionlib.SimpleActionServer('fake/position', RotationAction, ❹
                                     execute_cb=rotation_callback,
                                     auto_start=False)
    a.start()

    # Start everything
    rospy.spin()
```

❶ Initialize the actuator, and do any setup you need to make it work.

❷ Subscribe to a topic for volume commands.

❸ Announce a service to control the light.

❹ Announce an action to control the rotational position.

The `import` statements deserve a little extra attention:

```
#!/usr/bin/env python

from fake_actuator import FakeActuator

import rospy
import actionlib
from std_msgs.msg import Float32

from sensors.srv import Light,LightResponse
from sensors.msg import RotationAction,RotationFeedback,RotationResult
```

The first statement imports the previously defined service definitions for the light, `Light` and `LightResponse`, which we discussed. The second statement pulls in the definitions for all of the messages related to the rotation action interface, also discussed previously. We need all three to make the action work.

Design 1: Continuous Actuation

We can treat the volume control on our fake actuator as an example of continuous actuation; we're going to constantly send it volumes—floating-point numbers in the range 0 to 1—and it's going to set the volume appropriately. The commands are one-way: we're going to set the volume, but there's no feedback on what the current volume is. If we wanted to confirm that the volume actually did get set, then we would use a service call, similar to the example in the next section. However, for now, we're going to assume that the volume will always get set correctly. We're also implicitly assuming that setting the volume is something that happens quickly and is not buffered by the actuator; that is, that the device is capable of responding to a volume-setting request before the next request comes in. If this isn't the case, then one of the other designs might be more appropriate.

So, we're going to continually send volume commands to the device, and the volume is going to get set quickly. In this case, a topic is a good choice for the communication mechanism. Since we're going to be sending floating-point numbers corresponding to the fraction of total volume to set, we've chosen to use `Float32` for the message type. We could have defined our own unique message type for this: say, one called `Volume` and containing a single-floating point number. However, using a more generic type makes it easier to use the topic interface, since we don't have to convert from a `Float32` published by other nodes into the new data type.

We've chosen to name the topic `fake/volume`. It's a common practice, when a single device has a number of different interfaces, to use a namespace like this. All interfaces for the device start with `fake/` and end with a descriptive name.

As you might imagine, the code for the callback connected with this topic, shown in Example 15-7, is quite simple. All we do is call the volume-setting function with the value from the message. In this case, we're multiplying the value by 100, since the device expects an integer from 0 to 100 and the topic delivers a floating-point number between 1 and 0. We're also capping the range of the value we pass on to be between 0 and 100, so that the volume stays within the bounds expected by the device. The callback is a natural place to do this sort of conversion and bounds checking. It's also a good place to enforce software limits on your hardware devices. For example, if you never wanted the volume on the device to go above 80% of maximum, this would be the place to make that happen.

Example 15-7. The topic callback for the volume control

```
def volume_callback(msg):
    actuator.set_volume(min(100, max(0, int(msg.data * 100))))
```

The `set_volume()` call in Example 15-7 deserves some extra explanation, because it's a bit gnarly. We're taking the value in the message (which is a `float` between 0 and 1), scaling it up to a number between 0 and 100, then converting it to an integer with the `int()` function. We're then clipping it to the range 0 to 100, just case we got bad data in the message. The `max()` function returns `0` if the scaled value is less than zero, and the value itself otherwise. This establishes a lower bound. This value then goes through the `min()` function, which returns `100` or the value, whichever is lower. These two steps ensure that the resulting value passed to `set_volume()` is an integer between 0 and 100, inclusive.

Design 2: Infrequent, Instantaneous Actuation

ROS networking is "best effort," and there's always a (small) chance that a message sent over a topic won't get received and acted upon. ROS topics are built on TCP sockets, which have guaranteed delivery, but a message can still be lost if the subscriber's message buffer overflows. The chances of this are small, at least for well-designed code, but it can happen. If you're sending frequent commands, and one of them doesn't make it through, then the assumption is that it isn't the end of the world; as long as packets are only dropped occasionally, they're being sent often enough that it won't cause any serious problems.

However, if you're only sending commands occasionally, losing one of them is a bigger deal, and you'd like to be sure that they all get through. In this case, the right thing to do is to use a service call. This allows you to issue a command to the actuator and wait until you get an acknowledgment back, often containing information on whether or not the command was successful.

The light on our fake sensor is a good example of the sort of actuator that should use a service-call interface. Turning the light on or off is a discrete operation that, presumably, we won't be doing at a high frequency. The code for the service callback, shown in Example 15-8, is almost as simple as the code for the topic callback in the previous section.

Example 15-8. The service callback for the volume control

```
def light_callback(request):
    actuator.toggle_light(request.on)
    return LightResponse(actuator.light_on())
```

All that the code does is pass on the command (a Boolean representing the desired state of the light) to the device API. It then returns a Boolean with the current state of the light. The node calling the service can compare the command to the return value, and verify that everything worked as expected. The service definition is shown in Example 15-9; it's simply a single Boolean parameter to the service call, representing the desired state of the light, and another Boolean for the return value, representing the actual state of the light after the call.

Example 15-9. Light.srv

```
bool on
---
bool status
```

Service calls are synchronous; the calling node has to wait for a response from the server. This is fine if the command doesn't take long to perform or if the calling node can afford to wait. However, it can cause problems if the command takes a long time to execute and you don't want to wait for it to finish. In this case, you should use an action interface for your actuator.

Design 3: Infrequent, Extended Actuation

As we learned in Chapter 5, action interfaces are similar to service interfaces in that they allow the calling node to be sure that the command was received and acted upon. However, since actions are asynchronous, they don't require the calling node to wait for the command to finish. This is ideal for actions that can take a long time. A great example of this is the navigation stack: we don't want to have to wait until the robot navigates to a goal location, but we do want to know when it gets there.

In our fake actuator, the set_position() function sets a desired rotational position. However, the actuator has a limited rotational speed and cannot instantaneously move from one position to another. This makes it a good candidate for an action interface. The code for the action callback is shown in Example 15-10, and the action definition is shown in Example 15-11.

Example 15-10. The action callback for the volume control

```
def rotation_callback(goal):
    feedback = RotationFeedback()
    result = RotationResult()

    actuator.set_position(goal.orientation)
    success = True

    rate = rospy.Rate(10)
    while fabs(goal.orientation - actuator.position()) > 0.01:
        if a.is_preempt_requested():
            success = False
            break;

        feedback.current_orientation = actuator.position()
        a.publish_feedback(feedback)
        rate.sleep()

    result.final_orientation = actuator.position()
    if success:
        a.set_succeeded(result)
    else:
        a.set_preempted(result)
```

Example 15-11. Rotation.action

```
float32 orientation
---
float32 final_orientation
---
float32 current_orientation
```

We begin by allocating a `RotationFeedback` and a `RotationResult` to return incremental feedback on progress and the final position of the actuator, respectively. Both of these are floating-point numbers and correspond to positions of the actuator.

Next, we pass the requested position to the device API, which starts the actuator turning. Then, we loop until the actual position of the actuator is close to the requested position. On each pass through this loop, we check to see if the action has been preempted (and break the loop if it has) and send back the current position as periodic feedback to the calling node. We use a `Rate` instance to loop at 10 Hz. Finally, if the action was not preempted, we set its status to `succeeded` and return the final position of the actuator.

This allows the calling node to issue a rotation command and not have to wait until it completes. It still gets periodic updates and notification of success or failure through the use of callbacks.

Summary

In this chapter, we've seen how to take a new sensor or actuator and write a wrapper for it to bring it into the ROS ecosystem. For sensors, once you decide on the message type, the delivery mechanism (topic, service, or action), and how to access measurements from the sensor, writing a wrapper is quite straightforward. For actuators, the mechanism is (largely) determined by how you are going to interact with the device. Topics are often a good choice if you're going to be constantly sending commands and can afford to lose a message occasionally. If you are going to send commands less frequently, or really need to make sure the commands were acted on, you should use a service (for things that happen quickly) or actions (for things that happen more slowly).

Once you bring something new into ROS, the next step is to tell people about it. As we'll see in Chapter 22, one of the strongest parts of ROS is the community of people contributing to it. If you bring some new hardware into the ecosystem, you should think about hosting the code in a public place, writing up some documentation and a wiki page, and telling the community about it (see Chapter 22 for details on how and where to do this). This will let others benefit from your hard work and will make ROS even stronger and better than it already is.

Now that we've seen how we can add individual new sensors and actuators into ROS, the next few chapters look at how you can bring whole new robot platforms into the ecosystem.

## CHAPTER 16

Your Own Mobile Robot

One of the most rewarding (if occasionally frustrating) robotics projects you can undertake is to build your own robot. There are lots of great robots out there, but sometimes there isn't one that suits your specific needs. Or perhaps you just want to have the experience of designing and building a robot yourself. Whatever the reason, once you've built your amazing custom robot, how do you go about controlling it with ROS?

In this chapter, we'll walk through the steps of connecting a new robot (albeit one inspired by a very old robot) to ROS, allowing us to then use the libraries and tools that we've discussed throughout this book. While we're framing this chapter as a guide to ROS-controlling your from-scratch custom robot, it applies equally well to any robot that isn't already "ROS-ready," whether a robot built from a kit of parts or an off-the-shelf robot that doesn't yet have ROS support (an increasingly rare occurrence).

TortoiseBot

We're going to build a new indoor mobile robot. For inspiration, we look to one of the very earliest such robots, which was called Elsie (Figure 16-1). Elsie was one of a series of robots built in the late 1940s by Grey Walter, a British neurophysiologist (or perhaps cybernetician). A pioneer in his field, Walter built robots as part of his study of animal behavior. He believed that by building machines that exhibit complex, life-like behavior, we can learn about how natural organisms work. This area of study would eventually come to be called *artificial life*.

Figure 16-1. Grey Walter's Elsie, one of a series of "Tortoise" robots built in the 1940s

Walter's robots were amazing technological and scientific feats: hand-built, analog machines capable of randomly wandering around a room, avoiding (or at least bouncing off) obstacles, and returning to a charging station when their batteries ran low.[1] Walter's tortoise was built on a tricycle chassis, with two passive rear wheels and one steered and driven front wheel. Coupled to the front wheel was a photo diode that caused the robot to steer toward light sources (but, through clever electrical integration, to prefer not to get too close).

Because of their dome-like protective shells and their plodding movements, Walter called his robots *tortoises*. In homage to Walter's work, in this chapter we're going to build a *TortoiseBot*. Well, we won't actually build it, but we will explain what you need

---

1 Except for being hand-built and analog, they might remind you of a certain robot vacuum cleaner that came along 50 years later.

to know to control it from ROS, were you to build it yourself—and we will build a simulation model of it.

The steps to using ROS to control a TortoiseBot, or pretty much any new robot, are:

1. Decide on the ROS message interface.
2. Write drivers for the robot's motors.
3. Write a model of the robot's physical structure.
4. Extend the model with physical properties for use in simulation with Gazebo.
5. Publish coordinate transform data via `tf` and visualize it with `rviz`.
6. Add sensors, with driver and simulation support.
7. Apply standard algorithms, such as navigation.

In the following sections and into the next chapter, we'll go through each step, explaining the decisions that need to be made along the way. At the end, you'll be ready to get your own custom robot (regardless of whether it bears any resemblance to the TortoiseBot) running ROS.

ROS Message Interface

The first thing that we need to do is to get control of the mobile base. We want to write a ROS node that will communicate with the mobile base hardware, in whatever manner is available, then present to the rest of the system a standard ROS interface. This is a common and core concept of ROS: *abstraction*. Whatever the particulars of a specific robot, in ROS we want to make it look and interact like other robots to which it is similar. Then we can reuse an entire ecosystem of tools and libraries that are designed to work with a standard interface.

The defining characteristics of the TortoiseBot are that it is mobile and that it is confined to driving on the ground (as opposed to climbing walls or flying). More specifically, because of its kinematic configuration, the TortoiseBot can move in the ways that a tricycle can: it can translate forward and backward (along its x-axis), it can yaw (rotate about its z-axis), and it can do combinations of the two. The TortoiseBot cannot translate side to side (y-axis) or up and down (z-axis). Neither can it roll or pitch its body (rotation about its x- or y-axes, respectively). So, fundamentally, it is sufficient to control the TortoiseBot by sending it a pair of desired velocities:

vx
> Linear velocity along the x-axis (by convention, positive is forward).

vyaw
> Rotational velocity about the z-axis (by convention, positive is counterclockwise).

In return, we would expect the robot to report its position and orientation in the plane as (*x*, *y*, *yaw*).

To represent robots like the TortoiseBot, the ROS community has arrived at the following ROS message interface, which is supported by a huge variety of mobile platforms:

geometry_msgs/Twist (cmd_vel *topic*)
> The desired velocity of the robot, sent as a command to the robot.

nav_msgs/Odometry (odom *topic*)
> The position and orientation of the robot, sent as data by the robot.

Let's see what's in each of those message types, using the rosmsg show command, starting with geometry_msgs/Twist:

```
user@hostname$ rosmsg show geometry_msgs/Twist
geometry_msgs/Vector3 linear
  float64 x
  float64 y
  float64 z
geometry_msgs/Vector3 angular
  float64 x
  float64 y
  float64 z
```

That's simple enough: three linear velocities for translations along each axis, and three angular velocities for rotations about each axis. We don't actually need some of the fields (specifically, linear/y, linear/z, angular/x, or angular/y), but it's easy enough to ignore them and just take the values that we can use.

Now for nav_msgs/Odometry:

```
user@hostname$ rosmsg show nav_msgs/Odometry
std_msgs/Header header
  uint32 seq
  time stamp
  string frame_id
string child_frame_id
geometry_msgs/PoseWithCovariance pose
  geometry_msgs/Pose pose
    geometry_msgs/Point position
      float64 x
      float64 y
      float64 z
    geometry_msgs/Quaternion orientation
      float64 x
      float64 y
      float64 z
      float64 w
  float64[36] covariance
```

```
geometry_msgs/TwistWithCovariance twist
  geometry_msgs/Twist twist
    geometry_msgs/Vector3 linear
      float64 x
      float64 y
      float64 z
    geometry_msgs/Vector3 angular
      float64 x
      float64 y
      float64 z
  float64[36] covariance
```

 Many ROS messages contain a field called header, which has the type std_msgs/Header. The header is used to communicate two pieces of information that are necessary for the correct interpretation of many types of data in a robot system: at what time the data was produced and in what coordinate frame it is represented. The header is treated specially in a few ways in ROS, notably in the tf library, which provides tools for converting many types of data between coordinate frames. As a result, you can easily perform what would otherwise be complex operations, like converting range scans acquired at different times from different lasers into a common coordinate frame for processing.

That's an imposing message format, with a lot of fields to fill out. Fortunately, as with the geometry_msgs/Twist message, we can leave a lot of them empty. To report the robot's position and orientation, we only really need to fill out the pose/pose/position and pose/pose/orientation fields, ignoring the covariance fields (which are only needed for downstream components that reason about uncertainty). Within pose/pose/position, we only need to fill out x and y. Working with pose/pose/orientation is little more complex: even though the robot can only rotate about one axis (z), we need to construct a valid quaternion that represents a 3D orientation. Constructing and working with quaternions is outside the scope of this book; luckily there are lots of great tutorials online, as well as various helper utilities within ROS (a good place to start is the documentation for tf (*http://wiki.ros.org/tf?distro=indigo*)).

While we can ignore unneeded fields, it certainly seems like the cmd_vel/odom interface is overkill for our simple TortoiseBot, which just roams around on the ground. We could easily define a much simpler message interface for the TortoiseBot that includes just the fields that make sense for our robot. But then we wouldn't be compatible with other robots, or the tools and libraries that are designed to work with them. This is a common point of tension: when deciding what ROS interface to present, we must weigh specificity against interoperability, looking for the best fit for our robot that will give us the greatest ability to reuse existing tools and libraries. In the case of a mobile robot, it's much more powerful and flexible to use the cmd_vel/odom interface, which can represent arbitrary poses in 3D, with uncertainty. A common set of tools can operate on just about any mobile robot that uses this interface, whether it drives on the ground or flies in the sky.

As a result, the ROS community has settled on this interface for mobile robots, including simple ones like our TortoiseBot. We'll follow suit.

Hardware Driver

Now that we know what ROS interface to support, we need to actually write the node that will control the robot's motors and read from its encoders (sensors on the motors that measure how much each motor has turned). The details of this step, which is to write a driver, are very much dependent on how the robot hardware is designed and how you can communicate with it. There will be some kind of physical interface, such as USB, along with some kind of communication protocol, which is often custom. If you're lucky, there will also be some code that implements the communication protocol, in which case you could be saved a lot of effort (or not, if the code isn't structured or licensed in a way that makes it easily reusable).

Whatever the communication details, you'll likely need to do some math in your driver node to convert between the robot's native representation of commands and data and the cmd_vel/odom ROS interface that we're going to support. For a robot like the TortoiseBot, this interface is sometimes referred to as the "unicycle model" because it treats the robot as a one-wheeled vehicle that can control its forward and turning speeds independently. The robot is not actually a unicycle, of course, so some translation is needed. For example, the robot might natively operate on a per-wheel basis, accepting desired velocities for individual wheels and reporting back individual wheel rotation data. In that case, your node will need to perform the necessary trigonometric calculations, using knowledge of the kinematic configuration of the robot (wheel diameters, axle lengths, etc.) to convert between individual wheel states and overall robot states. This calculation is usually straightforward; for more complex cases, consult a textbook that covers robot kinematics.

We can't provide general-purpose driver code for controlling a mobile base, but there are many examples within the ROS ecosystem to look at. For the rest of this chapter, we'll proceed under the assumption that you have written a driver node that supports the cmd_vel/odom interface and will discuss the other steps that are needed for ROS integration. The following steps, starting with writing a model, can all be tried out in simulation, without any hardware or drivers.

Modeling the Robot: URDF

To use our TortoiseBot with many standard ROS tools, we need to write down a *model* of the robot's kinematics. That is, we need to describe the physical configuration of the robot, such as how many wheels it has, where they are placed, and which directions they turn in. This information will be used by `rviz` to visualize the state of the robot, by `gazebo` to simulate it, and by systems like the navigation stack to make it drive around the world in a purposeful manner.

In ROS, we represent robot models in an XML format called Unified Robot Description Format (URDF). This format is designed to represent a wide variety of robots, from a two-wheeled toy to a walking humanoid. URDF is similar to the Simulation Description Format (SDF), which we used to build Gazebo environments around existing robots in Chapter 11 and Chapter 14. While SDF includes extra features that are useful in simulation, URDF is required by most ROS tools, and Gazebo can understand it in addition to SDF. So, it's best to model a new robot using URDF.

In this section, we'll walk through constructing a URDF model for the TortoiseBot. For complete coverage of URDF syntax and features, consult the URDF documentation (*http://wiki.ros.org/urdf?distro=indigo*).

To model the TortoiseBot, let's consider its essential components:

- One chassis
- Two rear wheels, attached to the chassis
- One front caster, attached to the chassis
- One front wheel, attached to the front caster

You can imagine these components forming a tree: the chassis is the root, with connections to each of the rear wheels and the front caster, which in turn is connected to the front wheel. In fact, URDF is only capable of representing robots whose kinematics can be described by a tree; looping structures are not allowed (fortunately, with the exception of a certain class of manufacturing robot, looping structures are fairly uncommon in robots).

We will translate this tree-like narrative description of the TortoiseBot into the language of URDF, which is focused primarily on links and joints:

- A *link* is a rigid body, such as a chassis or a wheel.
- A *joint* connects two links, defining how they can move with respect to each other.

Let's start our TortoiseBot model with one link for the chassis, shown in Example 16-1.

Example 16-1. Model of the TortoiseBot chassis

```xml
<?xml version="1.0"?>
<robot name="tortoisebot">
  <link name="base_link">
    <visual>
      <geometry>
        <box size="0.6 0.3 0.3"/>
      </geometry>
      <material name="silver">
        <color rgba="0.75 0.75 0.75 1"/>
      </material>
    </visual>
  </link>
</robot>
```

This short model declares one link, called base_link (this name is more common than chassis in ROS systems), which is visually represented by a box (a rectangular solid) that measures 0.6 m × 0.3 m × 0.3 m. As with all URDF links, by default, the origin of this box is its center; this fact will be important later, when we start attaching joints at offsets from links. We give the box a color that we call "silver," defined in the commonly used RGBA space, which combines levels of red, green, and blue to form a color (the A is for *alpha*, which represents transparency, where 0 is transparent and 1 is opaque). To see what this model looks like, save that code to a file called *tortoise-bot.urdf*, and use roslauch urdf_tutorial/display.launch to visualize it:

```
user@hostname$ roslaunch urdf_tutorial display.launch model:=tortoisebot.urdf
```

You should see rviz pop up, showing you a single oblong silver box, similar to Figure 16-2.

> Another handy tool for visualizing URDF model structures is urdf_to_graphiz. It parses a URDF file to produce a topological graph representation of the model, showing how links and joints are connected. Try it on your TortoiseBot model by running urdf_to_graphiz tortoisebot.urdf, then opening the resulting *tortoisebot.pdf* file with a PDF viewer.

Next let's add the front caster. We can represent it as another oblong box, oriented vertically and attached to the front of the chassis, as shown in Example 16-2.

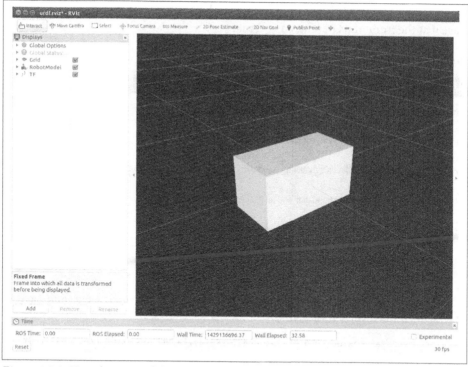

Figure 16-2. Visualization of the TortoiseBot chassis

Example 16-2. Code for the TortoiseBot front caster and joint

```
<link name="front_caster">
  <visual>
    <geometry>
      <box size="0.1 0.1 0.3"/>
    </geometry>
    <material name="silver"/>
  </visual>
</link>

<joint name="front_caster_joint" type="continuous">
  <axis xyz="0 0 1"/>
  <parent link="base_link"/>
  <child link="front_caster"/>
  <origin rpy="0 0 0" xyz="0.3 0 0"/>
</joint>
```

This snippet of URDF declares a second link, front_caster, along with a joint, front_caster_joint, which connects the front_caster to the base_link. The joint is continuous, which means that it can rotate indefinitely in either direction about a given axis, which in this case is z-axis (determined by the axis tag). The joint types supported by URDF are listed in Table 16-1. The `origin` of the joint is offset in x to place it at the front of its parent, `base_link`.

Table 16-1. Joint types supported by URDF

Name	Description
continuous	A joint that can rotate indefinitely about a single axis
revolute	Like a continuous joint, but with upper and lower angle limits
prismatic	A joint that slides linearly along a single axis, with upper and lower position limits
planar	A joint that allows translation and rotation perpendicular to a plane
floating	A joint that allows full six-dimensional translation and rotation
fixed	A special joint type that allows no motion

Add the new code to *tortoisebot.urdf*, before the closing `</robot>` tag, and save it. Then launch the display tool again:

```
user@hostname$ roslaunch urdf_tutorial display.launch model:=tortoisebot.urdf
```

Now `rviz` will show you both links, with red, blue, and green markers designating the origin of the caster link, similar to Figure 16-3.

The caster looks like it's in the right place, but how can we check whether the joint is working correctly? Fortunately, the URDF display tool can help. Launch it again, this time with the extra argument `gui:=True`:

```
user@hostname$ roslaunch urdf_tutorial display.launch model:=tortoisebot.urdf \
    gui:=True
```

Now, in addition to `rviz`, you'll get a small control GUI called the `joint_state_publisher`, similar to Figure 16-4.

The `joint_state_publisher` can be used to control our newly defined joint. Slide it back and forth, and in `rviz` you should see the front caster rotate back and forth with respect to the chassis. As you can already, the URDF display tool, along with the control GUI, provides an invaluable way of checking, debugging, and fixing a URDF model.

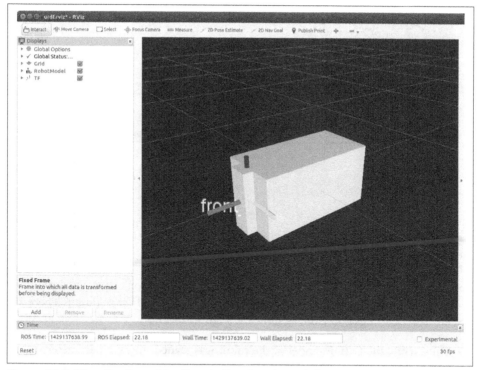

Figure 16-3. Visualization of the TortoiseBot chassis, with front caster

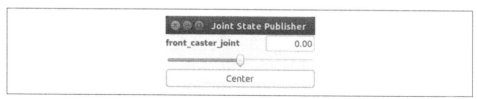

Figure 16-4. joint_state_publisher GUI for one joint

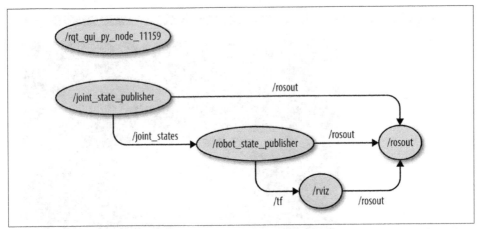

Figure 16-5. rqt_graph view of the nodes involved in visualizing and actuating the Tor-toiseBot model

Let's stop to consider what's happening under the hood: we don't have a real robot, or even a simulation of a robot, so what is the `joint_state_publisher` doing? There are actually several things going on, as shown in Figure 16-5:

- On startup, the URDF model of the robot was loaded into the parameter server, under the standard name `robot_description`. To see the version that's in the parameter server, try `rosparam get /robot_description`.

- The `joint_state_publisher`, in response to the slider state in the GUI, is publishing `sensor_msgs/JointState` messages on the `/joint_states` topic. Each message declares the position of each joint in the system. Try `rostopic echo /joint_states` to see the data for yourself.

- Another node, the `robot_state_publisher`, read the URDF model from the parameter server and is subscribed to `/joint_states`. This node combines the 1D position of each joint with the kinematic model to calculate a tree of 6D (position and orientation) coordinate transforms that describe where in space the robot's links are with respect to each other (in other words, it performs *forward kinematics*). This tree of transforms is published as `tf2_msgs/TFMessage` messages on the `/tf` topic.

- Finally, `rviz` also read the URDF model from the parameter server and is subscribed to `/tf`, allowing it to visualize the positions and orientations of the robot's links.

This arrangement may seem overly complex, but its modularity allows for significant reuse of the pieces. For example, the `robot_state_publisher` is commonly used with robots (both real and simulated) to handle the common task of forward kinematics, allowing the authors of robot drivers to publish just the individual joint state information and not the full coordinate transform tree. And, as you've already seen, `rviz` is used extensively in ROS development, especially for visualization of data related to coordinate transforms. So, the URDF display tool is really just a combination of commonly used ROS tools with a simple frontend GUI that allows you to supply fake joint position information. This kind of reuse is a hallmark of the ROS philosophy (originally the Unix philosophy): build small reusable tools, then configure and combine them to do what you need.

Getting back to our TortoiseBot model, let's add the wheels, starting with the front wheel, shown in Example 16-3.

Example 16-3. Code for the TortoiseBot front wheel and joint

```
<link name="front_wheel">
  <visual>
    <geometry>
      <cylinder length="0.05" radius="0.035"/>
    </geometry>
    <material name="black"/>
  </visual>
</link>

<joint name="front_wheel_joint" type="continuous">
  <axis xyz="0 0 1"/>
  <parent link="front_caster"/>
  <child link="front_wheel"/>
  <origin rpy="-1.5708 0 0" xyz="0.05 0 -.15"/>
</joint>
```

This URDF snippet declares a new link for the wheel itself, represented as a cylinder, and a new continuous joint to connect the wheel to the caster. Note that the origin of the joint is offset in y and z to move it to the front bottom of the caster, and also rotated about x to put the round part of the wheel on the ground. Run the display tool again to check the result. Now you'll have two sliders in the `joint_state_publisher` GUI, one for the caster joint and one for the front wheel joint. Try them both to check the rotation axes and directions.

Finally, similar to the front wheel, let's add the rear wheels, shown in Example 16-4.

Example 16-4. Code for the TortoiseBot rear wheels and joints

```
<link name="right_wheel">
  <visual>
    <geometry>
      <cylinder length="0.05" radius="0.035"/>
    </geometry>
    <material name="black">
      <color rgba="0 0 0 1"/>
    </material>
  </visual>
</link>

<joint name="right_wheel_joint" type="continuous">
  <axis xyz="0 0 1"/>
  <parent link="base_link"/>
  <child link="right_wheel"/>
  <origin rpy="-1.5708 0 0" xyz="-0.2825 -0.125 -.15"/>
</joint>

<link name="left_wheel">
  <visual>
    <geometry>
      <cylinder length="0.05" radius="0.035"/>
    </geometry>
    <material name="black"/>
  </visual>
</link>

<joint name="left_wheel_joint" type="continuous">
  <axis xyz="0 0 1"/>
  <parent link="base_link"/>
  <child link="left_wheel"/>
  <origin rpy="-1.5708 0 0" xyz="-0.2825 0.125 -.15"/>
</joint>
```

This URDF snippet adds two more wheels with continuous joints offset so as to be attached to the back end of the chassis, one on either side. Launch the display tool to see the result, which should look similar to Figure 16-6. Play with the sliders in the `joint_state_publisher` to check all four joints.

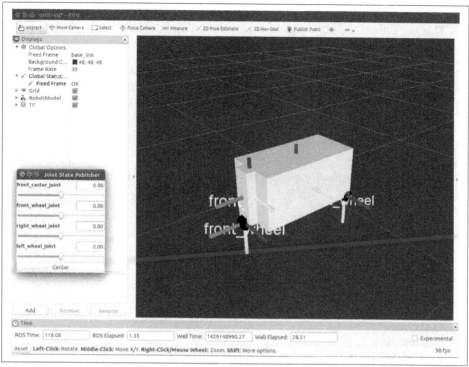

Figure 16-6. Visualization of the complete TortoiseBot model

We now have a good kinematic model of the TortoiseBot. You may have noticed that it's not very pretty, and indeed, the visual appearance of robot models can be greatly improved through the use of high-quality *meshes*, but we won't cover that topic here. Instead, we'll proceed with how to simulate a TortoiseBot.

Simulation in Gazebo

Our URDF model of the TortoiseBot captures the kinematics and visual appearance of the robot, but it doesn't say anything about the physical characteristics that are needed to simulate it. To simulate a TortoiseBot in Gazebo, we need to add two new tags to every link in the model:

`<collision>`
 Similar to `visual`, this tag defines the size and shape of the robot's body, for the purpose of determining how it will interact with other objects. The collision geometry can be identical to the `visual` geometry, but it's often different; e.g., you may use a complex mesh for a good visual appearance, but a set of simple shapes (boxes, cylinders, etc.) for efficient collision detection.

`<inertial>`

This tag defines the mass and moment of inertia of the link, which are needed to move it according to Newton's laws.

To add collision geometry, given the simplicity of our visual model, we just duplicate the visual geometry. Go through your *tortoisebot.urdf*, adding for each `<visual>`/`<geometry>` tag a sibling `<collision>`/`<geometry>` tag, with the same shape and size. For example, the `base_link` with collision information would look like Example 16-5. Note that you don't need to add a `<material>` tag for the collision body.

Example 16-5. Code for the TortoiseBot chassis, with collision information

```
<link name="base_link">
  <visual>
    <geometry>
      <box size="0.6 0.3 0.3"/>
    </geometry>
    <material name="silver">
      <color rgba="0.75 0.75 0.75 1"/>
    </material>
  </visual>
  <collision>
    <geometry>
      <box size="0.6 0.3 0.3"/>
    </geometry>
  </collision>
</link>
```

To add inertial data, we need to determine the mass properties of each link. Doing this for a real robot can be surprisingly difficult. While resources like detailed CAD information can be a good guide, it's often necessary to measure the system physically, either through disassembly and analysis of each component, or through carefully designed experiments with the complete system. In lieu of such experiments, it's common to use informed estimates of mass properties and to refine them over time.

For our purposes with TortoiseBot, we'll get reasonable simulation behavior if the masses are in the right order of magnitude. To keep things simple, we'll give the chassis a mass of 1.0 kg, the caster 0.1 kg, and each wheel 0.1 kg. For help with computing inertia matrices, we can consult some well-known formulas (*http://bit.ly/moments_of_inertia*) for computing moments of inertia for objects of various shapes, including boxes and cylinders. Using those formulas, we computed the inertia values shown in Example 16-6 for the chassis box, in Example 16-7 for the caster box, and in Example 16-8 for each wheel cylinder. Add each block of XML inside the corresponding link(s) in your *tortoisebot.urdf*.

Example 16-6. TortoiseBot inertial data for the chassis

```
<inertial>
  <mass value="1.0"/>
  <inertia ixx="0.015" iyy="0.0375" izz="0.0375"
           ixy="0" ixz="0" iyz="0"/>
</inertial>
```

Example 16-7. TortoiseBot inertial data for the caster

```
<inertial>
  <mass value="0.1"/>
  <inertia ixx="0.00083" iyy="0.00083" izz="0.000167"
           ixy="0" ixz="0" iyz="0"/>
</inertial>
```

Example 16-8. TortoiseBot inertial data for each wheel

```
<inertial>
  <mass value="0.1"/>
  <inertia ixx="5.1458e-5" iyy="5.1458e-5" izz="6.125e-5"
           ixy="0" ixz="0" iyz="0"/>
</inertial>
```

Don't worry if you don't find these values to be intuitive or meaningful. Your authors don't, either; nor do many people who work professionally on simulation of rigid body dynamics. What's important is to have a general idea of how to approximate them.

 When working with inertial values, here's a great way to visually debug things is in Gazebo: click on View→"Center of Mass/Inertia" to see a visual representation of the inertia matrix and mass for each link in your robot. If the inertial data is very different from (e.g., much smaller or larger than) the visual or collision geometry, then you have a problem.

Now we're ready to load our TortoiseBot model in Gazebo. There are a few different ways to do this. Because we want to use some ROS tools with our simulated robot (as opposed to working solely within Gazebo), we'll follow this pattern, using roslaunch to automate things:

1. Load the robot's URDF model into the parameter server.

2. Launch Gazebo (e.g., with an empty world).

3. Use a ROS service call to spawn an instance of the robot in Gazebo, reading the URDF data from the parameter server.

This process might seem a little roundabout, but it's actually a very flexible way of doing things. For a start, it gets the URDF model onto the parameter server, where it can be accessed by other nodes. By convention, the URDF model is stored in the parameter server under the name /robot_description (you can use another name for this parameter, but then you'd have to change the default settings for many tools). Once it's on the parameter server, the URDF model can be used by tools like rviz, which needs the model to visualize the robot, or a path planner, which needs the model to know the robot's shape and size. A well-written ROS tool will never make assumptions about the physical structure of a robot, but rather will read the URDF model from the parameter server and configure its behavior based on the model.

At this point, we need to organize our code into a ROS package, which we'll call tor toisebot. So, create a directory in your workspace called *tortoisebot*, add an appropriate *package.xml* file, then move your *tortoisebot.urdf* file in there. Now we're going to add a roslaunch file that will execute the preceding steps to launch Gazebo with a TortoiseBot in it. The roslaunch code is shown in Example 16-9.

Example 16-9. tortoisebot.launch file to bring up Gazebo with a TortoiseBot model

```
<launch>
    <!-- Load the TortoiseBot URDF model into the parameter server -->
    <param name="robot_description" textfile="$(find tortoisebot)/tortoisebot.urdf" />
    <!-- Start Gazebo with an empty world -->
    <include file="$(find gazebo_ros)/launch/empty_world.launch"/>
    <!-- Spawn a TortoiseBot in Gazebo, taking the description from the
         parameter server -->
    <node name="spawn_urdf" pkg="gazebo_ros" type="spawn_model"
          args="-param robot_description -urdf -model tortoisebot" />
</launch>
```

In this launch file, we load the URDF file into the parameter server as /robot_description, then use a helper launch file from the gazebo_ros package to run Gazebo with an empty world. With the model data loaded into the parameter server and Gazebo running, we use the helper tool spawn_model, also from the gaz ebo_ros package, to ask Gazebo to spawn an instance of the TortoiseBot, reading URDF data from the /robot_description parameter.

Save that file as *tortoisebot/tortoisebot.launch* and give it a try:

```
user@hostname$ roslaunch tortoisebot tortoisebot.launch
```

You should see Gazebo pop up, with a TortoiseBot, similar to Figure 16-7. Hooray!

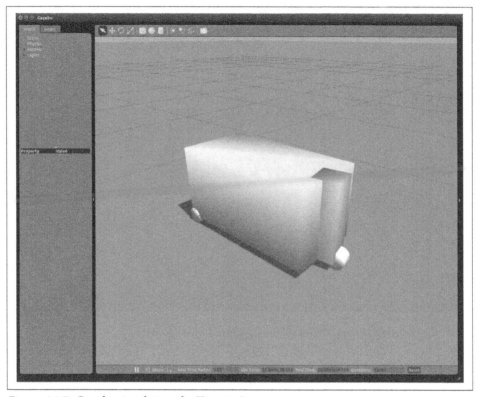

Figure 16-7. Gazebo simulating the TortoiseBot

Use the Gazebo GUI to explore your robot. For example, if you select View→Wireframe and View→Joints, you can see the structure of the robot, similar to Figure 16-8. You might wonder how, in a physics-based simulation, the caster link and the chassis link can interpenetrate each other. The reason is that by default Gazebo disables collision checking between links that are part of the same model.

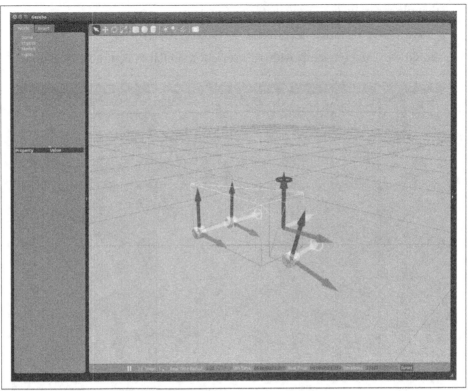

Figure 16-8. Wireframe and joint view of TortoiseBot in Gazebo

Now that we have a simulated robot, let's control it. But how? Recall from earlier in this chapter that we expect robots like the TortoiseBot to support the cmd_vel/odom interface to take commands and report position. On the real robot, that interface would be implemented by a hardware driver. In simulation, we need to do something similar, but fortunately easier: we'll load a Gazebo plugin. In particular, we'll load a differential drive plugin that will allow us to control the TortoiseBot via cmd_vel messages, which the plugin will convert into appropriate velocities for the left and right wheels. (At this point, we're diverging from the mechanical design of Grey Walter's Elsie, which was driven with motors on the front caster and wheel, not the back wheels. We don't have an off-the-shelf plugin to implement cmd_vel on top of that arrangement of motors, so we'll cheat a bit and drive the robot with motors on the back wheels.)

To load the differential drive plugin, we need to add another block to the TortoiseBot URDF model, shown in Example 16-10.

Example 16-10. Extra URDF code to load the differential drive plugin for TortoiseBot

```
<gazebo>
  <plugin name="differential_drive_controller"
          filename="libgazebo_ros_diff_drive.so">
    <leftJoint>left_wheel_joint</leftJoint>
    <rightJoint>right_wheel_joint</rightJoint>
    <robotBaseFrame>base_link</robotBaseFrame>
    <wheelSeparation>0.25</wheelSeparation>
    <wheelDiameter>0.07</wheelDiameter>
    <publishWheelJointState>true</publishWheelJointState>
  </plugin>
</gazebo>
```

In the configuration of the differential drive plugin, we're telling it to control the left_wheel_joint and right_wheel_joint. We're also telling it how large the wheels are and what the distance is between them, and that the base of the robot is called base_link (an improved version of the plugin could in many cases infer this data from the model). Finally, we tell the plugin to publish /joint_states messages for positions of the wheels.

Insert that XML snippet into *tortoisebot.urdf*, anywhere inside the <robot> tag, then relaunch with roslaunch tortoisebot tortoisebot.launch. Gazebo will look the same, but now there's a plugin ready to help us drive the robot with messages sent to cmd_vel. Check that it's there with rostopic:

```
user@hostname$ rostopic info cmd_vel
Type: geometry_msgs/Twist

Publishers: None

Subscribers:
 * /gazebo (http://rossum:57336/)
```

That looks good, so let's try sending a command. We can do it manually via rostopic, sending velocities of 0 m/s for translation along the x-axis and 0.5 rad/s for rotation about the z-axis:

```
user@hostname$ rostopic pub -1 cmd_vel geometry_msgs/Twist \
  '{linear: {x: 0.0}, angular: {z: 0.5}}'
```

You should see the robot rotate in place, counter-clockwise (which is the direction of positive rotation about the robot's z-axis). It's nice that we can dig down and send commands directly like this with rostopic, but it's not a great way to drive a robot. Instead, let's use the teleop_twist_keyboard tool, which reads keypresses and publishes corresponding cmd_vel messages (we could also use the custom teleop program that was covered in "Keyboard Driver" on page 112):

```
user@hostname$ rosrun teleop_twist_keyboard teleop_twist_keyboard.py
Reading from the keyboard  and Publishing to Twist!

Moving around:
   u    i    o
   j    k    l
   m    ,    .

q/z : increase/decrease max speeds by 10%
w/x : increase/decrease only linear speed by 10%
e/c : increase/decrease only angular speed by 10%
anything else : stop

CTRL-C to quit
```

Use the keys displayed on the screen to move the robot. Drive it forward and backward, and turn it in place. Note how, especially when you change directions, the motion of the caster and its effect on the behavior of the robot are captured by Gazebo. We didn't program in anything about the caster swiveling around; it just follows from first principles of physics, given the model that we built.

 When you're working with a mobile robot that's roaming around in Gazebo, you can keep it automatically in the center of the camera view: in the model tree on the left side of the Gazebo GUI, right-click on the name of the robot and select "Follow".

We know that the cmd_vel interface is working to command the robot; let's check that the odom interface is working to provide position data from the robot. We can do that with rostopic, checking specifically for the pose/pose field of the message:

```
user@hostname$ rostopic echo /odom/pose/pose
position:
   x: 3.03941689732
   y: -2.43708910971
   z: 0.185001156647
orientation:
   x: 4.91206137527e-06
   y: 2.22857873842e-06
   z: -0.913856008315
   w: -0.406038416947
```

You should see a stream of such position and orientation values that change over time as the robot moves. Those messages are being published by the differential drive controller, which is converting the observed motion of the robot's individual wheels into motion of the robot's body, in the same coordinate frame as the velocities that we commanded via cmd_vel.

Summary

In this chapter, we began the process of integrating a brand new robot into ROS. We discussed standard ROS interfaces for mobile robots, considered the issues of writing hardware drivers, then built a functional model of the TortoiseBot, including the physical properties necessary to simulate it. In the next chapter, we will build further on the TortoiseBot, visualizing it with `rviz`, adding sensors, and running standard algorithms such as navigation.

## CHAPTER 17

Your Own Mobile Robot: Part 2

In Chapter 16, we learned how to add a new mobile robot, the TortoiseBot, to ROS. We decided on topic APIs, built a complete Gazebo model, and used low-level velocity commands to drive it around in simulation. In this chapter, we'll take the next big step by getting the TortoiseBot to navigate autonomously (in simulation). To get there, we'll take a series of smaller steps:

- Visualize and verify transform data.
- Add a laser sensor.
- Configure and incorporate the navigation stack.
- Use rviz to localize the robot and send navigation goals.

Verifying Transforms

Recalling the setup with which we ended the previous chapter, we can launch a simulation of the TortoiseBot like so:

```
user@hostname$ roslaunch tortoisebot tortoisebot.launch
```

That launch file will start a Gazebo simulation of the TortoiseBot in an empty world. Now it's time to use rviz to visualize the state of the (simulated) robot. Leaving Gazebo running, start rviz in the usual way:

```
user@hostname$ rviz
```

You might wonder why Gazebo and rviz are separate programs. They look pretty similar: both give you a 3D view of a robot and allow you to visualize various aspects of the robot and its environment. They are separate programs because they play very different roles: Gazebo *simulates* a robot, while rviz *visualizes* a robot. Gazebo is a substitute for a real robot in a physical environment, computing the effects of forces and generating synthetic sensor data. While the 3D GUI is a key feature of Gazebo, it is also optional; for applications like continuous integration testing, Gazebo is often run without a GUI. The job of rviz, on the other hand, is to visualize the state of a robot, whether physical or simulated in Gazebo, by talking to its sensors and presenting the results. In other words, rviz shows you what the robot *thinks* is happening, while Gazebo (or looking at your physical robot) shows you what is *really* happening.

To visualize our robot, we need to configure some aspects of the rviz display (after making these changes, when exiting rviz, you should click Save when prompted so that you start with the same configuration next time):

- In Displays→Global Options, set "fixed frame" to "odom." That way, we'll be able to see the robot move around with respect to its odometric origin.

- In Displays, click the "Add" button, then select "RobotModel" and click "OK". That will cause rviz to read the TortoiseBot's URDF model from the parameter server and display it.

The result will be similar to Figure 17-1, which doesn't look great. The robot's chassis and caster links seem to be there, but not in the right positions with respect to each other, and the wheels are nowhere to be seen. In addition, rviz is unhappy: in Displays→RobotModel, the status is Error, and there are messages complaining about a lack of transforms between various links.

The problem is that we are not publishing coordinate transform data. Like many ROS tools, rviz requires that information about the relationships between different coordinate frames be provided via tf2_msgs/TFMessage messages on the /tf topic. We need to provide the necessary messages, which is easy to do, in two steps:

1. Publish sensor_msgs/JointState messages for all of the robot's joints on the /joint_states topic

2. Use the robot_state_publisher (which we encountered when building and debugging our TortoiseBot model in "Modeling the Robot: URDF" on page 281) to convert the /joint_states messages to corresponding /tf messages.

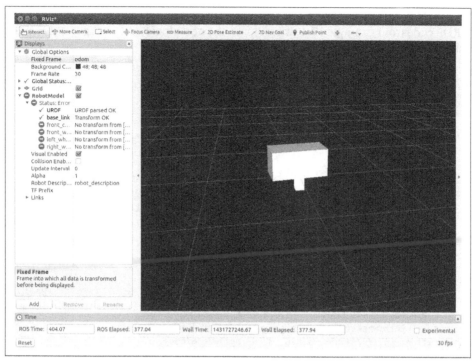

Figure 17-1. Visualization of the TortoiseBot with missing transforms

Let's check what is already being published on /joint_states:

```
user@hostname$ rostopic echo /joint_states
header:
  seq: 110218
  stamp:
    secs: 1102
    nsecs: 357000000
  frame_id: ''
name: ['right_wheel_joint', 'left_wheel_joint']
position: [0.5652265431822379, 3.7257917095603696]
velocity: []
effort: []
```

We see the positions of the right and left wheel joints being published repeatedly, but nothing about the caster joint or front wheel joint. Why is that? Looking back at *tortoisebot.urdf*, notice this line, within the configuration of the differential drive plugin:

```
<publishWheelJointState>true</publishWheelJointState>
```

That line tells the differential drive plugin to publish /joint_states messages for the two joints that it is controlling. Fair enough, but we also want /joint_states messages for the other two joints, which are passive. Fortunately, there's another Gazebo plugin that we can use here: the joint state publisher. In *tortoisebot.urdf*, add the URDF code from Example 17-1, which loads the new plugin and configures it to publish data for the caster and front wheel joints.

Example 17-1. Extra URDF code to load the joint state publisher plugin for TortoiseBot

```
<gazebo>
  <plugin name="joint_state_publisher"
          filename="libgazebo_ros_joint_state_publisher.so">
    <jointName>front_caster_joint, front_wheel_joint</jointName>
  </plugin>
</gazebo>
```

Relaunch *tortoisebot.launch*, and try listening in on /joint_states again:

```
user@hostname$ rostopic echo /joint_states
header:
  seq: 10698
  stamp:
    secs: 53
    nsecs: 502000000
  frame_id: ''
name: ['left_wheel_joint', 'right_wheel_joint']
position: [0.17974448092710826, 0.09370471036487604]
velocity: []
effort: []
---
header:
  seq: 10699
  stamp:
    secs: 53
    nsecs: 502000000
  frame_id: ''
name: ['front_caster_joint', 'front_wheel_joint']
position: [0.2139682253512678, 0.6647502699540064]
velocity: []
effort: []
```

Now we can see position data for all four joints. It's arriving interleaved in different messages, but that's not a problem. With the /joint_states data verified, it's time to add robot_state_publisher. In *tortoisebot.launch*, add the following XML code:

```
<node name="robot_state_publisher" pkg="robot_state_publisher"
      type="robot_state_publisher"/>
```

Relaunch again, then start `rviz`. The result will be similar to Figure 17-2, which looks much better. The wheels and caster are in the right location, because now `rviz` is receiving the required transform data via `/tf` messages.

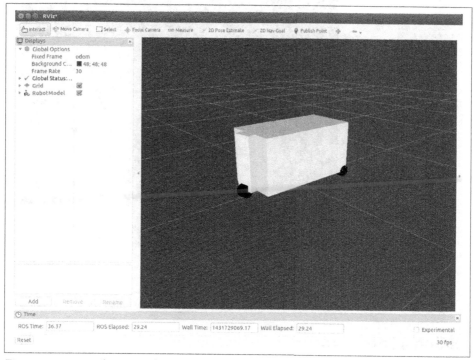

Figure 17-2. Visualization of the TortoiseBot with transforms

If you'd like, you can inspect the messages that are published by `robot_state_pub` `lisher` in the usual way: `rostopic echo /tf`. But we can do better than that, by asking `rviz` to show us the data. In Displays, click "Add", select "TF", then click "OK". You will see the familiar red/green/blue axis origins pop up, with labels telling you their names. To see things a little more clearly, let's make the robot semitransparent: in Displays→RobotModel, set Alpha to 0.5. The result will be similar to Figure 17-3.

Now that we've confirmed that transforms are being handled properly, it's time to add a sensor to our robot.

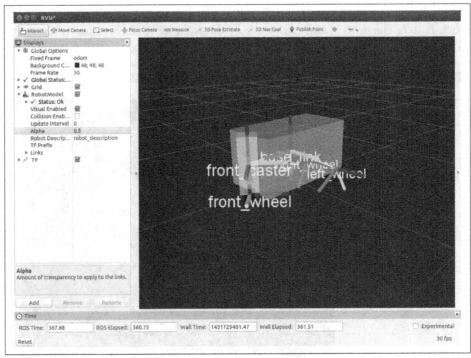

Figure 17-3. Visualization of the TortoiseBot with transforms visualized

Adding a Laser Sensor

Still one of the most popular sensors for mobile robots, *laser range-finders*, or simply *lasers*, are very handy devices. A laser gives you a pretty accurate view of the world around you, and while it's just a single slice, that slice turns out to contain plenty of information for a robot that roams around a world with lots of continuous vertical structure (like walls and doors). In this section, we're going to add to our TortoiseBot a laser similar to those made by Hokuyo, whose sensors are widely used on robots today (for more on lasers, refer back to "Laser scanners" on page 85).

If we were building a physical robot, this is where we would buy the sensor, physically bolt it to the robot, then hook up power and data. Because we're working in simulation, we can just edit some URDF. First, we need to add the link that will represent the sensor, plus a joint to attach it to the robot. The URDF code in Example 17-2 adds a small cube representing the laser, attached to the top center of the robot chassis; insert this code in your *tortoisebot.urdf*. Note that, as with other parts of the robot, we must provide reasonable mass and inertia values for the laser; without that information, we cannot incorporate the laser into a physics-based simulation like Gazebo.

Example 17-2. Extra URDF code to define a link and joint for the laser sensor

```
<link name="hokuyo_link">
  <collision>
    <origin xyz="0 0 0" rpy="0 0 0"/>
    <geometry>
      <box size="0.1 0.1 0.1"/>
    </geometry>
  </collision>
  <visual>
    <origin xyz="0 0 0" rpy="0 0 0"/>
    <geometry>
      <box size="0.1 0.1 0.1"/>
    </geometry>
  </visual>
  <inertial>
    <mass value="1e-5" />
    <origin xyz="0 0 0" rpy="0 0 0"/>
    <inertia ixx="1e-6" ixy="0" ixz="0" iyy="1e-6" iyz="0" izz="1e-6" />
  </inertial>
</link>

<joint name="hokuyo_joint" type="fixed">
  <axis xyz="0 1 0" />
  <origin xyz="0 0 0.2" rpy="0 0 0"/>
  <parent link="base_link"/>
  <child link="hokuyo_link"/>
</joint>
```

You can confirm the result by launching Gazebo again (and, optionally, rviz). But so far, all we did was add the physical representation of the laser; we haven't told Gazebo that it should behave like a laser. To do that, we need to use the <sensor> tag, which allows us to define and configure a sensor. Shown in Example 17-3 is the URDF code required to attach a laser sensor to the TortoiseBot.

Example 17-3. Extra URDF code to define a laser sensor

```
<gazebo reference="hokuyo_link">
  <sensor type="gpu_ray" name="hokuyo">
    <pose>0 0 0 0 0 0</pose>
    <visualize>false</visualize>
    <update_rate>40</update_rate>
    <ray>
      <scan>
        <horizontal>
          <samples>720</samples>
          <resolution>1</resolution>
          <min_angle>-1.570796</min_angle>
          <max_angle>1.570796</max_angle>
        </horizontal>
      </scan>
```

```
            <range>
              <min>0.10</min>
              <max>30.0</max>
              <resolution>0.01</resolution>
            </range>
          </ray>
          <plugin name="gpu_laser" filename="libgazebo_ros_gpu_laser.so">
            <topicName>/scan</topicName>
            <frameName>hokuyo_link</frameName>
          </plugin>
        </sensor>
      </gazebo>
```

Here are the key points of this block of code:

- First, we create a sensor of type `gpu_ray` (which means that it will be simulated on your computer's GPU, which is more efficient than using the CPU), and attach it to the `hokuyo_link` that we created previously.

- Then, we configure the sensor to behave similarly to a Hokuyo laser: publish new scans at 40 Hz, take 720 samples per scan over a field of view of 180 degrees, and scan from a minimum of 0.1 m to a maximum of 30 m.

- Finally, we load the GPU laser Gazebo plugin and configure it to publish data from the laser via `sensor_msgs/LaserScan` messages on the `scan` topic. For more information on this and other Gazebo plugins, check the `gazebo_plugins` documentation (*http://wiki.ros.org/gazebo_plugins?distro=indigo*).

Let's check the result of attaching the laser. Add the code from Example 17-3 to your *tortoise.urdf*, then relaunch. To give the laser something to look at, use the Gazebo GUI to drop a cylinder somewhere in front of the robot, as shown in Figure 17-4.

Start `rviz` and configure it to show the laser data: in Displays, click "Add", select "LaserScan", and click "OK". Then, in Displays→LaserScan, set the topic to /scan. You should see a visualization of the laser scan similar to Figure 17-5.

In the Gazebo GUI, trying moving the cylinder around, and inserting and moving other objects, while checking the effect on the laser scan display in `rviz`. You can also try driving the robot from the keyboard with `teleop_twist_keyboard`, as we did in "Simulation in Gazebo" on page 289.

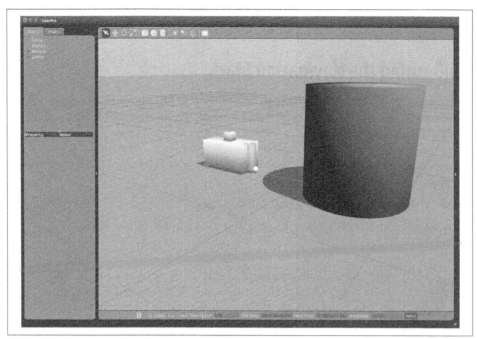

Figure 17-4. Simulation of the TortoiseBot with an obstacle for the laser to see

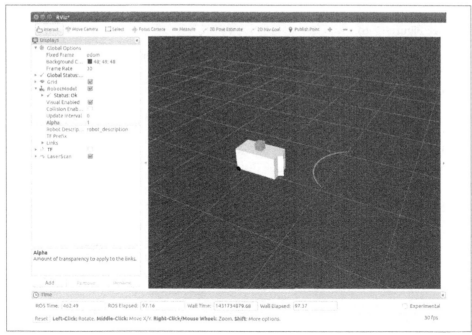

Figure 17-5. Visualization of laser scans from the TortoiseBot

We now have a simulated robot with good transform and laser data, so it's time to add autonomous navigation.

Configuring the Navigation Stack

We're going to give the TortoiseBot the ability to autonomously navigate with a known map (i.e., we're not going to build a map). To add navigation to a robot, we need to launch three new nodes:

- `map_server`, to provide the static map against which the robot will localize and plan
- `amcl`, to localize the robot against the static map
- `move_base`, to handle global planning and local control for the robot

> The theory and operation of the ROS navigation stack are explained in Chapter 10; in this section, we're specifically covering the process of configuring navigation for use on a new robot.

To run `map_server`, we need a static map. Let's reuse the map from Chapter 9, which was created by a mobile robot roaming around in a reasonably complex office building, (see Figure 17-6).

That map is stored in the `mapping` package that we created previously. To have `map_server` provide this map, add the following XML code to your *tortoisebot.launch* file, inside the `<launch>` block:

```
<node name="map_server" pkg="map_server" type="map_server"
      args="$(find mapping)/maps/willow.yaml"/>
```

We also need to put our TortoiseBot into a 3D simulation world that matches the 2D map we're using. Fortunately, there is just such a world in the `gazebo_ros` package, with a launch file ready for our use. In *tortoisebot.launch*, remove the line that includes `empty_world.launch` and substitute the following line, which instead includes *willowgarage_world.launch*:

```
<include file="$(find gazebo_ros)/launch/willowgarage_world.launch"/>
```

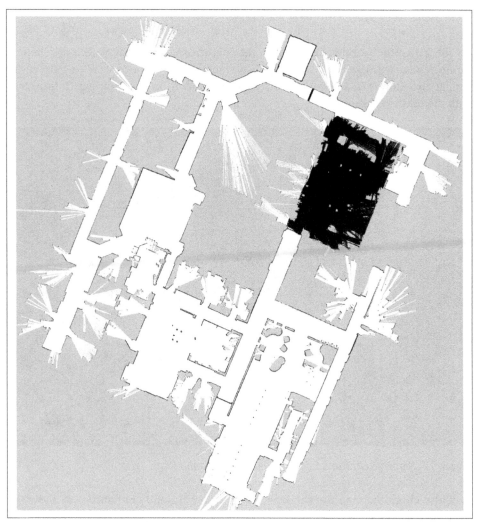

Figure 17-6. Map of an office building, to be used for navigation

Now that we're using a nonempty world, we care about where the TortoiseBot gets placed. Previously, when spawning a TortoiseBot with `spawn_model`, we didn't specify a position, so the robot was placed at the origin of the world. Given the office environment provided by *willowgarage_world.launch*, it will be helpful to put the robot in an open area where we can easily localize it. A convenient position, relative to the origin of the world, is +8 m in x and –8 m in y. To place the robot at this position, remove the line from *tortoisebot.launch* that calls `spawn_model` and replace it with the line shown here, which specifies values for the robot's x and y position (in the same way, you can also specify a z position and/or an orientation):

```
<node name="spawn_urdf" pkg="gazebo_ros" type="spawn_model"
      args="-param robot_description -urdf -model tortoisebot -x 8 -y -8" />
```

To check that the world is loaded with the robot placed correctly within it, relaunch *tortoisebot.launch*. Use the Gazebo GUI to change your point of view to get a result similar to Figure 17-7, in which you're looking down on the building from above, with the robot visible.

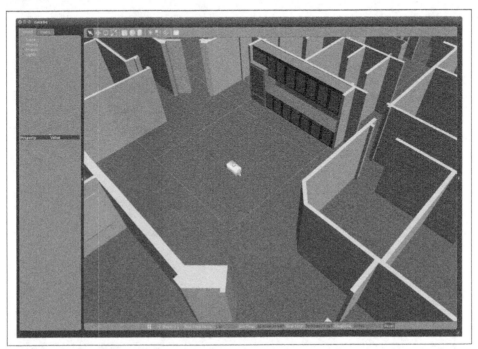

Figure 17-7. TortoiseBot in an office building in Gazebo

Let's also check that `map_server` is working. Run `rviz` and configure it to show the map: in Displays, click "Add", select "Map", and click "OK". Then, in Displays→Map, set the topic to /map. In addition, in Displays→Global Options, change the fixed frame to `map`. You should see the 2D map appear, similar to Figure 17-8.

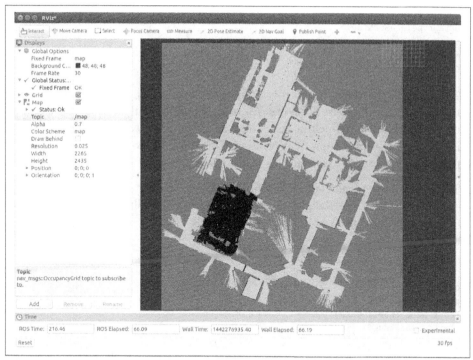

Figure 17-8. The static map displayed in rviz

With our robot ready to go in a simulated office building, and a `map_server` providing a matching static map, we need to launch `amcl`, which will localize the robot within the building, using the map. While `amcl` is extremely configurable and generally does need to be tuned for good performance, for our purposes, we can use the example configuration for differential-drive robots, which is provided as a launch file in the `amcl` package. Add the following line to your *tortoisebot.launch* file:

```
<include file="$(find amcl)/examples/amcl_diff.launch"/>
```

Now it's time to set up `move_base`. As explained in Chapter 10, `move_base` is a complex node, with a variety of opportunities for configuration. Fortunately, its default configuration is pretty close to what we need, leaving just a handful of things for us to change. First, we need to set the parameters that will be common to both the global and local costmaps that are used by `move_base`. Create a file called *costmap_common_params.yaml* and insert the YAML code from Example 17-4.

Example 17-4. costmap_common_params.yaml

```
footprint: [[0.35, 0.15], [0.35, -0.15], [-0.35, -0.15], [-0.35, 0.15]]
observation_sources: laser_scan_sensor
laser_scan_sensor:
```

```
sensor_frame: hokuyo_link
data_type: LaserScan
topic: scan
marking: true
clearing: true
```

We first define the shape of the robot's footprint as a rectangle (you can add more points to make a different 2D polygon), using the outer dimensions of the chassis plus caster. Then we define our laser to be an observation source. As a result, data published on the scan topic will be used to update the costmaps, both inserting obstacles (marking) and asserting free space (clearing).

With the common parameters established, we need to configure the global and local costmaps separately. For the global costmap, create a file called *global_costmap_params.yaml*, and insert the YAML code from Example 17-5.

Example 17-5. global_costmap_params.yaml

```
global_costmap:
  global_frame: map
  robot_base_frame: base_link
  static_map: true
```

We tell the global costmap to use a static map (to be provided by the map_server) and that it should do its reasoning in the map frame, while it should consider the canonical frame of the robot to be base_link.

The local costmap requires only a slightly different configuration; create a file called *local_costmap_params.yaml*, and insert the YAML code from Example 17-6.

Example 17-6. local_costmap_params.yaml

```
local_costmap:
  global_frame: odom
  robot_base_frame: base_link
  rolling_window: true
```

Whereas the global costmap uses a large static map, we tell the local costmap to use a small rolling window: the robot always remains at the center of the window, with obstacle data outside the window being discarded, and potentially reobserved later, as the robot moves. We also tell the local costmap to reason in the odom frame, in which the robot's pose may drift, but tends to vary smoothly, as compared to the map frame, in which the pose can make discrete jumps. These two differences cause the local costmap to be more suitable for local obstacle avoidance, in which what's happening right now, near the robot, is far more important than either where the robot thinks it is in the world, or what the static map (which might be outdated, after all) says.

We also need to configure the base local planner, which does the actual work of planning paths and computing control commands. Create a file called *base_local_planner_params.yaml*, and insert the YAML code from Example 17-7.

Example 17-7. base_local_planner_params.yaml

```
TrajectoryPlannerROS:
  holonomic_robot: false
```

In this case, we're setting just one parameter, to tell the planner that the TortoiseBot is not holonomic (because it is differential-drive; for more on types of mobile robots, refer back to "Actuation: Mobile Platform" on page 77).

With all the configuration established, it's time to modify the launch file to run move_base. Add the code from Example 17-8 to your *tortoisebot.launch*.

Example 17-8. Extra XML code to launch move_base

```
<node pkg="move_base" type="move_base" respawn="false" name="move_base"
      output="screen">
  <rosparam file="$(find tortoisebot)/costmap_common_params.yaml"
            command="load" ns="global_costmap" />
  <rosparam file="$(find tortoisebot)/costmap_common_params.yaml"
            command="load" ns="local_costmap" />
  <rosparam file="$(find tortoisebot)/local_costmap_params.yaml"
            command="load" />
  <rosparam file="$(find tortoisebot)/global_costmap_params.yaml"
            command="load" />
  <rosparam file="$(find tortoisebot)/base_local_planner_params.yaml"
            command="load" />
</node>
```

In this part of the launch file, we start the move_base node and configure it with the parameters from the YAML files that we just created. Note that we load the *costmap_common_params.yaml* file twice, once in the global_costmap namespace and again in the local_costmap namespace; we separated those parameters exactly because we would require them in two places and didn't want to duplicate any code.

That's all the configuration required; let's get this robot moving!

Using rviz to Localize and Command a Navigating Robot

With all the changes incorporated, launch *tortoisebot.launch*, which will bring up a TortoiseBot in the simulated office building, with the navigation stack ready to run. As described in Chapter 10, we need to give amcl a reasonable initial estimate of the robot's pose within the map that corresponds to its actual location in the building. That's easiest to do with a GUI, so also start rviz. It will be helpful to see how amcl's particle filter evolves as the robot moves, so go ahead and enable the `rviz` visualization for it: in Displays, click "Add", select "PoseArray", click "OK", then set the topic for the new display to `/particlecloud`.

Work with the points of view in Gazebo and `rviz` until you have them roughly aligned and can match where the TortoiseBot is in the Gazebo world to where it should be in the `rviz` map. In `rviz`, click the "2D Pose Estimate" button, then click and drag in the map to set the robot's position and orientation, as shown in Figure 17-9.

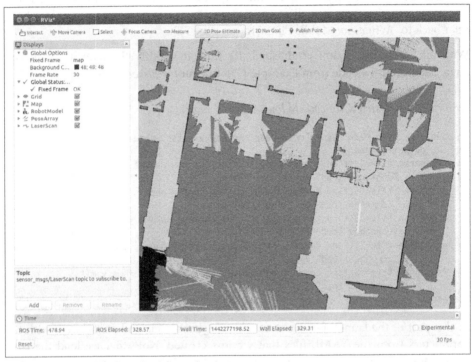

Figure 17-9. Setting the robot's initial pose in rviz

In `rviz`, the robot's pose will jump to approximately the pose that you provided, with a surrounding cloud of arrows showing the distribution of poses being tracked by `amcl`, as seen in Figure 17-10. You can judge the goodness of the estimate by checking how the laser scan visualized in `rviz` matches with the map. If the laser scan looks badly misaligned, just set the pose again. In general, you should provide the best initial pose you can, but it doesn't have to be perfect, because `amcl` uses a fairly robust probabilistic localization algorithm. Nothing is happening yet in Gazebo; we're just telling the robot where it is, not asking it to move anywhere.

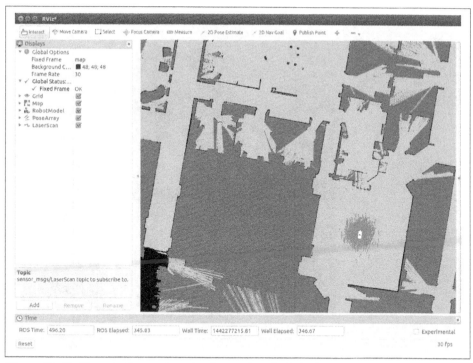

Figure 17-10. The robot's pose in rviz after setting the initial pose

With the robot localized in the map, it's time to make it drive. In rviz, click the "2D Nav Goal" button, then click and drag in the map to set a goal pose for the robot, as shown in Figure 17-11. The robot will start moving in Gazebo, and rviz will be updated with the robot's estimated pose and laser scan data, as shown in Figure 17-12.

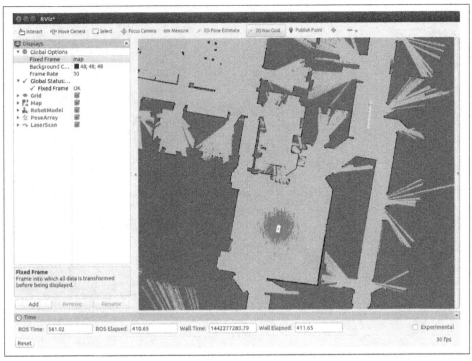

Figure 17-11. Setting a navigation goal pose in rviz

It works; hooray! Now it's time to experiment. When the robot reaches the goal (or before), give it a new goal somewhere else. Try giving a new pose estimate on the fly. See what happens when you give it a very bad pose estimate, somewhere else in the map. Give it a navigation goal in a location that's unreachable.

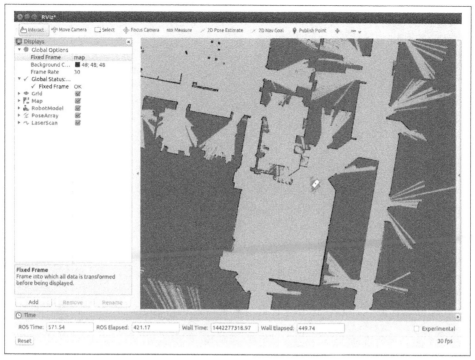

Figure 17-12. The robot navigating toward its goal, with the red localization particle cloud converging on a higher-confidence estimate

Summary

In this chapter, we started with a working simulation model of a mobile robot and turned it into an autonomously navigating robot. We did this without writing any procedural code, but rather by providing configuration information (via XML and YAML). That's the power of ROS: standard, flexible tools like `robot_state_pub lisher`, `amcl`, and `move_base` can be configured and combined to produce useful behavior on a wide variety of robots, even one that we just built ourselves.

Of course, if you experiment more than a little with the system that we built, you'll find that the TortoiseBot's navigation isn't perfect. It doesn't always get through doorways, sometimes gets lost (becomes mislocalized), and might occasionally get stuck. The next step would be to dig into the documentation for the navigation stack and configure it carefully for our robot. Each of the nodes that we're using in this chapter offers extensive configuration options, from noise models in `amcl` to acceleration limits and planning horizons in `move_base`. The defaults and example configurations that we relied on were enough to produce a working system, but each robot requires some parameter tuning to get really solid navigation performance.

## CHAPTER 18

Your Own Robot Arm

In Chapters 16 and 17, we learned how to add ROS support for a new mobile robot, from modeling and simulation to autonomous navigation. Here we're going to follow the same pattern, but this time for a robot arm, or manipulator. We learned about manipulation in general and how to use an existing ROS-supported robot arm in Chapter 11. Now we'll walk through how to add a new robot arm, including configuring MoveIt to perform path planning.

CougarBot

We're going to build a new manipulator. For inspiration, we go back to the earliest industrial robot arms, which were produced by the Unimation company in the 1960s. Founded by George Devol and Jospeh Engelberger, Unimation provided robot arms first to General Motors, then to other companies and industries, forever changing the nature of manufacturing worldwide. In 1966, Engelberger introduced robots to the general public when he appeared on the *Tonight Show* with one of his machines, demonstrating for Johnny Carson how a robot could pour a beer, conduct an orchestra, and putt a golf ball. Shown in Figure 18-1 is one of Unimation's later models, from its PUMA (Programmable Universal Machine for Assembly) series of robot arms.

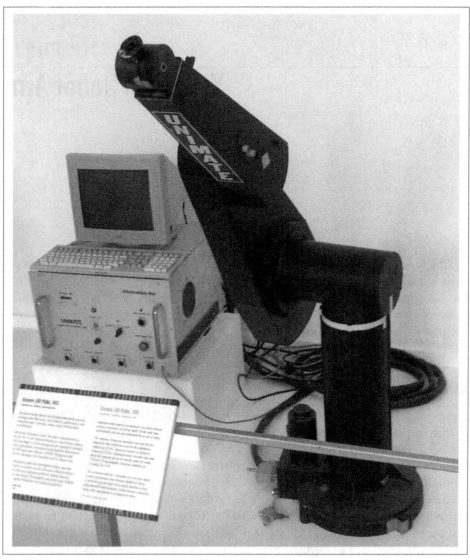

Figure 18-1. An example of Unimation's PUMA series of robot arms (source: Wikimedia Commons (http://bit.ly/500_puma))

In honor of the contributions made by these early machines, we'll create a similar robot arm, called CougarBot. The steps to create the CougarBot robot arm are very similar to what we did when creating the TortoiseBot mobile base:

1. Decide on the ROS message interface.

2. Write drivers for the robot's motors.

3. Write a model of the robot's physical structure.

4. Extend the model with physical properties for use in simulation with Gazebo.

5. Publish coordinate transform data via tf and visualize it with rviz.

6. Add sensors, with driver and simulation support.

7. Apply standard algorithms, such as path planning.

ROS Message Interface

We saw in Chapter 16 that the standard ROS interface to a mobile robot is the cmd_vel/odom topic pair, which allows us to send velocity commands and receive odometry updates. The analogous interface for a robot arm is:

control_msgs/FollowJointTrajectory (follow_joint_trajectory *action*)
    Command a trajectory for the arm and monitor its progress.

sensor_msgs/JointState (joint_states *topic*)
    Publish the current state of each joint in the arm.

The follow_joint_trajectory/joint_states ROS interface allows us to, in a portable manner, observe and command a robot arm's joints. Let's see what kind of goal message we can send to the follow_joint_trajectory action:

```
user@hostname$ rosmsg show control_msgs/FollowJointTrajectoryGoal
trajectory_msgs/JointTrajectory trajectory
  std_msgs/Header header
    uint32 seq
    time stamp
    string frame_id
  string[] joint_names
  trajectory_msgs/JointTrajectoryPoint[] points
    float64[] positions
    float64[] velocities
    float64[] accelerations
    float64[] effort
    duration time_from_start
control_msgs/JointTolerance[] path_tolerance
  string name
  float64 position
  float64 velocity
  float64 acceleration
control_msgs/JointTolerance[] goal_tolerance
  string name
  float64 position
  float64 velocity
  float64 acceleration
duration goal_time_tolerance
```

Wow, there's a lot going on there. It looks like we can define a trajectory by any combination of position, velocity, acceleration, and effort targets, along with time parameterization and tolerances to obey along the way. Fortunately, as we'll see later, it's easy to construct simple trajectories without filling out every field.

Let's look at the `joint_states` side of things:

```
user@hostname$ rosmsg show sensor_msgs/JointState
std_msgs/Header header
  uint32 seq
  time stamp
  string frame_id
string[] name
float64[] position
float64[] velocity
float64[] effort
```

This message is more straightforward, just reporting the current position, velocity, and effort of each joint. We'll read and plot this data later.

Hardware Driver

To implement the `follow_joint_trajectory/joint_states` interface for a physical robot, we need to write a node that will communicate with the robot hardware. The details of that driver node will depend on how the robot works and how we can communicate with it. As with mobile robots, a robot arm will usually offer some physical interface, often serial or network, along with a protocol for exchanging messages over that interface. Ideally, we can find a reusable library that implements the protocol, which we can wrap into a ROS node where we will handle any necessary data transformations, such as unit conversions.

We can't provide general-purpose driver code for controlling a robot arm, but there are many examples within the ROS ecosystem to look at. For the rest of this chapter, we'll proceed under the assumption that you have written a driver node that supports the `follow_joint_trajectory/joint_states` interface, and discuss the other steps that are needed for ROS integration. The following steps, starting with writing a model, can all be tried out in simulation, without any hardware or drivers.

Modeling the Robot: URDF

Now it's time to write down a physical model of the CougarBot, as a URDF file. This model will be used by rviz to visualize the robot, by Gazebo to simulate it, and by MoveIt to plan motions for it.

Let's start with the kinematics. Looking at Figure 18-1, we see that the defining characteristics of this robot arm are that:

- The base is rigidly attached (e.g., bolted) to a work surface.
- After the base, the first joint is a "hip" that swivels the "torso" from side to side.
- The next three joints are the "shoulder," "elbow," and "wrist," which respectively swing the "upper arm," "lower arm," and "hand" up and down.

So, our robot model will need five links (base, torso, upper arm, lower arm, and hand) connected by four joints (hip, shoulder, elbow, and wrist). Let's start modeling it. For simplicity, we'll use a combination of cylinders (a series of tubes, if you will) for the links; more sophisticated models, including highly detailed surface meshes, could be used to improve the accuracy and visual realism of the model.

We'll start with the base, which is rigidly attached to a work surface. We represent this arrangement in URDF by creating a special link called world and connecting the base, modeled as a squat cylinder, to it with a fixed joint. This URDF code is shown in Example 18-1.

Example 18-1. Model of the CougarBot base link, fixed to the world

```xml
<?xml version="1.0"?>
<robot name="cougarbot">
  <link name="world"/>
  <link name="base_link">
    <visual>
      <geometry>
        <cylinder length="0.05" radius="0.1"/>
      </geometry>
      <material name="silver">
        <color rgba="0.75 0.75 0.75 1"/>
      </material>
      <origin rpy="0 0 0" xyz="0 0 0.025"/>
    </visual>
  </link>
  <joint name="fixed" type="fixed">
    <parent link="world"/>
    <child link="base_link"/>
  </joint>
</robot>
```

Note that we used the `<origin>` tag in the `<visual>` element to offset in *z* the point of reference for the base link from its default in the cylinder's center to its bottom. That offset will make it easier to reason about where to attach the next joint, and we'll do the same thing for subsequent links. To see what this model looks like, save that code to a file called *cougarbot.urdf*, and use `roslauch urdf_tutorial display.launch` to visualize it:

```
user@hostname$ roslaunch urdf_tutorial display.launch model:=cougarbot.urdf
```

You should see `rviz` pop up, showing you a single squat cylinder, similar to Figure 18-2. You can see the effect of the `origin` offset in the placement of the coordinate axes at the bottom of the cylinder.

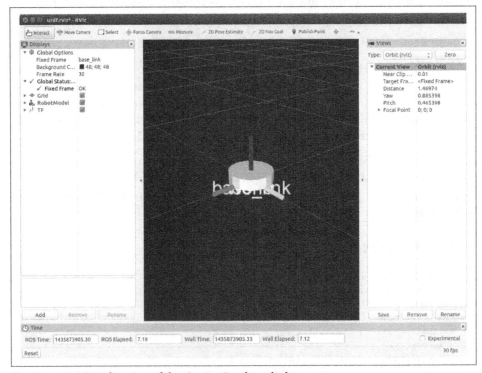

Figure 18-2. Visualization of the CougarBot base link

With the base link in place, we'll add the torso link and hip joint, as shown in Example 18-2.

Example 18-2. URDF code to add the CougarBot torso and hip

```
<link name="torso">
  <visual>
    <geometry>
```

```
        <cylinder length="0.5" radius="0.05"/>
      </geometry>
      <material name="silver">
        <color rgba="0.75 0.75 0.75 1"/>
      </material>
      <origin rpy="0 0 0" xyz="0 0 0.25"/>
    </visual>
  </link>
  <joint name="hip" type="continuous">
    <axis xyz="0 0 1"/>
    <parent link="base_link"/>
    <child link="torso"/>
    <origin rpy="0 0 0" xyz="0.0 0.0 0.05"/>
  </joint>
```

The torso is a tall, thin cylinder, connected to the base via the hip, which is a continuous joint that rotates indefinitely about the z-axis. Add this code to *cougarbot.urdf*, and check the result with the URDF visualizer, this time with the joint control GUI enabled:

```
user@hostname$ roslaunch urdf_tutorial display.launch model:=cougarbot.urdf \
    gui:=True
```

The hip slider in the GUI will swivel the torso back and forth. Next are the upper and lower arm. We can model each as a thin cylinder with the same radius as the torso, but shorter. From the robot's point of view, the upper arm is connected via the shoulder to the right (or outside) of the torso, and the lower arm is connected via the elbow to the left (or inside) upper arm. The URDF code for these new arm components is shown in Example 18-3 and Example 18-4.

Example 18-3. URDF code to add the CougarBot upper arm and shoulder

```
  <link name="upper_arm">
    <visual>
      <geometry>
        <cylinder length="0.4" radius="0.05"/>
      </geometry>
      <material name="silver"/>
      <origin rpy="0 0 0" xyz="0 0 0.2"/>
    </visual>
  </link>
  <joint name="shoulder" type="continuous">
    <axis xyz="0 1 0"/>
    <parent link="torso"/>
    <child link="upper_arm"/>
    <origin rpy="0 1.5708 0" xyz="0.0 -0.1 0.45"/>
  </joint>
```

Example 18-4. URDF code to add the CougarBot lower arm and elbow

```
<link name="lower_arm">
  <visual>
    <geometry>
      <cylinder length="0.4" radius="0.05"/>
    </geometry>
    <material name="silver"/>
    <origin rpy="0 0 0" xyz="0 0 0.2"/>
  </visual>
</link>
<joint name="elbow" type="continuous">
  <axis xyz="0 1 0"/>
  <parent link="upper_arm"/>
  <child link="lower_arm"/>
  <origin rpy="0 0 0" xyz="0.0 0.1 0.35"/>
</joint>
```

Add this code to *cougarbot.urdf*. The last kinematic element that we need is the hand, attached via the wrist to the end of the lower arm. For variety, we'll model the hand as a box, as shown in Example 18-5.

Example 18-5. URDF code to add the CougarBot hand and wrist

```
<link name="hand">
  <visual>
    <geometry>
      <box size="0.05 0.05 0.05"/>
    </geometry>
    <material name="silver"/>
  </visual>
</link>
<joint name="wrist" type="continuous">
  <axis xyz="0 1 0"/>
  <parent link="lower_arm"/>
  <child link="hand"/>
  <origin rpy="0 0 0" xyz="0.0 0.0 0.425"/>
</joint>
```

After adding this code to *cougarbot.urdf*, visualize it again via `roslauch urdf_tuto rial display.launch` with the joint control GUI enabled, then use the `hip`, `shoul der`, `elbow`, and `wrist` sliders to move the robot model around, as shown in Figure 18-3.

Now we're getting somewhere; that looks like a pretty decent robot arm. With the CougarBot's structure settled, let's get this robot into simulation.

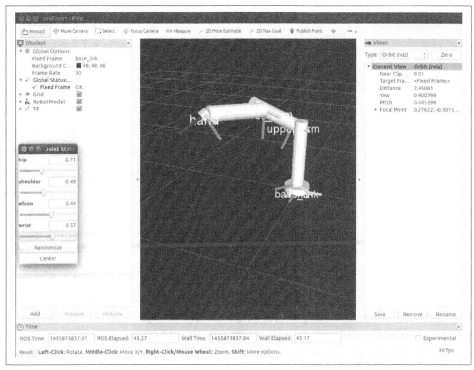

Figure 18-3. Visualization of the CougarBot base, torso, upper arm, lower arm, and hand

Simulation in Gazebo

In the previous section, we created a visual kinematic model of the CougarBot, capturing the sizes and positions of the links and joints. That's enough information to visualize the robot in `rviz`, but to simulate it in Gazebo, we need to add the collision geometry and inertial properties of each link.

To add collision geometry, given the simplicity of our visual model, we just duplicate the visual geometry. Go through your *cougarbot.urdf*, adding for each <visual>/ <geometry> tag a sibling <collision>/<geometry> tag with the same shape, size, and origin. For example, the `base_link` with collision information would look like Example 18-6. Note that you don't need to add a <material> tag for the collision body.

Example 18-6. Code for the CougarBot base, with collision information

```
<link name="base_link">
  <visual>
    <geometry>
```

```
      <cylinder length="0.05" radius="0.1"/>
    </geometry>
    <material name="silver">
      <color rgba="0.75 0.75 0.75 1"/>
    </material>
    <origin rpy="0 0 0" xyz="0 0 0.025"/>
  </visual>
  <collision>
    <geometry>
      <cylinder length="0.05" radius="0.1"/>
    </geometry>
    <origin rpy="0 0 0" xyz="0 0 0.025"/>
  </collision>
</link>
```

To add inertial data, we need to determine the mass properties of each link. To keep things simple, we'll give each link a mass of 1.0 kg. For help with computing inertia matrices, we can consult some well-known formulas (*http://bit.ly/moments_of_inertia*) for computing moments of inertia for objects of various shapes, including boxes and cylinders. Using those formulas, we computed the inertia values shown in Example 18-7 for the base, in Example 18-8 for the torso, in Example 18-9 for the upper arm and lower arm (they're identical), and in Example 18-10 for the hand. Add each block of XML inside the corresponding link(s) in *cougarbot.urdf*.

Example 18-7. CougarBot inertial data for the base

```
<inertial>
  <mass value="1.0"/>
  <origin rpy="0 0 0" xyz="0 0 0.025"/>
  <inertia ixx="0.0027" iyy="0.0027" izz="0.005"
           ixy="0" ixz="0" iyz="0"/>
</inertial>
```

Example 18-8. CougarBot inertial data for the torso

```
<inertial>
  <mass value="1.0"/>
  <origin rpy="0 0 0" xyz="0 0 0.25"/>
  <inertia ixx="0.02146" iyy="0.02146" izz="0.00125"
           ixy="0" ixz="0" iyz="0"/>
</inertial>
```

Example 18-9. CougarBot inertial data for the upper arm and lower arm

```
<inertial>
  <mass value="1.0"/>
  <origin rpy="0 0 0" xyz="0 0 0.2"/>
  <inertia ixx="0.01396" iyy="0.01396" izz="0.00125"
```

```
           ixy="0" ixz="0" iyz="0"/>
  </inertial>
```

Example 18-10. CougarBot inertial data for the hand

```
<inertial>
  <mass value="1.0"/>
  <inertia ixx="0.00042" iyy="0.00042" izz="0.00042"
           ixy="0" ixz="0" iyz="0"/>
</inertial>
```

Note that, in every link for which we used the `<origin>` tag to offset the point of reference for the `<visual>` and `<collision>` elements, we used the same `<origin>` tag for the `<inertial>` element. In this way, we ensure that the visual, kinematic, and dynamic representations of the robot are consistent, which suits our purposes with the CougarBot (there are situations in which you might want them to diverge from each other).

At this point, we need to organize our code into a ROS package, which we'll call cou garbot. Create a directory in your workspace called *cougarbot*, add an appropriate *package.xml* file, then move your *cougarbot.urdf* file in there. Now we're going to add a `roslaunch` file that launches Gazebo with a CougarBot in it. The `roslaunch` code is shown in Example 18-11.

Example 18-11. cougarbot.launch file to bring up Gazebo with a CougarBot model

```
<launch>
  <!-- Load the CougarBot URDF model into the parameter server -->
  <param name="robot_description" textfile="$(find cougarbot)/cougarbot.urdf" />
  <!-- Start Gazebo with an empty world -->
  <include file="$(find gazebo_ros)/launch/empty_world.launch"/>
  <!-- Spawn a CougarBot in Gazebo, taking the description from the
       parameter server -->
  <node name="spawn_urdf" pkg="gazebo_ros" type="spawn_model"
        args="-param robot_description -urdf -model cougarbot" />
</launch>
```

In this launch file, we load the URDF file into the parameter server as `/robot_description`, then use a helper launch file from the gazebo_ros package to run Gazebo with an empty world. With the model data loaded into the parameter server and Gazebo running, we use the helper tool spawn_model, also from the gaz ebo_ros package, to ask Gazebo to spawn an instance of the CougarBot, reading URDF data from the `/robot_description` parameter.

Save that file as *cougarbot/cougarbot.launch* and give it a try:

```
user@hostname$ roslaunch cougarbot cougarbot.launch
```

You should see Gazebo pop up, with a CougarBot, similar to Figure 18-4. Hooray!

Figure 18-4. Gazebo simulating the CougarBot

However, the robot is just lying there, collapsed. What happened? We asked Gazebo to simulate a robot arm having links with mass connected to joints. But we didn't say anything about how to *control* those joints. In the absence of any torque being applied to the joints, as a motor would do, the robot is limp, with the links falling under the force of gravity like a in rag doll (but obeying the kinematic and dynamic properties of the model).

Recall from "Simulation in Gazebo" on page 289 that for the TortoiseBot we added to the model a Gazebo plugin to support differential drive control via the cmd_vel/odom interface. Obviously, differential drive isn't right for our robot arm. For the Cougar-Bot, we need something to help us control all its joints via the follow_joint_trajectory/joint_states interface. For this purpose, we're going to use two plugins: the ros_control plugin will accept new desired trajectories via follow_joint_trajectory, while the ros_joint_state_publisher will publish the joint_states data.

To make the joints move, we need the ros_control plugin. Adding this plugin takes some effort. To understand why, it's important to know that all the control code we're going to use in simulation is also used with real hardware. To make this work, the controllers and supporting infrastructure require extra abstraction and configuration, both of which add complexity. In exchange for the additional complexity, we get the ability to run the same code in simulation and on real robots, which is a great trade-off to make.

First, for every joint in our URDF model, we need to define a matching *transmission*. The transmission models what happens between the output of a motor and the joint to which the motor is attached. Transmissions often involve a gear reduction to account for the mechanical gearbox that is used to increase the torque available from an electric motor, which is naturally a high-speed, low-torque device. A transmission can also include more complex phenomena, such as mechanical coupling among joints. Shown in Example 18-12 is the code to define a simple transmission for the CougarBot's hip joint. To learn more about this and other types of transmission, consult the documentation for URDF (*http://wiki.ros.org/urdf/XML/Transmission?distro=indigo*).

Example 18-12. URDF code to add a transmission for the hip joint

```
<transmission name="tran0">
  <type>transmission_interface/SimpleTransmission</type>
  <joint name="hip">
    <hardwareInterface>PositionJointInterface</hardwareInterface>
  </joint>
  <actuator name="motor0">
    <hardwareInterface>PositionJointInterface</hardwareInterface>
    <mechanicalReduction>1</mechanicalReduction>
  </actuator>
</transmission>
```

This block of code defines what is essentially an empty transmission, with a gear reduction of 1. It's unrealistic, but will meet our needs for simulating a CougarBot. Add that URDF code to your model, anywhere inside the <robot> tag. Then add the analogous transmissions for the other three joints, shown in Example 18-13.

Example 18-13. URDF code to add transmissions for the shoulder, elbow, and wrist

```
<transmission name="tran1">
  <type>transmission_interface/SimpleTransmission</type>
  <joint name="shoulder">
    <hardwareInterface>PositionJointInterface</hardwareInterface>
  </joint>
  <actuator name="motor1">
    <hardwareInterface>PositionJointInterface</hardwareInterface>
    <mechanicalReduction>1</mechanicalReduction>
  </actuator>
</transmission>
<transmission name="tran2">
  <type>transmission_interface/SimpleTransmission</type>
  <joint name="elbow">
```

```
      <hardwareInterface>PositionJointInterface</hardwareInterface>
    </joint>
    <actuator name="motor2">
      <hardwareInterface>PositionJointInterface</hardwareInterface>
      <mechanicalReduction>1</mechanicalReduction>
    </actuator>
  </transmission>
  <transmission name="tran3">
    <type>transmission_interface/SimpleTransmission</type>
    <joint name="wrist">
      <hardwareInterface>PositionJointInterface</hardwareInterface>
    </joint>
    <actuator name="motor3">
      <hardwareInterface>PositionJointInterface</hardwareInterface>
      <mechanicalReduction>1</mechanicalReduction>
    </actuator>
  </transmission>
```

With the transmissions defined, we can add the ros_control plugin, as shown in Example 18-14

Example 18-14. URDF code to load the ros_control plugin

```
<gazebo>
  <plugin name="control" filename="libgazebo_ros_control.so"/>
</gazebo>
```

Add that code to your *cougarbot.urdf*. Next we'll choose which of the controllers offered by ros_control we're going to use and configure it. For our purposes, we need something that will accept trajectories of joint positions (as opposed to, say, velocities, accelerations, or other goals or constraints). Create a new file in your cou garbot package, call it *controllers.yaml*, and insert the YAML code shown in Example 18-15.

Example 18-15. YAML configuration of a controller for CougarBot

```
arm_controller:
  type: "position_controllers/JointTrajectoryController"
  joints:
    - hip
    - shoulder
    - elbow
    - wrist
```

This file defines a new controller, called arm_controller, of type position_ controllers/JointTrajectoryController, that controls all of of our robot's joints. The following is the XML code required to load the contents of this file via rosparam into the ROS parameter server, where other tools can access it:

```
<rosparam file="$(find cougarbot)/controllers.yaml" command="load"/>
```

Add that code to your *cougarbot.launch*. Now we actually need to spawn our newly configured controller. By default, ros_control starts without any controllers running, waiting to be told what to do. Here is the XML code required to use the control ler_manager/spawner tool to spawn our arm_controller:

```
<node name="controller_spawner" pkg="controller_manager" type="spawner"
    args="arm_controller"/>
```

Add that code to your *cougarbot.launch*. Now, let's get this robot moving! Launch the simulation again. You should get a different result this time, similar to Figure 18-5.

Figure 18-5. Gazebo simulating the CougarBot, with the controller running

The robot is now no longer just lying there, but rather is maintaining the configuration that we specified when we built the model. That's the result of our new controller, which by default will try to keep each joint at its zero position. We can tell it to go somewhere else by sending a new command to the follow_joint_trajectory interface. How can we do that? Let's start by looking at the list of available topics:

```
user@hostname$ rostopic list
/arm_controller/command
/arm_controller/follow_joint_trajectory/cancel
/arm_controller/follow_joint_trajectory/feedback
/arm_controller/follow_joint_trajectory/goal
/arm_controller/follow_joint_trajectory/result
/arm_controller/follow_joint_trajectory/status
```

```
/arm_controller/state
/clock
/gazebo/link_states
/gazebo/model_states
/gazebo/parameter_descriptions
/gazebo/parameter_updates
/gazebo/set_link_state
/gazebo/set_model_state
/rosout
/rosout_agg
```

We can see that the /arm_controller namespace contains several topics that look interesting. The follow_joint_trajectory namespace contains the topics that make up the action interface, which is how the controller is normally used. But it also offers a command topic; let's get more information on that one:

```
user@hostname$ rostopic info /arm_controller/command
Type: trajectory_msgs/JointTrajectory

Publishers: None

Subscribers:
 * /gazebo (http://rossum:42185/)
```

We saw the trajectory_msgs/JointTrajectory message in "ROS Message Interface" on page 321 when looking at the type of goal accepted by the follow_joint_ trajectory action. Now let's try to construct and publish a message of that type. The minimum information that we need to provide is the ordered list of joint names that we want to control, and a trajectory containing at least one point. Each trajectory point needs to define a position for each joint, along with a target time (measured from the start of execution of the trajectory) by which that point should be reached. That's not so much data, so we can publish it via rostopic at the command line, telling each joint to move to a new angle, and get there in 1 second:

```
user@hostname$ rostopic pub /arm_controller/command \
  trajectory_msgs/JointTrajectory \
  '{joint_names: ["hip", "shoulder", "elbow", "wrist"], points: \
  [{positions: [0.1, -0.5, 0.5, 0.75], time_from_start: [1.0, 0.0]}]}' -1
```

You should see the robot arm smoothly move to the new configuration, as shown in Figure 18-6. Controlling a robot like this is similar to how an animator might create key frames for a character. We specify the configuration that the robot should achieve and let something else (in our case, the controller that we attached to the arm) fill in the intervening details.

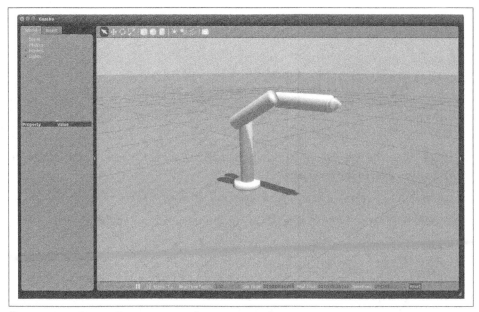

Figure 18-6. CougarBot arm moved to a new configuration

Try modifying the rostopic call to send the robot to other configurations, as well as adding more points to form a longer trajectory. Interesting, but that quickly gets tedious. Typing out lists of joint angles at the command line is not a great way to control a robot arm. We need to continue working on our CougarBot until it's planning paths for itself.

Verifying Transforms

In the previous section, we used the ros_control plugin to provide the follow_joint_trajectory interface to control the arm. Now we'll use the ros_joint_state_publisher plugin to provide the joint_states interface to send out the current state of the arm.

Adding the ros_joint_state_publisher plugin is easy. We just need to tell it the list of joints for which it should publish state data. In our case, we want all of them: hip, shoulder, elbow, and wrist. Add the code in Example 18-16 to your *cougarbot.urdf*, anywhere inside the <robot> tag.

Example 18-16. Plugin to publish joint state data

```
<gazebo>
  <plugin name="joint_state_publisher"
          filename="libgazebo_ros_joint_state_publisher.so">
    <jointName>hip, shoulder, elbow, wrist</jointName>
  </plugin>
</gazebo>
```

To check that the plugin is working, launch *cougarbot.launch,* then echo the joint_states data to the console:

```
user@hostname$ rostopic echo /joint_states
```

You should see a stream of messages showing you the position (angle) of each joint:

```
header:
  seq: 2946
  stamp:
    secs: 29
    nsecs: 632000000
  frame_id: ''
name: ['hip', 'shoulder', 'elbow', 'wrist']
position: [0.0002283149969581899, 2.4271024408939468e-05, \
           -6.677035226587691e-05, 1.7216278225262727e-06]
velocity: []
effort: []
```

The position values should be near zero, because that's where the controller is trying to keep the arm. They might change slightly over time, much like a in real robot that is fighting against gravity to hold its position.

Let's go ahead and add the familiar robot_state_publisher, which will do forward kinematics on the joint_states messages and robot model to produce tf messages. Here is the XML code to launch the robot_state_publisher:

```
<node name="robot_state_publisher" pkg="robot_state_publisher"
      type="robot_state_publisher"/>
```

Add that code to your *cougarbot.launch* and relaunch it. Now we're ready to visualize the state of the robot, so also launch rviz. In rviz, choose base_link as your "fixed frame", and be sure to add the RobotModel and TF displays. You should see the robot, with its TF frames visualized, similar to Figure 18-7.

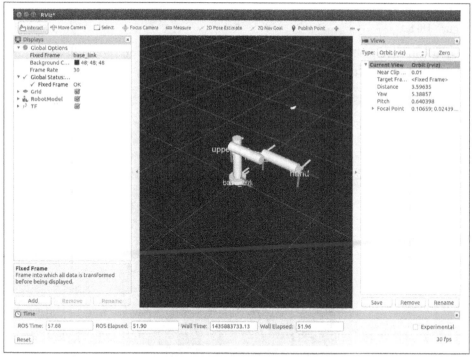

Figure 18-7. Simulated CougarBot arm, visualized live in rviz

To check that everything is working, let's also plot the joint_states data using rqt_plot (see also "Plotting Data: rqt_plot" on page 392):

```
user@hostname$ rqt_plot '/joint_states/position[0]' '/joint_states/position[1]' \
    '/joint_states/position[2]' '/joint_states/position[3]'
```

You should see a live combined plot of the four joint positions, all near zero. Now let's send that simple trajectory again:

```
user@hostname$ rostopic pub /arm_controller/command \
    trajectory_msgs/JointTrajectory \
    '{joint_names: ["hip", "shoulder", "elbow", "wrist"], points: \
    [{positions: [0.1, -0.5, 0.5, 0.75], time_from_start: [1.0, 0.0]}]}' -1'
```

You should see the robot model move to the new configuration in rviz, similar to Figure 18-8.

And, if you were paying attention to the `rqt_plot` window, you should have seen the joint angles diverge from zero to their new respective goals, similar to Figure 18-9.

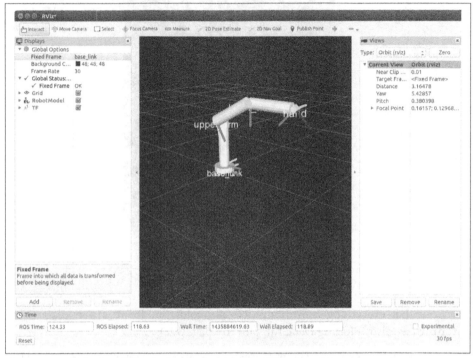

Figure 18-8. Simulated CougarBot arm, visualized live in rviz

Now that we have our CougarBot supporting the `follow_joint_trajectory/joint_states` interface, we can put MoveIt on top to do path planning.

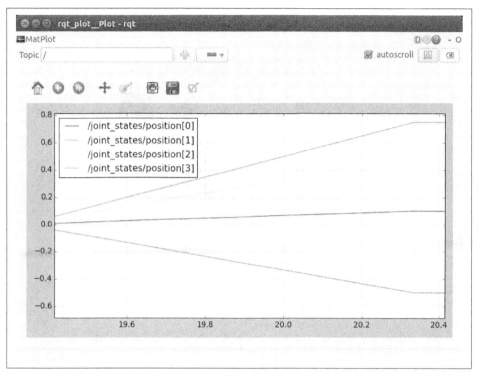

Figure 18-9. Plot of CougarBot joint angles during trajectory execution

Configuring MoveIt

MoveIt is a library of tools for motion planning and control. Though similar in spirit to the navigation stack, which we configured for the TortoiseBot in "Configuring the Navigation Stack" on page 308, MoveIt is a more complex system, with extensive opportunities for configuration. To help with configuration, MoveIt provides a graphical tool called the Setup Assistant. Let's start to configure MoveIt for CougarBot by launching the Setup Assistant:

```
user@hostname$ roslaunch moveit_setup_assistant setup_assistant.launch
```

You should see an introductory screen similar to Figure 18-10.

Click "Create New MoveIt Configuration Package," then browse to your *cougarbot.urdf* file, and click "Load Files." You should see a model of your robot appear on the right side of the Setup Assistant window, similar to Figure 18-11.

Figure 18-10. The MoveIt Setup Assistant

Figure 18-11. The CougarBot model loaded into the MoveIt Setup Assistant

Now we're going to work our way through the sections on the lefthand side of the Setup Assistant window, clicking on each one:

Self-Collisions

In this section, click the "Regenerate Default Collision Matrix" button. MoveIt will examine the robot model and also randomly sample many possible configurations to help decide when collision checks should and should not be performed. Collision checking is very expensive, so it's important to be able to avoid it when possible.

Virtual Joints

Nothing to do here.

Planning Groups

We need to create one planning group, which will cover the entire arm. Click "Add Group." For "Group Name," fill in "arm" (really, any name will do). For "Kinematic Solver," select "kdl_kinematics_plugin/KDLKinematicsPlugin." This plugin provides a generic inverse kinematics solver, which isn't the most efficient way to do things, but it will work fine for our purposes. Click "Add Joints," then select and add all five joints, and click "Save." You should see a result similar to Figure 18-12.

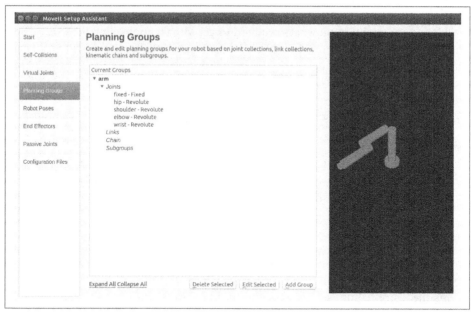

Figure 18-12. The Planning Groups configuration step in the MoveIt Setup Assistant

Robot Poses
> Nothing to do here.

End Effectors
> We need to tell MoveIt which link of the robot we'll be planning for; let's use the hand link. In "End Effector Name," fill in "hand" (again, any name will do). In "Parent Link," select "hand," then click "Save."

Passive Joints
> Nothing to do here.

Configuration Files
> We need to tell MoveIt where to create a new ROS package that contains the new configuration files. In "Configuration Package Save Path," provide a path to a new directory called *cougarbot_moveit_config* that is a sibling to your existing *cougarbot* directory, then click "Generate Package."

That's it for the Setup Assistant; quit it by clicking "Exit Setup Assistant." Now we have a new package, called `cougarbot_moveit_config`, which contains various launch and YAML files. Trying out all the launch files is outside the scope of this book; consult the MoveIt documentation (*http://moveit.ros.org/*) for a complete introduction to the generated files.

We'll focus our attention on what's required to get MoveIt controlling the CougarBot. The last thing we need to tell MoveIt is how our arm controller is configured. In *cougarbot_moveit_config*, create a new file, *config/controller.yaml*, and insert the YAML code shown in Example 18-17.

Example 18-17. YAML code to configure MoveIt to use the CougarBot arm controller

```
controller_manager_ns: /
controller_list:
  - name: arm_controller
    action_ns: follow_joint_trajectory
    type: FollowJointTrajectory
    joints:
      - hip
      - shoulder
      - elbow
      - wrist
```

In this file, we're telling MoveIt where to find the `follow_joint_trajectory` action server that's being provided by the `ros_control` plugin, as well as which joints should be controlled. There's one more file to edit: in *cougarbot_moveit_config*, open *launch/cougarbot_moveit_controller_manager.launch.xml*, which was autogenerated empty by the Setup Assistant, and insert the XML code shown in Example 18-18.

Example 18-18. Extra XML code to load MoveIt's controller configuration

```
<launch>
  <param name="moveit_controller_manager"
         value="moveit_simple_controller_manager/MoveItSimpleControllerManager"/>
  <param name="controller_manager_name" value="/" />
  <param name="use_controller_manager" value="true" />
  <rosparam file="$(find cougarbot_moveit_config)/config/controllers.yaml"/>
</launch>
```

This file sets several parameters, including loading the contents of the *controllers.yaml* file that we just created.

That's it; MoveIt is configured! Now, how do we actually use it?

Using rviz to Send Goals

Launch the CougarBot simulation as usual:

> user@hostname$ **roslaunch cougarbot cougarbot.launch**

Also launch MoveIt, using the configuration that we just created:

> user@hostname$ **roslaunch cougarbot_moveit_config move_group.launch**

Now the simulated robot is running, with MoveIt ready to accept goal poses and do path planning. We just need to bring up rviz in a? with a? suitable configuration to send those goals. Fortunately, MoveIt provided us with such a configuration. Launch rviz like so:

> user@hostname$ **roslaunch cougarbot_moveit_config moveit_rviz.launch config:=True**

Note that you could combine these three steps into one by writing a new launch file, called *all.launch*, as shown in Example 18-19.

Example 18-19. One launch file to rule them all

```
<launch>
  <include file="$(find cougarbot)/cougarbot.launch"/>
  <include file="$(find cougarbot_moveit_config)/launch/move_group.launch"/>
  <include file="$(find cougarbot_moveit_config)/launch/moveit_rviz.launch">
    <arg name="config" value="True"/>
  </include>
</launch>
```

Whichever way you launch everything, you should see rviz with some new features provided by the MotionPlanning display, as shown in Figure 18-13

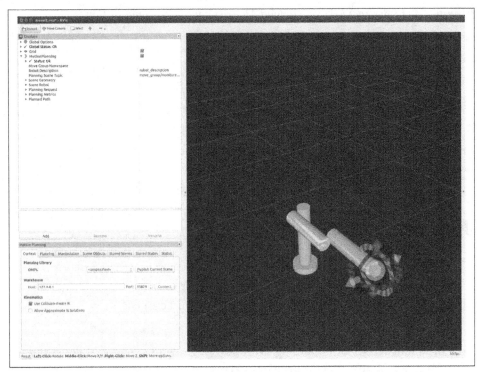

Figure 18-13. CougarBot visualized in rviz with the MotionPlanning display

There is a lot that you can do with this interface. We'll just cover basic planning and execution. First, in the Motion Planning→Context window, select "Allow Approximate IK Solutions." We do this because our robot's one-degree-of-freedom wrist makes it difficult to interactively specify a strictly reachable pose. For this reason, robot arms usually have a two- or three-degrees-of-freedom wrist.

Click on Motion Planning→Planning. Now we're ready to start playing with the robot. In the rviz window, the multicolored marker attached to the robot's hand allows you to translate and rotate the hand in space. As you do that, the inverse kinematics (IK) solver is trying to find a configuration of the robot arm that will put the hand where you want it. The configuration that it finds will be visualized for your review, as shown in Figure 18-14.

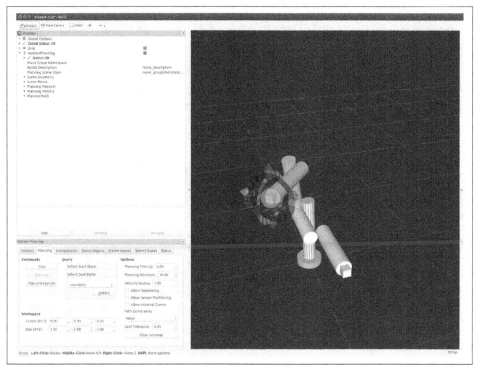

Figure 18-14. Using rviz to define a goal configuration

With the goal configuration selected, click "Plan." You should see a planned trajectory from start to goal being played back repeatedly in `rviz`. So far, nothing is moving in Gazebo; we're just visualizing the trajectory in `rviz`. To execute the trajectory on the robot, click "Execute." The robot should move in Gazebo, following the trajectory promised by `rviz`.

Try other goal configurations by dragging the hand marker around. If you're having trouble getting to a configuration, remember to use both the rotation and translation handles on the hand marker. It might help to imagine what combination of joint rotations would be required to reach a configuration that you have in mind. You can also try random configurations: under "Select Goal State," select "<random valid>" then click "Update." Repeat this procedure until you find a goal configuration that you like, then click "Plan and Execute" to move the robot there.

Summary

In this chapter, we learned how to build a model of a robot arm from scratch, including all the details need to visualize and simulate it. We further attached a controller to the arm, then configured MoveIt to plan and execute trajectories on the arm based on goal poses for the robot's hand—and we were able to do all of that by specifying and configuring models in XML and YAML, without doing any procedural programming. It's a good demonstration of how Gazebo, rviz, MoveIt, and other ROS tools can be combined to provide significant power to the developer of a robot system.

Of course, our CougarBot is not ready to ship yet. For a start, we haven't added any sensors. Path planning is good, but it's far more useful when you're using it to avoid running into obstacles. MoveIt supports obstacle-aware path planning; we just need to add a sensor (probably a Kinect-like depth camera) to the CougarBot model, then extend our MoveIt configuration to subscribe to that sensor stream and use the resulting data to create an environment model in which to do path planning. Check the MoveIt documentation (*http://moveit.ros.org/*) for tips on doing just that.

At this point, we have learned how to model and control new robots with ROS. In the next chapter, we'll cover a different, but equally important, kind of integration, which is adding a new software library to ROS.

## CHAPTER 19

Adding a Software Library

A common step in building a robotics application is adding an existing software library that provides an important capability. Depending on your application, you might want to give your robot the ability to recognize certain objects, or detect people, or (as we'll do in this chapter) speak. There are many good libraries (many of them open source!) out in the world implementing such algorithms that you could use on your robot. Whenever possible, we recommend that you try the existing libraries, especially the ones with strong reputations for reliability and support. While it's always tempting to build your own, and while in some cases you may eventually end up doing so, you'll get going more quickly—and learn more about what exactly you need—by starting with an existing system that does most of what you want.

Many libraries that are relevant to robotics have already been integrated with ROS, such as OpenCV (*http://wiki.ros.org/vision_opencv?distro=indigo*), PCL (*http://wiki.ros.org/pcl?distro=indigo*), and MoveIt (*http://wiki.ros.org/moveit?distro=indigo*). These libraries, and the code that makes them easy to use in a ROS-based robot, form a vital part of the overall ROS ecosystem. Much of the value in using ROS is having ready access to the right tools for the job, especially libraries of useful algorithms. Still, you'll probably find some library that you need but that hasn't yet been integrated.

In this chapter, we'll discuss how to integrate an existing software library (whether it's one that you wrote or a third-party package) with ROS. Between the content of this chapter and the examples provided by the many ROS-connected libraries already available, you'll be ready to tackle the next integration project on your own.

Make Your Robot Talk: pyttsx

From Robbie the Robot to C3PO, we have come to expect our robots to talk with us. While (at the time of writing) there are still some fundamental challenges to overcome on the path to creating truly conversational machines, giving your robot the ability to speak is easy, fun, and can even be a handy debugging tool. Consider all those times when the robot is just sitting there, refusing to move, and you're wondering why. While ROS offers great software tools for helping you to understand what's going on (Chapter 21), to use those tools you need to be looking a screen, not the robot. What if the robot could talk to you, telling you what state it's in, what it's waiting for, or something else?

Fortunately, following decades of research in speech synthesis, there are now multiple text-to-speech (TTS) software packages that you can use off the shelf, as black boxes. In this section, we'll work with the Python `pyttsx` module, which provides a unified way to interact with TTS systems that are commonly available on various operating systems.

 Our goal in this section is to explain the process of integrating with a library like `pyttsx`. If you want a ready-to-use ROS node with speech synthesis capabilities, try the `sound_play` package (*http://wiki.ros.org/sound_play?distro=indigo*).

First, let's make sure that we have `pyttsx` installed. On most systems, `sudo pip install pyttsx` will do the job; for special cases, consult the `pyttsx` documentation (*http://pyttsx.readthedocs.org*). To make sure that it's working properly, let's try one of their example programs:

```python
#!/usr/bin/env python

import pyttsx
engine = pyttsx.init()
engine.say('Sally sells seashells by the seashore.')
engine.say('The quick brown fox jumped over the lazy dog.')
engine.runAndWait()
```

Save that code to a file and run it:

```
user@hostname$ python pyttsx_example.py
```

You should hear the two sentences spoken through your computer's audio system. If you have trouble at this step, check your speaker/headphone connections and volume settings; after that, consult the `pyttsx` documentation.

Now we have a working executable program that will speak a couple of sentences; how should we wrap it up into a general-purpose ROS node? We need to decide a few things:

- What type of topic/service/action interface will the node provide?
- What parameters should be exposed?
- How will we integrate the ROS event loop with the `pyttsx` event loop?

We start by defining the action interface that we'll use to interact with our node.

Action Interface

Because the act of converting text to speech takes time—possibly many seconds for long sentences—it's a good candidate for an action server (see Chapter 5). That way, we can send goals (what we want to say), get notification when they've been said, and even cancel a sentence that is in progress.

Let's decide on the message type that will be received as a goal by our `pyttsx` node. As always, we should first consider using an existing message, especially if it's already being used by a similar node. In this case, the most similar example is the `sound_play/soundplay_node.py` node, which subscribes to messages of type `sound_play/SoundRequest` (*http://docs.ros.org/api/sound_play/html/msg/SoundRequest.html*). But that message has a surprisingly large number of fields and flags. The complexity of the message comes from the fact that the `sound_play/sound play_node.py` node does more than just text-to-speech (and that it's somewhat specific to the PR2 robot). We could use that message type, but it's overkill for our application.

So, we'll design our own goal message type. We know that we need it to contain a `string` field that will be the sentence to be spoken. Let's start with that, then add more fields later as needed. Similarly, we can leave the feedback and result empty, because this node won't have that much status to report. Example 19-1 shows the action definition, also available in the *action* directory of the `basics` package (refer back to Chapter 5 for help with *.action* file syntax).

Example 19-1. Talk.action

```
# The sentence to be spoken
string sentence
---
# No result content needed
---
# No feedback content needed
```

With the action interface settled, we need to decide what kinds of configuration we should offer.

Parameters

Consulting the pyttsx documentation (*http://pyttsx.readthedocs.org*), we see that we can change various settings, such as the volume and rate of speech, and the voice that is used. Those settings are all good candidates for parameters, which the user can set when launching the node (see "Parameter Server" on page 119).

Let's start by exposing the volume and rate of speech, because we can reasonably expect that a user might want to modify them. That's what parameters are for: the knobs that you expect users will want to be able to adjust easily and/or frequently, without modifying any code. For each parameter, we need to decide its data type and its default value (i.e., what we will do if the user doesn't set a value). In our case, the easiest thing is to just mirror how the volume and rate parameters are used in the underlying pyttsx library:

volume (float32)
> Floating point volume in the range of 0.0 to 1.0 inclusive. Defaults to 1.0.

rate (int32)
> Integer speech rate in words per minute. Defaults to 200 words per minute.

We should also add a parameter to control whether the node will preempt a sentence that is currently being spoken when a new sentence is received. Interrupting the speaker might not be the nicest thing from a user interaction point of view, but it's a good capability to have, and we want the developer to have control over that behavior. Our new parameter is:

preempt (bool)
> Whether to preempt in-progress speech in response to a new goal. Defaults to false.

Now we know what the external interface to our node will look like, both for control (action server) and configuration (parameters). Next we will determine how to design the internal structure of the node to bridge between the `pyttsx` library and the `rospy` library.

Event Loops

A common issue when integrating an existing software library into a ROS node is how to manage event loops. Often, the library will have its own way to manage execution and may even want you to give up control of your `main()` function. Every situation will be a little different, but it's often the case that you'll need to separate the library's event loop into its own thread. That's usually easy enough, but it's also important to ensure that the event loop can be properly and safely stopped at the right time.

For the `pyttsx` node, we'll create a separate thread for its event loop, and we'll structure that thread in such a way that we can reliably shut it down. Here's the code for that thread:

```
def loop(self):
    self.engine.startLoop(False)
    while not rospy.is_shutdown():
        self.engine.iterate()
        time.sleep(0.1)
    self.engine.endLoop()
```

In this thread, we check whether it's time to shut down in between repeated calls to the library's `iterate()` function, which causes the event loop to turn over once, processing the next event. We could instead call the library's `startLoop()` function with the argument `True`, which enters an internal processing loop, but then we would need to have the right machinery in another thread to call `endLoop()` at the right time.

While the details of this interaction are specific to the `pyttsx` library, the underlying characteristics are shared by many libraries. For example, it's common to see both the "endless loop" call (`startLoop(True)` in the case of `pyttsx`, or `ros::spin()` in the case of `roscpp`) and the "do one loop" call (`iterate()` in the case of `pyttsx`, or `ros::spinOnce()` in the case of `roscpp`). The right way to use the library's event mechanisms will depend on how they work and your requirements.

Having decided on the action interface, parameters, and event loop structure, we're ready to write our `pyttsx` action server node.

The Speech Server

Example 19-2 shows the code for a full speech synthesis node. Don't worry if it looks intimidating; we're going to step through each part of the program.

Example 19-2. pyttsx_server.py

```python
#! /usr/bin/env python
import rospy
import threading, time, pyttsx
import actionlib
from basics.msg import TalkAction, TalkGoal, TalkResult

class TalkNode():

    def __init__(self, node_name, action_name):
        rospy.init_node(node_name)
        self.server = actionlib.SimpleActionServer(action_name, TalkAction,
          self.do_talk, False)
        self.engine = pyttsx.init()
        self.engine_thread = threading.Thread(target=self.loop)
        self.engine_thread.start()
        self.engine.setProperty('volume', rospy.get_param('~volume', 1.0))
        self.engine.setProperty('rate', rospy.get_param('~rate', 200.0))
        self.preempt = rospy.get_param('~preempt', False)
        self.server.start()

    def loop(self):
        self.engine.startLoop(False)
        while not rospy.is_shutdown():
            self.engine.iterate()
            time.sleep(0.1)
        self.engine.endLoop()

    def do_talk(self, goal):
        self.engine.say(goal.sentence)
        while self.engine.isBusy():
            if self.preempt and self.server.is_preempt_requested():
                self.engine.stop()
                while self.engine.isBusy():
                    time.sleep(0.1)
                self.server.set_preempted(TalkResult(), "Talk preempted")
                return
            time.sleep(0.1)
        self.server.set_succeeded(TalkResult(), "Talk completed successfully")

talker = TalkNode('speaker', 'speak')
rospy.spin()
```

Let's look at the code piece by piece. First we do some standard imports, including the Talk action message types that we'll need and the pyttsx module. We also import the standard threading module, which we'll need to manage the event loop thread:

```python
import rospy
import threading, time, pyttsx
import actionlib
from basics.msg import TalkAction, TalkGoal, TalkResult
```

Next we create a class, TalkNode, which will make it easier (or at least cleaner) to store some state about the node, including the speech engine. In the constructor, we initialize the node, create the action server, initialize the speech engine, then create and start the thread that will run the event loop:

```
class TalkNode():

    def __init__(self, node_name, action_name):
        rospy.init_node(node_name)
        self.server = actionlib.SimpleActionServer(action_name, TalkAction,
          self.do_talk, False)
        self.engine = pyttsx.init()
        self.engine_thread = threading.Thread(target=self.loop)
        self.engine_thread.start()
```

Now it's time to handle parameters, then start the action server. The volume and rate parameters get passed directly to the library; we'll keep the preempt parameter for ourselves:

```
        self.engine.setProperty('volume', rospy.get_param('~volume', 1.0))
        self.engine.setProperty('rate', rospy.get_param('~rate', 200.0))
        self.preempt = rospy.get_param('~preempt', False)
        self.server.start()
```

 A leading tilde character in a parameter name, such as ~volume, indicates that the parameter is *private* to the node, which means that it will be stored in and retrieved from the node's namespace, as opposed to its parent namespace (which is the default). It is good practice to keep parameters local to the node using them whenever possible. If our node is named speaker, then the volume parameter will be stored in the parameter server as /speaker/volume (unless the node is itself pushed down into a namespace, in which case the parameter name would be further qualified).

We already went over the code for the loop() function that runs in a separate thread. Let's look at the code for the goal callback, do_talk(). On receipt of a new goal, which is a sentence, we pass the sentence to the speech engine:

```
    def do_talk(self, goal):
        self.engine.say(goal.sentence)
```

Having asked the speech engine to say the sentence, we need to monitor it for completion. Also, if preempt was set, we need to check for a preemption request. If the current goal is to be preempted, then we call stop() on the engine, followed by a second loop to wait for confirmation that it's stopped, and finally a report back to clients that the preemption was accomplished. Otherwise, when the speech engine has finished saying the sentence, we report that success:

```
        while self.engine.isBusy():
            if self.preempt and self.server.is_preempt_requested():
                self.engine.stop()
                while self.engine.isBusy():
                    time.sleep(0.1)
                self.server.set_preempted(TalkResult(), "Talk preempted")
                return
            time.sleep(0.1)
        self.server.set_succeeded(TalkResult(), "Talk completed successfully")
```

Now that we have an action *server* that will accept commands to make the robot talk, we need to write an action *client* that will exercise it.

The Speech Client

A ROS node that activates the speech server is straightforward to write. Example 19-3 shows the code for a simple client program that tells the server to say "hello world" a few times.

Example 19-3. pyttsx_client.py

```
#! /usr/bin/env python
import rospy

import actionlib
from basics.msg import TalkAction, TalkGoal, TalkResult

rospy.init_node('speaker_client')
client = actionlib.SimpleActionClient('speak', TalkAction)
client.wait_for_server()
goal = TalkGoal()
goal.sentence = "hello world, hello world, hello world, hello world"
client.send_goal(goal)
client.wait_for_result()
print('[Result] State: %d'%(client.get_state()))
print('[Result] Status: %s'%(client.get_goal_status_text()))
```

In this program, following the usual initialization, we create an action client of the appropriate type, send a sentence as a goal, then wait for completion. That's the beauty of using an action server: we've wrapped up the non trivial behavior of synthesizing speech in an interface where we can just send it a string of words, then wait to be told that it's done executing. We've written the code; now it's time to test it.

Checking That Everything Works as Expected

Let's verify that our speech server and client work as intended. Open a new terminal, and start up roscore. In another terminal, start the server:

```
user@hostname$ rosrun basics pyttsx_server.py
```

In a third terminal, start the client:

```
user@hostname$ rosrun basics pyttsx_client.py
```

You should hear the words "hello world" repeated a few times. Let's try out those parameters. Stop the server, then run it again with a lower volume setting:

```
user@hostname$ rosrun basics pyttsx_server.py _volume:=0.5
```

Now run the client again, and you should hear the same words, but quieter. You can adjust the rate of speech in the same way. You can also experiment with the effect of the preempt parameter: try running the server with _preempt:=true, then run two instances of the client, each in a separate terminal. You should hear the speech begin on behalf of the first client, then be interrupted and start again on behalf of the second client (the effect will be more noticeable if you modify the second client to send a different string).

Summary

In this chapter, we discussed how to integrate an existing software library into a ROS system, which is often called for when building a robotics application. We worked with the relatively simple example of a text-to-speech system that has just one kind of input (the text to be spoken), but the basic elements apply equally well to other libraries: decide on the appropriate data types, and develop an interface (in this case an action interface); decide on the parameters that will be accepted; and decide how to integrate the library's event loop with your own.

Even this relatively simple example resulted in a useful node that could be deployed straight away on a robot (as long as the robot has speakers). The node could, of course, be improved and extended in a number of ways, from exposing more configuration of the speech engine (e.g., which voice is being used), to delivering detailed feedback to clients (e.g., notification of each word having been said). There's almost always more that could be exposed, and the art is in deciding what to leave out.

In the past few chapters, we've presented examples and discussed patterns for adding devices, robots, and capabilities to ROS. The ease with which the platform can be stretched and extended to cover new use cases is a key feature of ROS—but each new feature brings complexity, and writing good robot software is a challenging task to begin with. With that challenge in mind, the next few chapters will introduce some important tools and techniques that will help you to become an efficient and effective ROS developer.

## PART V

Tips and Tricks

## CHAPTER 20

Tools

Efficient software development requires good developer tools. Where would you be without your favorite editor, version control system, or testing framework? When developing robotics software, we of course rely on those tools, but we also add some new ones. These ROS-specific developer tools are designed to help you work with your robotics applications, including starting and stopping, introspection, and testing.

In this chapter, we'll cover commonly used ROS tools, explaining when and how to use each one. We will leave out the following tools, which are covered in the context of debugging in Chapter 21: `rosbag`, `rqt_bag`, `rqt_graph`, and `rqt_plot`.

The Master and Friends: roscore

We first encountered `roscore` much earlier in this book (see "roscore" on page 11), and have used it extensively since then. But it will be helpful to understand what exactly it does. When you run `roscore`, which is your first step in bringing up a ROS system, you're really starting three different tools:

- The *master*, which handles the name service.
- The *parameter server*, which holds key/value parameter data (see "Parameters: rosparam" on page 361).
- The rosout node, which aggregates debug messages from all other nodes (see "/rosout Versus /rosout_agg" on page 382).

The first thing that a ROS node does on startup is contact the master to register itself. That's why, if you try to start a node without a master, you'll get a warning, like this:

```
user@hostname$ python -c "import rospy; rospy.init_node('my_node')"
Unable to register with master node [http://localhost:11311]: master may
not be running yet. Will keep trying.
```

When registering with the master, each node supplies its own network address, which is where it can be contacted later by other nodes. The master maintains a table of these registrations, each one mapping the node name to its network address. For example, the node my_node might be listening for new connections at the address *http://localhost:61515*. The port on which a node listens (61515 in this example) is randomly assigned by the operating system when the node starts, which is why we need the master to keep track of where each node can be found. This mapping of node name to address is used constantly behind the scenes when nodes connect with each other.

In addition to registering itself with the master, a node registers each of its topic subscriptions and advertisements, and its services. When you advertise a topic by creating a rospy.Publisher, the rospy library registers with the master that your node is a publisher of that topic. That information is subsequently provided to each node that registers as a subscriber for the topic (by creating a rospy.Subscriber). Given the publisher list for a topic, each subscribing node will contact each publishing node to negotiate a connection over which to receive messages for that topic. Thereafter, the message data is sent directly from publishers to subscribers, without involving the master. For services, a similar mechanism is used to keep track of names and addresses of servers, allowing clients to find them by name.

With its critical role in name lookup, the master is the one centralized aspect of an otherwise distributed ROS system. As such, it is also a potential point of failure. If you kill the master, the situation is usually unrecoverable. Already running nodes and existing topic connections will persist, but new nodes can't be started, and new connections can't be made. Because there is no easy way to reconstruct the state previously held by the master, you will likely need to restart your entire ROS system following the death of the master. If the master is only temporarily unreachable—e.g., because a robot moves out of wireless range—then the system should resume normal operation when the master becomes reachable again. Fortunately, the master is a robust, well-tested tool that is not prone to crashing.

It's common to keep a master running over an extended period of time, reusing it across multiple development and debugging sessions. This is fine to do, with the caveat that the master can accumulate stale state about nodes. When a node crashes, it won't deregister itself with the master and so will still show up, for example, when you run rosnode list (see "Introspection: rosnode, rostopic, rosmsg, rosservice, and rossrv" on page 369). Such stale state is usually not a problem, as the ROS tools and client libraries are designed to tolerate it, but it can be distracting. To purge the master of entries for nodes that are no longer reachable, run rosnode cleanup.

Parameters: rosparam

In the same process with the master (but functionally separate) is the *parameter server*. The job of the parameter server is to store configuration data in a network-accessible database. The parameter server maintains a dictionary of key/value pairs, in which the keys are strings and the values can be of (nearly) any type. Any node, including yours, can write to or read from the parameter server.

 Parameters are intended for *configuration*, not *communication*. If you try to use parameters to exchange high-volume or high-rate data between nodes, you will be sorely disappointed by the resulting performance. Instead, use topics for these purposes.

While parameter access is usually done from code (via `rospy.get_param()` and `rospy.set_param()`), it can be useful to operate on the parameter server from the command line, for which we use the `rosparam` tool. For example, to list the current parameters:

```
user@hostname$ rosparam list
/rosdistro
/roslaunch/uris/host_localhost__50387
/rosversion
/run_id
```

You can also operate on individual parameters, setting, getting, or deleting them:

```
user@hostname$ rosparam set my_param 4.2
user@hostname$ rosparam get my_param
4.2
user@hostname$ rosparam delete my_param
user@hostname$ rosparam get my_param
ERROR: Parameter [/my_param] is not set
```

Parameter values can be specified using any valid YAML string. You can put parameters into a namespace by either specifying a YAML dictionary or using the / separator:

```
user@hostname$ rosparam set my_dict "{message: 'Hello world', x: 4.2, y: 2.4}"
user@hostname$ rosparam get my_dict
{message: Hello world, x: 4.2, y: 2.4}
user@hostname$ rosparam set my_dict/message 'Goodbye world'
user@hostname$ rosparam get my_dict/message
Goodbye world
```

You can also dump parameter data to and load it back from a YAML file, optionally in a namespace:

```
user@hostname$ rosparam set my_dict "{message: 'Hello world', x: 4.2, y: 2.4}"
user@hostname$ rosparam dump data.yaml my_dict
```

```
user@hostname$ cat data.yaml
{message: Hello world, x: 4.2, y: 2.4}
user@hostname$ rosparam load data.yaml my_dict2
user@hostname$ rosparam get my_dict2
{message: Hello world, x: 4.2, y: 2.4}
```

In summary, rosparam is handy tool for inspecting and modifying the parameters that configure your ROS system.

Navigating the Filesystem: roscd

As we've seen throughout this book, ROS code is organized into packages, with each package in its own directory. It can sometimes be hard to remember where exactly in the filesystem a given package lives. To speed up moving around among packages, we use roscd, which changes to the directory containing a given package:

```
user@hostname$ roscd my_package
```

The roscd tool is part of the rosbash suite, where it is implemented as a bash shell function, rather than an executable program. To use roscd or other rosbash functions, you must be sure to source the bash-specific ROS setup file, for example:

```
user@hostname$ source /opt/ros/indigo/setup.bash
```

Another handy rosbash shortcut is rosed, with which you can edit a file in a ROS package without having to first change to the package's directory. The file will be opened in your favorite editor (as determined by the value of the environment variable EDITOR):

```
user@hostname$ rosed my_package my_file.cpp
```

The rosed tool will look for a file by the given name anywhere within the given package's directory.

Starting a Node: rosrun

Just like other resources, ROS nodes are stored in packages, where they are not in the default search path for executables (the environment variable PATH). As a result, depending on where a package sits in the filesystem, running a node might require you to use a long and difficult-to-remember directory prefix to specify where that node is on disk. Instead, you can use rosrun and just give the package name and node name:

```
user@hostname$ rosrun my_package my_node
```

Similar to rosed, rosrun will look for an executable file by the given name anywhere within the given package's directory. You can kill a node started via rosrun just as you would if you had run it directly, with Ctrl-C. The rosrun tool is part of the rosbash suite.

Starting Many Nodes: roslaunch

Starting nodes one by one with rosrun is good for testing and debugging, but most ROS systems comprise many nodes, and you don't want to have to start and stop them individually. You also don't want to have to remember which command-line arguments, name remappings, and parameters to provide to each node. Ideally, especially for complex systems, you would describe the desired set of nodes and their configuration in a file.

For this purpose, we use roslaunch, a tool that reads an XML description of a set of nodes, then launches and monitors those nodes. By convention, roslaunch XML files have the extension *.launch* and are called "launch files." For example, to launch both the talker and listener examples from the rospy_tutorials package, we would write the XML code shown in example Example 20-1:

Example 20-1. talker_listener.launch

```
<launch>
  <node name="talker" pkg="rospy_tutorials" type="talker" />
  <node name="listener" pkg="rospy_tutorials" type="listener" />
</launch>
```

> While roslaunch guarantees that all parameters are set prior to executing any nodes, there is no ordering when it comes to executing the nodes. Conceptually, all nodes start executing at around, but not exactly, the same time. If you need to sequence the execution of two nodes, use ROS communication between them.

We're asking roslaunch to start two nodes for us. In each <node> tag, we specify the containing package (pkg), the name of the executable file within that package (type), and the name that we want to assign to the node once it's running (name). Save that code to a launch file called *talker_listener.launch*, then pass it to roslaunch:

```
user@hostname$ roslaunch talker_listener.launch
roslaunch talker_listener.launch
... logging to
/home/user/.ros/log/99e865f8-314c-11e4-bf3a-705681aea243/
  roslaunch-localhost-36423.log
Checking log directory for disk usage. This may take awhile.
Press Ctrl-C to interrupt

started roslaunch server http://localhost:52380/
```

```
SUMMARY
========

PARAMETERS
 * /rosdistro
 * /rosversion

NODES
  /
    listener (rospy_tutorials/listener)
    talker (rospy_tutorials/talker)

ROS_MASTER_URI=http://localhost:11311

core service [/rosout] found
process[talker-1]: started with pid [36428]
process[listener-2]: started with pid [36429]
```

Now both the `talker` and `listener` nodes are running. To stop them, give a Ctrl-C to `roslaunch`, and it will take care of shutting everything down. It keeps careful track of all processes that it has launched and is thorough about stopping them before exiting itself. If a node is not responding properly to a shutdown request, `roslaunch` will forcibly kill it. This is a key feature of `roslaunch` and a reason to use it even for small ROS systems: in a distributed computing environment comprising multiple processes, it's important to be sure that after shutdown, they are all indeed stopped.

If there is already an instance of roscore running, roslaunch will use it. If not, roslaunch will start a roscore automatically and will kill it on exit.

You may have noticed that in the previous example, there were no messages printed to the console, which is surprising because both `talker` and `listener` are usually very chatty, printing to the each time a message is sent or received. In this case, there's no output because the default behavior of `roslaunch` is to direct nodes' output to log files to avoid cluttering the console. If you want to see the output from a node, set the attribute `output="screen"` in the corresponding <node> tag. For example, to see the output from the `listener` node, we would modify the launch file as shown in Example 20-2.

Example 20-2. talker_listener_screen.launch

```
<launch>
  <node name="talker" pkg="rospy_tutorials" type="talker" />
  <node name="listener" pkg="rospy_tutorials" type="listener" output="screen" />
</launch>
```

Then we'll see the usual console output from `listener` even when run by `roslaunch`:

```
user@hostname$ roslaunch talker_listener_screen.launch
...
process[talker-1]: started with pid [36626]
process[listener-2]: started with pid [36627]
[INFO] [WallTime: 1409517683.732251] /listener I heard hello world 1409517683.73
[INFO] [WallTime: 1409517683.831888] /listener I heard hello world 1409517683.83
[INFO] [WallTime: 1409517683.932052] /listener I heard hello world 1409517683.93
...
```

You can specify name remappings for a node in a launch file by using the <remap> tag inside the corresponding <node> tag. For example, we can remap our `talker/lis tener` pair to communicate over a different topic than their default, which is `chatter`, as seen in Example 20-3.

Example 20-3. talker_listener_remap.launch

```
<launch>
  <node name="talker" pkg="rospy_tutorials" type="talker">
    <remap from="chatter" to="my_chatter"/>
  </node>
  <node name="listener" pkg="rospy_tutorials" type="listener">
    <remap from="chatter" to="my_chatter"/>
  </node>
</launch>
```

It's also useful to specify parameters in a launch file by using the <param> tag. Most often, you'll be setting parameters for a specific node, which you can do by putting the <param> tag inside the corresponding <node> tag. For example, we could add a parameter in the namespace of the `talker` node as shown in Example 20-4.

Example 20-4. talker_listener_param.launch

```
<launch>
  <node name="talker" pkg="rospy_tutorials" type="talker">
    <param name="my_param" value="4.2"/>
  </node>
  <node name="listener" pkg="rospy_tutorials" type="listener" />
</launch>
```

Pass that file to `roslaunch`, then check the parameter value from another terminal:

```
user@hostname$ rosparam get talker/my_param
4.2
```

In this case, we're just setting a parameter in a node's namespace, then reading it back. More often, the node in question would read the parameter value and modify its behavior in some way. Because parameters are usually read by nodes on startup, roslaunch guarantees that all parameters specified in a launch file are set prior to launching any of the nodes.

It is common to separate a complex roslaunch configuration into multiple launch files that are easier to test, document, and maintain. These files can be composed through the use of the <include> tag. For example, we could separate the node declarations from Example 20-4 into two files, as shown in Example 20-5, which is included by Example 20-6. Note that the file attribute of the <include> tag should be relative to the location of a ROS package, which in this case is called basics.

Example 20-5. listener.launch

```
<launch>
  <node name="listener" pkg="rospy_tutorials" type="listener" />
</launch>
```

Example 20-6. talker_listener_param_include.launch

```
<launch>
  <node name="talker" pkg="rospy_tutorials" type="talker">
    <param name="my_param" value="4.2"/>
  </node>
  <include file="$(find basics)/launch/listener.launch"/>
</launch>
```

While these examples cover the most commonly used features of roslaunch, there are many more, such as namespace grouping, environment variable access, argument substitution, conditional evaluation, and launching on remote machines. For details on advanced features, consult the roslaunch documentation (*http://wiki.ros.org/ roslaunch?distro=indigo*).

Testing a Many-Node System: rostest

Testing is a critical aspect of any software system, and we strongly encourage the use of standard testing frameworks such as unittest or nose (Python) and Google Test (C++). These frameworks allow you to write test programs that exercise your code in various ways to ensure that it behaves correctly. But, while these frameworks are great for testing libraries in isolation, it can be difficult to write tests for an entire ROS system. For this purpose we use rostest.

The rostest tool is just an extension to roslaunch, adding the <test> tag to allow specification of a test program to be run alongside the other nodes. For example, if we wanted to test that the talker in our talker/listener system is working properly, we could extend the launch file as shown in Example 20-7.

Example 20-7. talker_listener_test.launch

```
<launch>
  <node name="talker" pkg="rospy_tutorials" type="talker" />
  <node name="listener" pkg="rospy_tutorials" type="listener" />
  <test test-name="test_talker" pkg="basics" type="test_talker.py" />
</launch>
```

This file says to `rostest`: bring up the nodes, then run the test program to check that everything is working. Given this file as input, `rostest` will launch the nodes just like `roslaunch` does. The difference with `rostest` is that, after launching the rest of the nodes, it will further launch the test node, which is expected to use one of the standard testing frameworks to verify that the rest of the nodes are working properly and to report its findings in an xUnit-format output file.

 If you declare multiple `<test>` tags in a single launch file, `rostest` will run them all, sequentially. For each test, `rostest` will ensure a clean environment by tearing down and restarting the nodes to be tested.

For example, the `test_talker.py` node referenced in Example 20-7 might have the contents shown in Example 20-8.

Example 20-8. test_talker.py

```
#!/usr/bin/env python

import sys, unittest, time
import rospy, rostest
from std_msgs.msg import String

class TestTalker(unittest.TestCase):

    def __init__(self, *args):
        super(TestTalker, self).__init__(*args)
        self.success = False

    def callback(self, data):
        self.success = data.data and data.data.startswith('hello world')

    def test_talker(self):
        rospy.init_node('test_talker')
        rospy.Subscriber("chatter", String, self.callback)
        timeout_t = time.time() + 10.0
        while (not rospy.is_shutdown() and
                not self.success and time.time() < timeout_t):
            time.sleep(0.1)
        self.assert_(self.success)
```

```
if __name__ == '__main__':
    rostest.rosrun('basics', 'talker_test', TestTalker, sys.argv)
```

In this test, we subscribe to the chatter topic, then check for receipt of a message on that topic that starts with a particular substring. If that condition is satisfied within 10 seconds, then we report success; otherwise, we report failure. In other words, we're verifying that the talker node is functioning as expected.

Let's look at the fundamental elements of this test, starting with the module imports:

```
import sys, unittest, time
import rospy, rostest
from std_msgs.msg import String
```

In addition to the usual imports in a rospy node, we're also pulling in the standard Python unittest module and the ROS-specific rostest module. Taken together, these two modules allow us to declare, run, and collect results from our test. Next we create the class that will contain our test(s):

```
class TestTalker(unittest.TestCase):

    def __init__(self, *args):
        super(TestTalker, self).__init__(*args)
        self.success = False
```

As usual when using unittest, we create a class that inherits from the unittest.TestCase class. Because we're going to signal success in this test asynchronously, we also declare a constructor that initializes a success flag (and explicitly invokes the unittest.TestCase constructor; to ensure proper setup for running tests). With the initial conditions in place, we write the test itself:

```
    def callback(self, data):
        self.success = data.data and data.data.startswith('hello world')

    def test_talker(self):
        rospy.init_node('test_talker')
        rospy.Subscriber("chatter", String, self.callback)
        timeout_t = time.time() + 10.0
        while (not rospy.is_shutdown() and
               not self.success and time.time() < timeout_t):
            time.sleep(0.1)
        self.assert_(self.success)
```

First, there's a callback function that, if provided a string message with the expected content, will signal that the test has succeeded. Next, we create a function that runs the test: create a node, subscribe to a topic using the previously defined callback function, wait for either success or a timeout, then report the test result via the uni ttest.TestCase.assert_() function. The name of our test function is important—

in this context, all functions with names beginning with `test_` are assumed to be tests and will be run as a result of running the overall test suite.

Finally, in this invocation of `rostest.rosrun()`, we're saying that this test is part of the `basics` ROS package, that the test is named `talker_test` (this name will be used to organize test results and should be unique within each package), and that the tests to be run are defined in the `TestTalker` class:

```python
if __name__ == '__main__':
    rostest.rosrun('basics', 'talker_test', TestTalker, sys.argv)
```

 The `roslaunch` tool will ignore `<test>` tags in launch files, so you can freely declare tests directly in launch files that you are actively using.

While this example test is intentionally simple, the same techniques can be applied to build sophisticated tests for complex ROS systems. The structure of a good ROS test is similar to that found in other software testing: set up the system to be tested, optionally stimulate it with input, then verify some expected output.

Introspection: rosnode, rostopic, rosmsg, rosservice, and rossrv

A core design principle of ROS is that it should be possible from outside the system to see as much as possible of what's going on inside. This introspection capability is made possible by the fact that both the master and the nodes can be remotely interrogated with regard to their state. While you can conduct this interrogation directly in code, it's usually more convenient to use the command-line tools that we'll present in this section.

To get started, let's define a simple system, consisting of a couple of nodes (Example 20-9).

Example 20-9. listener_add_two_ints_server.launch

```xml
<launch>
  <node name="listener" pkg="rospy_tutorials"
        type="listener" output="screen" />
  <node name="add_two_ints_server" pkg="rospy_tutorials"
        type="add_two_ints_server" output="screen" />
</launch>
```

Save that code to a file called *listener_add_two_ints_server.launch* and launch it:

```
user@hostname$ roslaunch listener_add_two_ints_server.launch
```

Now, imagine that you've just encountered this ROS system and you're trying to understand how it works. First let's see what topics are available, using `rostopic list`:

```
user@hostname$ rostopic list
/chatter
/rosout
/rosout_agg
```

So, there's a `chatter` topic (we'll ignore the /rosout and /rosout_agg for now; see "/rosout Versus /rosout_agg" on page 382). Let's see what type of message it carries, using `rostopic info`:

```
user@hostname$ rostopic info chatter
Type: std_msgs/String

Publishers: None

Subscribers:
 * /listener (http://hostname:53752/)
```

There's one subscriber to `chatter`, and the message type is `std_msgs/String`. Let's see what makes up that type, using `rosmsg show`:

```
user@hostname$ rosmsg show std_msgs/String
string data
```

Now we know that there is one subscriber to the `chatter` topic, named `listener`, and that it is expecting to receive messages of type `std_msgs/String`, each of which contains a field called `data` that is of type `string`. That's a lot of information to be able to gather at runtime, without any knowledge of how the system was configured. And it's enough information to allow us to publish a message to `listener` on the `chatter` topic, using `rostopic pub`:

```
user@hostname$ rostopic pub /chatter std_msgs/String\
  "{data: 'Hello world'}"
publishing and latching message. Press ctrl-C to terminate
```

In the terminal where you ran `roslaunch`, you should see a message from `listener` confirming receipt of the message, similar to this:

```
[INFO] [WallTime: 1409524634.817011] /listener I heard Hello world
```

The default behavior of `rostopic pub` is to publish and latch a single message. But we can publish multiple messages by using the `-r` option to specify the publication rate in Hz:

```
user@hostname$ rostopic pub -r 10 /chatter std_msgs/String "{data: 'Hello world'}"
publishing and latching message. Press ctrl-C to terminate
```

Back in the roslaunch terminal, you should see a stream of console output from listener, confirming receipt of each message.

> Like rosparam set, rostopic pub accepts message data in YAML, which allows you to publish complicated message structures directly from the command line.

So, we can introspect topics; now let's do the same for services. We start by listing the available services, using rosservice list:

```
user@hostname$ rosservice list
/add_two_ints
/add_two_ints_server/get_loggers
/add_two_ints_server/set_logger_level
/listener/get_loggers
/listener/set_logger_level
/rosout/get_loggers
/rosout/set_logger_level
```

Let's learn more about that add_two_ints service (we'll ignore the \logger services for now; see "Logger Levels" on page 378), using rosservice info:

```
user@hostname$ rosservice info /add_two_ints
Node: /add_two_ints_server
URI: rosrpc://localhost:53877
Type: rospy_tutorials/AddTwoInts
Args: a b
```

This service is being offered by the add_two_ints_server node and is of type rospy_tutorials/AddTwoInts. Let's see the request and response type definitions, using rossrv show:

```
user@hostname$ rossrv show rospy_tutorials/AddTwoInts
int64 a
int64 b
---
int64 sum
```

Now we know that the add_two_ints_server node is offering the add_two_ints service, which is of type rospy_tutorials/AddTwoInts, which accepts a request containing two integers and returns a response containing one integer. That's enough information to allow us to call the service directly, using rosservice call:

```
user@hostname$ rosservice call /add_two_ints "{a: 40, b: 2}"
sum: 42
```

Back in the roslaunch terminal, you should see some output from the add_two_ints_server node as it processes the request:

```
Returning [40 + 2 = 42]
```

In addition to topics and services, we can introspect nodes directly, starting with `ros node list`:

```
user@hostname$ rosnode list
/add_two_ints_server
/listener
/rosout
```

We can see our two nodes, `add_two_ints_server` and `listener` (we'll ignore the `ros out` node for now; see "/rosout Versus /rosout_agg" on page 382). Let's get more details on the `listener` node:

```
user@hostname$ rosnode info listener
Node [/listener]
Publications:
 * /rosout [rosgraph_msgs/Log]

Subscriptions:
 * /chatter [unknown type]

Services:
 * /listener/set_logger_level
 * /listener/get_loggers


contacting node http://localhost:53866/ ...
Pid: 38875
Connections:
 * topic: /rosout
    * to: /rosout
    * direction: outbound
    * transport: TCPROS
```

From this output, we can see the topics and services that are used by the node, as well as the active connections that exist between that node and others. We can check whether the node is responsive with `rosnode ping`, similar to how we use `ping` to check for a machine on the network:

```
user@hostname$ rosnode ping listener
rosnode: node is [/listener]
pinging /listener with a timeout of 3.0s
xmlrpc reply from http://localhost:54055/ time=1.947880ms
xmlrpc reply from http://localhost:54055/ time=3.143072ms
xmlrpc reply from http://localhost:54055/ time=3.656149ms
```

We can also remotely kill a node via `rosnode kill`:

```
user@hostname$ rosnode kill listener
killing /listener
killed
```

Back in the `roslaunch` console, you can see evidence of the node shutting down:

```
shutdown request: user request
[listener] process has finished cleanly
log file: /home/user/.ros/log/99e865f8-314c-11e4-bf3a-705681aea243/listener*.log
```

Summary

In this chapter, we covered the most commonly used ROS tools, learning along the way how to start, stop, configure, test, and introspect a ROS system. You now know what's happening under the hood when you run `roscore`, how to view and modify parameters with `rosparam`, how to get around your package directories with `roscd` and `rosed`, how to run a single node with `rosrun` and multiple nodes with `roslaunch`, and how to test a many-node system with `rostest`. You also know how to combine `rosnode`, `rostopic`, `rosmsg`, `rosservice`, and `rossrv` to gain an understanding of what's going on in a running ROS system, even when you don't have any a priori knowledge of how it's structured.

These tools are a key part of the value of ROS and will contribute significantly to your efficiency as a developer of ROS software. In the next chapter, we'll focus on debugging techniques, revisiting some of the tools covered here and introducing some new ones.

## CHAPTER 21

Debugging Robot Behavior

As you've no doubt noticed by now, robotics applications can be complex. In addition to the usual complexity present in any software system, you have sensors and actuators that are interacting in uncertain ways with the physical (or simulated) world. And, at least in a ROS system, you have a distributed processing graph with many independent processes that are interacting asynchronously through message passing. In short, there are many ways for things to go wrong, and it can sometimes be tricky to figure out what the problem is.

When you have everything ready, and you hit the "Go" button, and... nothing happens, what do you do?

Fortunately, ROS provides some powerful tools to assist you in debugging your applications. In this chapter, we'll go over the most commonly used tools, providing some debugging technique suggestions along the way.

Log Messages: /rosout and rqt_console

Just as you would with any other software, when a ROS system isn't behaving properly, you should first check for error messages. If you're in luck, then some part of the system will be telling you exactly what's wrong. Of course, the distributed nature of a ROS system makes error message handling a little more complex than with a single program.

If you're running a single program, you would reasonably expect to see error messages from that program pop up in a dialog window (if it's a graphical application, like a web browser) or be printed to the terminal where you ran the program (if it's a console application, like a compiler). But ROS is a distributed computing environment, with applications commonly comprising dozens of separate processes, the great majority of them lacking a graphical interface. How can you get error messages from all those processes?

You could go check each terminal from which you started a node, but what if you started a whole bunch of nodes in one terminal with roslaunch? Or what if you don't have access to the terminal where the nodes were started (e.g., if they were started on the robot as part of the boot sequence)? This situation is similar to that encountered by operating system services: they are started automatically, no one watches them, and yet they need a way to report errors. Operating systems solve this problem with a central message logging mechanism; for example, on Linux, most services log their messages to the file */var/log/syslog*. That's close to what we need, but we further require the ability to see messages generated anywhere on the network.

Generating Log Messages: /rosout

How can we share log messages (which could be errors, warnings, debugging information, etc.) throughout a ROS system? Naturally, we'll use ROS topics. Specifically, there's a special ROS topic, /rosout, that carries all log messages from all nodes. The /rosout topic is of type rosgraph_msgs/Log:

```
user@hostname$ rosmsg show rosgraph_msgs/Log
byte DEBUG=1
byte INFO=2
byte WARN=4
byte ERROR=8
byte FATAL=16
std_msgs/Header header
  uint32 seq
  time stamp
  string frame_id
byte level
string name
string msg
string file
string function
uint32 line
string[] topics
```

The rosgraph_msgs/Log message is designed to allow any node to publish a log message so that it can be viewed by anyone else on the network. You can think of /rosout as an enhanced print(): instead of just printing a string to the console, you send that string, along with a bunch of useful metadata, to anyone who wants to know about it. In fact, a well-written ROS node won't use print() at all, because those printed strings will be seen only by someone who happens to glance at the terminal where the node was started. Instead, ROS nodes publish their log messages to /rosout so that they can be seen by anyone.

Of course, it would be unreasonable to expect developers to construct and publish a rosgraph_msgs/Log message instead of just calling print(). So, the rospy client library provides functions that handle the rosgraph_msgs/Log publishing but are as easy to use as print(). For example, to warn of a potentially problematic power situation, you might do something like this:

```
if battery_voltage < 11.0:
    rospy.logwarn('Battery voltage low: %f'%(battery_voltage))
```

The rospy.logwarn() function does three things:

- Prints a formatted version of the warning to the console
- Prints a more detailed version of the warning to the node's own log file in ~/.ros/log on the machine where it is running
- Contructs and publishes to the /rosout topic a message that contains the warning, plus useful metadata about the node in which it's called

The battery warning might look like this on the console where the node is started:

```
[WARN] [WallTime: 1408299179.063983] Battery voltage low: 10.430000
```

It might look like this in the node's log file, assuming that the node is named battery_monitor:

```
user@hostname$ tail -n 1 ~/.ros/log/battery_monitor.log
[rosout][WARNING] 2014-08-17 11:12:59,063: Battery voltage low: 10.430000
```

And the corresponding /rosout message that is published might look like this (the level is rospy.WARN=4):

```
user@hostname$ rostopic echo /rosout
header:
  seq: 1
  stamp:
    secs: 1408299179
    nsecs: 063983
  frame_id: ''
level: 4
name: /battery_monitor
msg: Battery voltage low: 10.430000
file: <stdin>
function: <module>
line: 2
topics: ['/rosout']
```

In the rospy client library, there is one logging function for each logger level (we'll learn more about logger levels in the next section), in order of increasing severity:

```
rospy.logdebug()
```
Debugging statements, which nobody needs to see when the system is working properly.

```
rospy.loginfo()
```
Informational statements, which don't indicate a problem, but which might be helpful to users.

```
rospy.logwarn()
```
Warnings, which users should probably know about because they may affect the behavior of the system, but which do not indicate a failure.

```
rospy.logerror()
```
Errors, which users should know about because something has failed; however, the situation is recoverable.

```
rospy.logfatal()
```
Fatal errors, which users should definitely know about because the situation is unrecoverable.

When writing ROS code, you should always use one of the `rospy.log*()` functions instead of calling `print()` directly. They're just as easy to use as `print()`, and they offer you a much greater ability to debug your system, as we'll see in the next section.

Logger Levels

Each ROS node is configured with a *logger level* that controls how severe a log message must be for it to be printed, logged to a file, and published to /rosout. The logger levels correspond to the logging functions explained in the previous section, in order of increasing severity: `rospy.DEBUG`, `rospy.INFO`, `rospy.WARN`, `rospy.ERROR`, and `rospy.FATAL`.

The default logger level for a node is `rospy.INFO`, which means that messages that are at least as severe as `rospy.INFO` will be printed, logged, and published. As a result, by default, `rospy.DEBUG` messages are suppressed: effectively, `rospy.logdebug()` does nothing. You can think of it like the debug mode of a compiler or other tool: when you need detailed debug information, it's vital to be able to see it, but most of the time you don't want to be distracted by the extra output, nor do you want to pay the performance penalty associated with producing it. In ROS, the penalty is the time required to print to screen, write to file, and publish to /rosout. Because for debug messages none of this work is done by default, you can make liberal use of `rospy.log debug()` in your code without any impact on the system except when someone asks to see those messages.

When you do want to see the debug messages from a node, you need to change its logger level. If you have access to the code, you can make this change by passing the `log_level` keyword argument to `rospy.init_node()` when initializing the node. For example:

```
rospy.init_node('battery_monitor', log_level=rospy.DEBUG)
```

Following that initialization, the node will print, log, and publish messages that are at least as severe as `rospy.DEBUG` (which is all log messages). Usually, you would make such a change temporarily, only while you're actively debugging a problem with the node.

You can also change the logger level in the other direction. For example, if your node is making a lot of calls to `rospy.loginfo()`, and you want to focus on the warnings, then you could change its logger level to `rospy.WARN`:

```
rospy.init_node('battery_monitor', log_level=rospy.WARN)
```

Following that initialization, both `rospy.DEBUG` and `rospy.INFO` messages will be suppressed.

But it's not always convenient (or possible) to change the code in a node for debugging purposes, so ROS provides a service call mechanism for changing logger levels at runtime. Every ROS node advertises two services in its node namespace: `get_loggers` and `set_logger_level`. As the names suggest, these services allow you to, respectively, get and set a node's logger configuration. While you can of course call these services directly (e.g., with the `rosservice` command-line tool), it's easier and more practical in most situations to use `rqt_logger_level`, a graphical tool that allows you to browse and configure the logger levels for all nodes in a ROS system. Let's try it out:

```
user@hostname$ rqt_logger_level
```

You'll see a window similar to the image in Figure 21-1.

Using this GUI, you can change the logger level of any currently running node: click on a node, then a logger within that node, then the desired level. The new level will persist for the lifetime of the node, or until someone else changes it. If the node is restarted, it will go back to its default logger level.

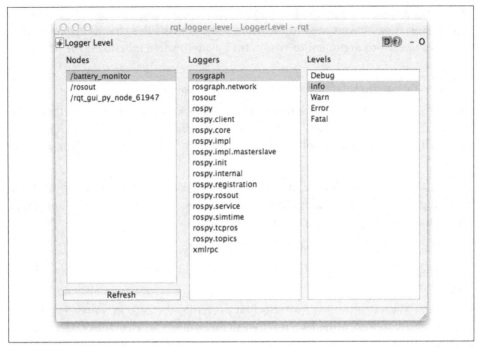

Figure 21-1. The rqt_logger_level GUI allows you to change the debugging logger level of any running ROS node

Using `rqt_logger_level` (or the underlying `get_loggers` service call), you'll notice that nodes expose multiple loggers, sometimes a dozen or more. That's because the log message mechanism is extensible, allowing the developer to create custom, even hierarchical loggers to organize the messages that are produced by different parts of a library or tool. Such custom use of log messages is beyond the scope of this book. For our purposes in debugging a ROS system, such as when configuring logger levels via `rqt_logger_level`, you want to work with either the logger named `rosout` (if the node was written in Python) or the logger named `ros` (if the node was written in C++).

Reading Log Messages: rqt_console

Now that we know how to generate log messages and configure logger levels, it's time to start reading the messages. As we've seen, nodes publish log messages to the `/rosout` topic, so we could access those messages by reading `/rosout` directly, either with a simple subscriber node or by calling `rostopic echo /rosout`. But in a large ROS system, there will be many log messages flowing through the network, and we need a better way to access them.

For this purpose, ROS provides the graphical tool rqt_console. You can launch it just like the other ROS tools:

```
user@hostname$ rqt_console
```

A window will pop up similar to the image in Figure 21-2 (in this case, we were running a simple node named battery_monitor that called rospy.logwarn() periodically in a loop).

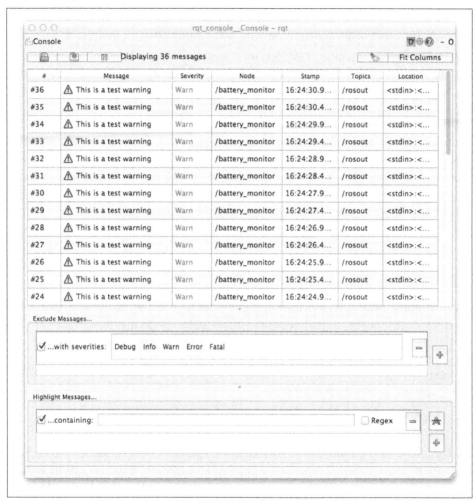

Figure 21-2. The rqt_console GUI collects and displays debug messages from all running ROS nodes in one console

You can heavily customize your view into the log messages using rqt_console. Here are some of the features that you're likely to find useful, especially when working with a large ROS system (there are many other features; check the documentation (*http://wiki.ros.org/rqt_console*) and experiment with the interface to see what's possible):

- Pause and resume message display, useful when messages are scrolling by too quickly to see.
- Clear the accumulated messages from the display, useful when retrying a failing operation.
- Double-click on a message to pop up a window with the full content of that message, for easier inspection and copying to the clipboard.
- Define filters to include or exclude messages from display based a variety of criteria, to allow you to focus on just errors, or just messages from one node, or any other criterion of interest.
- Save accumulated messages to a file, for offline analysis.

Your first step in debugging a misbehaving ROS system is to check for relevant messages (especially errors and warnings) with `rqt_console`. In fact, any time you're running an ROS system comprising more than a couple of nodes, you should have `rqt_console` up, so that you can quickly and easily consult it if something goes wrong. Note that `rqt_console` can only display the messages that it has received since it started running; starting `rqt_console` *after* a problem occurs usually won't tell you anything about what caused the problem.

/rosout Versus /rosout_agg

2107.140While nodes publish their log messages to /rosout, if we look under the hood, we'll see that `rqt_console` doesn't actually subscribe to that topic:

```
user@hostname$ rosnode info rqt_console
Node [/rqt_console]
Publications:
 * /rosout [rosgraph_msgs/Log]

Subscriptions:
 * /rosout_agg [rosgraph_msgs/Log]
```

So, `rqt_console` is publishing to /rosout (as do all ROS nodes), but it's subscribing to /rosout_agg, a different topic of the same type (`rosgraph_msgs/Log`). Why is that? To understand the reason, consider a large ROS system, with a hundred nodes running on multiple machines (this situation is not uncommon with complex robots such as the Willow Garage PR2). Each of those hundred nodes is publishing log messages to /rosout. To receive those messages, you need to establish a connection to each node. The time required to establish each connection is small, but when you do it a hundred times, the total time is not small. If a tool like `rqt_console` had to connect individually to each node, the delay during startup would be unacceptable: you might wait tens of seconds while the connections were established, and to complicate matters, along the way you would see messages from some nodes but not others, which could be misleading.

To avoid this sort of startup delay and lack of determinism, ROS provides a node called rosout (which shouldn't be confused with the topic by the same name, /rosout). The job of rosout is to subscribe to /rosout, taking in log messages via direct connections to all nodes in the system, then republish those messages on an aggregation topic, /rosout_agg. The rosout node is started automatically for every ROS system as part of roscore. As a result, rosout is already up and running before any other node, and so can establish /rosout connections to other nodes as they are started. Later, when a tool like rqt_console starts, it need only make a single connection to the rosout node over the /rosout_agg topic, after which it will immediately begin receiving the aggregated log messages from all nodes in the system.

Nodes, Topics, and Connections: rqt_graph and rosnode

In the previous section, we learned the first rule of ROS debugging: always check for error messages using rqt_console. Very often, when your robot refuses to move, somewhere in the system there's a node complaining about the underlying cause of the problem (e.g., "No laser scans received; is the sensor powered and connected to the computer?"). But it's not always that obvious.

A frequent cause of problems in a ROS system is missing or otherwise incorrect connections between nodes. In this section, we'll learn how to debug such problems, then walk through some situations that commonly arise.

Visualizing the Graph: rqt_graph

If you suspect that something is wrong with the connections in your system, your first step is to run rqt_graph, a graphical tool that queries and visualizes nodes and topics. To see how it works, let's start a pair of nodes that will communicate with each other. Start a roscore, then start an instance of rostopic to publish a string on the chatter topic, once per second (for clarity of demonstration, we're explicitly setting the node names using the __name argument so as to override the random names that would otherwise be generated to avoid name conflicts):

```
user@hostname$ rostopic pub /chatter std_msgs/String \
  -r 1 "Hello world" __name:=talker
```

In another terminal, start another instance of `rostopic` to listen to the `chatter` topic and print the received messages to console:

```
user@hostname$ rostopic echo /chatter __name:=listener
```

Now start `rqt_graph`:

```
user@hostname$ rqt_graph __name:=rqt_graph
```

A window will pop up similar to the image in Figure 21-3.

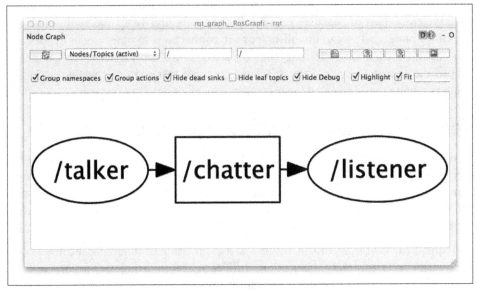

Figure 21-3. The rqt_graph GUI shows the current state of nodes and topics in a running ROS system

The nodes are displayed as ovals and the topics as boxes, with arrows showing the direction of the flow of messages. This display is the best way to get a high-level view of the structure of your system. As with the other graphical ROS tools, there are a variety of ways to configure the presentation of the data, some of which we'll explore in the upcoming sections.

First, let's get a view of the *entire* system: in the drop-down in the upper-left corner, select "Nodes/Topics (all)," then uncheck the boxes for "Hide dead sinks" and "Hide debug." The resulting graph looks like the image in Figure 21-4.

Now we can see the `rosout` node mentioned in the previous section, along with the `/rosout_agg` topic that it publishes for use by tools like `rqt_console`. We also see `rqt_graph` itself. In most cases, the default view, which hides these system nodes and topics, is appropriate, but it's good to know how to see *all* of what's going on.

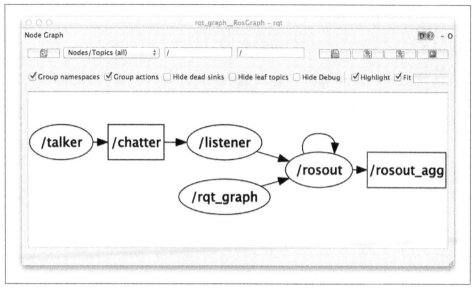

Figure 21-4. The options in rqt_graph allow you to reveal more or less about a running ROS system

Problem: Mismatched Topic Names

With the `talker`, `listener`, and `rqt_graph` nodes still running, let's add another publisher for `/chatter`. This time, though, we'll misspell the topic name:

```
user@hostname$ rostopic pub /chatter std_msgs/String -r 1 "Hello world 2" \
    __name:=talker2
```

Click the refresh button in `rqt_graph`, then select "Hide debug." You'll see something like the image in Figure 21-5.

From this view, it's clear what the problem is with the topic names. While in this case, it's a simple misspelling, more often it's a mismatch in naming convention (e.g., `laser` vs. `lidar`) or specificity (e.g., `camera` vs. `head_camera`). But the result is the same: a publisher/subscriber pair that you expect to be connected are not, because they disagree on the name of the topic over which they should be communicating. Diagnosing this problem is most easily done with `rqt_graph`, wherein the disconnected topics are easy to pick out. Having diagnosed the problem, the fix depends on how the system is structured: while code changes might be required, more often it's a matter of changing the topic name remapping arguments that were passed to one node or the other (in complex systems, those remapping arguments are stored in `roslaunch` files).

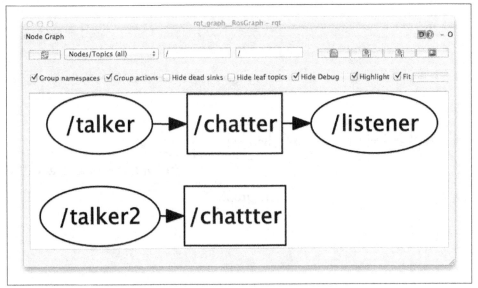

Figure 21-5. A missing connection caused by a misspelled topic name can be seen clearly in rqt_graph

Problem: Mismatched Topic Types and/or Checksums

Now let's add a third publisher, this time using the right topic name but the wrong topic type; instead of publishing a string, we'll send a 32-bit integer:

```
user@hostname$ rostopic pub /chatter std_msgs/Int32 -r 1 "3" __name:=talker3
```

Click the refresh button in rqt_graph. You'll see something like the image in Figure 21-6.

Everything looks good: talker and talker3 are both publishing via chatter to listener. But if we watch the terminal where we started listener, we see that it's receiving only the string messages from talker, not the integer messages from talker3. To dig in further, we'll use the command-line tool rosnode.

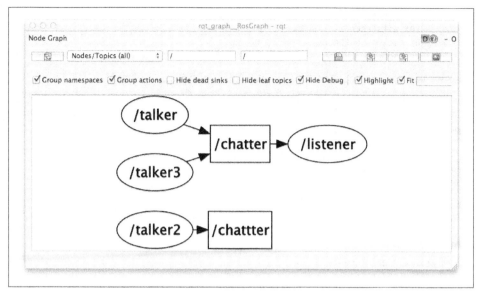

Figure 21-6. Two nodes are publishing to a subscriber, but they disagree on the message type; further investigation is needed

First, let's list the nodes in the system:

```
user@hostname$ rosnode list
/listener
/rosout
/rqt_graph
/talker
/talker2
/talker3
```

The problem is that `talker3` doesn't appear to be communicating with `listener`, while `talker` is working fine. Let's look at `talker` in more detail:

```
user@hostname$ rosnode info talker
Node [/talker]
Publications:
 * /chatter [std_msgs/String]

Subscriptions: None

Services:
 * /talker/set_logger_level
 * /talker/get_loggers


contacting node http://localhost:61515/ ...
Pid: 65904
Connections:
```

```
* topic: /chatter
  * to: /listener
  * direction: outbound
  * transport: TCPROS
```

Here we can see the chatter topic is listed as a publication of talker (which means that it's being advertised). We can further see that there is an outbound connection established on that topic from talker to listener, which means that data is flowing correctly. Now let's look at talker3 in detail:

```
user@hostname$ rosnode info talker3
Node [/talker3]
Publications:
 * /chatter [std_msgs/Int32]

Subscriptions: None

Services:
 * /talker3/get_loggers
 * /talker3/set_logger_level


contacting node http://localhost:61686/ ...
Pid: 66317
```

Here we can see that, while chatter is listed as a publication of talker3, there are no connections to listener, or to anyone else. That connection is missing from talker3 because the ROS type-checking mechanism refused to establish the connection when the two sides disagreed on what type should be used. During negotiation of a topic connection, the subscriber (in this case, listener) tells the publisher what type of message it is expecting; if that type does not match what the publisher is sending on that topic, then it drops the connection.

This kind of error-checking happens behind the scenes all the time in a ROS system. If types don't match, then connections are refused. The same thing happens when types match, but their checksums don't. For example, if you have a publisher/subscriber pair that agree on a topic name and type but have different definitions of the message type (often caused by different versions of the *.msg* file on different machines), then the connection between them will be refused. When there is a type or checksum mismatch, there are usually log messages that inform you of what has happened. For example, in the present example, talker3 produced this warning:

```
[WARN] [WallTime: 1408327763.423004] Could not process inbound connection:\
  topic types do not match: [std_msgs/String] vs.\
  [std_msgs/Int32]{'message_definition': 'string data\n\n', 'callerid':\
  '/listener', 'tcp_nodelay': '0', 'md5sum':\
  '992ce8a1687cec8c8bd883ec73ca41d1', 'topic': '/chatter', 'type':\
  'std_msgs/String'}
```

As mentioned previously, you should always check for such error messages first (with `rqt_console`, of course). But you should also know how to navigate your nodes' connection status by interrogating them with `rosnode`.

Problem: Incorrect Network Settings

In addition to type and checksum mismatches, connections between ROS nodes often fail because of incorrect network settings. There are many ways to misconfigure a network, and we are not going to address general network debugging in this book. Here, we'll cover a couple of cases that commonly arise in ROS systems, and we'll offer debugging procedures that can be repurposed for other situations.

Imagine that you're working with a mobile robot, with the `roscore` and various ROS nodes running on the computer carried by the robot. You're doing development and debugging on your laptop, which is connected via a wireless network to the robot's computer. For clarity, let's assume hostnames and IP addresses for the computers:

- Robot computer: `robby`, 192.168.1.2
- Laptop: `hal`, 192.168.1.3

For this configuration to work, nodes running on the laptop `hal` will have their environment variable `ROS_MASTER_URI` pointing to `robby`, because that's where the `roscore` is running. That could be done in `bash` using the `export` keyword:

```
user@hal$ export ROS_MASTER_URI=192.168.1.2
```

A common problem in this situation is that ROS topic communication will work in one direction but not the other. For example, subscribers on `hal` can receive data from publishers on `robby`, but subscribers on `robby` cannot receive data from publishers on `hal`. A particularly common example of this problem happens when running `rviz` on the laptop and the navigation stack on the robot: you can see the sensor data reported by the robot visualized in `rviz`, but you cannot set the robot's pose or send it navigation goals.

When you encounter this kind of situation, your first step is to use `rostopic` to check what hostname is being used by nodes running on each machine. Say that you're unable to send messages via the `/initialpose` topic (used to set the robot's initial pose) from `rviz` on `hal` to `move_base` (a node in the navigation stack) on `robby`. You should check the list of publishers and subscribers for `/initialpose`, which might look like this:

```
user@hostname$ rostopic info initialpose
Type: geometry_msgs/PoseWithCovarianceStamped

Publishers:
 * /rviz (http://localhost:56171/)
```

```
Subscribers:
 * /move_base (http://robby:53992/)
```

See the problem? The publisher, rviz, is telling potential subscribers that it can be contacted at the *hostname:_port address_* localhost:56171. The port number is probably fine (we'll talk more about that shortly), but the hostname is not. The move_base node, which is running on robby, will fail when it tries to contact rviz at localhost:56171, because rviz is running on hal. From the perspective of nodes running on robby, localhost means robby, not hal.

This is a classic example of a computer not knowing its own name: hal doesn't know its name, so it does the best that it can in topic advertisements by using localhost, which will at least make sense to nodes running on hal. In a properly configured network with properly configured machines, this kind of problem should not occur, but it is nonetheless fairly common. In general, every computer involved in a ROS system must know the name or address by which other the computers will be able to contact it.

If you can, you should fix the configuration of your computers and/or network so that they all use valid, externally addressable names. But that is not always possible (e.g., if you do not have superuser privileges on a computer). In that case, you can use some hooks that ROS offers to override its default name lookup logic. Specifically, you can set the ROS_HOSTNAME environment variable before starting nodes on the misconfigured machine. For example, to solve the specific problem described here, you would set ROS_HOSTNAME on hal before starting rviz:

```
user@hostname$ export ROS_HOSTNAME=hal
user@hostname$ rviz
```

Then the output from rostopic info /initialpose would include:

```
...
Publishers:
 * /rviz (http://hal:56171/)
...
```

That will be enough so long as the name hal can be resolved to an IP address. But if hal was assigned an address dynamically from a DHCP server, then it's possible that the name hal, while better than localhost, still won't be resolvable by nodes running on robby (again, this should not happen, but it does). In that case, you can specify the IP address explicitly using the ROS_IP environment variable:

```
user@hostname$ export ROS_IP=192.168.1.3
user@hostname$ rviz
```

Then the output from rostopic info /initialpose would include:

```
...
Publishers:
 * /rviz (http://192.168.1.3:56171/)
...
```

If that doesn't do it, then the problem is likely that the firewall settings on hal are preventing inbound connections on port 56171. By default, many operating systems use software firewalls that limit inbound TCP or UDP connections to a specific set of ports that are used to provide well-known services like ssh or http. Because ROS publishers might use any port, and because there are often many publishers using many different ports, ROS requires complete bidirectional connectivity between all pairs of machines, on all ports. An easy way to meet this requirement is to change your firewall to allow incoming connections on all ports (essentially, disable the firewall).

If you cannot or prefer not to change your firewall settings, then we recommend that you establish a *virtual private network* (VPN) between the computers in your network. Because the VPN is authenticated and encrypted, there is no need for a firewall to protect connections within it. There are multiple VPN tools to choose from; a widely used open source tool is OpenVPN, which creates a new network interface, with a new IP address, on each computer. If you use a tool like OpenVPN, then you should almost certainly set ROS_IP on all computers to ensure that they are advertising their VPN-specific IP addresses. The configuration of a VPN is outside the scope of this book, but there are many good resources regarding this topic online and in other books.

Sensor Fusion: rviz

In the previous sections, we covered problems related to error reporting and connection handling. What if all of the nodes are connected properly, and they're not raising any errors, but the robot is still not behaving properly? A good place to start is using rviz to visualize the relevant sensor data from the robot. You can start rviz just like the other ROS tools:

```
user@hostname$ rviz
```

The details of what to visualize will depend on your application. In addition, rviz is a powerful tool, and its heavily configurable feature set is outside the scope of this book. Here a few tips to help with debugging common problems:

- Visualize data from multiple sensors simultaneously. For example, if you're using a laser and a depth camera, visualize them together in a common coordinate frame and look for differences. Assign a different color to each sensor to make it easy to distinguish them.

- Increase the decay time on a sensor stream to check it for consistency over time. For example, if you're using a depth camera on a mobile robot, try setting the decay time for the depth camera point cloud to five seconds, then move the robot around and check the consistency of consecutive scans.

- Visualize each stage of a sensor-processing pipeline. For example, if you are running camera images through a series of filters, be sure to publish the image output of each filter so that you can check the intermediate results in addition to the final result.

- Wherever you can, publish visual debugging messages using the `visualization_msgs/Marker` type. This message allows you to create, modify, and delete geometric shapes of various of kinds. For example, if you are estimating the pose of an object from sensor data, then publish that estimated pose as an arrow so that you can visually check the result against other sensor data.

Plotting Data: rqt_plot

While `rviz` is the right tool for gaining a high-level view of the sensor state of your system, sometimes you want to examine individual values. If you are debugging the behavior of a position controller for a joint in a robot arm, for example, you might want to examine the time series of computed torques, or the position errors, or some other quantity. For this purpose, we use `rqt_plot`, which supports 2D plotting of any numeric data that is published in a ROS system.

As an example, Example 21-1 shows a node that generates a sine wave on the topic /sin, of type `std_msgs/Float64`.

Example 21-1. sine_wave.py

```
#!/usr/bin/env python

import math, time
import rospy
from std_msgs.msg import Float64

rospy.init_node('sine_wave')
pub = rospy.Publisher('sin', Float64)
while not rospy.is_shutdown():
  msg = Float64()
  msg.data = math.sin(4*time.time())
  pub.publish(msg)
  time.sleep(0.1)
```

Run `sine_wave.py`; then in another terminal, run `rqt_plot`, telling it to plot the `data` field of the /sin topic:

```
user@hostname$ rqt_plot /sin/data
```

You'll see a continuous plot of the sine wave, similar to the image in Figure 21-7.

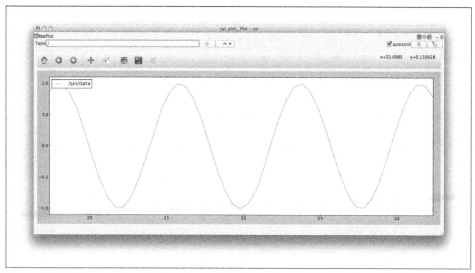

Figure 21-7. The rqt_plot GUI produces 2D plots of any numeric data published in a ROS system

It's often helpful to plot multiple values at the same time to compare how they vary over time. Example 21-2 shows a node that generates a cosine wave on the /cos topic, also of type std_msgs/Float64.

Example 21-2. cosine_wave.py

```
#!/usr/bin/env python

import math, time
import rospy
from std_msgs.msg import Float64

rospy.init_node('cosine_wave')
pub = rospy.Publisher('cos', Float64)
while not rospy.is_shutdown():
  msg = Float64()
  msg.data = math.cos(4*time.time())
  pub.publish(msg)
  time.sleep(0.1)
```

With sine_wave.py still running, run cosine_wave.py; then in another terminal, run rqt_plot, this time asking it to plot data from both topics:

```
user@hostname$ rqt_plot /sin/data /cos/data
```

Now you'll see a continuous plot of both waves, with the expected phase difference between them, similar to the image in Figure 21-8.

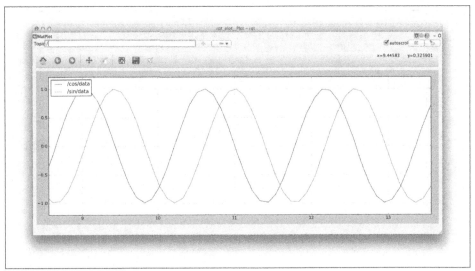

Figure 21-8. The rqt_plot GUI can plot multiple data values simultaneously

The `rqt_plot` GUI offers a number of features, including stopping and starting plotting, panning and zooming, configuring subplots, and exporting images.

Data Logging and Analysis: rosbag and rqt_bag

The complement to live data visualization, data logging is also a vital debugging tool. It is common in ROS systems to log data to file for later analysis and playback. Data logging works as you might expect: subscribe to the topic(s) that you want to log, and then write incoming messages to disk. In fact, you could easily write your own node to log data for your application.

However, you shouldn't write your own logger, because ROS provides a powerful, general logging tool called `rosbag`. The `rosbag` tool is able to log data of any type from any ROS topic, all to a single file. By convention, the resulting log files have the extension *.bag* and are referred to as "ROS bags," or simply, "bags."

Logging and Playing Back Data: rosbag

Let's see how to record data from one topic. Start a `roscore`, then run `rosbag`, telling it to record from the `chatter` topic and write the output to a file call *chatter.bag* (we are giving a specific filename here for clarity; in general, you should let `rosbag` auto-generate a timestamp-based name for its output file):

```
user@hostname$ rosbag record -O chatter.bag /chatter
[ INFO] [1408922392.770333000]: Subscribing to /chatter
[ INFO] [1408922392.773664000]: Recording to chatter.bag.
```

In another terminal, use rostopic pub to publish at 10 Hz to chatter:

```
user@hostname$ rostopic pub /chatter std_msgs/String -r 10 "Hello world"
```

Let rostopic pub run for about 10 seconds, then kill both it and rosbag record. Now you should have a file called *chatter.bag*, which contains the messages that were published to the chatter topic. Let's look inside it:

```
user@hostname$ rosbag info chatter.bag
path:        chatter.bag
version:     2.0
duration:    12.9s
start:       Aug 24 2014 16:23:54.80 (1408922634.80)
end:         Aug 24 2014 16:24:07.70 (1408922647.70)
size:        14.1 KB
messages:    130
compression: none [1/1 chunks]
types:       std_msgs/String [992ce8a1687cec8c8bd883ec73ca41d1]
topics:      /chatter   130 msgs    : std_msgs/String
```

The rosbag info command interrogates the bag and presents the metadata, including time and duration and the number and types of messages contained within it. Here we can see that we captured 130 messages of type std_msgs/String on the chatter topic. If we had logged multiple topics and/or types (which is common), those names would be listed as well.

Playing back the data from a bag is just as easy as recording it. With your roscore still running, start up rostopic echo to be ready to print the messages to console:

```
user@hostname$ rostopic echo /chatter
```

Nothing happens yet, because there is no publisher of data on the chatter topic. Now use rosbag play to read the bag and play it back:

```
user@hostname$ rosbag play chatter.bag
[ INFO] [1408923117.746632000]: Opening chatter.bag

Waiting 0.2 seconds after advertising topics... done.

Hit space to toggle paused, or 's' to step.
```

In the terminal where you ran rostopic echo, you'll see the messages displayed on the screen:

```
data: Hello world
---
data: Hello world
---
data: Hello world
```

```
---
...
```

The console output from `rostopic echo` will continue until all of the data in the bag has been played back, at which point `rosbag play` will exit.

This example is intentionally simple, but the underlying system is very powerful. Using `rosbag`, you can record the message stream from any ROS topic, then play it back later. To the subscribing nodes, the messages will be indistinguishable from the original publications. As a result, you can often test and debug large parts of your system exclusively from logged data in bags. A very common use case is to play back a bag along with the relevant nodes from your application, and visualize the result in `rviz`.

The `rosbag` tool offers many options.Here are some tips on usage:

- To record all data within a ROS system, run `rosbag record -a`. But be careful with this option, because in a large system, you could easily log immense amounts of data. Besides the disk space and CPU cycles consumed by `rosbag record` itself, subscribing to all topics can have a nontrivial performance impact on the rest of system, especially for nodes that do not compute certain results unless there is at least one active subscriber (common for image-processing pipelines).

- Bags are internally composed of *chunks* that can be compressed to save disk space. To compress the data while recording, run `rosbag record -j /topic`. To compress an existing bag, run `rosbag compress topic.bag`. Compressed bags can be read by `rosbag play`; they will be automatically decompressed on the fly during playback.

- To continually play back a bag in a loop, run `rosbag play -l topic.bag`. This option is useful when testing processing pipelines.

- To have `rosbag play` also publish the time associated with each message on the special `/clock` topic, run `rosbag play --clock topic.bag`. But note that handling of timestamps with the playback of logged data can be tricky. For example, the times published to `/clock` will be in the past, from when the bag was created, and not all nodes are robust to backward jumps in time.

Whether you're trying to understand what went wrong in a particular situation where the robot misbehaved or you're tuning the parameters of your perception pipeline, bags are an important part of any development and debugging process.

Visualizing Bags: rqt_bag

Similar to how you use `rqt_graph` to inspect the structure of a ROS system, it can be helpful to inspect the structure of a bag. For this purpose, ROS provides the `rqt_bag` tool. You can run this like the other ROS tools, giving it the name of a bag to operate on:

```
user@hostname$ rqt_bag chatter.bag
```

A window will pop up looking something like the image in Figure 21-9.

Figure 21-9. The rqt_bag GUI allows you to visually inspect and operate on logged data

Using `rqt_bag`, you can see at a glance how many topics were recorded and how frequently messages on each topic were received, and you can introspect the contents of the messages. You can play back and optionally loop over the entire bag or a section of it, or you can step through it one message at a time. You can also save a section of the bag as its own bag, allowing you to work with a particular sequence of messages.

Analyzing ROS Bags with Other Tools: rostopic echo -b

It's common to work with data from ROS bags in other, non-ROS tools, such as gnuplot, GNU Octave, or MATLAB. For this purpose, you'll often want to produce a text presentation of the data that can be easily parsed by other tools. Fortunately, this ability is built into `rostopic echo`; just tell it the name of the bag to read from:

```
user@hostname$ rostopic echo -b chatter.bag /chatter
data: Hello world
---
data: Hello world
---
data: Hello world
---
...
```

That format is easy enough to read, but not that easy to parse. So, let's add the -p argument to produce a comma-separated format that starts with an explanatory header:

```
user@hostname$ rostopic echo -p -b chatter.bag /chatter
%time,field.data
1408922634801335000,Hello world
1408922634901209000,Hello world
1408922635001016000,Hello world
...
```

Redirect that output to a file:

```
user@hostname$ rostopic echo -p -b chatter.bag /chatter > chatter.csv
```

and you're ready to read the data into your favorite processing tool. You can also process the data yourself in Python using the `rosbag` library; some useful examples are listed in the `rosbag` cookbook (*http://wiki.ros.org/rosbag/Cookbook*).

Summary

In this chapter, we covered a variety of tools and techniques that will help you when debugging your ROS system. We use these custom tools because robotics is a challenging endeavor, combining the complexity inherent in any software with the need to interact asynchronously with the physical world. Writing good robotics software is hard, and there are many more ways to get it wrong than right.

While we use custom tools, the principles of debugging a ROS system are the same as debugging any other system: when something goes wrong, you first need to understand what is happening and why. The key is to gain visibility into the workings of the system, which is what the tools described in this chapter provide. Once you can see what's going on, you're on the path to figuring out how to fix it.

## CHAPTER 22

The ROS Community: Online Resources

In this book, we have explained how to use the libraries and tools that make up ROS. Along the way, we have implicitly been making the argument that you should use ROS for your next robotics project because of the technical merits of the software. But that's only part of the story.

As with any large open source project, much of the strength of ROS derives not from the software itself, but from the community that develops, uses, and supports that software. If ROS were a finished product—a complete system that satisfied everyone's robotics needs—then the community would not play such a prominent role. But ROS is not finished: it is a living ecosystem of code and documentation, with thousands of people around the world constantly fixing, improving, and extending it. In this chapter, we'll introduce you to the online resources through which you can connect with the ROS community and hopefully become a contributor yourself.

Etiquette

First, let's talk about good online etiquette. It's easy to get right, as most of us do most of the time: just behave in a reasonable manner. But it's also easy to become frustrated when something isn't working properly, or at least not the way that we think it should work. For those times, here are a few points to keep in mind:

- Assume *good faith* on the part of your fellow community members. The bug that you found was just a mistake. The missing documentation that you need was just an oversight. The delay in responding to your question is just because we're all busy. And the seemingly caustic response that you received is just a misinterpretation of tone. We'll make more and quicker progress by giving everyone the benefit of the doubt.

- Don't repeat questions on mailing lists or forums. The original question will have been seen, and if you haven't gotten a response then likely nobody has had time to answer yet. Alternatively, it could be that nobody knows the answer. In any case, repeating questions is poor form.

- Don't try to raise the priority of your question or issue by demanding a fast answer or listing personal deadlines (homework, project, etc.). Doing so is unlikely to generate sympathy, and may even have the effect of slowing down the response.

We're all involved in this project because we want it to continue to succeed. Our contributions will make the greatest if we collaborate politely and generously.

The ROS Wiki

The online hub of the community is the ROS wiki (*http://wiki.ros.org?distro=indigo*). The wiki contains information about ROS as a whole (e.g., installation instructions) and documentation specific to ROS packages, including all of the tools and libraries described in this book. The wiki is also your entry point to other online resources (repositories, trackers, etc.).

The backbone of the wiki is a set of package pages, each named *http://wiki.ros.org/ <package name>*. For example, to find documentation on the rospy package, you would go to *http://wiki.ros.org/rospy?distro=indigo*. The package pages follow a consistent format and are partially autogenerated from metadata that is extracted from the packages' code (see Figure 22-1). In addition to introducing and explaining the purpose and usage of the package, a good package page will offer links to related resources, such as tutorials, troubleshooting guides, change logs, and API documentation.

The wiki is editable by anyone, including you, and we rely on the collective efforts of the community to maintain and update it. Developers do their best to write good documentation for their packages, but documentation can almost always be improved by users. When you see an opportunity to improve a page in the wiki, whether it's a minor typographical edit or the addition of an entirely new tutorial, please do!

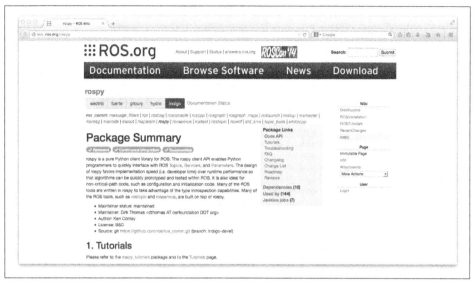

Figure 22-1. The ROS wiki: the home for information and documentation about ROS software

ROS Answers

When you have a question about ROS—from "How do I do X?" to "Why doesn't Y work like Z?"—you should visit ROS Answers (*http://answers.ros.org*). ROS Answers is a Q&A forum, similar in functionality to Stack Overflow but scoped to ROS (see Figure 22-2). Because it is designed specifically to handle questions and answers, ROS Answers is the best way to address troubleshooting queries.

Figure 22-2. ROS Answers: the Q&A forum for the ROS community

Before asking a question, be sure to search for similar questions that have been asked in the past. While you might be the first to encounter a particular problem, it's often the case that someone else has been there before and asked about it at ROS Answers. If you don't find an answer to your question in the archive (which at the time of writing contained more than 18,000 questions), then by all means ask it. Here are some guidelines for asking good questions:

- Be as specific as possible. If you're asking how to do something, give as much context as you can; it may be that, given information about your goal, someone will suggest an alternative approach. If you've encountered unexpected behavior (e.g., something appears to be broken), then provide steps to reproduce that behavior.

- Where appropriate, include error/warning messages, relevant code snippets, debugger backtraces, bags and other log files, as well as images and/or videos that demonstrate the problem.

- Provide relevant type and version information for your system. At least the ROS distribution name (Hydro, Indigo, etc.) should be included. Depending on the nature of the question, it may be helpful to include names and versions for specific ROS packages, the underlying operating system, and/or your hardware.

- When including output from a program, such as error or warning messages, always copy and paste them, rather than re-typing them. Small typing mistakes can make a big difference, and it's important to see the exact output.

Like the wiki, ROS Answers is editable by everyone, including you, and we rely on the community to answer questions. If you know the answer to a question, answer it!

Trackers (Bugs and Feature Requests)

It may happen that the answer to your question at ROS Answers is something like, "Yes, that looks like a bug," or perhaps, "No, that capability hasn't been implemented." Or it could be that you have independently identified a bug or missing feature. In any case, bugs and feature requests should be reported to the appropriate issue tracker.

Because of the distributed nature of ROS code, there is no central issue tracker for ROS. Rather, each package or collection of packages has its own issue tracker. To find the right issue tracker, you first need to decide in which package the problem lies. It's OK if you're not sure; make your best guess, and the issue can be migrated later if needed. Go that package's page in the wiki (*http://wiki.ros.org/<package name>*), where you should find a link for reporting bugs and requesting features. If such a link is not available, follow the link for the source, which will take you to the repository containing the code; from there you can navigate to the issue tracker for that repository.

To file a good bug report or feature request, start with the guidelines given in the previous section for ROS Answers. And if you can, try to supply a patch that fixes the bug or implements the feature. The best issues, and the ones that are serviced most promptly, are those that come with patches.

Like the wiki and ROS Answers, the ROS issue trackers are open to everyone, including you. If you see a bug that you can fix or a feature that you can implement, please do!

Mailing Lists and Special Interest Groups

The primary ROS mailing list is *ros-users@lists.ros.org*. List archives and subscription information can be found at *http://lists.ros.org/mailman/listinfo/ros-users*. The *ros-users@* list is used only for announcements and discussions of general interest to the ROS community. If you have released a new ROS package or are hosting a ROS-related event, then post it to *ros-users@*. On the other hand, if you have a question about how to use ROS, or have found a bug, use ROS Answers and/or the issue trackers, as explained in the previous sections.

Within the ROS community, there are various subcommunities that focus on specific topics, from embedded systems, to driver development, to robot arms. These subcommunities self-organize into special interest groups, or SIGs, which have their own mailing lists and discussion forums. Information on ROS SIGs, including a list of active groups and advice on creating a new group, can be found on the wiki (*http://wiki.ros.org/sig*).

Finding and Sharing Code

As with issue trackers, there is no single repository for ROS code. Instead, code is distributed throughout many different repositories, often on a package-by-package basis. This arrangement allows for maximum flexibility in how and where code is stored, what licenses are applied, and how development and releases are handled. To find the repository that contains the code for a particular package, follow the source's link from that package's page in the wiki.

People often ask the question, "How can I contribute my new package to ROS?" The answer is: put the code in publicly accessible repository, then tell the community about it. You can use your favorite version control tool and keep your code wherever you like (though it is highly recommended that you use `git` and host the code at Git-Hub (*https://github.com*), which is where most existing ROS software is hosted. To have your repository indexed for inclusion in the ROS wiki, you just need to provide a few pieces of information; for details, see the tutorial (*http://bit.ly/doc_generation*) on the ROS wiki. You're not giving the code to ROS so much as letting the ROS community know where to find it.

Summary

In this chapter, we covered the online resources that allow you to connect with and join the ROS community. Whether you have a troubleshooting question, a bug to report, or a new package to announce, communicating with the community is easy to do. ROS is a collaborative effort, driven by the needs and contributions of the community. Get involved, don't be shy, and let us know what you're working on.

## CHAPTER 23

Using C++ in ROS

We chose to use Python for this book for a number of reasons. First, it's an accessible language for people without a lot of computer science background. Second, it has a lot of useful stuff in the core packages, which lets us concentrate on higher-level concepts. Third, ROS has strong support for Python. Fourth, we wanted to pick a single language for all of the examples in the book, and Python seemed like a reasonable choice.

However, sometimes you're going to want to use another language for your ROS development. Maybe some library that you need to use doesn't have Python support. Maybe you're more comfortable developing in another language. Maybe you want the (often slight) speed advantage that a compiled language brings. In this chapter, we're going to look at how the API in C++, one of the other supported languages, differs from the Python API, and how you can translate the examples in this book to C++. All of the idioms and design patterns for C++, and any other language that has a ROS API, will be the same: we're still going to use callbacks, we're still going to pass messages over topics, and so on. However, the syntax and specific data structures will be a little different. Once you learn how to map the Python examples onto your language of choice, then you'll be able to easily translate examples from one language to another.

The two best-supported language APIs in ROS are for Python and C++. In this chapter, we'll concentrate on the C++ API, but many of the things that we talk about will apply to APIs in other languages. Once you figure out the syntax and data structure differences, things will start to look the same, and you'll be able to change languages at will.

When Should You Use C (or Some Other Language)?

When should you use C++, or one of the other supported languages? The short answer is: when it makes your life easier. Since ROS is inherently a distributed system, it's easy to mix nodes written in different languages within the same system, with the messaging system (topics, services, and actions) acting as the glue that holds everything together.

Sometimes you will have a sensor or actuator with an API in C or C++, and it will be much easier to wrap this up into a ROS node if you use C++. Or, if you're new to Python but have years of C++ coding experience, you might just be more efficient writing code in C++. Similarly, if you're making extensive use of code that's written in C++, then it's easier to wrap this up in a C++ node. You might even be forced to use C++ because you're maintaining or extending a package that someone else wrote in C++.

Sometimes, especially if you're doing complex mathematical calculations, you'll want to write a node in C++ to make it faster. Be careful about this, though, since Python libraries like scipy are already very well optimized and will most likely be running the same code as your C++ implementation under the hood. Python does introduce some slowness, but you should be objective when you make the decision to implement something in C++. A C++ node might be faster than a similar Python node, but does the speed increase justify the extra development time of writing and debugging the C++ node?

Whatever your reasons for using C++ in ROS, whether they're driven by programming language zealotry or by cold, hard facts, let's look at how to write and build a ROS node with C++.

Building C++ with catkin

The main difference between C++ and Python (for our purposes, at least) is that C++ is a compiled language, while Python is an interpreted one. This means that you're going to be interacting more with catkin and the ROS build system when you're using C++. Every time you make a change to your code, you're going to have to recompile it using catkin_make, and depending on the changes that you've made, you might also have to edit some other files.

This need to recompile is, in our opinion, one of the reasons to prefer Python for development. You can iterate on changes faster with Python because you don't have to recompile your code. ROS is a big software system, and if your node is complex and has many dependencies, your compile might take a few minutes. This will inevitably slow down your development process a bit.

Putting our biases to one side for the moment, let's look at the files you need to edit when using C++.

package.xml

The *package.xml* file is the place where you declare all of your dependencies. When using C++, you have to declare both a build and a runtime dependency on roscpp:

```
<build_depend>roscpp</build_depend>
<run_depend>roscpp</run_depend>
```

You can either do this manually, by editing the file, or have catkin_create_pkg do it for you when you create the package:

```
user@hostname$ catkin_create_pkg <package name> roscpp
```

You'll also need to add in dependencies, both build and runtime, for any additional packages that you use in your node, just as you did when using Python.

CMakeLists.txt

You'll also need to add to the *CMakeLists.txt* file, so that the build system knows what you're trying to do and where to find things. In particular, you need to modify the file in the directory where your *src* directory lives (where your *package.xml* file also lives), not the one at the top of your catkin workspace. Suppose you're going to build a node called minimal from a single source file, *minimal.cpp*. You first have to let the build system know about the executable, and all of the files needed to build it:

```
add_executable(minimal
  src/minimal.cpp
)
```

This tells the build system that you're going to build an executable called minimal from the file *minimal.cpp*. If you have more than one executable in your package, you need to add lines like this for each one. If an executable is built from more than a single source file, you need to list these files in the body of add_executable().

You also need to tell the build system about any link dependencies that you have. At a minimum, this will be the set of dependencies that catkin has worked out for you, based on the build dependencies in your *package.xml* file:

```
target_link_libraries(minimal
  ${catkin_LIBRARIES}
)
```

Again, you need to add lines like this for each of the executables you build. Once you've got this information in place, then you're ready to build your node.

catkin_make

To build your node, invoke `catkin_make` from the root of your `catkin` workspace. This will build your code, and make sure that everything that you depend upon is up to date. To make things easier on you, you should structure your directories according to ROS Enhancement Proposal (REP) 128 (*http://www.ros.org/reps/ rep-0128.html*). Basically, this means that there should be a directory called *src* in your catkin workspace directory. Individual package directories should live in this *src* directory. Within a package directory, there should be a *package.xml*, a *CMakeLists.txt*, and another *src* directory (where your source code actually lives):

```
catkin_workspace/
  src/
    CMakeLists.txt
    package_1/
      CMakeLists.txt
      package.xml
    ...
    package_n/
      CMakeLists.txt
      package.xml
  build/
  devel/
```

You invoke `catkin_make` from *catkin_workspace*. This will build your `minimal` executable and place it in *catkin_workspace/devel/lib/<package name>/minimal*.

Now that we've seen how to build a C++ node, let's look at what goes into the node itself, and how to translate from the Python examples in this book to C++.

Translating from Python to C++ (and Back Again)

To understand how to translate from the Python examples in this book to C++, you only really need to know three things: how a node is put together, how the three communication mechanisms are defined, and how to translate the data structures from one language to another. We'll start by looking at how to write a minimal node in C++.

A Simple Node

Example 23-1 shows the code for a minimal C++ node in ROS.

Example 23-1. minimal.cpp

```
#include <ros/ros.h>  ❶


int main(int argc, char **argv) {
  ros::init(argc, argv, "minimal");  ❷
  ros::NodeHandle n;  ❸

  ros::spin();  ❹

  return 0;
}
```

❶ Include the basic ROS header information.

❷ Initialize the node, and give it a name.

❸ Create a node handle.

❹ Give control over to ROS.

All ROS C++ nodes need to include the *ros.h* header file. Nodes are initialized by a call to init(), giving the command-line arguments and a name for the node. Then, we create a node handle that allows us to create topics, services, and actions. We didn't have to explicitly create a node handle when using Python, since the language was able to do it for us behind the scenes. This is one of the recurring themes when using C++: things often need to be more explicitly specified.

We need to add both build and runtime dependencies on roscpp to the *package.xml* file, and modify our *CMakeLists.txt* to contain the information shown in Example 23-2.

Example 23-2. CMakeLists.txt

```
cmake_minimum_required(VERSION 2.8.3)
project(cpp)

find_package(catkin REQUIRED roscpp)


add_executable(minimal src/minimal.cpp)
```

```
target_link_libraries(minimal
  ${catkin_LIBRARIES}
)
```

In this example, our package is called cpp. Once all of this information is in place, we can cd to our top-level catkin workspace and invoke catkin_make. This will compile our code and make sure all of the dependencies are up to date. Once this is done, we can find the resulting executable in *devel/lib/cpp/minimal*, and we can run it with ros run as usual:

```
user@hostname$ rosrun cpp minimal
```

Topics

Example 23-3 shows how to set up a topic publisher in C++. The basic approach (set up the node, define the publisher, publish in a loop) is the same as in Python, but the details are a little different.

Example 23-3. topic_publisher.cpp

```
#include <ros/ros.h>
#include <std_msgs/Int32.h>  ❶


int main(int argc, char **argv) {
  ros::init(argc, argv, "count_publisher");
  ros::NodeHandle node;

  ros::Publisher pub = node.advertise<std_msgs::Int32>("counter", 10);  ❷

  ros::Rate rate(1);  ❸
  int count = 0;

  while (ros::ok()) {  ❹
    std_msgs::Int32 msg;  ❺
    msg.data = count;

    pub.publish(msg);  ❻

    ++count;
    rate.sleep();  ❼
  }

  return 0;  ❽
}
```

❶ Include the definition of the message we're going to use.

❷ Create the publisher.

---

❸ Create a `Rate` instance to control the publishing rate.

❹ Loop while the node is alive.

❺ Create a message and populate its data field.

❻ Publish the message.

❼ Wait for a while.

❽ Return success.

The two notable parts of this code are the creation of the topic publisher, and the loop condition. To create a publisher, we use the syntax:

```
ros::Publisher pub = node.advertise<std_msgs::Int32>("counter", 10);
```

This is a function defined as part of the `NodeHandle` class, templated on the type of message that's being sent. The parameters are the topic name, and the buffer size. The loop condition:

```
while (ros::ok()) {
```

will evaluate to true as long as the node is running and has not received a Ctrl-C to shut it down.

The corresponding topic subscriber node is shown in Example 23-4, and is even simpler.

Example 23-4. topic_subscriber.cpp

```
#include <ros/ros.h>
#include <std_msgs/Int32.h>

#include <iostream>


void callback(const std_msgs::Int32::ConstPtr &msg) {  ❶
  std::cout << msg->data << std::endl;
}


int main(int argc, char **argv) {
  ros::init(argc, argv, "count_subscriber");
  ros::NodeHandle node;

  ros::Subscriber sub = node.subscribe("counter", 10, callback);  ❷

  ros::spin();
}
```

❶ Define the callback function.

❷ Create the subscriber.

As with the publisher, the subscriber is called on the node instance, but this time we don't need a template argument since it can be calculated from the type of the callback parameter. The three arguments are the topic name, the buffer size, and the callback function.

The trickiest part is the callback function:

```
void callback(const std_msgs::Int32::ConstPtr &msg) {
```

This function should have a return type of void, and a single argument that is a const reference to a const pointer to the message type. In this instance, the message type is std_msgs::Int32, and this has a type of ConstPtr defined within it. In general, the argument for a callback dealing with messages of type *T* should have an argument of type const *T*::ConstPtr &. When building the message definition, catkin will make sure that the type ConstPtr is defined for your message types. Note that ConstPtr is a reference-counted smart pointer. You're not expected to call delete() on this when you're done with the message.

 Although we've used one particular signature for the callback here (using ConstPtr), there are actually several that will work just as well (they all resolve to the same underlying types). We suggest that you use signatures like this in your code, but don't be surprised if you see a different, but equivalent, signature in someone else's code.

Note that, when accessing the data from the message, you should use the dereferencing operator ->:

```
std::cout << msg->data << std::endl;
```

As you can see, the basic structure and idioms of a C++ node are the same as those of a Python node, even if the syntax is a little different. This is also true for services and actions.

Services

Defining and using services is largely the same as defining and using topics. Example 23-5 shows how to define the word counting service from Chapter 4 in C++.

Example 23-5. service_server.cpp

```
#include <ros/ros.h>
#include <cpp/WordCount.h>
```

```
bool count(cpp::WordCount::Request &req,   ❶
           cpp::WordCount::Response &res) {
  l = strlen(req.words);
  if (l == 0)
    count = 0;
  else {
    count = 1;
    for(int i = 0; i < l; ++i)
      if (req.words[i] == ' ')
        ++count;
  }

  res.count = count;

  return true;
}


int main(int argc, char **argv) {
  ros::init(int argc, char **argv, "count_server");
  ros::NodeHandle node;

  ros::ServiceServer service = node.advertiseService("count", count);   ❷

  ros::spin();   ❸


  return 0;
}
```

❶ Define the callback function.

❷ Create the server.

❸ Give control over to ROS.

The main differences here are that the callback function takes two arguments: the request, of type WordCount::Request, and a response, of type WordCount::Response. Again, these are provided automatically when you build the service definition. The return value is placed in the response argument, and the callback returns true or false, indicating success or failure. Once again, we advertise it through the node handle.

Example 23-6 shows how to use the service.

Example 23-6. service_client.cpp

```
#include <ros/ros.h>
#include <cpp/WordCount.h>
```

```
#include <iostream>

int main(int argc, char **argv) {
  ros::init(argc, char **argv, "count_client");
  ros::NodeHandle node;

  ros::ServiceClient client = node.serviceClient<cpp::WordCount>("count");   ❶

  cpp::WordCount srv;   ❷
  srv.request.words = "one two three four";

  if (client.call(srv))   ❸
    std::cerr << "success: " << srv.response.count << std::endl;   ❹
  else
    std::cerr << "failure" << std::endl;

  return 0;
}
```

❶ Create the service client.

❷ Create a data structure for the request and response.

❸ Call the service, testing for success.

❹ Access the response through the data structure.

Again, we make a call on the node handle, templated on the service data type, to set up the client. We then create an instance of the service data type, and fill in the request information. The actual service call is made using the `client.call(srv)` call, which will return true if successful, and false otherwise. Note that it is the responsibility of the service server to return this value. Finally, we can access the results of the call through the data structure's `response` field.

Summary

In this final chapter, we've seen how to translate some of the Python code from the rest of the book into C++. All of the idioms and design patterns that we've talked about previously are the same, regardless of the language that you write your code in; only the syntax and details change. Once you learn how to make these cosmetic changes, you should be able to switch from Python to C++ and back again with ease.

Of course, we've only scratched the surface of the C++ API in this chapter. Dealing with it completely would take a whole other book. However, if you're already familiar with the language, then you should be able to take this chapter in one hand and the

ROS wiki documentation in the other, and start crafting your own ROS nodes in C++. Or, you can choose a simpler life, and stick with Python. Your choice.

Index

Symbols

A

B

About the Authors

Morgan Quigley is a cofounder of the Open Source Robotics Foundation (OSRF), which develops and maintains the Robot Operating System (ROS). He came to OSRF after receiving a PhD in computer science at Stanford University, where he created one of the ancestors of ROS as part of the Stanford AI Robot (STAIR) project in 2006 and 2007. As it became clear that the future of robotics software was in collaborative development, this effort led him to cofound the ROS project with many other engineers. His research interests include robot software systems, open source software and firmware, embedded systems design, mechatronics, and sensor design.

Brian Gerkey is cofounder and CEO of OSRF. Prior to joining OSRF, Brian was Director of Open Source Development at Willow Garage. Previously, Brian was a Computer Scientist in the Artificial Intelligence Center at SRI, and before that, a postdoctoral research fellow in the Artificial Intelligence Lab at Stanford University. Brian received his PhD in computer science from the University of Southern California (USC) in 2003, his MS in computer science from USC in 2000, and his BSE in computer engineering, with a secondary major in mathematics and a minor in robotics and automation, from Tulane University in 1998. Since 2008, Brian has worked on the ROS Project, which develops and releases one of the most widely used robot software platforms in robotics research and education (and soon industry). He is founding and former lead developer on the open source Player Project, which continues to maintain widely used robot simulation and development tools.

Bill Smart is an associate professor at Oregon State University, where he codirects the Robotics program. His research interests span the areas of mobile robotics, machine learning, human–robot interaction, and the interaction between robotics and the law. Bill has been writing software for robots for over two decades, and doing active research and development of robot software architectures for over 15 years. At Oregon State University, he codirects the Robotics program and teaches classes in robotics and computer programming at both the undergraduate and graduate levels. He has been a ROS user since the beginning and was involved in some of the early planning workshops for the system. In 2010–11, he spent a 15-month sabbatical at Willow Garage, developing software for PR2 robots and enjoying the weather in California.

Colophon

The animal on the cover of *Programming Robots with ROS* is a Salim Ali's fruit bat (*Latidens salimalii*). Named after the famed Indian ornithologist, the Salim Ali's fruit bat remains a rare species about which little is known, more than 60 years since it was first collected and mistaken for a short-nosed fruit bat. Confined to rainforests at the southern tip of the Indian Peninsula, in the vicinity of the Western Ghats mountain range that runs along the Arabian Sea, the Salim Ali's fruit bat is one of the more endangered species in a region acknowledged as one of the world's most biodiverse.

Members of the megabat suborder to which fruit bats belong do not feed on insects. Rather, they use long tongues to slurp out the nectar of flowers, or use specially adapted teeth to bite into fruit, from which they often drink only the juice. The consequence of the fruit bat's frequent interaction with flowers is a mutually beneficial relationship known as *chiropterophily*, in which the flowers rely on herbivorous bats to carry pollen from one flower to another. The megabat's consumption of fruit—primarily figs or the fruit of the bead tree, in the case of the Salim Ali's fruit bat—also perform the function of dispersing seeds.

By mechanisms that are not clear, the fruit bat's herbivorous nature has deprived almost all members of the Megachiroptera suborder of the ability to use echolocation. It is possible, according to some research, that the economy of energy achieved by insectivorous bats, whose flight activities also seem to physiologically prepare the bat for the vocalizations that act like submarine pings in echolocation, is not as easily realized by the heartier-meal-eating and generally bigger fruit bats. The megabats' larger eyes and keener sense of smell appear to compensate.

The last 25 years of the Salim Ali fruit bat's history have seen its status as a species threatened by extinction change from "rare" to "critically endangered" to the more optimistic "endangered." Research has indicated that there is a greater population and range than was previously recorded, and efforts have been made to discourage the private owners of the land on which the bat maintains roosts from hunting it as a pest or for its rumored medicinal value. However, the outlook for the survival of the species is still not bright, as humans continue to encroach on and fragment its primary habitat.

Many of the animals on O'Reilly covers are endangered; all of them are important to the world. To learn more about how you can help, go to *animals.oreilly.com*.

The cover image is from Cassell's *Natural History*. The cover fonts are URW Typewriter and Guardian Sans. The text font is Adobe Minion Pro; the heading font is Adobe Myriad Condensed; and the code font is Dalton Maag's Ubuntu Mono.

Have it your way.

Get even more for your money.

Join the O'Reilly Community, and register the O'Reilly books you own. It's free, and you'll get:

- $4.99 ebook upgrade offer
- 40% upgrade offer on O'Reilly print books
- Membership discounts on books and events
- Free lifetime updates to ebooks and videos
- Multiple ebook formats, DRM FREE
- Participation in the O'Reilly community
- Newsletters
- Account management
- 100% Satisfaction Guarantee

Signing up is easy:

1. Go to: oreilly.com/go/register
2. Create an O'Reilly login.
3. Provide your address.
4. Register your books.

Note: English-language books only

To order books online:
oreilly.com/store

For questions about products or an order:
orders@oreilly.com

To sign up to get topic-specific email announcements and/or news about upcoming books, conferences, special offers, and new technologies:
elists@oreilly.com

For technical questions about book content:
booktech@oreilly.com

To submit new book proposals to our editors:
proposals@oreilly.com

O'Reilly books are available in multiple DRM-free ebook formats. For more information:
oreilly.com/ebooks

O'REILLY®

CPSIA information can be obtained
at www.ICGtesting.com
Printed in the USA
LVOW03s0718171215

466910LV00014B/49/P